PENGUIN BOOKS

SHADOW WARRIOR

David Francis Everett was born in Tasmania in 1962. He joined the army at age fifteen, and the Australian SAS Regiment at twenty-one. He left the army in 1986, and went on to have various adventures, a few of which have inspired this, his first book. He now lives 'out bush' in Australia's vast north.

dangerousdaveeverett.com

SHADOW WARRIOR

DAVID EVERETT

with KINGSLEY FLETT

PENGUIN BOOKS

PENGUIN BOOKS

Published by the Penguin Group
Penguin Group (Australia)
707 Collins Street, Melbourne, Victoria 3008, Australia
(a division of Pearson Australia Group Pty Ltd)
Penguin Group (USA) Inc.
375 Hudson Street, New York, New York 10014, USA
Penguin Group (Canada)
90 Eglinton Avenue East, Suite 700, Toronto, Canada ON M4P 2Y3
(a division of Pearson Penguin Canada Inc.)
Penguin Books Ltd
80 Strand, London WC2R 0RL, England
Penguin Ireland
25 St Stephen's Green, Dublin 2, Ireland
(a division of Penguin Books Ltd)
Penguin Books India Pvt Ltd
11 Community Centre, Panchsheel Park, New Delhi – 110 017, India
Penguin Group (NZ)
67 Apollo Drive, Rosedale, North Shore 0632, New Zealand
(a division of Pearson New Zealand Ltd)
Penguin Books (South Africa) (Pty) Ltd
Rosebank Office Park, Block D, 181 Jan Smuts Avenue, Parktown North,
Johannesburg 2196, South Africa

Penguin Books Ltd, Registered Offices: 80 Strand, London WC2R 0RL, England

First published by Penguin Group (Australia), 2008
This edition published 2009

Text copyright © Flett Media 2008
Photographs copyright © David Everett 2008

The moral right of the author has been asserted

All rights reserved. Without limiting the rights under copyright reserved above, no part of this publication may be reproduced, stored in or introduced into a retrieval system, or transmitted, in any form or by any means (electronic, mechanical, photocopying, recording or otherwise), without the prior written permission of both the copyright owner and the above publisher of this book.

Cover and text design by David Altheim © Penguin Group (Australia)
Typeset in 12/18pt Fairfield by Post Pre-press Group, Brisbane, Queensland
Printed and bound in Australia by Griffin Press

National Library of Australia
Cataloguing-in-Publication data:

Everett, David (David Francis)
Shadow warrior / David Everett.
Camberwell, Vic. : Penguin Group (Australia), 2008.
9780143010654 (pbk.)
Everett, David (David Francis) Criminals – Australia – Biography.
Guerrillas – Burma.

355.0092

penguin.com.au

In memory of Kate and Adam

This story is as true as my memory can make it. Some events and characters have been altered to keep a few blokes in the shadows.

The hardiest soldiers be either slain or maimed, [or], if they escape all hazards, and return home again, if they be without relief of their friends, they will surely desperately rob and steal, and either shortly be hanged or miserably die in prison.

Thomas Harman, A *Caveat or Warning for Common Cursitors*, 1566

CONTENTS

ABBREVIATIONS

2IC	second in command
ABSDF	All Burma Students Democratic Front
AG	Adjutant-General
ANFO	ammonium nitrate fuel oil
APC	armoured personnel carrier
BMI	Burmese Military Intelligence
CO	commanding officer
CQB	close-quarter battle
CT	counter terrorism
DS	Directive Staff
GP	general purpose
GPMG	general purpose machine gun
IOU	Initial Orientation Unit
HF	high frequency
HK	Heckler and Koch
HQ	headquarters
KNDO	Karen National Defence Organisation
KNLA	Karen National Liberation Army
KNU	Karen National Union
LUP	lying-up place
MSU	Metropolitan Security Unit
NCO	non-commissioned officer
NDF	National Democratic Front
OC	officer in charge
OP	observation post
PT	physical training
RAEME	Royal Australian Electrical and Mechanical Engineers
RPG	rocket-propelled grenade
RTU	return to unit
RV	rendezvous point
SHU	Special Handling Unit
SLR	self-loading rifle
TRG	tactical response group
TRW	Tribal Refugee Welfare in Southeast Asia
VOTP	violent offenders treatment program

PROLOGUE

The dog was a German shepherd, about two years old, big and woolly but still goofy like a pup. Baz and I were in cheap overalls and balaclavas, hiding behind the shed in a backyard next door to the target house. The owner of that house was the manager of the Hoyts Carousel cinema complex in Perth, and we were going to grab him and his wife out of their bed, and at gunpoint take them back to his office and make him open the safe.

It was the end of the Australia Day long weekend and people had been flocking to the air-conditioned cinemas to escape the oppressive summer heat. The safe would be packed with cash. Going through the front door with guns blazing is for born-to-lose desperados. Nabbing the manager at home and bringing him in to open the safe was the only way to go.

We'd been hanging out in the shadows for four hours, waiting for the man of the house to come home. I'd been watching the cinema complex for a couple of weeks, learning this bloke's routine and I knew he knocked off at 11 p.m. He alternated weekends with his assistant manager, and it was pure luck that he was on for the long weekend. At 11.30, right on cue, his car came into the drive. Baz and I watched the couple have tea, wash the dishes and then slip into their routine before bed. The last light to go off was at the front left-hand corner of the house, so we figured this was most likely their bedroom. We gave them about an hour to get settled.

I blew a silent whistle and the dog ran over, sniffing and barking, each time I blew it. The silly mutt wasn't sure if it should attack us or play. Baz had mixed up some bait out of sodium cyanide, which was supposedly fast acting and would suck the oxygen out of the dog's blood in less than sixty seconds. They reckon it's painless, but you never really know. We flirted with the idea of getting friendly with the mutt in the hope he'd stay quiet. But it was too risky. Baz dropped the bait over the fence and the dog scoffed it down. It took a couple of waltzing staggers before its legs collapsed. It gave one long sigh and was dead. The first obstacle was overcome.

The main concern after the German shepherd was the proximity of the neighbour's house. With only a two-metre gap between the buildings, we'd have to keep noise to a minimum. Neither Baz nor I had seen any outside evidence of a burglar alarm and this was the era before motion-sensor lights cost twenty dollars at your local hardware store, so we were clear to move in closer. I scaled the fence carefully and crawled up the side of the main bedroom window. They had been renovating so there was a lot of junk in the yard, and I had to quietly move this stuff out of the way.

Once level with the bedroom window, I propped and listened. It was a hot night and I could hear a fan blowing inside. This would aid us by covering any small noises we made as we gained entry. I signalled for Baz to move over, and sure enough, despite his bulk, he moved like a cat.

We both did a 360-degree crawl around the house to get a good feeling for the layout. No security-alarm stickers on any of the windows was another good sign. We didn't risk trying to look inside the main bedroom window since the side of the house was lit up by a street lamp. A dark head-shaped silhouette against the window would be a bit of a giveaway. Instead, I used a small dentist's mirror to peer over the window sill. I could see two figures lying on the bed.

We hadn't set any hard and fast plans for a covert way into the house. We thought it would be better to decide on the night after we'd had a good look around. A last resort would be to knock on the door and force our way in as soon as it was opened, or failing this, we could smash it in with a sledgehammer. Very noisy and high risk, but we were confident we could do it quickly enough to prevent the couple from calling for help. A single loud noise is not usually enough to rouse neighbours. Going in quietly was obviously the preferred option, and the lock on the back door looked like it could be picked. We crawled up to it and ran a compass around the edges of the doorframe to check for reed switches or other magnetic switches that would trigger an alarm when the door was opened. The compass needle wasn't disrupted.

One last look around to confirm that we had no nosy neighbours and I began to work on the lock. It took me a couple of minutes to pick it and we were in. Using the full weight of my body to prevent any jerky movements, I very slowly swung the door open, just in case they had motion sensors in the house. My small pen-light torch had tape over the lens with a pinhole cut in it. This provided sufficient light to inspect the interior and everything looked clear – no alarms.

Baz had moved around to the front to check for unexpected visitors and restrain any occupants who might have heard me picking the lock and decided to flee via the front door. We were linked up by two-way radios with ear plugs and boom mikes. These gave the advantage of hands-free operation in case we had some restraining to do, as well as being virtually silent. I wasn't able to source any radio sets capable of sending an encoded signal that weren't conventional hand-held walkie talkies: anybody on the same frequency or using a radio scanner could listen in while Baz and I talked. This was only a minor issue really since we used only single-word codes to communicate and never referred to each other by name. Police were 'poppies', security guards 'slacks', and 'shut down' meant a compromise and to abandon the job. There wasn't a need to talk much anyway as we'd rehearsed the job hundreds of times, with plans for all the different scenarios that might crop up and a few that never would. The real value of the radios would come if one person was compromised and was able to warn the other to take off before the police arrived.

The back door led to a hallway that divided the house in two. It was an old federation-style house, which would probably be a nice home when the renovation was finished; that's if they felt safe there any more. The old jarrah floorboards were creaky, so I had to move very slowly, gently testing each place I put my foot before committing my body weight to it. It took me more than half an hour to check each room in the house except the main bedroom.

Once I'd cleared the house, I relocked the back door, moved up to the front and gave Baz a quick 'okay' on the radio. I unlocked the front door, again being careful to avoid any telltale loud clicks, and let the big fella in. The noisy fan in the bedroom gave plenty of cover for our movements, but I was still worried about Baz's bulk on the floorboards. Again, he proved me wrong by moving like a ballerina. We didn't need to talk. I signalled that the house was clear and that we only had the one bedroom to contain. The front door was closed and relocked.

We moved into position outside the bedroom door. I took out my pistol and Baz unsheathed his shotgun. Neither of the weapons was loaded – this wasn't a dinkum armed robbery. We'd chosen the shottie for its barrel diameter; looking down the unfriendly end of it would cause maximum intimidation. The pistol was for show, too. We agreed beforehand that our escape routes and early-warning systems were so good that it would be fairly easy to do a runner if we were compromised. There was just no way we were getting into a firefight with the coppers. Being a successful criminal depends on the fact that police resources are spread fairly thinly. You leave such little evidence that pursuing you further becomes counter-productive. Kill a police officer and you will be hunted down by every man and woman wearing a uniform for the rest of your days. Besides, in our own weird way Baz and I had some respect for other people who served.

I nodded, then turned the handle and swung the door open. We were prepared to bust in if needed but the door had no security chains or locks on it. I flicked on the light and stepped quickly over to the left side of the bed, and Baz went to the right. We raised our weapons and leant into them like we meant to shoot. Here was the moment that the success of the job hinged on. We had to suppress them fast but quietly. Forget that gentleman outlaw 'I'll be your robber for the evening' polite bullshit; that's for the movies. You swamp them with such force and aggression that you squash any tiny thought they, and especially the bloke, might have of putting up a fight. We were both charged up, ready to scare the shit out of them the second they woke up.

But we got nothing; they both continued to breathe deeply and steadily. Sound asleep with the light on and two black-masked, armed hoodlums standing in their bedroom with guns at the ready. Baz gave me his 'what the fuck do we do now?' look. According to the plan, they were both supposed to wake up and put their hands in the air without making a sound. Baz took the initiative and shook the manager awake.

He lifted his head with a start, blinked a couple of times and then the colour – quite visibly – drained from his face. He let out one long incoherent scream, which woke his wife. She screamed as well, only louder. I guess we had overdone the intimidation because they both just tripped into full-blown hyperventilating panic. We tried to calm them, speaking as soothingly as we could but nothing worked; in fact, they just screamed louder. I suppose a soothing-voiced bandit in a balaclava with a gun is still a bandit in a balaclava with a gun.

The situation was spinning fast out of control. In a war zone a rifle butt to the mouth would have shut them both up, but despite the escalating tension, we kept our sense of fair play and stuck to the rule that you can't do things like that to non-combatants. Baz made the smart move; he put the shotgun down and jumped on top of the bloke's upper body, pinning him on the bed. If we thought the woman was screaming loudly before, then we were wrong because she really let rip then. I didn't have any choice but to do the same to her, putting my hand across her mouth and pushing her back on the bed, still talking as soothingly as I could.

The manager twisted his mouth free of Baz's grip and shouted at me.

'Get the fuck off her, you fucking mongrel! She's bloody pregnant!'

If there were ever a turning point in my life, this was it. If I look back on all the lawless and dangerous things I have done, that moment on a hot January night, when I saw the look in that terrified woman's eyes, stands out as the one when I started to change my opinion of myself, and realise that somewhere along the way I had disconnected from the rest of the world.

I can't pinpoint exactly where the disconnection had occurred. I didn't lose respect for the law or people in general; I just had the sense that the rules didn't apply to me. Back then a few of us ex-SAS blokes had brushes with the law. This might have had something to do with our training and our motto: *do what you want but don't get caught*. But it was clear that my view of the world had become distorted – to the point where killing a pet and sticking a gun in someone's face was an acceptable means to an end. And even though this was a defining moment, I still had to unlearn a few things before I was capable of any regret.

PART I

The Road to the Regiment

TASMANIA

The first person I ever shot was my sister Mary. It was 1974, I was eleven years old, and that little air rifle was my pride and joy. Home on school holidays, we'd been at each other all day, as only brothers and sisters can be, calling each other stinky-bum, fart-face and the like. Mary upped the ante by smashing an egg on the top of my head and rubbing it all over my face. I ran for my air rifle and she ran squealing out the front door. Those fibro walls don't block much sound and our screaming match had attracted half the kids in the street. Mary was out on the gravel road teasing me in front of an audience, while I held a pretty good defensive position on the front verandah.

'Go on, Davey, have a shot,' she giggled. 'You haven't got the guts and ya can't shoot for shit anyway, ya little maggot.' She turned and wobbled her backside like a belly dancer.

I lined her up with the barrel, breathed out slowly, and squeezed the trigger. A little puff of dust lifted from the centre of her right buttock, followed a second later by a sharp *thwack* that echoed down the street. After that was a moment of stunned silence. Every eye in that little pack of kids turned to me in horror and then to Mary, who still had not moved a muscle. The quiet was broken by this blood-curdling wail. Both legs kicked out straight in front of her and she hit the road with an almighty thump, like someone had pulled her chair out. Then she sprung up, pressed her hands to her bum and ran around like she was on fast-forward. The wail was like a siren – I don't remember her taking a breath. The slug didn't penetrate the thick jeans she was wearing, but I reckon it must have still stung like a bastard.

All the mums in their aprons came out of their front gates and into the street, craning their necks like it'd all been choreographed. Most of the kids scattered for the hills, and I bolted over the back fence and down into the swamp. Mary's friends helped the wailing heroine back into the house. Nobody could believe I had done it, especially me.

We were living in the town of Luina on the west coast of Tasmania, where Mum and Dad both worked at the nearby tin mine. I knew that once Mum had gotten the phone call from the other kids she'd be home in less than ten minutes. There had been a few dos and don'ts laid down when I was given the rifle and, while my parents hadn't been specific, I was pretty sure that shooting my sister in the bum was one of the don'ts. Mum dished out most of the punishment in the house, and I knew I could handle a walloping from her, but it was Dad who made the big decisions, and if he put his foot down, I'd lose the rifle. That was the main worry.

From my hiding place, I heard Mum's car on the gravel. She pulled out again about ten minutes later, so I crept up to the house. A table had been dragged across the front door as a barricade and the back door was locked, but I got in the bathroom window easily enough.

The girls spotted me as I came into the kitchen; they pulled the table away from the front door and stampeded, screaming, out of the house again. I noticed Mary was moving pretty fast; she had forgotten to limp until she was well clear of the front yard. They started teasing me from the road again but this time from a lot further back, outside the effective range of the air rifle.

I decided to do a runner until things cooled off, so I grabbed a can of baked beans, some matches, a blanket and water bottle and was gone, just after I buried the gun where I knew it wouldn't be found. Hitching was easy, one of our main forms of transport in those days. I waved down a truck and got a lift up to the east of town – a place called Waratah, which in the 1800s had been home to the biggest tin mine in the world. Following an old cart track over the hills for an hour had me deep into the rainforest. I found a spot to camp on the bank of a dam, got a little fire going, heated up the can of beans, wrapped myself in the blanket and settled in for the night.

I've spent a fair bit of time on my own, out in the bush or on the run, and I suppose I started early. The Waratah expedition wasn't even my first time. Mum still tells the story of waking up in the middle of the night to find me missing. I was three years old at the time, so there was a bit of a panic until they spotted me running bare-arsed across a freezing paddock with a box of matches in my hand, trying to light a fire.

When I woke up in Waratah the next morning the outside of the blanket was stiff with frost, but I was warm enough inside. I walked out to the road and got a lift back to the edge of town on a mine truck. I sneaked up to the house, moving from cover to cover until I made it to the woodshed. I waited until I heard Mum get up to start breakfast. With the major threat occupied for a while, I crept up, opened my parent's bedroom window, and whispered to Dad. 'Hey, Dad, is Mum still angry? Should I come in or come back later?'

'No, mate, she's still pretty stroppy. But you better come in anyway and take what's coming to you.' He looked relieved to see me more than anything, but was still pretty stern. 'And we're going to have a talk about that air rifle later on.'

I decided to show myself at the kitchen window but keep one foot out the back gate. I was dirty, shivering and covered in burrs; I did my best to look hungry as well. Mum spotted me through the window and looked me up and down for a few seconds before calling out. 'Where've you been?'

'Out camping.' I said, trying to sound sorry for myself.

'How'd you get back?'

'Hitched.'

'You hungry?'

Right then I knew I'd be safe for a while. I went inside and sat at the kitchen table. Everyone else ignored me as if nothing had happened.

Sometimes when you misbehave as a kid it pays to do it big – I reckon my parents were too shocked to be angry. All I got was a lecture on controlling my temper. Dad made me retrieve the air rifle, then locked it in his cupboard and said it would be chopped up if I ever shot anyone again. It was the talk of the town for ages and everyone got a good laugh out of it. Mary says she's forgiven me now.

I was born in January 1962, in Campbelltown, Tasmania. I was the second of four kids and spent my whole childhood in the mountainous mining areas on the north-east and west coasts. My parents were both from Western Australia. It seems that as a kid Dad had been a fairly adventurous sort, spending his time fishing, riding horses and climbing the cliffs near Kings Park. He joined the 10th Light Horse Brigade at the start of World War Two, and then transferred to the air force when the mounted infantry disbanded. He was trained as a wireless operator/gunner on the twin-engine Beaufort bombers in Victoria and then in Winnipeg, Canada, before flying bombing raids over Europe in the last two years of the war. Dad wouldn't talk about the war and hated those American movies that glorified it. Aside from saying that he 'lost a lot of good mates', he took all his stories to the grave.

Something about Canada pulled him back there after the war, and it was there he learnt the mining game. It took his father's death to bring him back to Western Australia in 1947. After the funeral he kept wandering and got a job as a pearl diver up north in Broome. Those were the days when they used the heavy canvas suit and bell helmet to harvest pearls. It was dangerous work and deaths among the divers were common. After being circled and bumped by a huge tiger shark one morning, he decided there must be easier ways to make a living and started work at a lead mine near Onslow. In a historical exhibit in Darwin I saw a picture of my dad and his mates outside the Onslow pub taken in 1958, watching a nuclear test blast, conducted by the British, in the Montebello Islands.

My mum had grown up in Onslow, and it was her family who owned the mine. She met my dad at one of the local dances, and they were engaged within a few months. It must have been hard working for your father-in-law, so after getting married they moved into a fibro shack at Storeys Creek in Tasmania, where they had heard that work was available in the underground tin and wolfram mine.

It might seem a harsh existence by today's standards, living in those little fibro and tin houses. It was cold for most of the year up in the mountains, so family life tended to centre on the kitchen and its wood stove. Even in later years when we got a TV, it would take a special show to get us out of the kitchen after dinner. We'd read or play board games instead. Dad taught Mary and I to roast chestnuts on the edge of the fire, which was tricky because if you let them get too hot, they'd explode. One exploded in my dad's mouth once, which everyone except him thought was wildly funny.

Both Mum and Dad worked once I went to school, so Mary and I were expected to pitch in with most of the household chores, like getting the chooks' eggs and chopping wood. I was the sort of kid who was keen to muck in and help out anyway, so this was no problem for me. A bit too keen sometimes: I remember once helping Dad fix the car and pouring a can of water instead of oil into the top of the engine. It took him a while to drain that out, but all he said was, 'That's not where the water goes, mate.'

He'd always let me help out – it wouldn't be just handing him tools like with some dads. He always gave me an important task and had the patience to let me make a few mistakes before getting it right. Making home-brewed beer, we'd mix all the ingredients by hand in stainless-steel tubs salvaged from old washing machines. My job was to collect and clean the old bottles, then I graduated to helping with the mix. I put too much sugar in the first batch, and the family was woken one night by a series of loud bangs as the bottles exploded one by one in the cellar under the house.

It was a pretty lethal brew when Dad got the mix right. Some Friday nights he'd have a few workers over from the mine and, once the commercial beer had run out, he would start serving his own 'Snow's Special Bitter' (he'd been nicknamed Snow in honour of his white hair). Half an hour later and he'd have to drive them all home.

I suppose it's easy to think back and create a few myths, inevitably turning your father into a hero. But I reckon it was the same patience and firmness he showed with me that made him well respected by the blokes who worked for him in the mines. Having come through the ranks himself, he had empathy for the workers and was probably a better judge of what a man could achieve in a day's honest work than the management types who had never gotten their hands dirty. Most blokes busted a gut trying to please him, and he never had to crack the whip to get them to perform. One time I was with him on site, in the freezing cold and pouring rain, and he spied a bloke drilling rock, trying to break down the crusher stockpile. Dad saw that he didn't have any gloves, so he told me to take his own over to him. 'You serious?' the bloke asked incredulously when I told him the gloves were from the boss.

He set a high standard for leadership, my dad. Ever since, I haven't had much time for people in authority who lack integrity – and this has got me into trouble more than a few times.

It might have taken me until I was eleven to shoot someone, but my first brush with the law came when I was five years old. We had moved to a little town, Rossarden, 8 kilometres down the mountain from Storeys Creek, the year before I started school. Dad had been promoted to shift boss at another underground tin mine. The Rigby boys lived down the hill from us, and one day we decided to take the afternoon off school and head down to the local creek for a swim. The teacher noticed our absence and alerted the Rigbys' dad and Sergeant Black, the local copper. Sergeant Black was actually a friendly old fella, but even the friendliest of coppers have a way of being hard-faced and scary when they need to be. He pulled up at the creek in his brand-new Toyota four-wheel drive and bellowed out, 'You boys get over here!' He then gave us each a kick in the pants before putting us in the back of his vehicle for a ride up to the police station. The lockup was just a brick shed with barred windows and a steel door, but it was pretty intimidating to us kids, and we were terrified.

'This is where you'll end up if you wag school again!' he said, as he slammed the steel door on us. My first jail term lasted about twenty minutes, but it had the desired effect. I never wagged school again.

If I'd grown up in suburbia, I'd have probably got in a lot more trouble, maybe even skipped the army and gone straight to jail. But, as it was, we were surrounded by plenty of places to run wild. Mary and I could rove for miles. There were plenty of creeks to muck around in and caves to explore; we'd even sneak onto the mine site and climb down the airshafts, using candles to light the way. I'm still not a big fan of civilisation.

I know I was a difficult kid to bring up. Mum gave me plenty of beltings, which just toughened me up and probably made me harder to control, but such was the parenting style of the day. The only time I could outrun her was when she was pregnant. I ran amok when Mum was carrying my younger sister, Kate, but Mum had a long memory and once she was mobile again, she caught me after I'd broken some eggs and gave me a belting that more than made up for the previous nine months.

In contrast, the only time I can remember really upsetting Dad was when I ran off with his mate's rifle. Every Sunday Dad would visit the single men's camp to have a beer or two. I first started going down with him to have my hair cut by Uncle Tony, an old Italian chap, whose hand clippers used to yank out by the roots as much hair as they sheared. Still, the packet of PK chewing gum he gave me at the end of it went some way to helping me to forget the pain.

One time at the camp we visited another one of Dad's mates, Richard 'Dicky' Bird. He had two .22 rifles: one was a French pump action and the other was a single-shot bolt action. I think I'd been a gun and army nut since seeing my first war movie, much to my dad's annoyance, so I wanted to have a shot as soon as I saw them. I wouldn't let it rest until I was given a go.

I couldn't hold the rifle up by myself. Dad and Mr Bird cut a small sapling down so I could rest the rifle in its V, and then I had my first ping at a tin can. It became a regular event and those Sundays couldn't come around fast enough. I'd be issued five rounds to fire, and rapidly progressed from an upright tin can to firing at the base of an overturned one.

I reckon if they don't want young blokes to be attracted to guns, then they shouldn't make them so fine looking. I loved everything about them – from the way they smelled to the noise they made. I even loved cleaning them; after shooting, we'd spend ages oiling the mechanism, cleaning the bore with a 'pull-through' rag, and polishing the woodwork.

By the age of eight I was bored with hitting tin cans and asked my dad if I could go hunting black jays, Tassie's version of a crow.

'Yeah, sure you can,' he said. 'Just as soon as you can put five rounds through a matchbox at twenty yards.'

Dad knew this was nearly impossible, and I knew it too. It was his way of saying I was too young to go wandering on my own in the bush with a gun. I was crushed – for a few minutes – then I devised a cunning plan.

I tried to fool Dad and Mr Bird by shooting the matchbox from a yard away, but they spotted the powder burns almost immediately and told me to stop being a cheating little ratbag. I reckoned they must have been spying on me. The next Sunday I used my mate David Olsen's rifle to put five rounds in the matchbox, this time from a few yards back to avoid the telltale powder burn. I was going to use my own five rounds to go shooting after I had shown Dad and Mr Bird the evidence of my marksmanship, but then I began wondering how I'd explain the spare rounds. Eventually the whole scam got a bit too much for my eight-year-old brain, so I just took off without asking.

I don't know whether it's because of some link to our primitive past, but that absorbing pleasure of walking quietly through the bush with a gun, senses all switched on, looking for a target, has never left me. Some blokes are just born hunters, I guess. The black jays were making a racket up at the town dump, so I gave chase and completely forgot about time. I must have walked 6 or 7 kilometres – those bloody birds kept flying off before I could get my sights on them. I gave up after a few hours and shot my five rounds at bottles at the dump, then hiked back to the camp.

When I got back Dad was furious. He thought that I'd had an accident and had been all over the place looking for me, as had most of the fellows from the camp. It was around three o'clock in the afternoon and we had well and truly missed Mum's Sunday roast lunch. Dad didn't yell at me or hit me – I reckon he was one of those fellas who are a bit afraid of their own temper. Instead, he just stared at me like he was summing up my character in a new way. That cold glare was more effective than a million smacks on the bum.

'Just tell the truth, son,' was all he said. Disappointing him felt like the worst thing in the world.

Missing Mum's Sunday roast was something you just didn't do in our family. She ripped into Dad as soon as we got home, thinking he'd stayed up at the camp for a few extra beers. I couldn't let that injustice stand so I piped up. Trying to be helpful, I told her the reason we were late was that I was off on my own in the bush with a rifle. For some reason this just made Mum angrier and she started giving Dad a long lecture about his responsibilities as a parent. I backed slowly out of the room and put myself to bed to the sounds of Mum talking loudly over the top of Dad's ever more feeble protests. It put paid to my shooting for a while.

My other passion as a child was heavy machinery. If it was big, belched smoke and made heaps of noise, I loved it. A huge bulldozer would churn up the track behind our place almost every day. Sitting high up in the cab would be big Macka Watson. He had those weathered, craggy features that only a lifetime of working outdoors, drinking and smoking could create. Another mate of Dad's, he'd generally stop and have a chat on his way to the mine's sawmill. Whenever I heard the roar of that big diesel engine and the clanking of its tracks, I'd run out and hang around, waiting for the offer of a ride that never came. Eventually I worked up the courage to ask.

'No worries, my little mate. Jump up,' Macka boomed, and that was that. Every time he came past after that I'd race out and flag him down. Macka was half deaf from a lifetime of operating machinery – these were the days before hearing protection – and he never spoke quietly, always in a booming, gravelly roar. He was my mate and even said that if I kept it a secret between us, then it was okay to call him by his first name when no one else was around. In those days there was no way a child would dare to call an adult by their given name only. It was always Mr Watson or Uncle Fred or whatever. This privilege, our little secret, made me fiercely loyal to him. He had seven or eight children of his own and lived down in the main township. I remember his older boys had been called up and went to fight in Vietnam; they always took the time to have a chat with me whenever they came home. Just like Dad, they wouldn't tell me what happened over there, much to my annoyance as I loved hearing war stories.

By the time I had managed to scramble up the tracks and onto the seat in Macka's bulldozer, I would be covered in dirt and happy as a pig in mud. I've never lost this knack for getting dirty; stuff just sticks to me. I'd be elated, sitting up there, grinning at the roar of the engine and the clanking tracks, thinking *if only my mates could see me now*. It must have been a real pain in the bum for Macka to be bailed up every time he went past our house, but he never showed any signs of annoyance.

I badly wanted a drive but didn't reckon Macka would let me; I asked anyway. Again, to my surprise, he said okay straightaway. I didn't understand about throttles, gearboxes and all those other gadgets, but I'd seen the way he pushed the pedals and pulled the sticks and thought it looked easy enough. I had to perch almost half-off the seat to reach the pedals, and when I put my hands on the sticks I could feel the powerful vibration of the engine. We lurched off down the track. I tried to be serious and adult about it, but I couldn't stay deadpan and a huge grin kept splitting my face. Macka just laughed. I managed to knock a tree over, and when Macka let me off I raced back down the track to inspect the results: a splendid effort, indeed.

It wasn't long before I started going out with Macka and his mate, Dusty King, for the whole day. Mum and Dad were usually happy to let me go. I guess they figured it would help burn off some of my excess energy. I had to stay in the truck or on the dozer while they were working. I suppose it was a dangerous place for a little fella to be wandering about, but at the time it was magical to watch the brute power of that dozer pushing the logs around.

One Sunday I was halfway out the door, yelling to Mum that I was off with Macka, when, for no particular reason, she called me back in and told me to stay around home. She gave me a few jobs to do but nothing that was going to fill a whole day, so I took off and hitched a ride out to the logging site. I figured if Mum asked, I'd tell her I was playing down near the swamp. After a hard day's work, Macka and Dusty offered to take me back home, thinking I'd get a thrill from being dropped home in the truck, just like Dad getting home from work. But I knew if I turned up in the truck, I'd be in trouble.

'Ah, thanks anyway, Macka,' I said, trying to sound casual. 'I reckon I'll just walk back.'

'Don't be bloody silly, you little bugger,' he boomed. 'It's too dark; your dad would have me guts for garters if I let you walk now.'

I was cringing when we turned up in the truck at the side of the house. Mum was out in the veggie garden.

'G'day, Macka,' she called out with a big smile. 'You want some veggies?' I was relieved as she gave Macka and Dusty some cabbages and carrots, and thought I was off the hook. Mum and I smiled and waved as they drove away, but as soon as they turned the corner she dropped the smile, grabbed me by the scruff of the neck and whacked my bum like she was beating dust out of a rug. I reckon I was sore for a week after that, and I was banned from going on the truck for ages.

Our next move, from Rossarden to the tin and wolfram mine at Luina, was another promotion for Dad. It was a much bigger mine than the one at Rossarden: instead of relying on underground shafts, it had a spiralling underground decline with haulage trucks bringing out the ore. We had a slightly larger place than we had at Rossarden, with four bedrooms, but like all the houses up there it was made of fibro cement with a tin roof. The extra space was timely, because, as well as Mary, myself and Kate, we now also had my little brother, John.

By the time I was thirteen, Mum and Dad had to decide between sending me to the secondary school in the next town, Savage River, or to a boarding hostel attached to the high school at Wynyard, about 70 kilometres away. My parents were keen on us kids getting the best education they could afford, and they had already sent Mary to a boarding school in Launceston. The school in Savage River seemed like an outpost for the education department and a dumping place for all its problem teachers, so they chose the hostel in Wynyard and a new adventure began. The timing was probably perfect. I had always been a fairly independent kid, and so I had no great fear of leaving the comforts of home behind me.

I don't remember having any problems adjusting to high school. Most of the blokes had similar backgrounds to mine and we all loved the bush. If anything, I had more fun than at home because there were more friends to go on adventures with. Besides that, I was just past puberty; I had a new hobby and it wasn't hunting or fishing. All the girls at the hostel wore bras and most were really pretty.

The hostel itself was split into a north and south wing – one for the boys and the other for the girls – with the dining, living and kitchen areas in the middle. We often had midnight food raids on the kitchen and it didn't take us long to work out that the doors to the girls' dorms were unlocked as well. Having teenagers with raging hormones sleeping only a few yards from each other with no security was just asking for trouble, I reckon. Then again, a 12-foot-high electrified razor-wire fence probably wouldn't have been enough to stop us.

Louise Mulcay had blonde hair, big blue eyes, long tanned legs that she always showed off with mini skirts, and breasts that I could not stop staring at. She was a year older than me and in the popular group. I'm not sure what smooth pick-up line I used, but I remember asking her if she would go with me, and she said, 'Okay.' Nothing much changed, of course, besides the fact that everyone knew we were now 'going together'. We would hold hands and pash occasionally, but as far as I was concerned, having a girlfriend was a bit overrated. Then I heard about one of the senior guys sneaking down at night to see his girlfriend and figured I may as well try it, too.

That night I waited about an hour after lights out, and then crept down the hall and across the dining room. Once in the girls' dorm I crawled on hands and knees, keeping below the level of the beds. I stopped for a while to listen, but couldn't hear any talking, just deep breathing and soft snoring. I crawled up to the first bed that, in the dark, looked like it contained someone about the same size and shape as Louise. I had to get my face right up to hers to see if I had the right girl. I didn't, and had to check a few more before I found Louise's bed. She blinked a couple of times when I woke her up, and then regarded me with those calm blue eyes for a few seconds before pulling her covers back and saying, 'Jump in.' I was in midair, halfway through my Fosbury flop onto her bed, before she could finish saying 'in'.

I wish I could remember more about that first time. I was lacking in knowledge, but Louise had some experience and was able to channel my enthusiasm into the right areas. I can recall the incredible sensation of heat as I slid inside her. A few minutes later I was lying there, with my head spinning, thinking *so this is what all the fuss is about*. I was hooked. I was up and ready to go again about thirty seconds after that. We had a long night.

I averaged about three hours' sleep for the next four nights before Louise decided not to speak to me any more. I reckon she'd just wanted me for my body. This didn't worry me in the slightest because by that stage there was already another girl showing interest. I kept this up well into my third year of high school and was always nodding off during afternoon classes, but then at lights out I always seemed to find the energy to visit one of the young ladies.

One weekend I went home and arrived back at the hostel by bus on Sunday night. As I walked up the drive, I saw the light on in the housemaster's office. *Somebody is in trouble*, I thought.

That somebody was me.

'Everett,' Mr Walker called out ominously as I walked past the door. 'Come in here right now.'

Mr Walker was usually a friendly old bloke who rarely raised his voice, more like an older brother than someone in charge. But he had a grim look on his face that night.

'We've found out about your night-time activities, David,' he said. 'I suggest you phone your parents and get them to collect you. You may stay here tonight but are hereby expelled.'

By then it had been going on so long that I was surprised he hadn't known before. I'd assumed that he was turning a blind eye. I denied everything at first, but after I spoke to Dad on the phone, I decided to tell the truth. All was revealed except for the names of the girls. I found out later that there had been one girl who was keen on me, but, frankly, had a face like a squashed frog and there had been no way I was going to put her on my midnight roster. She'd dobbed me in.

A few days later, after a dressing-down from Mum and Dad, we had a meeting with the headmaster. He said that I could still attend school as long as I could arrange private boarding in the town. This was easily done and I continued my schooling as an external boarder.

My life at school didn't change all that much afterwards. I still managed to get out with my old mates from Luina, shooting and fishing most weekends. Almost all of us had guns by that age, but we weren't old enough to get driver's licences. One night we'd planned to go shooting, but couldn't find any of the older kids who would take us in their car, so I borrowed a tractor that belonged to one of the geologists who worked at the nearby mine. To get it started I shorted out the starter motor with a screwdriver, after disengaging the engine stop lever, and we roared off up the road, making sure to veer off into the bush whenever we noticed headlights coming the other way. I'm not sure what other motorists would have made of a tractor on the road with five gun-toting young blokes clinging to the back.

Magnet Valley was just over the next mountain range, and it was the only flat, green area among the tall timber for miles. We spotted a wallaby and all jumped off the tractor and charged after it, firing wildly. It probably sounds like a disaster waiting to happen – a bunch of teenagers all running around the bush with guns – but we were all country kids who had grown up with rifles and were fairly sensible. By that age natural selection tends to have taken care of the idiots. Not that we didn't have the odd close shave. I had the animal in my sights at one point and was taking up the pressure on the trigger when Steve Street popped his head up right in front of me.

'Ayyy!' I yelled out of shock. I remember his eyes were three times their normal size as he turned around and looked straight down the barrel of my gun. He went white and aged about ten years in five seconds.

We got the wallaby eventually, cruised back to Luina and parked the tractor, with no one the wiser. Three days later, the bloke who owned the tractor, John Coates, called out to me quietly as I walked past.

'Have a good night's hunting the other night did you, young Mr Everett?' We all banded together and gave him ten dollars for fuel, and he was happy.

Shooting, fishing, riding bikes and chasing girls took up most of my high-school weekends. Despite all the fun I'd had, my school results were okay. I was no genius but scored above-average marks, with maths my best subject. But ten years cooped up in a classroom was more than enough for me. By 1977 I had to decide on a career. I had no ambition for university. It was either an apprenticeship at the mine or joining the army. Most parents want life to be better for their kids than it was for them, so it was natural for Mum and Dad to encourage me away from the mines. I could tell that Dad, in particular, preferred the army for me. Being keen on guns made it an easy choice in the end. At the ripe age of fifteen I sat my tests and was accepted to join the Australian Army as an apprentice mechanic. I was to report to the Army Apprentices School in Balcombe, on Victoria's Mornington Peninsula.

Mum and Dad came to see me off on the ferry, Mum variously smiling, trying not to cry, and crying, and Dad hanging back.

Mum scolded him. 'Come and give your son a hug,' she said.

We embraced stiffly. 'Just look after yourself, son.'

I sat at the back of the *Empress of Tasmania* as she left Devonport Harbour and began ploughing through the huge swells of the Bass Strait towards Port Phillip Bay and Melbourne. Looking back on the receding green hills of my home island, I was thrilled to be setting out on the next big adventure. I had an exhilarating sense of freedom, which is a little ironic considering the number of years I was about to spend in institutions like the army and prison.

REAL SOLDIERING

Every army in the world has a similar method of breaking in new soldiers. Their brutally effective techniques have been honed over centuries. As soon as you get off the bus, you're made to run at double time: you get less than ten minutes to eat your meals and less than five hours' sleep per night. Barracks, uniforms, latrines and rifles are all to be kept spotless. Punishment for the slightest evidence of sloppiness is severe. They exhaust you physically and mentally until you can't remember who you are.

The apprentices school in Balcombe was called 'Boys Town' and was the dumping ground for every psychologically tired soldier in the Australian army. Most of the corporals, sergeants and warrant officers at Balcombe were good blokes, but there was also a handful of psychopaths that the army couldn't hide anywhere else. They set to work on us young fellas like a pack of sharks.

Some recruits, especially among the city boys, were crying for their mums by the second night – it was either grow up fast or ship out. Within a few days the harassment had the desired effect on me: I stopped thinking of home and pretty much anything else that the instructors didn't want me to think about. My new world was the army, and my new god was Platoon Sergeant Dave 'Molly' Mansfield, six-foot-one of pure rage. A Vietnam veteran, he was built solid like an ex-rugby player – all muscle and hard fat. He had a handlebar moustache, a mean glare and could go from deadpan to volcanic in the twitch of an eye.

Early on someone whispered a joke while we were on parade and I made the mistake of grinning when Sgt Mansfield was looking. He walked a couple of strides past me before lunging back with terrifying speed. He put his face so close to mine that I could smell last night's beer on his breath.

'Wipe that smile off your mug, Everett!' I was sprayed with his saliva as he shouted. 'Or I'll punch those teeth so far down your throat you'll have to stick a toothbrush up your arse to clean them!' I believed him.

One night during my second month at Balcombe, while I was walking back from the mess, I heard a drowsy voice singing weakly. I didn't recognise the tune; not sure the bloke singing did either. I followed the sound of the thin voice.

I found this big, fat bloke draped over the bottom of our barracks stairs, as pissed as a fart. It took me a few seconds to realise that this was Mansfield. I'd never seen anyone as legless as this before, let alone someone in authority. With no clue on how to handle the situation, I got some of the senior apprentices to help, and it took six of us to lift him into the back of a car. We drove him home.

Sgt Mansfield came to when we reached his house and he invited us all inside. Two of the bigger seniors propped him up and the rest of us followed closely in case he toppled over.

'Oh, come on, Dave. When is enough going to be enough?' his

wife asked, choking back tears, as we trooped into the kitchen. She looked drawn and tired.

'Shuddup, woman, and get these boys a beer!' he roared. 'Drink up, boys. That's an order.' Like all drunks, he needed company.

We stood around, embarrassed, while he mumbled barely coherent stories about Vietnam. Luckily, after a while, he stumbled off to the toilet and that gave us our opportunity to evacuate. We felt really sorry for his missus. Sgt Mansfield said nothing about it the next morning; it was drill as usual.

I reckon young blokes need role models – older men they can look up to. At the time my world view did not allow for a platoon sergeant to be falling-down drunk. Seeing someone who I thought of as invincible making a goose of himself had a real impact on me. Most blokes take a few years to lose their illusions about military life, but I noticed some pretty big cracks in its façade early on.

My time at Balcombe didn't feel like real soldiering. Having been raised on a diet of World War Two movies, I'd expected to be charging around the bush with a great big bayonet sticking out of the end of my bolt-action Lee Enfield rifle. I was a bit disappointed to be issued with a self-loading rifle. Most blokes back home frowned on rapid shooting; it was seen as a waste of ammunition and showed you up as a poor marksman. 'One shot, one kill' was always one of my dad's mantras. Of course, now, having been in combat, I can see the benefit of sending a lot of bullets down range towards the enemy, and you'd never catch me with a bolt-action rifle in a firefight.

The infantry training only took up a small portion of my time anyway; we were at Balcombe to learn a trade. I studied hard for my motor mechanic's ticket, and at the end of 1979 I was posted to the Adelaide Workshop Company, a Royal Australian Electrical and Mechanical Engineers (RAEME) base. This was another rest home for sad and burnt-out old soldiers, but by now I had learnt how to negotiate these sorts of blokes.

I was mad keen to work on armoured personnel carriers (APCs), as they were the closest things to tanks that I'd seen. An APC is designed to transport troops into battle while offering some protection from enemy fire, shrapnel and land mines. We used the 13-tonne box-shaped American M113, which began its life in the Vietnam War and is still in use today. It is a fully tracked vehicle, which means you steer with two sticks rather than a wheel. It was a simple arrangement: the right stick locked the right track when you pulled it back; the left stick did the same with the left side. You simply put the automatic gearbox in drive, plant your foot on the accelerator pedal and away you go, adjusting direction by pulling on a stick. Pull both sticks back and you stop; crank one stick right back and you spin around like a top. You could make adjustments in direction by pulling back slightly on one stick to slow the track on that side. I knew this because we had repaired them from time to time in Adelaide, and I always managed to get my hands on the sticks for a drive. When I was roaring along in one of these huge things it took me back to the cabin of Macka's dozer in Tasmania.

My trade certificates were issued at the end of my time in Adelaide, and I got the posting that I'd had my eye on: the 106 Field Workshops at Damour Barracks in Coopers Plains, on the south side of Brisbane. The 106 also had a forward repair workshop over at Enoggera Barracks in the northern suburbs of Brisbane, and they did a lot of repairs on APCs from 3/4 Cavalry Regiment. I got over there as fast as I could.

I met Don Watts on my first day there, and I was teamed up with him as soon as I walked into the place. Don, a fitter armourer, was the same height as me, but he was barrel-chested and solid with muscle where I was still a skinny weed. He had a couple of years' more experience than me in the trade and was working on an APC.

'Welcome aboard, mate,' he said with a smile. 'Let's get this transmission swapped over because I want to take this big bastard out for a spin in the hills.'

We got the job done fast, fired up the APC and headed off – two kids barely out of their teens, roaring through the bush in 13 tonnes' worth of valuable army equipment. I drove and Don sat up in the turret as the de facto commander. Having only one driver in an APC without an observer in the turret was a great way to get in trouble with the military police. Not far off the access road Don spied a couple of abandoned cars.

'Enemy straight ahead,' bellowed Don. 'Engage! Engage!'

I drove into the first car head on, doing about 40 k's an hour. I thought we'd go flying over the top of it, crushing it underneath like you see tanks do in the movies, but the APC just ploughed the car along the ground and slightly crushed its side. Not impressed with that, I backed off and prepared for a frontal attack. I drove one track of the APC up over the bonnet and then the roof of the car, tipping us at an alarming angle. One bloke had told us about how he'd heard you could spin an APC around to grind a car into scrap, so we gave that a try. We kept the track on the car locked and drove the other at full revolutions. We spun in a demented circle, grinding the car down into chunks of torn metal – it was pure destructive mayhem. I drove back and forwards over the wreck a few times until it was completely flattened. I then swapped places with Don and he did a similar job on the other car.

'I say, Dave,' Don giggled at his best fake-officer speak. 'It looks like some idiot has just run over these two cars with a tank. Let's get out of here.'

We powered back up the track, both laughing like mad pirates, until we were interrupted by a loud bang from the depths of the machine. I pulled back hard on both steering sticks to stop. The APC swung around on one tread and slammed into a bank on the side of the track. We were lucky this all happened on a flat area; further down the road we could have tipped the whole machine over. Don was as white as a sheet. I reckon I was the same.

It didn't take long to find the problem. In our rush to take the APC for a ride, we'd forgotten to tighten the bolts on one of the drive-shaft couplings; the super-charged V6 Detroit diesel drove its 350 horsepower through this coupling to the drive-wheels, and as it came loose, the drive shaft had thrashed around and beaten itself to death against the armour-plated hull. The shaft was shredded into metal splinters and it had gouged fist-sized chunks out of the armour plating before disintegrating. I knew I'd tightened the bolts on my side and so I reckoned it was Don who had slipped up, but being the mechanic, it was my job to check both. I blamed Don anyway. We had a quick shouting match over who was the biggest idiot before settling down to work out a plan of action to cover our butts. We were going to be in deep shit if we didn't think fast.

Luckily, the drive shaft was the only thing damaged. Don knew of an old drive shaft that was lying around in the workshop collecting dust, so I agreed to walk back to see if I could grab it without drawing too much attention to myself. Trotting back down the track we had just come up, I passed a couple of mechanics from the ambulance unit that was stationed near us. Their faces long, they were standing next to the flattened remains of the two cars.

'G'day fellas,' I said. 'Jeez, what's been going on here?'

'Ah, we left these cars up here so we could use them for parts and some idiot's run over them with a tank,' said the saddest-looking one.

Just then a couple of APCs from the 3/4 Armoured Regiment drove past. 'Probably one of those dickheads,' I said, jerking my thumb at the passing vehicles. 'Bloody bucket-heads probably tore 'em up for fun – the bastards.'

They looked at me suspiciously. I probably still had a mad glint in my eyes; time to change the subject.

'Anyway, my truck has broken down up the road. You reckon youse blokes could give us a lift back to the workshop?'

Back at the workshop I scrounged the spare drive shaft and returned to where Don was waiting patiently. It took us an hour to change over the shafts and drive back, slowly. No one found out, and all in all it was an excellent first day on the job.

The Damour Barracks were just down the road from the stadium where the 1982 Commonwealth Games were held, and most of my unit were either employed by the games as drivers or away on exercise. I had twisted an ankle and was doing odd jobs around the workshop when a brand-spanking new armoured-fitters track (a modified M113 APC) arrived on the back of a truck. When the truckie asked around for someone to drive it off the back of his trailer I jumped behind the controls before anyone else could volunteer.

After backing it off the truck, I drove it down the narrow concrete ramp at the side of the unloading bay. I noticed the fence on one side of the ramp shaking as I passed through. The truckie had a funny look on his face when I got off the ramp, but he didn't say anything to me. He just jumped in his cabin and took off fast.

I decided to do the sensible thing and park the unit's valuable new machine somewhere secure – right after I had taken it for a spin. I drove toward a hill at the side of the camp that led down to a main road and a set of traffic lights – this was the site of one of our unit's favourite pastimes. From the top of the hill, I could see a queue of civilian cars waiting for a green light. I took off down the hill, with the APC belching black diesel smoke and roaring like a freight train, heading straight toward the row of cars. The motorists must have been sure that they were about to be crushed. You could see their cars edging forward, trying to get out of the way of what must have looked like an inevitable crash. They couldn't see that the track I was following veered left at the bottom of the hill; a tracked vehicle can turn much sharper than a car with wheels. At the last moment I cranked on the left stick, sending the 13-tonne monster skidding sideways around the corner, and careering up the track and out of sight in a plume of black smoke. After having my fun, I parked the new machine and got back to work. Ten minutes later Staff Sergeant Wilson ran up to me.

'Everett,' he puffed, 'did you just rip down a fence with that new APC?'

Over towards the unloading ramp we saw a gang of serious-looking men in blue overalls, wearing side-arms (pistols) and radios. They were inspecting a few gaping holes in the fence. I winced as I remembered the fence shaking as I backed down the ramp.

Still, it was just a fence. I was wondering what the big deal was when the Officer in Charge (OC) came running over. When an officer runs you know it's serious.

'I've just had the SAS on the phone screaming blue murder,' he said, fuming. 'Someone driving an APC has breached their security.'

We didn't know the SAS counter-terrorism team had been using the empty warehouse next to our workshops as a staging area during the Commonwealth Games. And I'd just ripped down their perimeter fence. When we strode over for a look the guys in blue overalls retreated back into the shadows.

Sgt Wilson and the OC started pontificating about how they'd have to bring in civilian contractors to fix the fence and how many thousands of dollars that would cost, while I went back to the workshop and dragged over the portable power jack.

'What are you doing, Everett?' the OC demanded.

'Fixing the fence,' I replied, 'and it won't cost you thousands of bucks either.'

'Well, get it done right away,' he said, and he and Wilson both stormed off.

I stretched the wire back into place, and using some barbed wire that I'd pinched from the back fence of the base, where no one would notice a few strands missing, I threaded the gaps together. After about three hours' work, the fence looked a bit rough but the gaps were no more.

The OC came over and had a look, shook his head, informed me again that I was an 'idiot', and headed back to his office to telephone the Regiment boys. I stood over at the workshop and watched them come out to inspect the fence, then go back in again. They must have been satisfied that no one could sneak into their compound through the mended hole – indeed, all the terrorists would have to do instead was jump over the back fence where the barbed wire was now missing.

That first contact with the SAS stirred my interest. All that secrecy was fuel for a young, inquisitive mind. I had heard of the SAS by then: there'd been an officer by the name of Zot Simon back in Balcombe who never said a lot, which was unusual for an officer. Zot wore a sandy beret with a winged dagger badge on it. When I'd asked about him they had said he was a 'super soldier' from WA. I'd heard about the North Vietnamese Army nicknaming the SAS 'phantoms' due to their ability to sneak around undetected. I was curious.

By the time of the Commonwealth Games incident I had just about had it with the army. I was barely twenty years old and felt my life was draining away, like I might stick my head into an engine bay one day, pull it out twenty years later and be left wondering where my youth went. It had only been a year with the 106 and I didn't reckon I'd have the patience to see out two.

As far as real soldiering went, RAEME was a bit of a joke. We took part in annual shooting exercises and the occasional military exercise, but these mainly involved securing perimeters, building defences, doing clearing patrols and running around in 'ready-reaction' groups, rehearsing what would happen if our base came under attack. Most of the older mechanics figured that if this scenario actually played out, it would be easier just to go and hide in an APC, while the 'grunts' in the infantry did all the fighting. But most of us young fellows fantasised about getting into a firefight. It was all a bit half-hearted and average for me – I wanted to take on something serious.

Don and I were working on a Land Rover one day, and I was having a whinge, talking about my plans to go AWOL before the upcoming Christmas leave. Don might have become a little tired of my complaints by this time. He put down his spanner.

'Look, Dave, if you are that bored, why don't you come and have a crack at SAS selection with me?'

Don had tried to get in to the SAS the year before with another RAEME bloke called Tracey Wilson. Don had failed the first running test, but Tracey had gone all the way and was the first bloke from our section to make it.

'Yeah, right,' I said, and kept working. Don and Tracey had solid builds and were good sportsmen. I was skinny and still looked about fourteen. The SAS recruiters would laugh me all the way back to Enoggera. Still, Don had planted a seed.

'So, what do they get up to in the SAS, anyway?' I asked.

'Mate, they spend all day shooting and blowing things up. They travel everywhere, get the best gear and they are paid twice what we get,' he replied.

This all sounded much better than spending the rest of my life sweating under a hot engine cover coated in grease. 'So, how fit do you have to be?'

'You just have to run heaps,' Don explained. 'Toughen up your feet, learn to navigate cross-country, and just have the heart to keep going.'

I had got Rastus, my alsatian pup, from Tracey Wilson before he left to join the Regiment, so figured I knew Tracey well enough to give him a call that night. When I spoke to him I could tell he had been instructed to give no detail about what happened on the selection course, but he gave me some good tips on how to train.

I turned up to work the next day and told Don that I was going to give it a go.

At the 106, towards the end of every month, we held a Friday afternoon 'Mug of the Month' award ceremony. The award went to someone who had stuffed up in the previous month, and their prize was to stand up and receive a liberal bagging from one and all. Apart from the times when I really deserved it, like the SAS perimeter fence episode, I probably received more than my fair share of these. I was the skinny little bloke who looked like I should be in school and not the army, so most blokes found me an easy mark. I learnt to take it with a smile; most of it was good-natured, anyway.

That November, after the Commonwealth Games, Staff Sergeant Wilson seemed to take particular pleasure in standing up in the wet mess (the camp boozer) to announce the award.

'Ladies, gentlemen and soldiers, can I have your attention please?' He had to shout over the din and wait for everyone to quieten down, as we were all well on our way to being drunk. His voice was dripping with sarcasm as he continued. 'It has come to our attention that a member of our ranks has decided to try out for the SAS Regiment. This fellow considers himself hard enough to be a member of the elite.' Wilson paused while a few ironic cheers died down. 'This has come as a great surprise to me because as far as I can tell, he is a scrawny, pigeon-chested little weed. This month's Mug of the Month goes to David Francis Everett.'

There was an explosion of laughter. As I looked around the room, I could sense more than a bit of vindictive pleasure being taken. I wasn't as thick skinned as I thought, so although I laughed along, the determination to prove them wrong was like stone in my gut.

The pre-selection running test and interview for the Regiment were set down for late January. These weren't part of the real selection yet, just a way to chop out the pretenders who wouldn't be able to handle the real course. Even so, I started training in earnest. In recruiting me to try out with him, Don got more than he bargained for: I wanted to train twice as much as he did. Most afternoons after finishing work, he'd suggest that we go for a beer, but I'd push him to come running instead. The test was to run 3.2 kilometres in fifteen minutes – in jungle greens, boots and webbing, while carrying your self-loading rifle. Don and I marked out a course for us to practise on, and in a few weeks we had our time down to thirteen minutes.

On the day of the first run test and interview about three hundred guys rolled up, and this was just for the Brisbane area. I was as nervous as I'd ever been, and when we started the run I set off at a sprint, mainly just to avoid being trampled by the huge pack. Don and I ran together, and twelve-and-a-half minutes later we sprinted over the line. About half the blokes didn't make it, so that left 150 of us for the interviews.

On the interview panel there were three officers from the Regiment and an army psychologist. Chris 'Rock' Roberts, the Commanding Officer at the time, fired out most of the questions.

'So, why do you want to join our Regiment?' Lieutenant Colonel Roberts asked, while looking me up and down.

'I want to learn proper soldiering, sir, and I want to do it with the best in the army,' I fired straight back. I'd had this answer prepared, ready to go.

'You're just a mechanic, aren't you?' he asked. 'From RAEME?'

'That's right, sir.'

'I suggest you transfer to a rifle battalion and learn some *soldiering* there and reapply in twelve months.'

'No, sir,' I replied firmly. I had nothing to loose; I really couldn't have given a stuff about the regular army at this stage. 'That would be a complete waste of my time, sir. Why learn tactics that I'm going to have to unlearn when I join the Regiment anyway, sir?'

Lt Col. Roberts just glared at me while the psychologist asked me a few more questions. I can't be specific, but the questions were obviously aimed at making sure that I was a balanced individual, and not some nutter who might eventually misuse his training to aid a two-year crime spree – or something like that. If they were going to make me a superman, they had to be sure that I'd use my powers for good. I sometimes wonder what that psychologist thinks of that interview now.

They sent me out of the room while they got their heads together, and called me back in a couple of minutes later. Lt Col. Roberts spoke again.

'Everett, we've decided that you should go into a rifle battalion for a year. Then you should reapply.' He moved a piece of paper across the desk, signalling that this was the final word – 'next please'.

'I refuse, sir,' I said. He stared hard at me.

'Cheeky little bugger, aren't you?' He paused for a moment before reaching across for the piece of paper. 'All right, we'll give you a go, but I am saying right here that I have grave reservations about your ability to pass the selection course.'

'Thank you for the opportunity, sir.' I tried to hide the rush of elation. 'I'll do my best to give it 110 per cent.'

I saluted, did an about turn and marched out. Don marched past me on the way in. I gave him a wink, but no other clue as to how it had gone. I felt Don and I were really in this endeavour together, so I held back any real celebration until he came out of the interview beaming with a huge smile. We took off out of sight around the corner of the building and cut loose, backslapping and congratulating each other. Then we raced back over to the 106 workshop to tell the guys that we had made it to selection.

I had less than eight weeks to be ready, and so I started my training: running every night, pumping weights and working on my gut. Although I'd played a bit of footy and done some cross-country running as a kid, I'd never focused so hard on my fitness before. My twenty-one-year-old body responded fast and I stacked on muscle in a short time.

There wasn't enough time during the day to fit in all the training I needed to do, so of an evening I would don my greens and my webbing, strap on my pack, grab a steel pipe in place of a rifle and head out for a run. In between I worked on the other skills I'd need to get through the selection course – night map-reading and navigating on compass bearings. The hilly scrub that surrounded nearby Griffith University was the perfect place to practise; I got used to moving in the scrub at night and keeping to a bearing. Every morning I soaked my feet in methylated spirits, Condy's Crystals and urine to toughen up the skin against blisters. The webbing and shoulder straps of the pack chafed the hell out of me, so I attached some thick green felt to the inside of the straps and belts. This was the only modification I made to my equipment in preparation for the selection course and it did the trick.

Don didn't seem to be doing a lot of training. Every single night before I went out for my run I'd ask if he was coming. He always had something else to do.

'Look, Dave,' he snapped one night. 'Why don't you take care of your training and I'll take care of mine, hey?'

I still thought of us as a team, but I guess he had his reasons for telling me to bugger off. I just got on with my training. Later on I found out that Sgt Wilson had been taking bets on who would pass selection. The odds on me were very long. I copped plenty of shit in those eight weeks, and it was obvious that no one thought I'd stand a chance, but each little piss-taking comment just made me more determined. By the end of eight weeks I was as focused as I'd ever been in my life – no way was I coming back to 106.

SELECTION

It's four-thirty on a clear, cold autumn morning in the Hunter Valley, central New South Wales. A pack of us are running at top pace along a narrow bitumen road that winds through the bush and farming land. You can hear the hard thud of boots on the road, the rattle of webbing, the gasps, grunts, coughs and spits. Our breathing steams the cold air. This is the 14.2-kilometre battle-efficiency run, conducted with full webbing, greens and a rifle.

The first week of selection was coming to a close and nearly 100 blokes had already dropped out. I was pretty close to being next. My breathing was coming in ragged gasps, and the coppery taste of blood in my mouth, the deep ache in my chest and my desire to vomit all told me I was right at my limit.

When the body is in pain the mind goes looking for excuses, and I had a pretty good one. While I was gearing up for the morning's run, some bright spark in my hut suggested that I attach my water bottles to my belt by the hoops on the outside of their pouches, rather than by the bottles' metal rungs. These rungs would slip over the inside of the webbing belt and dig into the skin, causing blisters and open sores. Ditching them seemed like a good idea at the time, but just before halfway into the run one of the webbing loops tore loose and a bottle skidded off down the road.

Oh, shit was all I could think. I knew I couldn't leave equipment behind, as that meant an automatic fail. I immediately broke ranks and ran back to retrieve it. I bent down to scoop it up, stuffed it down the front of my shirt and ran like hell to catch up to the pack. There's a sort of mental glue in a group that keeps you running at a pace you would struggle with on your own. Sprinting to get back cost me a lot of energy but it was worth it.

Then the other loop broke.

The effort to rejoin my group a second time really took its toll. My legs were burning and I just couldn't get in enough air. At first there were a few inches between me and the bloke in front, then a few feet, and then I dropped off to the back of the pack. A wave of despair hit. For a moment I contemplated quitting, but I stamped hard on that thought and concentrated everything I had on chugging along as fast as my little legs could carry me.

As I came up toward the turnaround point, my mob came back past me and gave a few growls of encouragement. This, and reaching the turn, gave me a lift – my second wind came through and I increased my pace. I still wasn't fast enough to keep the racehorses in the group that had set off after ours from passing me. Their Directive Staff (DS) told me to tag along with them, but I couldn't lift my pace enough.

Then, some other dropouts from my group appeared up ahead. They had been spat out of the main pack and were struggling to hold their pace. Seeing that some of these buggers weren't invincible was a major morale boost. Before long the finish line came into view; I came in with plenty of time to spare. I grabbed a drink, flopped on the ground and enjoyed the huge boost in my spirits. It was a relief because anybody who failed this run was sent home straightaway. There was a long way to go, but I'd had the first clue that I might just be able to make it through. It was also the last time I tried any new kit without testing it first.

SAS selection had always been held in Western Australia, but the year I tried out they decided to hold the course in New South Wales to save the cost of transporting hundreds of blokes across the country and back again. Because of the large number of applicants there were two selection courses run back to back. The Queensland and West Aussie boys went first, with the rest a month or so later.

Don and I had taken the train down with the Brisbane boys and were part of the first batch to go into Singleton. We had a couple of days to kill before the course began, so I trained some more while most of the others went into town and got on the suds. They rolled back in on Sunday night looking very untidy. One bloke, Rolley, had himself a deep purple shiner on one eye – the result of a disagreement with one of the local boys over the affections of a lady. He was pounced on at the selection course's first meeting, and looked very sheepish as he was given a blistering verbal in front of the whole group.

Once the WA contingent had drifted in, there were 200 nervous blokes ready to face selection. We assembled on the lawn in front of the transit barracks. Everybody was trying to act cool while stealing glances at their competitors, sizing each other up. I was used to looking like a boy among men, but this time I really felt it. At that point a nagging doubt that I wasn't going to pass crept in and stayed at the back of my head for the duration of the course.

Compared to the British SAS, the Australian selection course is short and sharp. In Britain the approach is to wear a man down over a couple of months to see if he has staying power. In Australia the chaff is sorted from the hay in a few brutally demanding weeks. You can debate the merits of one over the other, but it's a no-win argument – time has shown that the same calibre of soldier comes out at the end. If you haven't got the athletic ability, heart and sheer mongrel doggedness to stick with it, you will fall by the wayside.

In the first week our daily 4.30 a.m. runs were followed by push-ups, breakfast, running, physical tests, running, map-reading, running, push-ups, first-aid training, push-ups, running, rappelling, running, push-ups, mental tests, push-ups, running, radio procedures, running, push-ups, swim tests, kit/weapon inspections, push-ups, running and more bloody push-ups. Throw in a couple of long route marches and you have people already leaving in droves – and the hard work hadn't even started yet. The tempo was twice what anybody was used to and was designed to build up the stamina of those who had done the training and to get rid of the pretenders who hadn't.

The time for the 3.2-kilometre run test we'd done to gain selection was dropped from fifteen minutes to twelve. Mark Gommers, a six-foot, solid-built bloke from an engineering battalion, was the only one to pass the first run and he did it easily. The rest of us were flopping around after, shattered, and convinced the course had been measured long. It didn't matter what you thought you knew, the distance had to be run again and again until you passed. I didn't pass until my third crack and was certain I'd be booted off.

My confidence took an even bigger battering when I failed the first swim test. We had to swim the length of a 25-metre pool wearing full army greens, boots and webbing, with a length of steel pipe slung over our shoulders in place of a rifle. At the end of the swim we had to tread water for two minutes. I finished the swim okay but sank when I tried to tread water. I didn't anticipate swimming on the course, and so I hadn't trained for it, and I was a poor swimmer to start with. I tried to keep afloat by bouncing off the bottom of the pool, but getting to the top again got harder each time, then impossible. It was probably comical to watch, but I wasn't laughing; I was too busy sucking in air. Eventually, it was go to the side of the pool or drown. I hauled myself out, and through my coughing and vomiting I heard the DS drone, 'Fail.'

Luckily, the failure rate must have been too high the first time round as they re-tested all us 'flops' the next day. I found out later that 80 per cent of the blokes who eventually passed selection failed this test. On the second time around we got two empty water bottles for flotation devices. I managed to tread water a little longer than my last effort, but I still sank inside the two minutes. I felt certain it was all over, and was surprised when they let me and a few other blokes through.

By the end of the first week all the running had taken its toll. General purpose (GP) army boots don't have cushioned soles and running on bitumen roads in them punishes your knees and ankles. The year after I went through the selection course the army medical board banned the boots from being used in running exercises because of all the leg injuries they created. This wasn't soon enough for me. After the battle-efficiency run, where I had dropped the water bottles, I developed an acute case of shin splints. It got more painful every time we ran, which was at least twice a day.

On the last run of that week every footfall felt like it would snap my shin. The best I could do was hobble along, steadily losing ground on the main pack. We were a couple of kilometres from camp when my old mate Rock (Lt Col. Roberts), Regiment CO and president of the Dave Everett Will Fail Selection Society, decided to join the run.

Rock was in his forties and carrying a bit of weight. I was embarrassed to see that he could keep up with me easily. He ran alongside me silently for a while, and the longer he didn't speak, the more certain I became that I was about to get a line ruled through my name.

'So, young Everett, what's going on?' He didn't even sound puffed. 'Going too fast for you, are we?'

'Slight shin problem, sir,' I replied, in my best chipper, can-do, voice. 'But it'll be righted soon enough.'

'When we interviewed you in January, you said something about *real soldiering*, and giving 110 per cent. Now you're using a little bit of shin pain as an excuse not to put in. You can stop now, just wait here by the side of the road and the DS will pick you up.'

'No, sir,' I blurted out. 'I'll finish.'

I hobbled a little faster. It felt like being kicked in the shins at each stride, and I was pretty sure I was doing myself some damage, but my anger overrode the pain. I managed to beat Rock home. He didn't look at me when he finished so I figured I was still in the game. However, I didn't reckon I would be able to run another day.

Luckily for me, I didn't need to run anymore. We were about to enter the next phase of our course, which involved stomping over great distances, carrying big loads on our backs.

We were told to prepare our kits for the cross-country navigation phase. We had to have a minimum of 35 kilograms' worth of material in our packs, including a PRC 25 radio set. Add to this a webbing kit and rifle and the total load hit 50 kilograms. It was obvious that the WA crew had been given tips from blokes already in the Regiment. Most had purchased top-dollar walking boots and commercial backpacks with ergonomic harnesses. Not me. I had only a standard-issue army pack. It was too small to stuff all my gear into, so I had bits of kit tied on all over the outside of my pack. The sight of this huge load being propelled by a pair of stubby legs provided plenty of material to the comedians in the group – 'Hey sonny, why don't you get your dad to carry his own pack?' It was all water off a duck's back to me, and as long as my system worked, it didn't matter.

After being dropped off at the base of some huge hills, we walked up to our starting point. Even this short climb was too much for some blokes and we lost a few more heads. Numbers were down to about eighty.

We were given a thorough briefing on what was to come in the next few days: the area of operation, safety procedures for if you got lost, and other details to ensure the smooth running of such an exercise. One thing was made very clear: stay off the tracks. If you are caught walking along on them, you will be failed. No arguments. You go straight home. I hadn't come this far to be failed on a technicality, so I followed this instruction to the letter, despite the temptation of a bit of easy walking.

There were DS sitting at fifteen different checkpoints, ranging from 10 to 15 kilometres apart. Most of the checkpoints were on the top of steep hills, many of them high above the cloud ceiling. The checkpoints on the flat weren't any easier to get to; they were usually in the middle of swamps or thick scrub. We were expected to make it to at least eight of them. It would be at least forty-eight hours of hard slog – the pressure was on.

We were getting a feed just before starting out when Rock came past and, within earshot of everybody, had another dig at me.

'So, young Everett, do you think you are going to get through?'

'Yeah, I said I was going to and I bloody well will . . . sir,' I shot back through my teeth. I spun on my heels and sat down next to Don with my tucker. I was still burning from the day before. I felt like I was being singled out, and to have nearly been chopped because of a simple injury seemed hugely unfair.

'Shit, Dave. You're gonna get kicked off the course! That was the CO you were talking to!' said Don.

I shrugged and kept eating. What's done is done.

I didn't have much time to dwell on whether I had stuffed up because not long after we got the whistle to get going. I heaved on my pack, staggered the first few steps while I got acquainted with its weight, and set off.

I began counting paces, checking my bearing and position on the map. I was inexperienced and still not totally proficient at map-reading, so I stuck rigidly to what I had been taught the previous week. It paid off. By nightfall the radio was squawking with lost soldiers.

On the way to my first checkpoint I was crossing a track when I met Wayne, one of the SAS cooks who was trying to get into the Regiment proper. It's a big stretch to go from working in the kitchen to being an elite soldier. He was walking right down the middle of the track.

'What are you doing? You'll get in the shit if you're caught,' I said.

'I know what I'm doing,' he reassured me. Wayne was heading to the same checkpoint as me and said he could get there faster by going along the tracks. We parted company, me on my compass bearing and him on the track. I beat him to the next checkpoint by a good ten minutes.

This checkpoint had been craftily placed on the side of a hill that was crisscrossed with tracks, none of which led to the clearing. The final approach was up a steep embankment, and you had to scramble through thick scrub. Night was falling, and my field of vision had shrunk to an area only as wide as my stride. I had to put complete faith in the compass bearing and in counting my paces. There I was, just counting steps in the dark. As I completed my last set of paces, just before I was about to look up to see if the clearing was where it was supposed to be, I bumped into the DS manning the checkpoint. It was satisfying to see my trust in the method paying off. It seems like a small thing now, but when you have the threat of being sent home constantly hanging over your head any victory is sweet.

The DS at the checkpoint grabbed some of my ammo. All afternoon blokes had been calling in on the radio, asking him to signal his position. He'd used up all his shells firing shots so they could home in for a bearing. It was a tough spot to find. There'd be a few more lost souls who he'd have to fire shots for that night. A couple of kilometres away I came across Mal, one of the officers on the course, stomping up and down a track, trying to get his bearings after he'd become completely bushed. We sat down with my map and I helped him locate the checkpoint by taking a back bearing off my line of travel. Mal headed off into the bush from the point where I had appeared; and that was the last I saw of him for a couple of days. He must have found the elusive checkpoint, though; he ended up passing the course.

Sticking rigidly to what I'd been taught had paid off, so I took this idea to ridiculous lengths. It was now pitch black and the glow of the luminous compass dial was my only light source. I couldn't see more than 6 inches in front of my face. I was pushing myself through the thick undergrowth of a tea-tree swamp when I bumped into a huge fallen tree that was blocking my route. The bloody thing was too high to crawl over, and I wasn't game to try and go around it, as there were tangles of vegetation along its length for as far as I could make out. To leave my line of travel and find it again on the other side would have been a fluke. The only way to get past was to squeeze under the small gap between the trunk and the ground.

I was exactly halfway through when I got jammed, thanks to the huge pack on my back. I flipped my arms and legs back and forwards like a turtle with a 50-kilogram shell. I was going nowhere. 'This is not fun anymore,' I remember squeaking as I lay there, face down in the mud, in pitch darkness, with bugs crawling all over me and not a sane soul for miles. I then cursed myself for sticking to the same plan I'd been patting myself on the back for only minutes earlier.

Just then, when I could feel myself going down mentally, my mood was broken by a radio call. Someone had gotten hopelessly lost, fallen into a swamp and was on the air asking what to do.

The fella had obviously gone so far off course that he was out of earshot of the DS's rifle shots. His mournful tone just begged for a sympathetic response. He was told gruffly to light a fire and wait until morning. I had a little chuckle and suddenly my own situation didn't seem too bad. At least I knew where I was and I hadn't fallen in any water. It occurred to me that the ground beneath was quite soft. A bit of digging under my belly and I soon made a hole deep enough to wriggle through. It was a relief to pop out the other side.

The next checkpoint took me past the main communications centre – where we had started. As I walked through, a DS grabbed me and said I should park up for the night. I ignored him and kept walking. One of the DS's jobs was to try to convince us to quit. At almost every checkpoint there'd be a DS being as soothing and friendly as possible, saying things like, 'It's okay, you can stop now. There's no shame in quitting; come and have a nice hot brew.' This time the DS called me back, insisting that he was dinkum. The call had gone out to every DS to pull in all pilgrims as they came through. I was still sceptical, so he dragged me over to the radio tent and repeated the message over the DS's private frequency. The message was acknowledged so I was convinced that he wasn't trying to 'rubber dick' me.

I was shown where to roll out my swag, and I reckon I was asleep before my head hit the ground. I woke at first light, got my kit together and made ready to leave. There was another bloke nearby who I recognised from my stint at the army apprentices school in 1977–78. We said g'day, and he asked me if I'd pulled the pin as well.

'Pig's arse,' I spluttered, wondering whether I hadn't been rubber dicked after all. I pulled on the pack and set off into the scrub in a bit of a panic, angry at myself for being so stupid. I didn't see that ex-apprentice again, so I guessed he had quit the previous day and was sleeping it off, waiting for a transfer in that morning.

I pushed on, bashing my way through thick scrub, either climbing or slipping and sliding down steep hills. One climb sticks in my mind. I had to crawl up a very steep embankment; I lost count of the number of times that I was nearly pulled over backwards by the weight of my pack. Just when I thought I was nearing the summit it opened up into another long climb. I was getting heavily tired now and was using all sorts of mind games to distract myself and to stay switched on. I imagined pizza and cold beer waiting at the top of the hill, or that I was with Sir Edmund Hillary on the final slopes of Mount Everest – anything to keep me pushing on. Finally I got to the top and Norm, the DS at the checkpoint, asked if I wanted to pull the pin. I was too knackered to come up with a witty reply, but I coughed back something along the lines of, 'You have to be bloody kidding. After walking all the way up here? Pig's arse. I'm not that much of a mug!'

He stared at me for what seemed like a minute. I stared back. Then we cracked up laughing. That was the first and last time I shared a laugh with a DS on that course. We had a bit of a yarn and, just for a moment, I enjoyed the view across the green hills that ran down to the Hunter Valley.

One of the blokes who'd already come through had left his protractor at the checkpoint before Norm's. The DS there had seen it drop out of his pack, but instead of letting the poor bugger know, he let him press on without it. He then radioed Norm to tell this bloke to come back and retrieve the lost protractor once he'd reached the top. On hearing this he dropped to his knees, stared at the ground for a while, then pulled out. It was a good lesson in staying aware, even when you are dead tired.

A few more steep climbs and I was getting near the end of the ordeal, but I had another problem by then. Dried sweat had stiffened the cotton of my trousers and my crotch was chafed red raw. It seemed that the hairs on the inside of my thighs were increasing the friction, so I dropped my pants for a bit of hairdressing with the mini scissors from my Swiss army knife. Me with my wedding tackle stretched out in one hand and the other carefully snipping away at the hairs beneath, would have probably looked to any passers-by like I had stopped right there, in the middle of SAS selection, to castrate myself.

Then, in my most vulnerable moment, I heard someone crash through the bush on the other side of the track. I looked up and spotted Rock. This was almost too much. My paranoia became full-blown – I was convinced he had it in for me and had just seen me playing with myself. I'd be sent home for sure. Rock turned and headed down the track; somehow he hadn't seen me. I pulled up my trousers, took a frantic compass bearing, shouldered my pack and headed off, fast.

'You! Soldier! What the fucking hell do you think you are doing? Stop right there!' Rock boomed at impressive volume.

I stopped in my tracks and looked back. I couldn't see Rock and it took a minute to realise that the person in the shit wasn't me. I needed to get to the next checkpoint, but I didn't want to miss someone getting a good bollocking. I crept up and peered through the scrub. About 30 metres in front of me were a couple of officers who the CO had sprung walking on the track. They were receiving one hell of a tongue-lashing. I hadn't seen brass told off before, and I certainly hadn't seen any with their bottom lips stuck out like that. As soon as the CO had moved off, I launched out of the scrub with an ear-to-ear grin.

'What's up, fellas?' I asked as innocently as I could. The two officers glared at me, then started to justify how it was much safer to walk on the track than to walk parallel to it in the scrub. It was a lame excuse. One of the mottos of the Regiment is *don't get caught*, and they did. Surprisingly one of them made it through the course, so he must have delivered his excuse convincingly – I'm pretty sure the same argument wouldn't have worked for a digger like me.

I pressed on to the next checkpoint. I'm not sure if it was the success of my scissor job or the quality of the distraction, but it no longer hurt down there. I made the last couple of checkpoints and completed that phase of the course a few hours after dark on the second day. By midnight the rest of those still in the game had straggled in. Graham Bremer, the senior non-commissioned officer (NCO) of the DS, called the remainder of us together for a briefing about what was next to come.

'Right, men, you've shown us you can navigate cross-country. Well done. Now you're going to cover the same distance you've just done but in half the time (twenty-four hours). That's averaging three-and-a-half kilometres per hour for those of you who couldn't do maths at school. There's no tricky navigation involved; it's a straight-ahead stomp. There is to be absolutely no talking or walking in groups. You do this alone. We kick off at first light, so you've got time for a few hours' kip. Right after you all give me two-hundred push-ups. Ready? One . . . two . . .'

We grabbed some rations and water before hitting the sack at about 1 a.m. I felt like I had only just got my head down when I was woken up before first light. We were issued maps, given the grid reference for the first checkpoint and turfed out.

The medics had taught us that wet socks softened the skin and created heat as you walked – all perfect conditions for blisters to form. On long marches blisters will cripple you better than anything else. For that reason I took five pairs of socks, and changed them every hour, hanging the sweaty ones on the outside of my pack to dry. It might have looked funny, but it was a wise move. I didn't develop any big blisters and any small ones were pricked, drained and squirted full of raw alcohol to dry them out. This stopped the fluid from creating friction between the skin layers, which would make the blister bigger and more painful. One neglected blister in the wrong place can see you sent home, regardless of how well you are coping otherwise. I was glad I had taken the time to toughen my feet before the course.

Although the route was cross-country, most of the 80 clicks followed a fire track that traversed the spine of a mountain range. The day was spent climbing and descending on a track that alternated between hard stone and soft sand. Just on nightfall I decided to have a rest and a brew. I spied Rolley, whose shiner from the night before the start of the course had faded, doing the same. Most of the blokes had ignored the no-talking rule so I wandered over for a yarn.

'Piss off,' he hissed. 'Go and sit away from me.' He was afraid of getting booted off for talking. Tiredness can intensify your emotions, and Rolley's dismissal stung. I felt like telling him to get stuffed, too. Instead I forced a smile and walked off down the track to have a brew by myself.

We both packed up and set off at the same time. We raced for the next 20 kilometres, overtaking each other time after time, all without saying a word. At one stage I thought Rolley was pushing a bit hard, like a horse that had the sniff of the barn door. It turned out he thought we were coming up to the last checkpoint, whereas I knew we had 17 clicks to go. Rolley beat me to the checkpoint, but just beyond it I spied him sitting dejectedly in the middle of the track, making a brew to try to lift his spirits.

He must have been crushed because as I walked passed he looked at me and started to have a whinge. 'Jeez, Dave. There's seventeen more to go.'

'Hooroo, mate. Not allowed to talk, eh?' I grinned as I blew past him.

Not long after that I started to pass some of the blokes who had cleared off in the morning and were now paying the price for not pacing themselves. Some blokes had even put up their hootchies to sleep for the night. They were either pretty confident or had thrown in the towel. Averaging more than 3 kilometres an hour over that distance is not impossible, as long as you keep going. Blokes who stopped for a kip thought they were doing themselves a favour, but they would wake up needing to hold 5 or 6 k's an hour for the rest of the course. This was pretty unlikely given the condition we were in after the first two weeks.

When Stewie Ellis, the DS manning one of the last checkpoints, offered me some water for my canteens, I didn't trust him: it seemed like another set-up. I later regretted not taking any because at three in the morning, with 9 clicks left to go, severe dehydration set in. My decision to knock back Stewie's offer really started to play on my mind. Even though it was freezing cold, I had a desperate thirst.

I caught up with a group who were climbing a fence that ran across the track. A bloke called Sully was among them, and he gave me one of his spare canteens. Talking about it with him afterwards, he reckoned that he didn't have much choice; the look on my face said I would have torn it off his pack anyway.

The boost I got from the water amazed me. I was off with a vengeance, and at about 4 a.m. I came to another checkpoint. Scotty, the DS there, told me I had finished and I could get my head down. I didn't trust this either; I reckoned there was one more to go. Something he said must have calmed my paranoia, though, and he managed to assure me that it was all over. I had just enough energy left for a relieved smile, and to find a clear patch of scrub and lie down.

By getting in at 4 a.m. I reckoned I had only just made it inside the set time limit. However, there were a few blokes who came in well after that who passed in the end. A couple of hours later the sun woke me, and I watched a few more blokes struggle in, including my mate Don, who'd had a sleep on the way.

Just after midday they told us to get ready to move out again. We were heading back down the way we had come. I looked around and everybody had sunken looks on their faces. I must have too. Trying to move again was excruciating; I walked like I was made of cardboard. Before we set off, they called out a couple of names, including Don's, and pulled these men aside. That was the last I saw of them.

We were down to fewer than fifty contenders now, and we all marched back along the same track we had suffered on the day before. Andy, one of the Brisbane boys, had rolled his ankle on the way and was hobbling along, but he was falling behind, fast.

We marched until dark when they let us make camp for the night. Andy hobbled in about half an hour later. He refused to pull out and take a ride in the ambulance. He was another short guy with attitude.

It started bucketing down, and it would continue all night and all the next day. We set off again at first light and it looked like we would be walking back the whole way. My feet had really started to give me trouble at this stage; my heels were deeply bruised and ached right down to the bone. I would have given anything for a pair of those flash hiking boots that some of the others were wearing. It was okay once I was walking, but it was sheer hell to get moving again each time I stopped.

The rain did not let up. It was coming in sideways and it was freezing cold. Another 20-odd clicks down the track and I started to struggle again. I'd felt defeated a couple of times before, but had managed to find some reserve of will and energy to push through it; this time, though, I doubted I had anything left to draw on. The group was strung out along the track. I was feeling at my lowest so I decided to take a break under a big old gumtree. Just then Andy came hobbling past, his face set grim. I thought for a moment about what he must be going through with his rolled ankle. I compared this to my sore feet and snapped out of it. A tough situation only gets miserable if you let self-pity creep in.

Warmed by a hot brew, I set off down the track again. Each step felt like someone was driving a nail into the bottom of my heel and they were definitely not choking up on the hammer. I reckoned I still had 40 clicks to go. About 10 clicks further on, after descending yet another bloody big hill, I came across another checkpoint. The DS walked up to me and asked how I was feeling.

'Oh, fine,' I said, trying to sound cheery, like I'd just walked down to the local for a beer, instead of having just walked more than 100 k's in a couple of days.

'Well, in that case, zip off around the corner and have a brew with the rest of the guys, and we'll head back into camp after the others roll in,' he said. I still had no trust in any of the DS's attempts to get me to relax, and thought, *Yeah sure – they've probably got beer on tap as well*, as I kept walking. To my surprise, when I rounded the corner I saw a fire going and blokes lounging around under shelters, pigging out on wild mushrooms and drinking brews. It was the end of the stomp. Thank God for that.

The thirty-two guys who remained faced the next back-breaking phase: the 'lucky dip'. We were put into eight-man teams, given one twenty-four-hour ration pack and assigned a series of tasks to be completed over the next few days. The tasks had a few things in common: they involved strength work and they were intensely frustrating – their aim was to break us mentally as well as physically.

The first task seemed straightforward enough: we had to carry around a bloody big log. The log had been nicknamed 'Jerkinoffsky's Rocket'. It weighed at least 150 kilograms and we had to carry it while weaving our way through dense bushland, all the time within eyesight of a perfectly good road. We then had to drag a quarter-tonne trailer along a track for what seemed like 10 k's – and the trailer only had one wheel. Following that we had to carry a huge army tent and the spare wheel for the trailer for about 20 k's through the scrub as well. Every half hour the DS demanded that the tent be erected in the thickest part of the scrub he could find. There were no tent poles so we had to cut our own.

For two days we were constantly harassed and pressured to stick to deadlines, and we only got the occasional short rest. They got this big fat bastard from somewhere, had him lie on a stretcher and made us carry him for miles. He smoked, ate, drank, farted and whined relentlessly the whole bloody way that we were being too rough on him. He was brave in taking up the task because we were very tempted to tip him out on the ground and give him a good kicking.

There was a Land Rover waiting at the end of the stretcher course, ready to take us back to camp. We all piled in, relieved at the thought of getting back to the camp and having some tucker. The DS drove about 100 metres up the road and then stopped. You would think that we would have been wise to the DS's tricks by now. But they got us again.

'We're out of fuel, boys. Get out and push.'

A collective groan went up. We pushed that vehicle up and down hills for the rest of that day and well into the night. Sheets of rain started to fall and the dirt roads were slick with mud. We stopped for a rest at the top of one particularly big hill. Everyone was short on water, and even though it was raining we didn't have time to collect any of it, so we were running around licking the leaves and trying to collect it in our hands. The DS must have felt sorry for us because he decided to go and get us some water to top up our supplies. We knew the Land Rover wasn't really out of fuel, but all the same it was demoralising to see him fire it up and drive away. He was back twenty minutes later with a drum of water.

After rehydrating, we pressed on with pushing the Land Rover to the next checkpoint. Being the smallest and lightest, I got the job of steering. I felt guilty and self-conscious about not pulling my weight, especially on the downhill runs when the DS wouldn't let the others aboard for a free ride. At the bottom of the hill the DS said that the group that had passed through before us had left a mess at the top. He ordered us back up the hill to clean it up. We set off, relieved to be free of the vehicle.

'Don't forget the Land Rover, boys,' he called out behind us. We had to try, I guess.

We pushed the vehicle back up the hill only to find the area spotless.

'Sorry, boys,' the DS said with mock sincerity. 'I just had another mob clean this place up and completely forgot. Off you go again, back down the hill – and take the vehicle.'

Our strength had almost gone. Every time a wheel went down a pothole we had to rock the vehicle back and forwards, and then push hard on the count of three to get it going again. This was happening more and more frequently as we got feebler. A group of grannies could have done better by this stage.

'All right, you weak bastards, I've had a gutful,' the DS snorted. 'Get in.'

We climbed in and roared off. It was 2200 hours. At the next checkpoint we piled out and were told to pitch a shelter and get some sleep. The only food I had left was a bit of flour. I mixed it with water and made a small piece of damper, which I heated on a stick over a hexamine fuel block. The chemicals from the hexamine gave it a foul-tasting crust. I was so hungry that it didn't matter.

Most of us were too wary of being rubber dicked to relax properly, but I gave in to a black wave of sleep. Seconds later the DS shouted us awake and told us pack our kit and prepare for a reconnaissance patrol. During the briefing, 'Trackman' Mal, the only officer in our group, was appointed our leader. He was tasked with the close-in reconnaissance of the mock enemy camp while we sat in the bush and kept watch.

This type of exercise is close to the Regiment's traditional role: cover long distances behind enemy lines with no support, then be switched-on enough to get in close without being detected. As we crept along I started losing control of my balance. It was like being drunk without the fun part. I figured I must have poisoned myself with that hexamine-flavoured damper. I hung in as best I could. The next time we had a break I whispered to a couple of the blokes nearest to me.

'Hey, are you feeling all wobbly?' I hissed as quietly as I could.

'Shit yeah,' one whispered back. 'I'm all bloody light-headed. I've had stuff-all to eat.'

It wasn't such a worry when I realised that we were all feeling that way and that I hadn't sent myself on a bad acid trip with the hexamine.

We found the camp and spread out in the bush, concealing ourselves and trying to stay awake while Mal did his recon. The DS observing the exercise came and stood right above me, staring down. I wasn't sure what he was up to so I sat dead still and stared straight back at him. This went on for about five minutes.

'Are you awake?' he whispered suddenly.

'Yes. Why?' I whispered back.

'Just checking. You looked asleep,' he said before disappearing back into the night. I started to worry about being reported for sleeping on patrol.

Not too long after this Mal came back, but he had lost the DS. The missing DS had our next instructions and we reckoned that losing us wasn't part of his plan. We saw an opportunity to sneak off, camp for the rest of the night and wait to be found. The DS would have to do all the explaining – not us. We were so thrilled by our little scam that we made too much of a racket. The DS walked out of the dark and tore strips off us.

We set off back to camp. I was just plodding along, keeping my attention on the back of the bloke in front of me. He was doing the same and whispered back that we had stopped. When he leaned forward to ask the bloke in front of him what was happening the bloke turned out to be a tree. We decided to stay with our new mate and wait to be found. Someone up ahead realised what had happened and retraced steps on a compass bearing to find us. The DS had run out of ways to abuse us by then and just growled. We eventually returned to camp just as the sun was coming up.

On our return we greeted our new orders – that we had to go on a 20-kilometre route march – with barely a whimper. After four days of being constantly on the go, we had entered that twilight zone of robot-like behaviour – we were beyond the stage of reacting to yet another brutal task. We were all struggling, but we pulled together, gave each other a rev-up and pushed on. I don't remember much from that final stomp.

We stalked into that final checkpoint as wary as cats. There was a table loaded with food, and nearby there was an empty bus. Surely this was another rubber dick.

'Get stuck in, boys,' said one DS, pointing to the table of food. None of us wanted to be the first to eat, but it gradually dawned on us that selection was over. Our stomachs had shrunk after ninety-six hours with almost no food, and so we all got gut aches on the bus back to camp. When we hopped out at the camp I was still expecting another trick, but the DS told us to get cleaned up and hit the sack. I sunk into the deepest sleep I can remember.

Of the 200 who had started three weeks before, only thirty had made it through. But the cruellest thing was yet to come. Only fourteen of us would be accepted into the Regiment. The others were out, and if they wanted to join up they would have to reapply and go through it all again next year.

The next morning we were summoned one by one before Captain Mick Silverstone, the DS in charge of selection, to be given the final verdict. I was nervous as I walked up to the office. To survive all that punishment and then miss out at the final interview would be tough to cop. I was pretty sure they'd fail me on my swimming. DS Silverstone was consulting some notes as I sat down.

'Everett, you have passed with above-average standard.'

I reeled a bit when he said this. It blew me away, in fact. But I kept listening.

'You contributed well both as an individual and team member. Your swimming needs improving and you will have to take remedial lessons in Perth. Do you wish to stay with RAEME or become a trooper?'

'I wish to join the Regiment, sir,' was the only reply I could muster.

That was that. I was in.

We were issued with leave chits and travel warrants for time off when we got back to our units. For the four weekends we had given up we were only given three days off in lieu. I was annoyed about this because we were all still exhausted and needed time to recover. The Brisbane boys and I decided to pull a scam, amending the '3' on our leave forms to an '8', giving us five extra days' leave. We figured there would be no questions asked as we were the only blokes from Brisbane who had got through. Nobody would be checking. We had earned it, anyway.

The next day, back in the orderly room of the 106, Sergeant Wilson was more than a little stunned when I handed him my paperwork. It was too much to expect a word of congratulation from him. He looked shattered; no doubt thinking of the money he had lost betting on Don.

'Well, what are you standing there for, Everett?' he said. 'You're on leave. Take off.'

Within half a day I had my feet up on the balcony of a Gold Coast holiday apartment, cold beer in my hand, with saltwater drying on my skin. It was a perfect Queensland day. Looking out at the deep blue Pacific Ocean the reality of what I had accomplished started to sink in.

Then the phone rang.

'Is that you, Everett?' It was Sergeant Wilson. There was a triumphant ring to his voice that gave me a sinking feeling. 'I was wondering why they would give you eight days off when they only gave Don three, so I rang the Regiment. You doctored your leave form, didn't you? Get your arse back here, you little prick. You are well and truly in the shit now.'

I should have known that pinhead would double-check everything. I reckon he rang them to see if I had actually passed the course. It was a gloomy drive back up to the barracks at any rate. My mind was clouded with pictures of all kinds of bad scenarios.

Walking into the duty room the next day, I was greeted by a beaming Staff Sergeant Wilson, looking like the chubby cat that ate the cream.

'You are truly fucked now, son. You will be charged and any plans of joining the SAS are out the bloody window.' I tried to act innocent as he gloated about his detective work.

'What's the drama about?' I interrupted, trying to stay calm. 'Nobody from my unit is due back from the bush for a week and there is nothing to do around here anyway. So who really gives a rat's arse if I took an extra five days? I'd be sitting on my bum doing zip anyway.'

'Bad luck,' he said. 'You can get your kit together and join the unit at Tin Can Bay on the next resupply. I'll be formally charging you. You can expect to see the OC when you get back.'

I got on the phone to the other blokes who had altered the forms as quick as I could. Most of them had speared off interstate to celebrate, so a lot of shifty dealing had to happen if we were to avoid having this thing blow up. Leave forms were retrieved and destroyed from a few company orderly rooms, using up a few favours in the process. It turned out that I was the only one who got burnt.

The formal hearing with the OC was held the following Friday. I was marched into his office with an escort and stood to attention in front of him. He read out the charge and called in his only witness – Staff Sergeant Greg Bloody Wilson. Wilson gave a summary of his actions after discovering the 'irregularity' in the paperwork.

Once Wilson had left the room the OC gave me a lecture. It was obvious he had consulted my bosses in the workshop and had done his homework on me. I was confined to barracks (CB) for eight days, but would still be allowed to join the Regiment.

Most blokes just slack off when they are CB. But I wanted to leave the place on a good note. I cleaned up the gardens around the boozers in the barracks and the living lines. Really got it looking spick and span. Everybody was pleasantly surprised when they saw how this lifted the place, so I left on good terms.

I finally caught up with Don as well. He confirmed that he had been kicked off the selection course for being late on that walk where he'd had a sleep.

'Mate, I should have done more training when you asked, instead of telling you to piss off.' He looked a bit sheepish as he shook my hand, but I had no hard feelings. He is a typical knockabout Queenslander in many ways and a good bloke. We still keep in touch and swap the occasional letter or Christmas card.

I had one more stop before heading west: parachute training school in Williamstown so I could pick up my static-line parachute training wings. This was the first opportunity we had to meet up with the blokes from the second selection course. There were about thirty of us all up – some weekend warriors from the reserve commando units in Sydney and Melbourne, infantry blokes from the battalions, engineers and one RAEME (me).

Our first training jump was above the Saltash drop zone and I was first to go. I had nobody to follow out the door. I remember wishing that first jump could have been out the side door of the plane – that way you wouldn't have been able to see out until the last minute. Instead, when the big Caribou opened its tailgate, I was standing on the edge of this yawning hole, watching the ground rush past 2000 feet below. The hard training kicked in when the green light went on. I didn't think too much and stepped out into the void.

I was ripped downwards by gravity and buffeted about by the wall of wind I was hitting at over 160 kilometres per hour. I counted to three and looked up, expecting to see my parachute streaming out above me. It wasn't. Instead it was in front of me. *Crikey*, I thought. *Nobody told me about this*. My hand gripped the reserve parachute handle. It was then I realised that you are supposed to count to three in three actual, whole seconds. Not the 'onetwo-three' I had rattled off in my hyped-up, adrenalin-fuelled state. The deliberate counting was aimed at avoiding what I had almost just done. Static-line chutes will always open up like that before the canopy fills properly.

Next thing I knew, the canopy banged open. It felt like my nuts had been driven back up into my body. The deceleration made me feel as if I was being dragged upwards by a giant hand. Then, other training drills kicked into practice and I made sure I was clear of other chutes and started preparing to land. After the cacophony of leaving the plane, it was a sensory overload in reverse: coping with the eerie silence, hanging there in the air, suspended a mile above the ground only by some rip-stop nylon and string.

I landed and executed what I thought was a pretty good parachute roll. *At least an 8.5 from the Russian judge*, I thought and bounced up, instantly addicted. Even having one of the instructors running over and telling me off for ten different things I had done wrong didn't dampen my enthusiasm. Thus began a love affair with parachuting.

We did another jump that day, and then that night we went to the air-force boozer and got on the suds. Most of us had been terrified and it felt good to share this with the other blokes. Knowing that you were not alone in your fears made them easier to cope with. Wayne, the Regiment cook who I had met walking on the track during selection, had made it this far, but was severely rattled from the first two jumps. Instead of coming out with us and letting off some steam, he stayed in his room and psyched himself out of jumping again. He dropped out of the course soon after.

I passed the course without any problems, got my jump wings and headed back up to say goodbye to the blokes at 106. Then I packed my kit and put my motorbike on a trailer behind my panel van. I headed out of town; it felt good to be setting off after all the effort I'd put in and all the hurdles I had jumped on the way. It finally hit me that I had made it into one of the world's elite military units. I had a 4000-kilometre drive across the continent to think about what was in store when I reached Swanbourne.

THE REGIMENT

I had heard that the Regiment was located in a nice spot in Perth, but I still wasn't prepared for the view when I came over the hill at Mount Claremont. It had to be every soldier's dream to be located next to one of the world's most beautiful stretches of beach. Oh, and make that a *nudist* beach. I rolled the van up to the security gate at Campbell Barracks, Swanbourne.

When the army first built Campbell Barracks during World War Two, Swanbourne was an out-of-the-way bit of coastal scrub next to a rifle range. Now it has been swamped by urban growth; the suburb's proximity to the long strip of white sand bordering the deep blue Indian ocean, golf course and nature reserve make it one of Perth's most exclusive areas. I think the nudists, who have been coming there since the seventies, probably feel a bit swamped, too.

The trooper at the gate took my name and checked it against a list. 'Everett, D. Let's see, you are to report immediately to the Squadron Sergeant Major.'

I entered the sergeant major's office, took one look at his face and knew that the Brisbane leave fiasco was not over. He glared at me and then came straight to the point.

'Everett, if you fuck up again, you'll be fucking fucked off the fuck out of here. Do whatever you fucking want but don't get fucking caught!'

I'd like to say that this was the most I've heard the word 'fuck' used in a single sentence, but it was pretty average for the army. With that welcome ringing in my ears, I was shown to my new home. Life as a Special Forces soldier had begun.

There have always been Special Forces in the military. Most people think that the tradition began when Lieutenant David Stirling and Australian Jock Lewes formed the British SAS in 1941. But the history of elite irregular units that patrolled behind enemy lines goes back much further. You can trace their evolution back to the long-range desert group (the SAS's predecessor) in World War Two, Lawrence of Arabia in World War One, the original commandos of the Boer War at the turn of the twentieth century, as well as to the American Civil War and War of Independence. Hand-picked groups of men have been conducting long-distance raids into enemy territory since we first chucked a spear.

Before I joined, my perception of the Regiment was shaped by my other army experiences. I wanted to get in because it seemed like bloody good fun and the best possible way to be a real soldier. I didn't become aware of the SAS mythology until after I left and I still don't buy it. Blokes in the Regiment aren't super-warriors. They are professional soldiers. Just like top-performing sportspeople, surgeons, lawyers, engineers or whoever, they strive to be at the top of the game.

Passing selection didn't earn us the right to wear the famous sandy beret with its winged dagger badge; the twenty-eight of us had a series of courses to pass before we would be admitted to the Regiment proper. I'd been forewarned about this, but some blokes were shocked to find out that for the next few months we would be pushed just as hard as during selection, with the threat of instant orders to return to unit (RTU) if we didn't pass. We were kept separate in draughty old World War Two-era huts as well, just to remind us that we weren't there yet.

First up was a rappelling course. One form of getting people in and out on a patrol is by rope from a helicopter. We learnt to make a makeshift harness, called a 'Swiss seat', out of a length of rope that wrapped around your legs and bum like a nappy. To insert, we attached our harness to the rope via a karabina and a metal friction device called a 'figure eight' and slid down the rope from the helicopter. To extract, each man hooks his harness to the rope hanging from the chopper and the entire six-man patrol is hoisted away on one long string. It would probably have been terrifying to anyone who was afraid of heights, but none of us had any problems. I was having a blast; it was just the sort of fun I had expected.

Next we learnt demolitions. Give explosives to someone with no training and the only thing they'll blow up is themselves. The course went on for five very intense weeks and involved lots of late nights studying the physics and chemistry involved. We first familiarised ourselves with all the different types of explosives, both civilian and military, that were currently used around the world. The theory was then applied to demolishing everything from the gearbox housing in a car to railway bridges and buildings, as well as breaching dam walls and sinking ships – all using the least amount of explosive as possible.

We were shown how to make explosives and detonators from common household items and how to trigger them with mechanical, electrical and chemical fuses. The final part of explosives training demonstrated how to lay explosive ambushes and booby-trap everyday items in homes, factories, aircraft and vehicles.

Weapons familiarisation was next. The Regiment teaches you how to handle almost every common military weapon in the world. For a gun-nut from Tassie this was Christmas and birthday rolled into one.

We started with the famous Soviet AK-47, favoured by communist armies and terrorists the world over. It pulls high and to the right, rusts easily, is very heavy, has a weird safety catch that you have to take your hand off the pistol grip to operate, and it goes to full automatic on the first click and semi on the second – otherwise, it is a very reliable weapon and makes for a good club when you run out of ammo.

The Regiment also had its own modified self-loading rifle (SLR) that we called 'the bitch'. It was fully automatic, had a shortened barrel with a pistol grip on the front stock, kicked like a mule, had immense man-eliminating power and was easily fired from the hip.

The American M-16 and its little brother, the CAR-15, both used smaller 5.56-millimetre rounds. These felt like pop guns and seemed boring when compared to the AKs. The 5.56-millimetre round won't drop a man as well as the 7.62-millimetre, but I still like them because they are light and you can carry heaps of ammo. We'd heard plenty of stories of North Vietnamese soldiers, high on amphetamines, taking more than ten hits from an M-16 before going down. This is not what you need in a firefight. The M-16 is also made with a few plastic parts and is not as robust as the SLR and AK-47.

We played with belt-fed machineguns, like the World War Two-era German MG-42 and the American M-60, whose action is a copy of the MG-42 and the .30 and .50 calibre Brownings. Generally these were used by the vehicle-mounted troops as they were too cumbersome to patrol with. We also used a range of submachine guns and several types of pistols and silenced weapons. The list goes on.

There had been some whispers that weapons training would be followed by a combat survival course; the rumours were that it was tougher than selection and if you were going to be sent home from the Regiment it would be during this stage. Nobody was allowed to tell us too much, but we'd heard that it involved living off the land for a month without any survival gear. At the time there was a major military exercise going on, with Americans, British and New Zealanders all involved. 'Kangaroo 1983' dealt with the scenario of Australia being invaded, and covered the whole top end of the country, from Port Hedland through Darwin to the Cape York Peninsula. The word came for us to be ready to leave at 0600 one morning. We were told that we were going up to act as the enemy for part of the exercise. Not a word was mentioned about the combat survival course, but nobody was fooled: we knew it was the start of the course. We acted dumb anyway.

After a three-hour flight, we landed in the fierce heat of Port Hedland and set up camp on the edge of an airstrip. As a bit of a public-relations exercise, the US Army had sent some of their 'Special Forces' guys to do the course with us. A couple of these blokes were green berets and the rest were CCT (combat control team) operators.

You have to understand one thing about the US military. It's mainly a catchment for people who can't function anywhere else. Much of their system pivots around raising the self-esteem of blokes who clearly aren't the sharpest tools in the shed. So they get medals for hitting the target on the shooting range, medals for passing basic training; they even have a medal for getting wounded called the 'Purple Heart'. They would probably have a medal for wiping your bum if they could decide what to call it.

It's the same with their Special Forces. It seemed like every second Yank I met was in some kind of Special Forces outfit. Of course, they do have some excellent soldiers and the couple of green berets who did the combat survival with us really knew their stuff. The CCT blokes, on the other hand, were all Arkansas farm-boys who chewed tobacco, strutted around, boasted about how good they were and generally fitted the stereotype of the arrogant Yank. Stupidity combined with an artificially inflated ego is a pretty lethal mix.

The night before departure they screened *The Green Berets*, starring John Wayne. You couldn't make a more ridiculous, over-the-top piece of propaganda if you tried. Not surprisingly, it's the only World War Two-style, patriotic, 'raise-the-flag' film ever made about Vietnam. We treated it as a comedy and laughed all the way through. But the Yanks were whooping and hollering and cheering on 'The Duke' like he was a real war hero. They all had their hands over their hearts at the end.

On the same night, right after the movie, they screened the last race of the 1983 America's Cup. The Yanks were chanting 'USA! USA!' right up until it became obvious that the Aussies were going to win. Then they started downplaying the whole thing, saying that they'd 'never heard of no goddamned America's Cup' until they came here. 'Y'all should come and play us in baseball.' I think the defeat might have punctured their collective self-esteem.

It was 3 a.m. and we were going to be moving in less than an hour, but I stayed up to watch that famous TV footage of Alan Bond (who I would meet in prison ten years later) with his arms in the air as if he were conducting a choir, signalling a crane to raise the keel of Australia II out of the water.

The DS in charge of the course gave a briefing at 4 a.m., telling us to prepare to set up a new camp. Unbelievably they still thought they had us fooled about what was happening next. That was until Tinlegs, one of the Brisbane boys, called out, 'Hey, boss! How do you cook a goanna?' Everyone, including the DS, cracked up laughing. The game was up.

We were issued parachutes and packed into a C130 Hercules aircraft, which took off into the darkness. All the windows on the plane were blacked out in an attempt to disguise which direction we were heading, but we all had compasses and it was no mystery that we were heading south. About one hour later I was just getting comfortable when I was jarred by the screeching of crash alarms. The familiar drone of the engines cut out and the nose of the aircraft dipped alarmingly.

Shit, we're going to crash, I thought.

There was chaos as the crew chiefs and the jump masters buzzed around, getting everyone ready to jump before we spudded in. The ramp went down amid the confusion, and the aircraft lurched unpredictably as it lost power. I clipped my harness to the static line as the jump masters raced down the rows of men frantically checking everyone's rig. Next thing they were spearing people out the back as fast as they could.

As soon as my chute popped, I twisted around to try to see where the Hercules would crash. No sooner had the last man exited than the bloody aircraft roared back to life and headed off up north. They'd fooled me again.

Spread out below were endless miles of red dirt and yellow spinifex grass as far as the eye could see. Even at 500 feet the air felt like it had come from a furnace. On landing we were met by a number of DS wearing American camouflage gear who officially welcomed us to the 1983 Combat Survival Course. They stripped us of our kits and sent us off on a 15-kilometre march, telling us to look for a small, muddy dam. We waited there for a couple of days before a DS reappeared, told us we were all useless and then sent us on a 20-kilometre route march to Mindaroo Station, which is 80-odd kilometres west of the coastal town of Onslow, where my mum was born. Once we reached the station, we were told to bunk down in an old shearing shed. We had two weeks of intense survival instruction ahead of us.

Survival is both a science and an art, and it takes years to learn properly. A couple of weeks' training would only cover the basics, so the DS focused on things we would face over the next month. One of the first things he covered was how to withstand interrogation. Even though they're not for real, in these sorts of courses the interrogation sessions can get pretty rough. I've been put in stress positions, bashed around, placed up to my neck in shit-pits and starved of food, water and sleep – all in the name of training. There is no magic psychological trick to learning how to withstand pain – you can't tell how you'll react to someone putting your nuts in a vice, but being familiar with torture methods means there will be fewer surprises if you get caught.

If being the operative word. We learnt basic escape and evasion techniques: how to stay hidden in the desert, how to make only small fires from old, dry hardwoods to avoid producing too much smoke, how to disguise shelters and how to navigate at night.

A botanist from the University of Western Australia taught us about the edible plants in the area, but this was a bit daunting: we seemed to drive more than 5 k's in one direction to look at a bulb or root, then 5 k's in another direction to find something else. Living in the desert would be tough if you were a vegetarian. Lucky for us there were plenty of kangaroos and sheep around. Without a doubt, water is the most crucial factor in survival; so we learnt where to dig in dry creek beds and how to make a still from any old metal drum to desalinate seawater, as well as how to make a solar still by digging a hole, filling it with green leaves and covering it with a sheet of plastic to catch evaporated water from the leaves.

After our two weeks at Mindaroo, we were herded into the back of covered trucks, sealed in so we couldn't see the direction and driven off into the bush. After a couple of hours bouncing on rough tracks, the truck slammed to a stop and a DS bashed on its side, screaming at us to get out. They lined us up and shouted at us to get our clothes off. Once we had stripped naked, one of the DS pulled on a rubber glove. A few years back blokes were known to smuggle button compasses, matches, small knives and any other piece of survival gear small enough to fit up the rectum. Of course, now these same fellows were running the course they knew just where to look. Nevertheless, I thought the threat of a rectal cavity search was just a joke, right up until the point when two DS grabbed me, bent me over and spread my legs. I don't care what you say, nothing is meant to go up your bum in that direction and the DS's finger hurt like hell.

Standing there, barefoot, naked and no longer virgins, we were each issued with a potato sack that would be our only clothing for the next few weeks, and put back into the trucks. We were dropped off alone at varying points of the compass and told in which rough direction it was back to Mindaroo. We had to be back before dark or we would fail the course. It was no use following the track – it took you on a winding 100-kilometre journey back to the station, where the trip was only 40 kilometres cross-country. There was no choice but to go overland, using the sun to navigate.

A couple of guys didn't make it in time, and we assumed they'd be booted off the course and RTU. Once we arrived, we were held until nightfall when we were given an obscure, far-off road junction as a mark and told to go cross-country again, this time using the stars to navigate. Everyone managed to turn up at that point, except the blokes missing from the previous day. It was straight back onto a truck and into Onslow. We were herded onto a boat and ferried out to a flat, rocky island. So far I had coped pretty well. The course was physically less demanding than selection, as the terrain was flat and we weren't humping huge packs. But the heat was fierce and dehydration was an issue: it was all about being smart, conserving energy and finding water. I suppose I was more confident by that stage; like everyone else there I had passed selection, so I knew I belonged. Although we could still be RTU at any point, the reality was that only a few blokes didn't make it through; whereas in the selection course there was someone bailing out every few hours.

We'd seen several big tiger sharks on the boat trip, so a few of us hesitated when the DS stopped 100 metres offshore and told us to swim in – they ended up having to boot a couple of blokes into the water. It came out in the debrief – after the course – that the DS had placed a couple of 44-gallon drums on the island, which we were supposed to use as stills for desalinating seawater. The problem was that there had been a cyclone a few weeks after that and the drums had disappeared. So by the time we arrived there was no water, and no way to make it. For the first two days we were stuck in 40-degree heat with nothing to drink except the blood of fish and turtles, which is pretty salty.

It was getting desperate; we stopped worrying about passing the course and starting wondering whether we'd survive long enough to make it off the island. A naval patrol boat happened to be passing by as part of the Kangaroo '83 exercise, and we signalled them with a fire. It turned out they assumed we were part of 'the enemy'. As they came toward the shore, we heard great percussive booms, like someone hitting a big bass drum; it was the sound of them firing at us with their 40-millimetre canon, using blanks, of course. Convinced that they'd killed us all, they sent a small contingent ashore with their umpire to claim victory. As soon as the bow of their little dinghy hit the sand, we roared out of the dunes, tackled them to the ground and stole everything that wasn't bolted down, especially their water. They must have thought they'd stumbled on some mad neanderthals. By this stage we were starting to look pretty wild. We had been eating relatively well, but the diet was almost totally protein so we'd all burned off any excess fat. With our skin parched from dehydration, we were cut like bodybuilders just before a competition. Our hair was matted and greasy, standing on end like we'd had electric shocks. To top off the look we were all coated from head to toe with a layer of fine red dust.

The biggest fellas in our team just sat on the Navy blokes to keep them still while we plotted how we were going to take the dinghy out to the patrol boat and raid that as well.

At that crucial moment the old fishing boat that had dropped us off appeared on the horizon. The DS had found the blokes who had got lost a few days back and were bringing them over to the island. The missing couple hadn't been RTU and were getting a second chance. The DS rescued the Navy blokes, probably side-stepping a major incident. They dropped off the two stragglers with an empty 44-gallon drum for a still, and then headed off to mend a few fences with the Navy boys, no doubt with the aid of grog.

At the same time, they dropped off – of all people – an army psychologist to accompany our group. This bloke was an officer who was writing a paper on the psychological hardship faced by military men surviving off the land. I reckon the only psychological hardship we faced was looking after this pinhead. He complained of being hot and thirsty after only a few hours, and the next morning he signalled the DS to pick him up and take him back to the luxury of the patrol boat. Some mothers do have 'em.

Back on the island we were just starting to enjoy ourselves. This area of WA has some of the best fishing in the world. Turtles and crabs were easy enough to grab, and as the tide went out plenty of fish were stranded in the small tide pools. With the water-supply issue solved, we spent the days in the shade and the nights fishing. We were quite comfortable. After a few days of monitoring this, the DS must have thought that we were looking a bit too relaxed. They ordered us back onto the fishing boat, took us to the mainland and drove us back out into the desert.

This time we were dropped off in groups of eight and told that we would have to survive off the land for a fortnight. There would be patrols out looking for us, and if we got caught then it would be 'into the bag' – Regiment slang for being captured and interrogated. Luckily, there were stacks of roos, goannas and bush tucker around to eat, so we wouldn't go hungry. It would be a case of having to keep on the move and stay hidden so we wouldn't be picked up.

The Yanks were shattered when we got dropped off in the desert again. They'd been told they would be heading back to the US once we left the island. They were ready to pack it in and go home. They weren't bad blokes, and we actually felt a bit sorry for them. We decided to give them a treat; we'd knock a sheep on the head and have a slap-up lamb dinner. This was taking a bit of a risk as we'd been specifically told that if we killed any sheep and were caught, then we'd be RTU.

After a few hours of searching the bush, we eventually found one old ewe; we surrounded her, each with some form of spear or club. The old sheep was quicker than she looked, and she threw a sidestep that would have done David Campese proud and burst through our circle. We all gave chase. The Yanks were the first to give up and start crying as their tucker took off over the hill. One by one we dropped by the wayside as this sheep ran around like it had an Apollo rocket up its arse.

I gave up after a few hundred yards and dropped to the ground, winded. Just as I was thinking how silly we were going to look in front of the Yanks, I heard pounding footsteps. I still have this image of a bloke called Kev running in hot pursuit of the ewe. He had found his second wind. His arms were pumping, knees lifting high, hair and spud sack streaming out behind him as he crested the hill and ran out of sight. Then I heard this breathless voice shouting out from the other side of the hill, 'For fuck's sake, you blokes! Come and bloody help me or it's gonna get away.' As one we rose and raced over the hill to find Kev wrestling with the ewe. Thank God Kev was a Kiwi.

One of the blokes gave the ewe a thump on the head with a nulla nulla and put it to sleep. Then we set about getting a fire started: we got a flat piece of hardwood for a base and a long, thin branch of softer wood for the drill. A small notch was carved in one end of the hardwood, with a tiny little depression to fit the end of the drill. The notch was filled with the fluffiest, driest grass we could find, and three of us got in a circle and took turns rubbing the stick between our palms. As one guy worked his hands to the bottom of the stick, the next guy would start at the top, keeping the drill spinning constantly. It was taking forever and our bellies started growling pretty loud. Just as the Yanks started moaning again a thin wisp of smoke appeared. They started cheering like it was the fourth of July. Lucky they didn't start chanting 'USA!' again or they would have been thumped. A bit of kindling was added and we soon had ourselves a decent fire with a nice pile of glowing coals. On went the sheep, wool and all. We covered her over with dirt to cook for a couple of hours.

Once the carcass was dragged out, it was easy to peel off the skin and get stuck into the meat and entrails. The meat was juicy and tasted as good as anything I've ever eaten. The Yanks were in tears of gratitude as they ate. As our stomachs quickly filled, talk came back around to the great hunt and Kev's heroic burst of speed.

'I don't know what he did with the ewe before I got over the hill, but when I got there they were both having a cigarette,' I said. We had a good laugh, which was great for morale. Afterwards, we lay around with full bellies, picking our teeth with twigs like kings after a feast.

Rubbing sticks together for fire was tedious work, so from then on we elected a fire watcher to carry some smouldering coals in an old tin can when we moved camp. This was just how the Aborigines used to do it – carry a few embers with them, rather than start from scratch every night. We'd make a thick shelter out of spinifex each night and have a small fire going, and then we'd huddle together for warmth as the temperature dropped, often to below zero. A couple of the Yanks persisted in asking for a big, roaring fire. We couldn't get it into their heads that doing this would give our position away. I thought to myself that if we got caught, it was unlikely that the Yanks would cop the same sort of flogging we would get in interrogation – they probably didn't care about getting caught as much as we did.

In the middle of the day, with the temperature climbing into the forties, we would try to find a shady place to lie down and avoid dehydration. Other army units weren't the only things hunting us – lie down in the wrong spot and thousands of huge ants would try to eat you alive. The trick was to creep really quietly to a shady spot where there weren't any ant trails. Roll over or hit the ground accidentally and they would be attracted by the vibrations and be all over you in seconds, and the next hour would be spent picking them out of every orifice in your body.

Once we got to know the area well, our hunting really improved. We got so successful at our kangaroo ambushes that there were legs of meat hanging from trees all around the place. We'd make jerky out of most of it and only used the fire to roast up the livers, which were a real delicacy. One day we were all spread out in the scrub trying to have a snooze when a mob of emus came into our midst. They were obviously curious about these strange-looking objects sprawled out in the scrub. One got too close for comfort, and as it bent down, I gave it a whack on the side of its head with my nulla nulla and dropped it like a stone. Next thing all the guys were up attacking the startled emus, most of whom made a hasty retreat, never to be seen again. The final score was cavemen: 2; emus: 0. I'd never eaten this half of our national emblem before. The meat was as tough as shoe leather, but made a welcome change from roo meat.

One day we heard the gunshot signals to come in, so we cautiously approached the pick-up point. The DS told us to stay in the bush while the Yanks were ordered into the truck. They were going home. Again they let rip with the whooping and hollering. Bloody Americans. To their credit, as they took off one of them threw a box out of the back of the vehicle. He had pinched one of the DS's private tuckerboxes and it was full of cereal, cans of baked beans and condensed milk, bread, peanut butter, Vegemite, spices, sugar and other goodies. We had another feast that night. The way we were going we'd have to watch our weight or we wouldn't fit into the spud sacks.

We had another week in the bush before we heard the three-rifle-shot signal again. At the designated pick-up point it was back into the trucks and we were driven out to the North-West Coastal Highway. We were turfed out on the side of the road, and the DS chucked a pile of assorted old military clothing in the dirt in front of us, telling us to get changed. We reluctantly parted with our spud sacks, which we'd grown fond of by that time, and sorted through the gear looking for things that would fit.

The DS then told us we had to be back in Perth – more than 1000 kilometres south – within twenty-four hours or we'd fail the course and be RTU. Everybody started hitchhiking. I teamed up with Henry Ford, as I called him, and we hitched north initially to get away from the main pack. One enterprising group caught up to one of the the DS, who was having a feed in a roadhouse, hot-wired his Land Rover and took off with it. When he realised what had happened the DS called the cops, got on the radio and threatened immediate dismissal from the course if the vehicle wasn't returned. Luckily, the boys were monitoring the frequency and took it back.

Henry Ford and I flagged down a road train and struck gold straightaway. The truckie was a good bloke but said he wasn't planning to go straight through to Perth. After we told him about our dilemma, he changed his plan and said we could do it without a break as long as one of us would share the driving. I hadn't driven a road train before but had been around trucks for ages. The only difficulty I had with the extra couple of trailers on the back was when we'd take corners. I flattened a few road signs before I learnt to go really wide. Luckily, the truckie was asleep at the time.

We got back to Swanbourne with nearly half a day to spare and were looking forward to a hot shower and a decent feed. As I walked into the duty room, half a dozen thugs dressed in black and wearing ski masks set on me. An almighty fight ensued. Unfortunately, I lost. I had mace sprayed in my face, then I was kicked to the ground, belted in the guts, maced again, handcuffed, and a bag was thrown over my head. That obviously wasn't enough: then they hurled me face-first into a wall. Bouncing off that produced a bagful of blood and snot as they dragged me coughing and spewing into an interrogation room. From the ruckus going on behind me I figured Henry had suffered the same fate. The DS did a tag team on us for the next twenty-four hours: stripping us naked, humiliating us, and slapping us awake whenever we dozed off. They wanted us to cough up any information about ourselves and members of our family – any information that would be useful to the enemy in a time of war.

We all handled the interrogation in different ways. The number one rule is: don't talk, act dumb and give nothing away. Macka, who I was to work for later in Queensland while I was on the run, was a supreme bullshit artist. He took the opposite tack and told a fantastical story about how he was just an engineer who was doing some prospecting in the bush when he was accosted by the rest of us and made to work as a slave for a month, carrying our packs, digging our latrine pits and cooking for us. He was so convincing I reckon the DS might have gone to check the records to see if he wasn't indeed some poor civilian we had picked up. Another bloke screamed blue murder every time they touched him, as if he had a broken arm, just like they had taught us in training.

One of the officers, Lieutenant Brian Fuge, actually lost the plot and tried to escape out of the room with his hands tied behind his back and the hood still over his head. 'Follow me, men,' he said as he ran past. Talk about the blind leading the blind. I heard a deep thud, and I wasn't sure if he had run headfirst into the wall or one of the DS had thumped him. He was quiet after that.

I stayed quiet and acted as lethargically as I could, trying to give the impression that I'd be too hard to communicate with and that there were much more interesting blokes to interrogate than me. I counted back the days we had spent on the course, trying to match them to the date that the next course was starting. I wanted to get some bearing on how long the interrogation would go on for. I was banking on it lasting around a week, but after twenty-four hours a DS ripped the hoods off us and said, 'That's it. The course is over. You are now on forty-eight hours' leave. Well done.'

It's hard to describe the surreal feeling you get after living like an animal in the bush for more than a month, under extreme pressure every moment, and then walking into a pub full of nicely dressed civilians laughing and drinking. We didn't feel like outsiders – more like aliens from another planet. Nobody in the pub came near us. We thought it was because we still had the wild bushman's stare in our eyes until we realised that we were giving off some of the fumes from the mace and making people's eyes sting. None of us met any nice girls that night.

After our two days off, it was on to the patrol course. We were really getting down to it now: patrolling is the essence of the SAS regiment, our bread and butter. Again, we were warned that only a high level of performance would prevent us from being shown out the gate. The initial phase ran for a few weeks and was conducted in dense scrub country in the south-west corner of the state. We spent the whole time drilling in SAS ambush and counter-ambush techniques, fire and movement, patrolling, infiltration, extraction, resupplying and working with the air force in close-country conditions. Then it was out into the desert to learn how to do the same activities in open country.

If you wanted to boil down the life of an SAS trooper, it would come to this: the six-man patrol. Before first light, we're up, packed and ready to move out within a matter of minutes. The six of us head out silently into the bush, staying hyper-vigilant, moving in synchrony like a twelve-legged animal. Every footstep is considered and measured for the amount of noise it will make. The movements appear slow and languid, as if we are half-asleep when we are anything but. Sometimes we move only a couple of kilometres in a day, but we are on our feet for most of the time, with up to 50 kilograms of gear hanging off our bodies.

If we get bumped (accidentally run into the enemy) this pace changes immediately. With no time to look for cover, it is a matter of turning around to send a murderous volume of fire down-range at the enemy. Not blasting away from the hip and emptying magazines on full auto like you see in the movies, but blokes firing single aimed shots, while others move back and then take over to maintain a continuous stream of fire. The idea is to create the impression of a much bigger force, so the enemy will get their heads down and give us an opportunity to clear off. Knowing when to turn the fusillade on and off to save ammunition is an art. Resupply is not always guaranteed because in most cases we are working deep in hostile enemy territory. Going over our drills like this, again and again, day after day, develops the skill level of the team to the point where the value of the unit is much greater than the sum of its parts.

During these drills, our team would normally lay up in a camp just before sundown. If the patrol was setting up observation posts, ambushes or demolition jobs, then we'd pull watches every few hours. Patrols can last from a week to a couple of months, and there is absolutely no glamour involved. It's bloody hard work and patrolling remains one of the toughest things I have ever had to do. There is the combination of extreme danger (either real or imagined), the need for concentration that this requires, and mind-bending boredom. This war within yourself – between the need to stay 100 per cent switched on and the urge to slack off – did more than a few blokes in. I remember most of that patrol course as just one big, long day repeated over and over; but a couple of incidents stand out.

We were just about to lay up one night when I heard a strange sound. The bush is rarely quiet, especially at sunrise or sundown, but the sound of the wind in the treetops, the creak of branches, the bird calls and the rustle of animals in the undergrowth all take on a familiar tone after a week or two. It's easy to pick out a noise that doesn't belong. It started as a soft mewing, which might have been a baby animal lost and calling for its mother, but then turned into a deep moan that was definitely human. Someone was in a lot of pain. It was coming from Tinlegs' position; I thought that to break patrol conditions and make that much racket he must have broken a leg. In between the moans there was a lot of grunting, so I reckoned he was trying to drag himself towards me.

As I moved over his way, the pitiable moaning stopped and soon after I spotted Tinlegs sitting on a log, looking shattered, with tears in his eyes. Still maintaining patrol discipline, I just raised my eyebrows to ask, 'What's up?' He lifted a shaky finger and pointed to a shiny brown turd lying on the ground. It was about a foot long and as thick as my wrist. It looked like a giant chocolate anaconda with layers of compacted shit for scales. The ration packs we ate on patrol contained a lot of egg whites and they made us constipated – which wasn't a bad thing, as human shit is a dead giveaway to a search party. Poor old Tinlegs had just given birth to about five days' worth of crap in one hit. I just smiled and moved back to my position. Tinlegs looked like he was in for a bout of postnatal depression. He's a politician nowadays.

The other incident that sticks in my mind happened out in the desert. We had set up an OP near a road, the LUP back in the scrub, and swapped shifts watching the road. I was stretching out in the LUP, half dozing, while another bloke heated up a brew on his hexamine-fueled stove. Why he wanted a hot brew in forty-degree heat was beyond me. Anyway, as he leaned over to stir the billy, a piece of camouflage scrimmage around his neck dangled into the flame and caught fire. He looked pretty comical as he tried, with increasing panic, to rip off his flaming necklace and beat out the flames at the same time.

I stopped laughing when the rest of the LUP, which was made of dead wood, sticks and spinifex, went up like a tin of petrol with a big whoosh. We threw our packs and rifles out past the flames and then flung ourselves through them, rolling madly in the dust, trying to put out our burning clothes. Oily black smoke was rising in a huge column above the burning LUP. We did a quick headcount to ensure everyone was out, and then desperately threw sand onto the flames. The enemy group was patrolling in helicopters as well as vehicles, and we expected to hear the thump-thump of chopper blades at any minute. To be caught out here meant going in the bag for the duration of the exercise, and nobody wanted that. The blokes from the OP came scurrying back, and the DS appeared out of nowhere and got stuck into us. Once the fire was doused, we camouflaged the area and shot through before anybody else could come to investigate. The only casualty of the whole affair was the necklace-wearer's bruised ego and my much-loved balaclava, which I sorely missed on the cold nights that followed.

Just like the combat survival course, the patrol course finished with another dose of interrogation, this time for a week and with experts flown in from Canberra to try to break us. Again, just when I had calculated that it'd continue for a while yet, the bag was ripped off my head and I was told it was all over. I had finally earned my sandy beret; it was issued in a small ceremony back at Swanbourne. I didn't feel any real sense of achievement. I don't remember even ringing my parents with the news. Earning a sandy beret was no excuse to relax, and I had no feeling of relief in passing the patrol course: I knew the pressure wouldn't ease off. They were always running the pencil over you at the Regiment. Some blokes had been RTU after more than five years for failing to come up to scratch in training. The pressure to perform would always be on.

I went back to Tassie on leave that Christmas. I was bored and restless at home in Luina. Mum says that it was then that she first noticed I had changed. Hanging around the house felt like a huge letdown after the fast tempo of the Regiment. I couldn't really talk about what I had been through. Back then people weren't that aware of the Regiment, so nobody in the general public, even my parents, understood what we had gone through to get this far; they just weren't able to relate to us. I left Tassie a few days early as I was itching to get back to barracks and begin life as a trooper.

At the time the SAS was made up of three squadrons: One Squadron conducted the counter-terrorism (CT) role, Two Squadron had the water-operations role, and Three Squadron had the vehicle-mounted role. Two and Three Squadrons both had a freefall troop attached. I put down for, and got into, Three Squadron's freefall troop.

I was welcomed in straightaway. The troop sergeant, Maurie Wesson, Captain Patterson, Squadron Sergeant Major Ian Rasmussen and Bill Forbes the OC were a great bunch of blokes. They illustrated how command should work in the rest of the army – there was no petty nitpicking over rules and regulations. Together we just worked out the best way to do the job and got on with it.

In my early days in Three Squadron I went to Williamstown to learn freefall skydiving. The freefall course was much easier than the static-line course I had done after selection, but I still managed to get into trouble.

At the time we were using round parachutes, which are almost impossible to manoeuvre when compared to the square (ram-air) chutes common nowadays. During one drill, the wind blew me miles off course and suddenly I had to make a choice between landing on top of trees, rocks, power lines or a tarmac road – and I didn't have much time to decide. I took the option of the road and pulled hard on the right toggle to take me upwind. Just before I landed, I chucked the steel ripcord handle away in case a late wind shift took me into the high-voltage power lines. I tried not to concentrate on those power lines, because sometimes if you think about an obstacle long enough, you'll hit it. I focused on the road as I came in to land. To no avail; I went right through them.

The buzz of the high-tension lines seemed to roar as I passed through them, and I thought, *I'm toast now*. I released my harness and dropped heavily, hitting the ground with a thud. The chute draped over the lines. Terry Hewitt, my instructor, raced through the scrub swearing and waving his arms. All I could think was that

I was in the shit, and so I instinctively jumped up to pull on the parachute, trying to untangle it. Big mistake: I heard a thunderous crack and a sheet of blue light blinded me. There was a maelstrom of sparks and smoke, and flaming nylon set alight the surrounding scrub. The entire district was blacked out. Terry thought I was dead, and so did I. I ran out of the cauldron, nearly knocking Terry over in my rush. I didn't even feel a tingle.

When not on intensive-training courses, we either trained or took part in exercises. We would shoot more rounds, blow up more buildings, ride more helicopters and jump out of more planes in one month than a regular soldier would during his whole military life. I had known the SAS would be a step-up in tempo from RAEME, but this was unreal.

I learnt that there was one more step up to make. Things have changed since my time, but back then the sharp end of the SAS was the counter-terrorism team. It was the only operational combat unit in the Australian army that was ready to deploy within two hours of notification to anywhere in Australia or in any of our protectorates. So, wherever the CT team went, each soldier had to carry live ammunition. All of us new guys wanted to be on the team – that was where the action was. I was excited when I found out that I'd been picked to join them.

If terrorists take over a target, there are generally two ways to get them: overtly, by simply assaulting the target – smashing, crashing and blasting our way in by any entry possible; or covertly, by gaining entry to the target silently. In this case, the first they'll know about us is when we put a bullet between their eyes, hopefully not shooting any hostages in the process.

We practised 'close-quarter battle' (CQB) in a purpose-built facility called 'the killing house'. It had thick panels of compressed hay for walls to stop any stray bullets. These walls could be moved and configured to suit whatever scenario we were acting out.

Step one was to learn to shoot fast and accurately – with instinct rather than aim. We fired hundreds of rounds each day with Heckler and Koch MP3s, K models and SDs (silenced) 9-millimetre submachine guns, and 9-millimetre Browning pistols. We gradually progressed from standing and shooting single shots on the range to moving and firing, then firing 'double taps'. A double tap is exactly what it sounds like: two rounds fired back to back in less than a second, aiming at the forehead of the target. We called it a 200 per cent kill rate.

The minimum requirement to pass the course was to be able to 'keyhole' both rounds in a double tap – that is, to have the holes from the two rounds overlap within a 5-centimetre area. This is difficult enough to do from close range while aiming, let alone walking around, not to mention all of the other degrees of difficulty: wearing full-body armour, gas mask, ballistics helmet and another 20 kilos of kit. Then factor in explosives, stun grenades and tear gas all being let off as we operated. It was hot, hard work, and the thrill soon wore off as the exercises were repeated time and time again.

Even the best of us took at least a week and several thousand rounds to come up to scratch. Shooting at this level required fine skills and these were easily lost. The only way to maintain them was to put thousands of rounds down the range each week in training.

I think the CT team cured me of being a gun-nut. Shooting had been such a treat when I was a kid, when ammunition was scarce and expensive. After a year and a half of unlimited ammo and the most advanced weapons in the world I'd had my fill.

The 'method-of-entry (MOE) house' was a two-storey structure with every type of door, window, vent or duct that we could possibly encounter in an operation. We learnt how to assemble explosive charges to blow our way through doors, windows, walls and anything else that might impede access to a target. We also practised covert entry, which included disabling locks and alarms and finding our way around all sorts of mechanical barriers – how to be a cat burglar, in other words.

After a month of practising in the MOE house, it was time for us to put it all together. We started with walk-throughs and entering from a single point and progressed to full-scale assaults with multiple entries, multiple targets and live ammunition. We often had to shoot across each other's line of travel, so not only did your skill level have to be exceptional, but you also needed to have absolute faith in the rest of your team.

The last element of CT training was the SAS marksman course. We learnt the basics of military sniping first, then the specialist techniques used by the Regiment. Bullets don't have a flat, straight trajectory; their fastest velocity is when they leave the muzzle, but after that they drop and go sideways. When I was growing up I used low-powered rifles over short distances and had learned to compensate for bullet drop and 'windage' by aiming slightly off target. The long-range and precise shooting required in CT work complicated the equation, and I'd have only seconds to figure out how to put a round in the head or chest of a moving or stationary target from hundreds of metres away.

We practised with the Parker Hale 7.62-millimetre rifle fitted with a Zeiss scope, which was the best of the bunch. We also used the HK PSG1s, which were tripod-mounted like a machinegun, and at 9 kilograms was nearly twice the weight of the Parker Hale, making it a pig to sneak around with. We also had a go with the huge American Barrett 0.5 rifle, which went off like a cannon, firing a round as long as your foot, and was capable of reasonable accuracy up to 3 kilometres away – just the thing for stopping cars or puncturing the armoured glass in an aircraft cockpit. A well-placed round from a Barrett could blow up an oil refinery.

At the completion of six months' CT training we were allocated to either the sniper team or the assault team. We all wanted the assault team, mainly because we thought that the hours we'd have to spend on a rifle range lying in the prone position would get tedious. I missed out and got the sniper team anyway, as did most blokes in our course. I was pretty annoyed at the time, but it worked out to be the best placement in the long run.

A sniper has to operate in both urban and rural environments, and so needs to carry gear to cover all contingencies. A sniper also acts as the eyes and ears for the assault teams, sending back information on a terrorist stronghold. In training we learnt how to get all the electronic surveillance gear in place, both in and around the target, as well as how to guide in the assault teams. Snipers are also responsible for delivering tear gas onto the target, so everyone had to be schooled in the use of this equipment. Sniping wasn't only restricted to land; we shot from helicopters, boats and ships, the variety of which made it a very hard skill to master. We operated independently of the assault teams and were often out of the barracks on exercises. The assault teams had to hold up in restricted areas on exercises and were confined to training in the killing house and MOE house in Swanbourne. Plus, the sniper team also got the chance to brush up on our CQBs every couple of months to keep our hands in, whereas the assault team didn't get to practise on the long guns.

I landed a job as one of the team drivers and, as well as my long gun, was issued one of the HK-SD submachine guns fitted with a scope for close-in, silent sniping. Being a submachine gun it fired 9-millimetre rounds that, in my opinion, were useless for sniping and too inaccurate, especially used for targets over 100 metres away and firing from helicopters. I don't reckon there is any room for taking chances with sniping, which was a point I regularly made to our superiors. But in the Regiment, as everywhere else in life, there are theorists who are attached to their fads, so we drilled with the HK; I'd hate to have to use it during the real thing.

In the regular army there is a massive gap in intensity between regular grunt work and when you are on exercises or training. In the Regiment there is a much narrower gap and the pace of training is relentless. In the CT team, there is no gap and every day is treated like the 'real thing'. For the next twelve months our feet didn't touch the ground. Nearly all the major exercises and operations were done in conjunction with the various state and federal police forces and agencies involved in counter terrorism. We had the chance to get to know a lot of people in powerful and important positions around the country.

We also got to know all the main office buildings, five-star hotels, government offices and parliament houses in every Australian capital city. Again, we did this incognito, wearing either suits or tradesmen's gear. We would look official and walk around with clipboards, checking out access points, places to set up a shooting platform and the like. We also had fun breaking into elevator shafts and rappelling down, without any workers or guests knowing we were there.

We practised getting to the target, carrying our long guns and other gear, in the midst of the general public. We'd wear long coats to cover the rifle if it was cold, but more commonly we'd dress as golfers or tradesmen, both of whom have an excuse to carry a long bag or piece of PVC piping. The scruffy backpacker disguise is also a great excuse to carry heaps of gear – I employed this technique myself later on when I was on the run.

It's bloody hard work setting up an OP on a target building without the bad guys seeing you. An experienced spotter will know straightaway that an open window is a threat, so we'd set up back from the window in a room facing the target. A hole would be cut in the glass, with a small suction cup attached, so that we could pop the hole in the window a second before we needed to shoot. We'd find dark corners and recesses in buildings and if there was no obvious stable shooting platform, we'd suspend the rifle from the roof in a harness.

You know those Hollywood movies where the roofs opposite the hostage building are lined with black helmeted snipers, all with their heads up over the parapet, aiming their guns down at the target? Those blokes would be drilled in seconds if the bad guys had their own snipers. The whole point of being a sniper in a hostage situation is for the enemy not to see you.

There is still an ongoing debate about who should have the CT role: army or police. To me it's simple: use soldiers to fight soldiers. Police usually have a branch dedicated to armed intervention, tactical response groups (TRGs) and the like. They are certainly proficient at what they do. But doing a run-in on junkies or deranged civilians is a far cry from going in against heavily armed, military-trained terrorists holding hostages.

In 1983 an Australian ex-infantryman named Mullins went on a rampage and the Queensland TRG decided to do an assault on the house he was holed up in. Mullins shot one of them dead and wounded two others with a CAR-15 before they nailed him as he was escaping through a floor hatch. If they had done their homework, they would have picked up that he'd reversed the doors so they opened out rather than in – this is one of the oldest tricks in the soldier's handbook. This delay in gaining entry probably cost the cop his life.

Say a gang of political extremists have taken over a building and are holding hostages. The police hand control over to the SAS when they can no longer guarantee the safety of the hostages. If you are ever thinking about pulling a stunt like this yourself, remember one very important thing: when the Regiment is called, your life is forfeit. Our mission orders were unambiguous. None of the people identified as terrorists at the time of the assault are to come out alive. They are all to be executed: no questions and no excuses. We are programmed, through thousands of hours of practice, to kill without thinking or hesitation. You are better off making your point and giving up while the police are still in control. Luckily, this has not yet happened in Australia, and I hope it never does.

A soldier, especially an SAS soldier, is not only fully prepared to kill to achieve the mission's aims, but also to die as well. Getting killed is part of the contract.

It's well known that the Regiment has lost more people in

training accidents than in warfare, and with the stunts we used to pull I'm amazed we didn't lose more. I was there the day that one bloke did get shot in training. The whole squadron was deployed to Woomera in South Australia, which was a top-secret rocket firing range in the 1950s. I can easily recall the day we got there, pulling up in our trucks on top of a huge plateau that dropped off into a large glimmering white salt lake that ran for hundreds of kilometres. The huge concrete launch pad rose up out of the gully and loomed over us. The buildings had been left untouched, as if the engineers had just up and walked away one day. All the old computers and test equipment was still inside the buildings as if they had only been used yesterday.

The launch control rooms were set back a kilometre from the site, and the assault teams practised live shoots inside these buildings as they were all made of concrete, so no rounds would fly out of the walls. While they were kicking doors down and charging around inside the buildings we practised rappelling off the launch pad and used it for sniping and gas-delivery practice.

A call came over the radio one day that someone had been shot. We raced over to the control buildings in time to see 'Boxhead', my old patrol sergeant from K-troop, being loaded into the chopper, looking very pale.

How he managed to get shot is still a mystery; it simply should not have happened. Two new guys had come into the CT team on the six-monthly rotations and were being put through their paces. In a simple room-clearing exercise one of them discharged his weapon and shot Boxhead right in the bum, the 9-millimetre parabellum round ripping into his right buttock and exiting near his groin. Luckily the bullet missed Boxhead's femoral artery because there would have been no way to stop the bleeding and he would have bled to death in two minutes. As it was he spent a few weeks in hospital and was back to full duties in a month or two.

Boxhead was the unluckiest bloke I knew. He was always getting blown up, shot or lots of bones broken spudding in on parachute jumps that went wrong. I had nearly blown him up myself once. A few months earlier a bunch of explosives had been close to its use-by date and the Regiment needed them disposed of, so we took them all up to Lancelin for a few days of good clean fun. We experimented with different ways of booby-trapping cars and making rockets that would explode hundreds of metres in the air, amongst other things.

I had managed to secure a 200-litre drum of avgas (aviation fuel) and rigged it to make a vapour bomb. This was done by inserting thirty TNT booster charges, threaded together on a length of detonating cord, into the drum. A short distance from the drum we put six sticks of plastic explosives set to detonate a quarter of a second later. The TNT would create a cloud of fuel vapour, which would be ignited into a massive fireball by the plastic explosive. We were using a non-electrical detonation system that fired a flash of heat down a very fine tube, as opposed to a charge of electrical current. It was technically the wrong method to set off a charge like this as the tubes only covered 50 metres and we needed to be more than 200 metres away to be safe. We thought we had solved the problem by joining four of the lines together, but sure enough, when the charge was cranked off it misfired at the join closest to the drum. When I went over with Boxhead to lay another line and make a better joint he said, 'Bugger it, Dave, let's just fire it from here.'

'Bit close, aren't we?' I said.

'Nah, she'll be right. Let's just set it off from here and be done with it.'

'OK, have it your way,' I replied, as I lay down in the sand and hooked up the initiator to the line. 'But you better get down.'

'Nah, she'll be right,' he said again.

'Last chance, mate. Sure you don't wanna get down?'

'Just fire the bloody thing, will ya?'

I flicked the switch and the mother of all fireballs exploded, sending a wave of searing heat and concussion over us. They saw the blast twenty kilometres away at the base camp. We were up and running like startled rabbits a second later and the blokes up on the hill were rolling around on the ground laughing their heads off when we got there. Apart from singed hair and smouldering clothes I was okay. Boxhead had severe sunburn, burnt hair, smoking clothes and a chunk of hissing shrapnel sticking out of his arm. How he hadn't got badly hurt was beyond me. That piece of steel could easily have taken his head off.

Boxhead was pissed off at me and reckoned I had overcharged the shot, but he had no comeback because he'd stood there like a shag on a rock when it went off. After he cooled down, we stitched him up and decided to keep it quiet to avoid the paperwork and any drama.

My eighteen months on the CT team went by in a blur. By the end of the stint I was looking forward to a break. It had been exciting at the beginning, but the repetition of the training was starting to wear thin. I was tired and getting bored. I suppose we were all like footy players who train every week and never get a game.

I'm pretty sure the Regiment is a very different place now. Real action, like the boys have seen recently in Iraq and Afghanistan, tends to strip away all of the petty bullshit. But when I was there in the early eighties, the Regiment had not been tested since Vietnam and the theorists had started to take over from the pragmatists. Some of the political bullshit and ego battles were starting to grate on me.

It was generally expected that after your first stint in the CT team it would be time to think long term about your army career; to start looking at what courses needed completing to 'lance up' and become a corporal, then to train to become a patrol leader and such. I looked ahead and couldn't picture myself having a long army career.

I was having a yarn with Boxhead about this one day and remember him saying, 'It's a career army now, Dave. We won't get a war in our lifetimes.' I wonder if Boxy remembers saying that now he has seen action in East Timor and Afghanistan.

I was hanging on by a thin thread, not sure of which choices to make in my life, when word started to spread through the Regiment about a bloke called Martin Donnelly. Martin had joined the Regiment after me. Originally from a tank battalion, he had to overcome the same prejudice I did. Blokes who weren't from the infantry were always on the back foot when it came to proving themselves in the Regiment. Martin hadn't helped himself by voicing some strong opinions that weren't welcomed by the officers. Then, in 1985, he left the SAS and went to Burma to help a minority group called the Karen fight a war of independence. Wounded in battle, he died in Australia after failing to recover.

The story was very sketchy, but by piecing together bits of

information that Martin had managed to pass on before he died, with other whispers travelling around the Special Forces community, we learned that Martin and a few other foreigners had been betrayed. They were set up to walk into an ambush by the very bloke who had hired them to join the Karen rebels. Hearing about any member of 'the family' unfairly copping it in the neck got our blood up. We talked it over amongst ourselves and everyone agreed that one of us should go up there and check it out.

I put my hand up to go. I had a couple of months' leave owing and applied for that on top of three months' leave without pay. I can look back now and be honest with myself: checking out Martin Donnelly's story was just an excuse. I was pretty sure that my future wasn't with the army, and leaving without seeing action left a major part of me unfulfilled. You'd probably have to be a soldier to understand that.

My leave came through and I booked a ticket to Thailand.

PART II

The Book of Gold

THE KAREN

'Somehow or other, I found myself sitting next to the SAS soldier who was introduced to us as Steve Wilson [my alias while with the Karen]. *At the close of breakfast I found myself asking Steve if there were any more like him. I liked the man for his feelings for the downtrodden and his wish to do something about it. In many ways he was similar to me in mind. I respected and appreciated him and thanked him for his generosity.'* From: *Rebel of Burma* by Constance Veronica Allmark.

Patpong Road, Thailand: a messy collision of East and West catering for every perversion on the planet. Tiny little village girls, looking like kids playing dress-up in their short skirts and heavy make-up, call out, 'Hey, Aussie, twenty dollar; me love you long time' as you walk past. Sleazy middlemen hand out laminated cards listing every sexual act you've ever thought of (and a few you haven't) as they beckon you to step inside smoky backrooms. Toothless, leathery old hippies – who came here in the seventies looking for nirvana, discovered cheap heroin and never left – wander about. Big-arsed Western tourists in starchy clothes walk down the dead centre of the street, like they're afraid they'll be sucked into one of the girly bars and disappear forever. Young backpackers of every possible nationality, postponing careers back home, in their uniform of T-shirt, shorts and sandals, get high on the sheer anarchy of it all.

Twelve hours earlier I had stepped off the plane onto the tarmac at Bangkok airport. A putrid wave of hot humid air hit and I heard the sounds of a million two-stroke motorcycle engines at full throttle. After the crisp dry air of Perth it felt like I'd stuck my head in a bucket of rotting fruit. I could taste exhaust fumes and sooty particles of dust in the back of my throat. After being assaulted by what seemed like a hundred taxi drivers at the airport, I chose the one who spoke the best English. As we inched our way along the clogged road to the city, he told me it was coming to the end of the dry season and they 'needed big rain' to wash out all the crap, rotting vegetables and dead bodies that were putrefying in the *klongs* (canals).

I checked in to a little hotel in the centre of town advertising five-dollar-a-night rooms and went to sleep coated in sweat, with the steady beat of the ceiling fan overhead. Sometime in the middle of the night I heard rustling and flicked on the light; cockroaches the size of my hand were scurrying over the floor. I wrapped myself in a sheet so they wouldn't be able to crawl on me and went back to sleep.

In the dawn light I woke to a crunching sound; thinking it was just another cockroach, I looked across to my bedside table and came face to snout with the biggest rat I have ever seen. He was casually munching on my packet of dry biscuits and giving me a hard stare, like he was pissed off I'd disturbed his breakfast. Here's another myth debunked: they don't teach knife throwing in the SAS. In fact, I doubt that anyone in the history of warfare has been killed by a thrown knife. Still, I carefully unfolded my Swiss Army knife and threw it at the big greasy bastard, hoping to pin him against the wood. The back end of the handle hit him and he just shook his head a couple of times and waddled off under the gap at the bottom of the door. I couldn't get back to sleep after that – I was too worried that the rat had gone to get his mates. I showered, dressed and headed off into the already noisy streets to see if I could track down a contact or two.

I'd been given a couple of numbers before I left. The Special Forces community worldwide is like one big family, and you are never more than a few phone calls away from someone who knows someone who can get you to the front line of a fight. Before I had left, I heard about a bloke called Baz who had known Donnelly prior to his time in the Regiment. I had heard that Baz was in Thailand at the request of Donnelly's parents. He'd been there for a month and was essentially on the same mission that I was – to find out what had really happened. He answered the phone with the richest Queensland drawl I have ever heard. He told me to meet him at the Madrid Bar at midday.

The Madrid was set back from Patpong Road in a little laneway. I walked in right on twelve o'clock and scanned the room, looking for Baz. A jukebox in the corner was blaring at full volume. The girls dancing on the bar wore tiny bikinis with little numbered discs so that you could order 'six beers, a bag of potato chips and number twelve' if you wanted. A close enough look at these girls and you could see stretch marks on their bellies. The disgrace of having a kid out of wedlock was the main reason behind most of them working in a place like this.

The bar was full of middle-aged Western men wearing camo trousers, those photographer-style vests with heaps of pockets, Hawaiian shirts and reflector sunglasses – the uniform of the mercenary on leave, it appeared. I ordered a beer and sat in the corner, overhearing snatches of conversations about 'The Nam', killing gooks and a whole bunch of other bullshit that a real soldier would never talk about. I looked around at the size of a few of the beer-guts and thought, *Jeez, if they are mercenaries, they must live pretty well out in the jungle.*

'Yeah, I was down there in Nicaragua,' said one bloke with a huge handlebar moustache. 'Killed me a bunch o' commies. Just got the word to head up to Iran – looks like we're gonna rock and rolla with the Ayatollah!'

I didn't know much about Baz except that he was ex-military and an Aussie; I was pretty sure that none of these big-talking bullshit artists propping up the bar were either. What on Earth would possess a person to leave their home and travel halfway across the world to sit in a sleazy bar and pretend they were a soldier of fortune? Could you get that bored with your own character that you had to try another one on for size? I noted most of them were American and I figured it was low self-esteem at work again. *Soldier of Fortune Magazine* has a lot to answer for feeding the fantasies of blokes like these. I thought that if this was one of Baz's favourite drinking holes, then I'd need to go looking for another contact – he was probably going to be another chair-borne commando.

Just as I was pondering this and swatting away the affections of a bar girl who looked about twelve, a tall, lean bloke with wiry bright-red hair, wearing rugby shorts, a maroon XXXX T-shirt and thongs, came into the bar. He took one long look around the room and then came straight up to me.

'You Dave?' he asked.

'Yep,' I replied. 'Jeez, you picked a good place to meet, mate. Any more wankers per square inch and we'd be in parliament.'

'Don't worry about these dickheads,' he said. 'This is Jimmy the Belgian's favourite watering hole. I figured we could ask around here and see if we can't track him down.'

'Who's Jimmy the Belgian?'

'The bloke who recruited Donnelly to the KNLA in the first place,' he said. 'I'm pretty sure he's the same bloke who gave him up to the BMI as well.'

'So, the KNLA, that's the Karen right? I asked. 'Who's the BMI?'

'Burmese Military Intelligence,' said Baz, starting to look a bit sceptical. 'How much do you know about this war anyway?'

'How much do I need to know?' I asked. Like every other ethnic minority in Asia, the Karen put their hand up for independence after the Japs left at the end of the war. They'd been punching on with the Burmese government ever since. 'They're just like the Tamils in Sri Lanka, aren't they?'

'Nah, mate,' said Baz. 'It goes a bit deeper than that. It goes right back to the book of gold.'

'What the fuck is the book of gold?' This was getting interesting.

'See, the Karen came down from Tibet centuries ago. Most people reckon they were in Burma before the Burmans themselves. The Karen look and dress a bit Tibetan to this day – you know, with the brightly coloured woollen clothes and stuff like that. They've mostly kept to themselves up in the mountains, so their culture has stayed fairly distinct from the Burmans, who originated in India and Bangladesh.'

'Very enlightening, mate, but what about this book of gold? Sounds like my kind of book.'

'Jeez, you're not real patient, are ya?' Baz's eyes narrowed. 'The book of gold contained the scriptures that were lost at the time of the migration down from Tibet. Some of the stories of these scriptures talk about Ywa, which sounds similar to the Hebrew word for God, Yahweh.'

Baz paused and stared hard at me to see if I was going to interrupt again or start taking the piss. I wasn't sure where he was going with this story, or what it had to do with the Karen war of independence, but I'd only just met the bloke and could see I was starting to irritate him. I gave him that open-handed conductor's gesture to continue talking.

'Now, 'cause the whole region is pretty strongly Buddhist and Animist, the Christian missionaries were struggling to get a foothold back at the turn of *last* century. They used the similarities between the book of gold and the bible to convert the Karen – well, not the Karen really, just their educated classes. It took the British nearly thirty years to subdue the country, but when they finally took over the place in the middle of the nineteenth century it was natural for Karen people to slip into most of the administrative positions because they'd been studying in Christian colleges and spoke good English.'

'So, if the Karen held positions of power right throughout the time Burma was a British colony, it'd give the Burmans a good reason to hate them,' I said.

'Exactly, mate. Now you're catching on,' said Baz. 'The Burmans had already formed an independence army to try to kick the British out before the Japs came along in 1942. The Burmans didn't need much of an excuse to start attacking Karen villages after that. The Karen stayed loyal to the British side during the Burmese campaign, acting as a resistance, attacking the Burmans and the Japs.'

'But if the Karen stayed loyal to the British, why didn't they get a better deal after the war?' I said. 'Why didn't they give the Karen a place at the table when they started talking independence?'

'The Karen leaders got too greedy,' said Baz. 'They realised that the Karen homeland wouldn't have much of an economy without a sea port, so they tried to claim the southern part of the country, which bordered the Andaman Sea. The British reckoned that would divide country too much, so they refused and the Karen didn't participate in any of the councils for independence. They formed their own council, the Karen National Union, and claimed their own independent state. They call this Kawthoolie, which means "land of flowers".'

I was impressed. 'Jeez, you're a fucken full bottle, aren't ya?'

'Well, I've been here a month and I like to read.'

'And what's the difference between the KNU and the KNLA?' I asked.

'The KNLA is the Karen National Liberation Army,' said Baz. 'They didn't really get going until after about 1949. The Burmese government raised a socialist militia who went on a murderous rampage right through Karen territory. The KNLA formed pretty much in response to that. At that point the head of the Tatmadaw, which is what they call the Burmese army, was a Karen bloke, General Smith-Dunn. He was ousted and replaced with a radical, nationalist, Karen-hating bloke called Ne Win.'

I'd heard of Ne Win. 'That's the bloke in charge of Burma now?'

'Yep,' said Baz. 'That's him. Anyway, some Karen battalions of the Tatmadaw came over to the Karen side after this and helped form the KNLA. They gave as good as they got in the early days, and at one point they pushed right across to one of the outer suburbs of Rangoon. This was the battle of Insein. They had to pull back because of lack of supplies and have been pretty much fighting an insurgency since then.'

So, there it was: ethnic intolerance with a bit of religious bigotry thrown in – the usual recipe. A blood feud that went back centuries.

'Where does Jimmy the Belgian fit in?' I asked.

Baz had found out that Jimmy the Belgian had been Martin Donnelly's recruiter to the KNLA. Martin had gone to help the Karen along with a bunch of other ex-military guys from Belgium, France and Germany. Most of these Europeans had been spat out by the French Foreign Legion and were travelling the world as guns for hire. Jimmy the Belgian had a few contacts in the KNLA and had set himself up as the middleman for blokes looking for a fight.

Martin and the Euros had hatched a plan with the Karen to capture an 84-millimetre Karl Gustav recoilless rifle from the Burmese. The Karl Gustav is a prized weapon and by far the best hand-held recoilless rifle available. It packs an enormous explosive punch for its size, and its exploding shell will spray shrapnel over 100 metres. The manufacturers in Sweden had an attack of conscience after they produced it and refused to sell it to anyone who was fighting an internal conflict – they probably had nightmares about the Karl Gustav being fired into crowds of protesters. The Burmese government got round this restriction and bought a bunch of them in Singapore. Word had reached the Karen that the Tatmadaw had one of these stored in a lightly guarded hilltop position.

Just as Martin and his mates were moving up on the position they were bumped by a big group of government troops firing from freshly built fortifications. The Tamadaw had been tipped off – Martin and his mates didn't stand a chance. One of the Frenchmen tried to lead a charge up the hill and was killed, along with more than a dozen Karen fighters. Shrapnel from one of the Karl Gustav's rounds sliced a piece of Martin Donnelly's skull clean off.

The surviving Karen troops saw him lying semiconscious; part of his brain was exposed. With a wound like that, you are not expected to recover – the brain starts to dry out and die. You convulse, and when glanced at in the heat of battle, this is easily mistaken for your death throes. The Karen troops ran back down the mountain leaving Martin for dead. Unbelievably, he came to and managed – walking and crawling – to make the 10 kilometres back to the exfiltration point. The guys waiting at the point must have been surprised to see him stagger in hours after the battle, with a couple of big leaves taped over the hole in his head.

Martin was taken back to the Thai border village of Mae Sot for treatment. It was there he was given a blood transfusion containing a virulent strain of hepatitis. This was what killed him a few months later back in Australia. Before he died, Martin had told a few people to find the Belgian. The Belgian was one of the few blokes who had known about the attack beforehand and so was probably the one who had tipped off the BMI. Martin had also told Baz that he reckoned that the Belgian had arranged the contaminated transfusion to silence him.

After Baz had finished telling Donnelly's full story, let's just say that I was really, really keen to meet this Jimmy the Belgian bloke. We looked around the bar and tried to work out from the snatches of conversation which of these blokes was most likely to know the Belgian. It turned out that they all did.

We endured an exhausting afternoon indulging the Madrid Bar pretenders and their tall tales of derring-do. Each bloke would force us to listen to him for at least half an hour before giving us essentially the same answer: the Belgian hadn't been seen in a while. One bloke confided that he was 'in the Company' and was involved in some black-ops in Laos. Such was his level of fantasy that he fully expected us to believe that a CIA agent would spill the beans to two strangers he had just met. Or maybe that is the way the CIA works, I dunno.

Then, just after we were about to give it up, we struck gold. We had picked up enough titbits about Jimmy the Belgian over the afternoon to pretend that we were old friends of his from the foreign legion. An old Frenchman, a Dien Bien Phu veteran, who was so plastered that he was only staying upright with the assistance of two bar girls, told us the hotel the Belgian was staying at. It was just down the road.

We bade farewell to all our new mates at the Madrid and jogged down to the hotel. Unbelievably, when we asked the girl behind the reception desk for Jimmy the Belgian's room, she handed us the key. He wasn't there, and the room looked like nobody had been there for a while. A good tip for spotting the pretenders who hang around the edge of wars is that they all have really nice gear. The Belgian was no exception. We helped ourselves. I picked up his camos and belt kit, which solved the problem of having to source these later.

Baz scored a pair of mini-binoculars and a superb Randal Model 1 fighting knife that cost about US$500 and that no proper soldier would ever use because they would be too afraid of losing it.

In the top drawer of the Belgian's dresser we found a pile of credit-card receipts. After quickly sorting these by date, we found that – apart from having a healthy appetite for young male prostitutes – the Belgian had recently bought a train ticket to Chiang Mai. This gelled with what we had heard in the Madrid Bar; a few blokes reckoned he might have scampered up there. I went back to my digs to pack and met Baz at the train station an hour later.

After the crowded, hot, smelly madness of Bangkok, Chiang Mai was like an oasis. The pace of life was more relaxed and the people smiling and gentle. On the train up both Baz and I had noticed how abruptly the landscape changed from the flat brown dry-season delta rice fields to the thick green forest of the foothills. Chiang Mai is also home to the Thai King's summer palace and has an ancient walled city that has been there for thousands of years. There are also several Buddhist monasteries in town, and the smiling orange-robed monks making their way around the streets just adds to the soothing quality of the place.

The combination of fresh mountain air and the need to sweat some of the booze and second-hand cigarette smoke out of our systems inspired Baz and me to go for a run early the next morning. Passing a large grassed area we spotted some parachutists landing so we ran over to say g'day. They were the Royal Thai Army Military Parachute Display Team training for the upcoming Australasian Armed Services Parachute Competition. Baz and I figured it would be useful to have some contacts in the Thai military so we hung around for the next few days and got to know them. I also figured if I stuck around long enough they might let me have a jump.

They were all officers, but they weren't bad blokes. Once I let on that I was from the Australian army and gave a few details about my background, they had a chute on my back and were leading me into the back of their Huey helicopter in no time. It was weird to one day be kicking around Bangkok on holiday and a few days later rising above the foothills under the distinctive double-bladed *whup whup* of the Huey. The rice fields that extended down to the delta and Bangkok looked like one continuous brown plain that ended abruptly with the deep emerald green of the Dawana Mountains. Gazing across the mountains into Burma I got my first look at the country that was to become such a big part of my life.

I couldn't enjoy the view for too long because I hadn't parachuted in over twelve months and jumping from a chopper can be tricky. Jumping from a plane, you instantly hit a wall of air at over 160 k's per hour. This gives you some purchase on the air and it's easier to get into a stable position to release your chute. Because a chopper is only flying at a few kilometres per hour when you jump, it's crucial to get a good 'arch' as you accelerate up to terminal velocity. As soon as I stepped off the skids, all the ingrained habits from training kicked in and I only missed the aim pad on the ground by a few metres. The past eighteen months I'd spent in the sniper team had been more about patience and stealth than full-on excitement. I had forgotten what a rush adrenalin could give. I was about to ask for another go when Baz reminded me what we were in town for.

We couldn't find anyone in Chiang Mai who knew the Belgian. It seemed that the local authorities also kept a tight rein on teenage prostitution, so we couldn't find a bar full of bullshit artists who would leak the sort of information we needed. After a couple of useless weeks snooping around, we decided to call it quits and head down to Mae Sot, about 800 kilometres north-west of Bangkok, which was known to be one of the main gateways into Burma.

Mae Sot is located on the Thai side of the Moei River, which, along with the Dawana Mountains, forms most of the official borderline with Burma. The Burmese town of Myawaddy is on the opposite riverbank. Mae Sot was once a large tin mining town; but as tin prices fell, mining operations slowed. The economy of Mae Sot got a second lease of life in 1962 when Ne Win, the Burmese military dictator, banned all foreign goods from entering Burma unless his government agencies were importing them. This created a huge black market in electronic goods and clothing, as well as simple luxuries like soap, shampoo and cigarettes. The taxing of these goods at the KNLA-controlled border 'gates' provided the KNU with cash to support their war effort. It's ironic that one of the main methods the military dictatorship uses to subdue its people also funds one of its biggest headaches – the Karen war of independence.

The streets of Mae Sot were like a scene from a Wild West movie, except one where the entire cast is Asian. Most of the tough-looking characters walking the streets were either smugglers or soldiers, coming from or going to the war. Not many people here spoke English. There were no backpacker hostels and white people were very rarely seen in the town. Baz and I were stared at everywhere we walked; some of our observers were curious, some suspicious and some openly hostile. The place was also full of BMI spies and no one trusted anyone. Everyone we asked about the Karen just shrugged their shoulders and laughed like they had never heard the word. But one day we got lucky. Walking down a small street just off the main thoroughfare, we spotted a sign written in English, which stood out amongst all the others with their Arabic-looking Thai script. 'Chemist' it said.

The little Thai woman behind the counter spoke flawless English, and it turned out that her husband, who owned the shop, was the doctor who had operated on Donnelly. Between his broken English and his wife translating his Thai, we learned that Donnelly had been carried into the surgery late one night, semiconscious, very dehydrated and close to death. As well as inserting a steel plate into his head, it had been necessary to give him a large-volume blood transfusion to counter the blood loss from his wounds and the massive dehydration from making the 10-kilometre journey to the exfiltration point. In this part of Thailand they didn't have the money for blood-screening facilities and most of the blood donors are street people who exchange a litre or two of their blood for a feed. This was probably the reason Martin picked up the hepatitis that killed him. Whether the BMI or Jimmy the Belgian had a hand in this, we will never know.

Through sheer luck we had solved part of the mystery, but we were still keen to make contact with the KNLA to get a firsthand report. The doctor's wife was a real chatterbox and without any prompting from us, in the course of the conversation, she'd mentioned a Karen woman who ran a small English-speaking school in the town. She also told us that the teacher's husband was a doctor in the KNLA. We had a Karen contact at last.

Rosie Kho Thaw's English School was just down the street from the main market. It was a small shopfront amongst restaurants, clothes stores and motorbike-repair shops. Rosie was teaching a small class of children and adults when I arrived, so I waited until the class had filed out onto the street before going in and introducing myself. In her late fifties, she had her hair pulled back in a tight bun and was wearing a sarong with a traditional Karen blouse made of finely woven cotton and intricately patterned gold bands.

I explained that I was hoping to speak to her husband and make contact with the Karen. I was expecting some reluctance on her part. She just smiled politely and told me to go back to the hotel and await a visit from her husband. Dr Kho Thaw, a small, well-dressed man, knocked on the door of our room the next evening.

'So, tell me,' he said in impeccable English that would have not been out of place in Oxford or Cambridge, 'how is Mr Donnelly? I do hope he is feeling rather better than the last time I saw him. That fellow is lucky to be alive.'

'Martin died a few months ago.' Baz explained about the hepatitis.

'Oh dear, that is very sad,' he said, his face grim. 'When we hadn't heard from him we assumed he had decided to pursue another line of work.'

The doctor gave us his version of Martin's story; how he had seen Martin at the exfiltration point, treated the head wound as best he could in the field and then sent him into Mae Sot for surgery.

'I am very saddened to hear of the fate of our good friend Martin. He was a very brave man.' He rose to leave. 'But if you will excuse me, I have a couple more patients to whom I must attend before I am to have dinner with my wife.'

'We were wondering if you could help us get to the KNU?'

I blurted out as he was leaving. 'Can you put us in contact with them? We'd like to get a firsthand account from some of the soldiers who were there.'

The doctor smiled, probably wondering if that wasn't the reason we had wanted to meet with him in the first place. 'I'll see what I can do,' he said politely before leaving the room.

The next morning Baz and I were sitting in an open-air café, enjoying a Pad Thai so spicy we were almost gagging, when an official-looking Asian gentleman in his 60s, accompanied by several young men all dressed in *longyies* (Karen sarongs) and T-shirts, approached us. I could tell by the way they held themselves erect and swung their arms as they walked that, despite the civilian clothes, they were soldiers.

The old man introduced himself as a sergeant-major in the KNLA. As we were to discover about most of the Karen officers, the sergeant-major spoke English with perfect diction. We were both a bit suspicious of him and worried he might be BMI, so we pretended to be English tourists; Baz putting on the worst cockney accent I had ever heard. He asked if we were enjoying our visit to Mae Sot. We swapped a bit of small talk before he asked what we were doing there and if we were interested in learning about the Karen revolution in Burma. We continued our charade, knowing it probably wouldn't fool him: if we had clocked him as a soldier, then he had probably done the same with us. He offered me his business card and melted back into the marketplace.

Dr Kho Thaw came through that evening, returning to our hotel with news of a meeting he had set up with the Karen liaison officer in Mae Sot, a Major So So. We told the doctor what had transpired at the café and he took a look at the card. He confirmed it did indeed belong to a warrant officer from the KNLA's 101 Special Battalion, which was a relief to us.

Baz and I were playing cards in our room the next morning when there was a light tap on the door. A young Karen bloke at the door said, 'You come now, please' and turned for us to follow him. We went through a maze of back alleys, people's backyards and houses and down laneways before emerging just a few hundred yards down the road. A blue Mercedes pulled up, the doors swung open and we were bundled inside and pushed down on the floor. We had a blanket placed over us, and then the car pulled away slowly.

After about ten minutes of sedate driving with a few turns, I could tell by the echo of the engine noise and the sudden darkness that we had pulled into a shed or garage. We were motioned out of the car, up a flight of stairs and into a room with polished teak floorboards, hand-carved wooden furniture, a huge slow-moving bamboo ceiling fan, and jade Buddha statues in every corner. Middle-aged and older men were sitting around in cane chairs drinking green tea.

We were introduced to Adjutant-General of the KNLA, General Lah Thoo (who we came to know as 'AG'), Major So So and David Thawkabaw, one of the personal assistants of KNU President, General Bo Mya. Lah Thoo had dark-stained teeth from chewing betel nut and would regularly spit a stream of black juice into a tin. Major So So was thickset with a face like granite and perceptive eyes that flicked from side to side and did not miss a thing. So So could have been the capo of a mafia family – he just oozed menace. Thawkabaw was slightly built, wore glasses and had the high forehead of an intellectual. He spoke the best

English of the group and addressed us, choosing his words very deliberately.

'So, gentlemen. You have decided to visit us. Now, what can we do for you?' He smiled thinly.

I had the sense that these men did not plan to give us a second more of their time than was necessary, in case we proved to be another in the stream of wannabe soldiers of fortune, religious do-gooders and dodgy freelance journalists.

I tried to be succinct.

'A friend of ours, Martin Donnelly, was fatally wounded on a mission with your army. We would like to visit KNU headquarters and speak with some of the soldiers who fought with our friend. His family would like to know more about how he was wounded.'

This sparked a debate that seemed to last for ages. The commanders were arguing back and forth in a mixture of Thai, Karen and Burman with the occasional phrase in English thrown in. Thawkabaw then addressed us.

'So, what can we do for you?' he asked again.

'We'd like to visit KNU headquarters,' I said again.

'But what can we do for you?'

'Help us find out what happened to our friend.'

'Where are you from?'

'Australia.'

'What is your occupation?'

'We are both soldiers.'

'What do you know of our struggle?'

'I know you are fighting for your independence against an oppressive regime.'

'What can we do for you?' he asked for the fourth time.

I was young and inexperienced with the Asian way of negotiation, and it took me a while to realise what they were really asking. I decided to go slightly out on a limb.

'We would like very much to visit and talk with the soldiers who fought with our friend Martin. But we are very sympathetic to your plight and are willing to help out any way that we can.'

When translated this set off another round of debate before Thawkabaw spoke to us again.

'How much money would you need to be paid for helping us?' he asked.

'Nothing; no money,' I replied, without looking across at Baz.

After another long debate, So So finished by making a short horizontal cutting movement with his hands, as if to say 'Okay, then it's settled'. Thawkabaw turned to us again and extended an invitation to attend the KNU headquarters at Manerplaw and speak with the General himself. We stayed at the KNU safe house while somebody was sent to the hotel to collect our gear.

Baz and I bunked down in a room at the back and were told in no uncertain terms to stay inside the house. We sat on our beds and swapped bemused looks. We had stepped into the deep end now and there was no going back.

INSURGENCY

Back when I first joined the CT team, we were about to fly out to do some aerial shooting and I was buzzing around, full of enthusiasm, unable to concentrate on anything else. Marty, one of my best mates in the Regiment, looked at me, shaking his head, and said, 'Dave, you are just an excitable boy.' He was right. It took me a while to develop the patience to cope with the relaxed Asian way of doing things. The two-week wait for the clearances and transport up to Manerplaw to be sorted was excruciating. I paced around looking for things to do while the big Queenslander just found a bunk to lie on and read all day.

Eventually we were woken early one morning and told to grab our gear, get in the back of a covered pick-up truck and stay out of sight. We went to another house where Adjutant-General Lah Thoo (AG) was waiting. AG was lively but obviously ancient; he'd been with the revolution since its inception in 1948 and took part in the battle of Insein. He'd also served with the British forces, fighting the Japanese during World War Two. AG was to be our chaperone into Kawthoolei, the liberated Karen State.

He pointed to another pick-up and gave us a black-toothed smile. 'You hide in back.' So we crawled in amongst sacks of rice and other supplies that were destined for Manerplaw. After many stops at Thai checkpoints, what seemed like hours later we came to a small Thai town of Ban Tha Song Yang, which was opposite the Burmese military outpost of Mae Tawah. This is where we left the bitumen road and started along a rough dirt track that followed the border. We pulled into the turnoff and parked under some trees. AG got out and beckoned us to join him. He put a pair of binoculars up to his eyes and pointed at a mountain about 3 kilometres away.

'Burmese army position,' he said. I had a look and saw a cleared area on the top of the mountain that was surrounded by tall bamboo fences.

Before we took off again, AG told us to stand on the tailgate of the pick-up and hold on to the canopy, as this would be a much easier way to ride the bumps on the track. Baz and I looked at each other and had the same thought: here we are on the main Karen supply route just over the riverbank from enemy-held territory and this old codger wants us to stand up in full sight. We weren't sure what would make the better target, my blond head or his blood-nut. Our concern seemed to amuse the old fella.

'No problem,' he cackled, 'they never come over this side of the river; too may problems for them if they do.'

This didn't convince us and we elected to lie down in the back again. A few kilometres down the track we decided that a sniper's bullet would be a better way to go than being slowly beaten to death by all the supplies bouncing around the vehicle. We banged on the roof and got AG to stop while we stood on the tailgate. The jungle was pretty thick, so we figured there'd be a chance to race off into the scrub if somebody tried to ruin our day. As we bumped and rattled along the track, we scanned every rock, tree and fold in the ground for a human shape or a rifle barrel. A couple of times we were seconds away from jumping off the truck and spearing into the jungle before a suspicious shape revealed itself to be just another rifle-shaped tree branch. While we were becoming nervous wrecks, the old fella just drove along looking bored. But then he wasn't going into a war zone for the first time. Being an old man who had spent nearly his entire life fighting, he probably figured that he was living on borrowed time anyway. You can't be a good soldier without accepting the likelihood of your own death, but the fatalism of the Karen soldiers – the almost-casual disregard for their own lives – never ceased to amaze me.

Even standing up it took a lot of concentration to absorb the shock of the bumps as AG drove along the track. We mostly cut through thick jungle, but we'd occasionally pass through small clearings covered by clusters of bamboo huts with thatched roofs. The people in these villages were living off small rice paddies and whatever they could scrounge in the jungle. AG said they were mainly Karen hill-tribe people who had fled the fighting in Burma to safety in Thailand.

A few hours and 436 potential ambushes later we finally emerged in an open valley on the banks of the Moei River. We pulled up at a transit depot that the KNU used to move supplies to their military bases along the Moei and Salween Rivers. A couple of bunkers, which stored supplies and fuel for the boats, were hidden away out of sight. These were being guarded by KNLA troops who were carrying submachine guns on slings hidden under their jackets (they were prohibited from carrying them in Thailand). The weapons ranged from near-new HK-MP5s to an old World War Two-era Thompson.

'Ahh, Dave, mate. Just quietly, why are these blokes armed if this is supposed to be neutral territory?' said Baz, looking bemused.

So much for the Burmese not crossing the border, I thought. It was later proved that Baz and I were not just being paranoid – during my time with the Karen, I heard that a few KNLA soldiers travelling that supply route did get popped by Tatmadaw raiding parties who had crossed the border.

As far north and south as I could see, the valley was ringed by huge white limestone peaks pushing out of green jungle. Flowering teak trees, bamboo and vines dipped into the swollen river. The thick humid air created a heavy, oppressive stillness. It felt like the lost world. I could easily see how the Karen has resisted the Burmese for more than seven centuries; it would be very difficult terrain to fight a war in.

We loaded our gear, along with rice sacks and fuel drums, onto a longboat and pushed off into the river. The longboat was the type that is commonly seen and heard on rivers all over Southeast Asia. They are well suited to navigating the often shallow and rocky fast-flowing channels of the rivers; they are about a metre and a half at their widest point and a good 10–15 metres long. They have a six-cylinder diesel-truck engine, gearbox and 10-metre drive shaft, all pivoting on a bracket attached to the stern of the boat. The driver can direct the thrust of the propeller at the end of the shaft by swinging the whole contraption around, making the boat very fast and manoeuvrable in the right hands. A 'number two' sits over the bow of the boat, guiding the skipper and fending off obstacles.

The engines have straight-through exhausts and sound like Mac trucks when cranked up and running at full throttle.

The rivers of Burma all pour into the Andaman Sea but they begin their journey thousands of kilometres away in the Himalayas, so there is a steady glacial flow even in the dry seasons. We followed the thick brown waterway as it snaked its way around the green mountains that towered over each bank. The jungle pressed so high and close on each side that at times it looked like we were roaring through a green tunnel. Again, Baz and I were on full alert, scanning the river bank on each side for threats. The driver of the boat hooked the tiller in the crook of his elbow so he could roll a cigarette, while AG leaned back against a sack of rice and went to sleep.

A couple of hours later we came around a bend and spotted a small settlement on the eastern bank. This was Manerplaw, the base of Karen operations in the region. The base had been hacked out of tall bamboo groves and was surrounded by huge tracts of tropical hardwood trees. Buildings, ranging from rickety bamboo shacks to good-quality teak houses, lined the high banks above the river. We pulled up to a landing point crowded with longboats and fuel drums. The base was bordered on the north, south and west by mountain ranges and the canopy of the jungle was too thick to see through from the air, protecting the base from aerial surveillance. Any invading army would have to get a great number of men and equipment across incredibly steep terrain and keep them supplied amid hostile locals who knew the country back to front – a demanding task. Something the Americans found out in Vietnam and the Russians discovered in Afghanistan.

The boat stopped briefly here to drop off supplies, and then we headed further down river to a Karen village called Too Wah Loo, which is located on the Thai side of the border. AG's residence was located there, and I think he wanted to get to know us a little better before we got any closer to their operation. We stayed a week at Too Wah Loo, where we met Captain Isaac and his wife Maggie. I was to form a long and close friendship with Isaac and his family over the coming years. He was one of the KNLA's logistical supply officers and a demolitions man.

The Christian missionaries certainly had an impact on the Karen culture. Although most Karen people remain either animist or Buddhist, Christianity plays a big role in the lives of many KNU leaders. In Too Wah Loo they held prayer meetings every night, to which Baz and I were invited as soon as we arrived. As we walked up the hill to the little wooden church, amid the early-evening cacophony from the jungle, we could hear the sweet harmonies of children singing drifting down through the trees.

We hung around the village for a few days, waiting for some news about meeting with the Karen soldiers who had fought with Martin Donnelly. The Karen people still lived mostly according to traditional customs that had evolved over thousands of years. Their isolation had left them mostly unaffected by Western culture. There was no television or pop music. Life was centred on the village and family. Respect for elders was paramount and people treated each other with dignity. Most people smiled and laughed constantly; it was rare to see anyone shouting and getting angry. I couldn't help but be affected by it all. As I walked around the village, playing hide and seek with a huge posse of kids who followed me everywhere, the villagers greeted me like a long-lost friend. I'd never experienced this kind of warmth and generosity before.

Eventually we were taken back up the river for a meeting with the Karen President. General Bo Mya was a big man with heavy jowls. He spoke no English so David Thawkabaw, the serious intellectual who had been at the first meeting in Mae Sot, was there to interpret. Bo Mya sat staring at us impassively as I again explained the purpose of our visit. He nodded once or twice, then spoke to AG for a few minutes. Thawkabaw then told us that we could stay as long as we liked. He'd most likely briefed the General beforehand, so our meeting was just a formality. We were one step closer to going to war. Baz and I hadn't even discussed the subject, but we both knew that finding out about Martin was only part of our reason for being here. We were going to help the Karen in their fight.

A smiling, muscular soldier, who we nicknamed Sampson, was assigned to us as an interpreter and guide. Sampson could have been an Olympic gymnast, I reckon; he was always demonstrating his amazing upper-body strength by walking on his hands and climbing ropes without using his feet. He took us up a steep, winding track that ascended the hill right behind the village at Manerplaw. Set amongst the trees on a small level clearing was the camp of the commando unit that Martin had been part of. The unit was commanded by a French army veteran who had married one of the local Karen girls.

We camped there for a few days and talked with most of the Karen officers and non-commissioned officers (NCOs) who had been on Martin's patrol. Their stories mostly confirmed what we had heard already. Jimmy the Belgian had indeed disappeared from Kawthoolei just prior to the job going down and he'd not been seen since. These stories were the last we'd hear about Jimmy the Belgian for a while. A few years after Baz and I had talked to the villagers about the Belgian, I heard that somebody had tracked him down – he was hiding out in a small village in northern Thailand. The bloke who got him must have had excellent sniper training because the Belgian was dropped from a few hundred yards away with a head shot. I guess justice was served in the end. The Belgian must have thought it was all a thrilling game, playing with people's lives like that, but there was a mile-long queue of people who wanted to take him out. He had been bound to get it in the end.

We could see that the Frenchman wasn't too comfortable with us hanging around his camp and talking with his commandos, so we thanked him for his time and made our way back down the track to Manerplaw. Baz and I sat around the next day, wondering what our next move was going to be. About midday Sampson came bounding into our hut and asked if we wanted to accompany a Karen fighting column as observers. A Tatmadaw Light Infantry Battalion had just swept through an area west of the Salween River, and the Karen needed to send a reconnaissance patrol to check on the local villages. The column would attack the Tatmadaw if the opportunity arose.

I did my best not to look too keen and glanced across at Baz, who was slung in his hammock with a book on his chest – he was a man who couldn't look keen if he tried.

' 'Ken oath we'll come along,' he said, without looking up.

Sampson gave a big grin and said, 'I'll find you some weapons.'

Sampson organised a selection of used rifles. I checked two M-16s – they looked pretty battered. One trick when checking for wear is to take the flash suppressors off and push a bullet down the end of the barrel. A new barrel should be a snug fit. If the gun has fired plenty of rounds, the diameter of the barrel will be worn fractionally wider and the bullet will rattle around inside the bore. The two M-16s were worn. The American M-16 is a good high-performance weapon. It's light, accurate and the smaller-bore NATO ammunition (5.56 as opposed to 7.62) means you can carry more rounds. But the plastic fantastic is not a good secondhand option, as they aren't very durable if they haven't been looked after – and I was yet to meet a Southeast Asian freedom fighter who knew how to look after a weapon properly. The AK-47 Sampson had for me was in good condition and, although a bit heavy for my liking, I figured it would be reliable.

Baz just picked up the first weapon he was given, a Belgian Fabrique Nationale FN FAL, and he'd go on this for the rest of the time he was with the Karen.

The next day we set out at first light down a well-used track in a loose column of around forty men. Baz and I stayed close to the rear. After a few hours, it was obvious that these blokes had no patrol discipline. Some were talking; I could hear gear rattling, and a few blokes were just walking along with their heads down, paying no attention to what was going on. I reckoned if I were on the other side with a few of my mates from the Regiment we would have chopped these blokes up by now. We stuck to the main tracks and apart from the odd stop to check for enemy presence there was very little forward scouting. Over time I learned that this area was the Karen's backyard. Their intelligence was very good and they could move on the main tracks with reasonable confidence of not being ambushed. But Baz and I didn't know any of this the first time and we felt very exposed.

I noticed a change come over the group just before nightfall on the first day. Weapons that had been carried one-handed over the shoulder or across the back of the neck were now in the ready position. All laughing and talking had stopped. Everyone was alert. We were approaching the first village on our route. The patrol fanned out off the track and into the jungle. We halted and everyone disappeared behind trees or into little gullies while they sent a few scouts in to check the village.

There is plenty of cover in thick jungle and you could have walked down the track, looking hard into the foliage and never have seen us. From my hiding spot I could smell smoke and the sickly odour of rancid fat that I would come to recognise as the smell of a rotting human corpse. Even straining to hear, I wasn't able to make out any sounds apart from the birds and monkeys. I looked across at Baz. The normally lethargic Queenslander was as alert as a blue heeler.

The forward scouts were back half an hour later, having checked the village for Tatmadaw and any landmines they might have left behind. The patrol leader waved for us to get up and move down to the track. As we walked into the village, Baz and I could only shake our heads in disbelief.

Every hut had been burnt to the ground. The embers were still hot and smoking, which meant the Burmese had probably left less than five hours before our arrival. Most of the villagers had fled into the safety of the jungle, but the few that had been caught by the Tatmadaw troops had been tortured, raped, mutilated and murdered.

One atrocity that still haunts me to this day was finding a baby, not more than a few weeks old, lying dead next to his mother. The baby had been bayoneted, shot and hacked into several pieces. His mother was nearby, naked, her head battered into a mess of pink and black pulp; she'd also been impaled, through the vagina, on a bamboo stake. No doubt she had been gang raped before the coup de grace had been delivered with the stake.

The other villagers who had been captured had fared no better. The Tatmadaw had tortured one old man shockingly. His lips, nose, eyelids and ears had all been hacked off. His eyeballs gouged out and squashed. They had pulped his testicles and roasted his feet over a fire. He must have died of shock when they were burning his feet as they'd left him there with his legs and what remained of his charred feet smouldering in the fire. They had nailed a young teenage boy to a tree by his ankles and flayed the flesh from his body with bamboo canes.

None of my training had prepared me for this. As I stood and watched the Karen soldiers bury the bodies, I looked down and noticed my left leg was shaking uncontrollably. The anger that consumed me at that moment was like a charge of electricity that took me over. The Tatmadaw had just made themselves another enemy. I remember thinking, what sort of piss-weak, cowardly, fucken bastards would do something like this? I've never lost that sense of rage. I still see that baby in my dreams from time to time.

There was no sense in this at all. The KNLA hadn't been operating anywhere near the village, so there was no intelligence to be gained by interrogating the villagers. The Tatmadaw simply would have had orders to sack and burn all Karen villages in the area, regardless of people's sympathies towards the KNLA. Even if there were some tactical advantage to scaring away these people from their traditional home, the cruelty shown by these scum was simply not human.

I looked across at Baz and could tell that he was affected strongly as well. The big Queenslander was a relaxed sort and not much fazed him. But his face was set like stone and he was never the same easygoing character after that. He spat on the ground.

'The mongrels,' he growled.

The logic of the oppressor, eh? The Tatmadaw's idea was to frighten the Karen into submission. It had the opposite effect. Not only did it harden the resolve of those who wanted to fight, but it made the others more reluctant to surrender. This terror was what the Karen could expect if they did lay down their arms.

The Karen's demands weren't extraordinary. They just wanted to maintain their cultural identity. Under Ne Win's rule, the Karen way of life was being eradicated. In schools they were forced to learn the Burman language and culture instead of their own. Any positions of responsibility and power within the government were exclusively reserved for the Burmans. The Karen people were fighting for the basic rights of self-determination and cultural survival. This had sustained the fighting spirit of the Karen people through decades of warfare. At that moment the Karen's cause became my cause, too.

We continued the patrol; we didn't bump into the Tatmadaw nor strike any more burnt villages. Back at the camp after four days of patrolling we approached Isaac and AG and asked them to speak to the president on our behalf. We proposed to stay for the next three months to assist the Karen with training. The president accepted our offer immediately and sent word back asking how much money we would require. We made it clear that we needed no payment beyond food and lodging and the opportunity to help the Karen cause.

Our initial assignment was based at the Frenchman's commando camp. One of the few Frenchies I have met in a war zone who is not an ex-legionnaire, his first name was Philippe and I can't recall his last name except that it sounded like 'Le Pew'. It took Baz about five seconds to christen him Pepé Le Pew, after the cartoon skunk. The commando camp was Pepé's little kingdom and the French tricolour flapped just below the KNU flag in the middle of the compound.

Despite the fact he had married a Karen woman, Pepé somehow became more French the longer he stayed in the camp. He had his tiger-striped camos tailor-made for him in Bangkok. They were so tight it looked like they'd been painted on. He insisted on shitting separately and had his own latrine dug away from the other pits. His had a corrugated-iron sheet set up to channel his turds away from the toilet squat and down into a pit. One day he made the whole unit stand to as he walked up and down the ranks, shouting at the men, accusing one of them of taking a shit in his latrine and not washing it away with water. As soon as the parade was over, Baz did a monster crap in his toilet and left it sitting right there on the corrugated iron. It looked like Pepé's head was going to explode with rage when he saw it the next day. 'Le Pew' indeed.

If Pepé had come from the French army, then their training must have been pretty shoddy, because he had some downright bizarre ideas about military strategy. An old army saying is that 'no battle plan survives first contact with the enemy', and this is especially true of the hit-and-run tactics of an insurgency. Pepé would concoct these elaborate plans that required every single decision to be made by him, with no flexibility for the sergeants in the field to change things on the fly. He would shout and scream and insist his instructions be followed to the letter. Then he'd leave the Karen to go and do the fighting. In the ill-fated mission that claimed Martin Donnelly's life, proper reconnaissance on the target would have revealed the freshly dug fortifications and the numbers of Tatmadaw waiting to ambush. The Frenchman's lack of planning most likely cost Martin his life as much as Jimmy the Belgian's treachery.

It was impossible for the Frenchman to admit he was wrong, even when he knew it. A claymore mine is a hemispherical-shaped mine that is designed to spray ball bearings in a wide arc. It's an American invention that comes with the helpful instructions 'Front Towards Enemy'. One night we were setting up a defensive perimeter on top of a small mountain and Pepé insisted the claymore mines be set facing out from the hill. I pointed out to him that this would cause the shrapnel to spray out over the heads of any advancing enemy instead of into their legs and torsos, inflicting the sorts of disabling wounds that mines are supposed to. Rather than lose face in front of the handful of soldiers who were helping set the mines, he blustered something about wanting to cause head wounds and stormed off.

Things were not going well for us at the commando camp and I reckon it was only respect for the Karen that stopped Baz from putting Pepé over his shoulder and chucking the little frog, tailor-made duds and all, into his own shit-pit. Luckily, Sampson had seen relations breaking down and spoke to the president. Isaac stepped in and asked if he could move Baz and I to a new training camp. We thanked Pepé for his most excellent instruction in French infantry tactics and headed back up the river.

It was obvious to Baz and I that the Karen troops were lacking in two main areas: reconnaissance and demolitions. Their poor knowledge of demolitions was forgivable because they didn't have access to many types of explosive. But we couldn't understand the poor quality of their reconnaissance work. We discovered over time that most of the troops were just farm boys – they didn't appreciate the advantage of having detailed information about the enemy. I could see the Karen improving their success rate enormously if they learned to set up proper observation posts, kept them manned continuously and fed back accurate info on enemy numbers, weapons and the type of fortifications.

There hadn't been much of this sort of training going on, so Baz and I decided that we'd build a camp and put together a team of instructors. Neither of us was on a Pepé Le Pew-style private-army ego-trip. We wanted to create a system that would continue long after we were gone. Right from the start the project was organised as a KNLA-run camp. The officers and NCOs ran the show with Baz and me in the wings, providing instruction and guidance.

The orders went out and men from battalions all over the Karen State were called in to participate in the camps. Priority was given to those who spoke some English. By the time everyone had assembled, we had about fifty trainees. A veteran of ten years' fighting was assigned as the commanding officer. He had a long pink puckered scar following the line of his jaw from an AK-47 round that had clipped his face. We called him 'Pacino' as a reference to the movie *Scarface*. Pacino was a bit of a legend in the Karen community and commanded absolute respect from the men. Sampson was appointed as his second-in-command.

The dry season was rapidly coming to an end, and the monsoons would soon be upon us. Before then, a training area and barracks had to be built from scratch. We nominated a level site that was near a freshwater stream, and the men set to work hacking down the jungle. The buildings were constructed almost entirely out of bamboo: bamboo poles lashed together with strips of bamboo fibre, bamboo slats for the floor and teak leaves strung together with more bamboo fibre to make the tiles for the roof.

Weapons, ammunition, explosives, uniforms, packs, webbing, blackboards, chalk, notebooks, food, medical gear and myriad other bits and pieces had to be collected so everyone would be equipped. Most of the gear came overland from Thailand, so we had some long waits to get what we needed. This wasn't the SAS with its almost-unlimited budget. We had to plan carefully, buy only what we knew we could afford and be creative with a few homemade alternatives.

Food was a constant problem. The staple diet was rice and fish paste, with chilli added to mask the foul taste of the latter. Baz and I were losing weight steadily, as were the rest of the troops, and most of them were undernourished to begin with. We set aside days to collect food from the jungle, and anything that we thought might supplement our diet was thrown into the cooking pot. If it crawled, ran or swam it was considered protein, and so monkeys, moles, river rats, toads, snakes and lizards were all added to the menu. We would sneak into the jungle at sunrise with silenced .22 rifles, find a monkey and drop him, so that when all his mates came over for a look we would get a full pot. In the wet season we ate fat, juicy toads, although we had to remember to skin them first – you can get a nasty rash if you don't. Our fishing expeditions took the form of throwing a hand grenade in the river; a line of blokes would be waiting to catch the fish as they floated to the surface.

We even snared a leopard once, but not without a tragic loss. The cat had tripped a landmine near the river and was badly wounded. One of the boys took a knife and went down to finish him off so he could bring back the meat. The boy was mauled to death before anyone could race down with a rifle and kill the beast. Even though they belong to relatively small cats, those claws can rip you up in no time. On some patrols I was more worried about the jungle cats than the Tatmadaw.

Over a few weeks it all started to come together, and once the basic accommodation was in place, we were set to begin instruction. The day before we were to start the demolitions course Baz broke out in a sweat, started vomiting and complaining of joint aches – all telltale signs of malaria. He was down for a week, so I took over his teaching role.

The Karen's arsenal of explosives was limited to what could be bought on the black market or stolen from the Tatmadaw. We had some gelignite, TNT, ammonium nitrate for mixing with diesel to make ANFO (the world's most commonly used explosive) and some plastic explosive that we salvaged from stolen claymore mines. I kept the instruction basic, with the main emphasis on handling the explosives and detonators safely. I wanted to get the guys to feel comfortable about using short fuses, so they could initiate a blast without panicking. Ten seconds is ample time to get to cover should the need arise to detonate a blast quickly.

We had not yet sorted out a proper water supply for the camp, so I decided that the first practical explosives lesson would be to blast some rock out of a spring on the side of a hill near our camp. This would create a small dam, one deep enough to cause sufficient pressure to push the water around the side of the hill, via pipeline, to the camp. I had the guys using a small slab of TNT at a time, so they each had a go at setting the fuse and getting behind cover quickly. We had just lit the first shot and retreated to cover when a boat appeared around a bend in the river. We were 100 metres above them up the hill, so there was no way they could be signalled and it was too late to pull the fuse. Just as they were going past, the charge blew and the boat was showered with rocks. The thick jungle vegetation stopped most of the bigger rocks, but the boat still got pelted.

The blokes on the boat must have thought it was a mortar attack; some of them leapt into the water, while others ducked for cover behind the gunwales. Luckily, they weren't armed or we would have copped a stream of lead. We had a good laugh at them, but we weren't laughing about half an hour later when a ready-reaction force from Karen headquarters pulled up in boats, armed to the teeth. We hadn't told anybody we were blasting that day, and the whole of headquarters had gone on general alert. I got in trouble for that, and we made sure to send a radio message to the duty officer at headquarters prior to each blast from then on.

TNT cost US$30 a kilo on the Thai black market and we needed lots of it for training. This was costing the Karen a small fortune, so Baz and I came up with another idea. We talked Isaac into ordering certain chemicals; we planned on showing the boys how to manufacture explosives – by far the cheaper alternative. A delivery arrived via boat from Thailand a few weeks later, and by the time we had put together our first batch we had the costs down to US$2 a kilo. Another advantage of making the final product ourselves was that TNT is very malleable towards the end of the manufacturing process: we could pour it into moulds for all types of applications, such as shaped charges for cutting metal and curved moulds for claymore mines. After a few weeks, we had quite an industry going; we trained up a new batch of soldiers to continue the work while we got back to the training.

Teaching demolitions has to be done in carefully measured steps, and the students have to know each step thoroughly before you can move on to the next one. Skip a stage and someone is bound to blow themselves up, and there's no coming back from that. Even though these boys were fast learners, teaching them took a long time – all instructions had to be translated into Karen dialects as well as Burmese. Some of the younger Karen blokes, who had come from the Irrawaddy delta region of Burma, could only speak Burmese because of the government's ban on teaching in their native tongue.

Malaria was also taking its toll. At any one time up to a quarter of the class would be in bed, shivering with fever and vomiting. Proper medical supplies were scarce, so only in the most severe cases did we use an intravenous glucose drip mixed with quinine. The local remedy was to make a stew from the intestines of a monkey that had been eating a certain type of bark, which contained traces of quinine. It was the vilest-tasting thing I have ever tried to swallow, but it seemed to work.

Most of the boys with malaria were only out of action for a couple of days, but the interruptions meant we had to run a lot of back-up night classes to get everyone up to speed. Baz and I were on the go fourteen to sixteen hours a day, but after a few weeks of hard work, the boys were confidently setting charges and safely handling the different types of explosives.

Weapons training was next on the agenda. Teaching someone to shoot is the easy part. All weapons will jam at some point and many a soldier has been killed by the enemy while frantically trying to clear a stoppage. The drill for clearing a breech and reloading the weapon has to be practised over and over again until the student can do it without thinking or panicking. Then it has to be practised while the student is blindfolded or in the dark. Then it has to be practised while the instructor distracts the student, making as much noise as they can muster, so that the soldier can clear the weapon under the same sorts of pressure as would be faced in battle. Clearing breeches is hard enough to master when you're only using the one type of weapon; the KNLA's armoury was like a military flea market – they couldn't afford to be too choosy when buying weapons. During the time I was there I did a run-down of their weapons store, which included Korean War-era Chinese SKS-type 56s, classic Russian Kalashnikov AK-47s, their Czech and Chinese copies (which are slightly different) and their stamped metal upgrade – the AKM and the more modern AK-74 version. They also had World War Two-era American M1 carbines, Garands, British Bren light machineguns and a funny-looking Sten gun with the magazine sticking out one side – being made of only 47 bits of mostly stamped metal, it looked like it was made from a kids' Meccano set. Then there were German Hecklers and Kochs, with a couple of Ruger Mini 14s, Israeli Uzis and Galils, Italian Barettas, Singaporean Ultimaxes and Belgian FNs. Of course, there were plenty of American M16s and their M203 variants, with the grenade launcher slung under the barrel, but most of these were pretty battered. Throw in a range of bazookas, light anti-tank weapons, mortars and recoilless rifles and you had a resupply and training nightmare.

Each of these rifles had a different breech and bolt configuration, so the drill for clearing stoppages was unique to each one. Baz and I were not looking forward to the repetition required in teaching the drill for each different weapon, not to mention all the halts for translation that would be needed. We were pleasantly surprised by how quickly the boys picked it all up, though, and in no time we had them swapping weapons and repeating the stoppage drills at high speed.

After hours of sitting around in our outdoor classrooms, Baz and I started to understand how the Karen were fighting this war. Most of the attacks were hit-and-run strikes conducted just before dawn. This meant charging into Tatmadaw trench-and-bunker systems and a lot of close-quarter shooting that usually developed into hand-to-hand fighting as the aged weapons inevitably jammed or the ammunition ran out. The bayonet hadn't been popular with the Karen; when things got nasty they tended to opt for a knife or else swinging their rifle as a club. Baz and I reckoned they could benefit from some bayonet training – using a 'pig-sticker' at the end of your barrel was a quicker and easier way of getting somebody than with a knife. The men's hand-to-hand fighting skills were also lacking, so a very basic unarmed-combat course was thrown into the curriculum as well. This was usually incorporated into the morning physical-training exercises.

The physical training was a bit 'counter cultural' to the Karen and they didn't appreciate the benefit of high fitness levels. The physical benefits are obvious – fit, strong soldiers are better fighters when they have to be, and, in the case of guerrilla warfare, get out of trouble faster when they don't want to be. Most people wouldn't understand the mental benefits, however. Fit soldiers have higher pain tolerance and stronger willpower – which is often the difference between prevailing and ending up dead or someone's prisoner.

We were pushing the men hard on a 10-kilometre run along the numerous jungle tracks that criss-crossed the area when one of the younger blokes slowed to a lazy-looking shuffle and dropped behind the main group. I reckon there are a few footy coaches who would love to bring an AK-47 to training because it really is a fine attitude-adjustment tool. I fired a couple of well-placed rounds in the shuffler's general direction to hasten his stride, but this bloke had no doubt been shot at before, several times, so it made no difference. Someone who slacks off is letting down the whole team, so to make my point I ordered the whole group to double back and take turns carrying him, piggy-back style, all the way back to camp. I ran beside him, calling him a weak, useless prick and other such classics from the army's abuse manual.

Afterwards, when everyone was off having a quick wash before class, the bloke in question, Wimbo, came marching over to my hut. Throwing his pack and kit down on the verandah, he mustered his few words of English, and shaking with rage said, 'No more. I finish.'

I was taken aback and didn't quite know how to respond. I could see all the other men look up with interest from the creek where they were washing. I beckoned Pacino over and asked him to interpret. He asked Wimbo to sit and talk, but he refused and stood stiffly at attention as he and Pacino exchanged some terse sentences in Karen. We learned that Wimbo had contracted tuberculosis as a child. TB is a highly infectious disease that leaves behind calcified lumps of scar tissue in the lungs. These can inflame from time to time and severely restrict the capacity to breathe. Wimbo wasn't swinging the lead on the run – he was struggling for oxygen.

Pacino, Baz and I decided right then to get the men together and list all their medical problems. It turned out that Wimbo was just the tip of the iceberg. As well as the commonly experienced malaria, there were several other cases of TB in evidence, along with gastroenteritis and exotic tropical diseases too numerous to mention. These blokes had all grown up without the benefits of the inoculations that Baz and I took for granted.

There was also a 'frank and open' exchange where Baz and I got the message that we were pushing them too hard, and that some of our motivational techniques were too abusive. I suppose we were trying to run the course like a mini-SAS selection, with the aim of the hard training to weed out malingerers. We came to realise that if these men had been malingerers, they wouldn't have joined the KNLA in the first place. Every Karen soldier was there because they wanted to fight. They had all seen family members or fellow villagers butchered by the Tatmadaw. They didn't need to be bullied into fighting well; they were there to protect their families.

Baz and I also got into our thick heads the importance of saving face in Asian culture. I apologised to Wimbo in front of the troops and explained that back in our country driving people hard was a way of thinning out those with poor commitment; we now understood that this was unnecessary. Wimbo stayed for the duration of the course, as did everyone else. Baz and I realised we were there to impart knowledge, not to build up an elite fighting unit, so we eased things up a bit.

I approached Isaac to see if we could order in a few basics to supplement the troop's poor diet. He agreed but said it would take a while to clear the money from the General as the KLNA had just spent a chunk of their budget on the mixed assortment of weapons I had reviewed. Baz and I kicked in our own funds to speed things along, and we were soon unpacking a consignment of milk powder, vitamin tablets, dried eggs, flour and yeast. We only managed to get a small amount but even that slight improvement in nutrition made a huge difference to how robust the men were and that lifted morale overall. The remarkable thing was that in the weeks after Baz and I stopped barking abuse at them the troops started to train harder than we could have pushed them. The physical training sessions became fun. Some mornings we'd kit the men up in all their fighting gear and take them on a run up to Pepé Le Pew's camp while carrying big logs on their shoulders. They'd stand outside the Frenchman's hut and recite 'Alouette' as they did their log exercises. The Karen blokes in the commando camp would come out laughing and clap along in time. It was funny to see Pepé stumble out of bed, bleary eyed, to see what all the commotion was about.

We were coming into the crucial phase of training now. It seemed that before Baz and I had arrived, the sum total of a Karen reconnaissance report was 'the enemy is over there – let's attack them now'. The disciplines of patrolling, ambushing and reconnaissance were foreign to them. A Karen soldier could watch an enemy position for a day and come back telling us that he had seen five soldiers collecting water. We would ask him how much water was being carried back inside the fortifications – to give a basic idea of enemy numbers. What was the patrol discipline like? If the patrol is casually strolling down to the river, making heaps of noise and not scanning the jungle, then you know they aren't expecting a visit. How did they get in and out of the fort? If they appeared to be following preset marks that might indicate a path through a mine field, what were the marks? Where were the machineguns located? What fields of fire did they have? Were there any mortar pits and where were they located? Which of the huts had telltale communications aerials sticking out of it? Were there any early warning devices? Were there any officers visible and which insignia were they wearing? Were there any gullies or natural formations that would make a good escape route following an attack? This was just for starters.

Teaching these skills was painstakingly slow but we had plenty of jungle to train in. Soon enough the troops were moving with absolute stealth and they observed their surroundings keenly.

One day we were returning from an extended patrol in the bush. We walked a familiar track that snaked down to the valley floor about 2 kilometres from base. The closer we came to home, the more relaxed our patrol discipline; nobody had ever been ambushed that close to base. I didn't want to be the first so I didn't relax completely, just enough to look around and enjoy the scenery. I'm a soldier, not a poet, so I'd rarely take the time to appreciate my surroundings. But this day I noticed the dappled light as it came through the jungle canopy, and the bright red, yellow and green flowers and huge butterflies flying between the trees. There was the murmur of talking and laughing rippling through the column as we all anticipated our first decent feed in more than a week. I was due back at the Regiment in Perth in less than a month's time, but suddenly it didn't feel like I was going home.

As final assessment for the course, we made the boys run a 14-kilometre route, including two river crossings, in full kit. Everyone passed; the troops were visibly stronger and fitter now. It was time to let them loose on the Tatmadaw.

We chose a few of the closest Tatmadaw hilltop positions and instructed teams of six to move in close and set up OPs. Sampson, Baz and I hung back, usually on the nearest hill, to observe the observers. We had a few extra men ready to let loose with some covering fire if things got nasty, but all the teams performed superbly. They were experienced soldiers after all – it was not as if we were showing them the enemy for the first time. But now they had better skills and more confidence. I remember watching Wimbo get so close to an enemy perimeter fence, after three hours of crawling like a caterpillar up the hill, that he almost got urinated on when one of the Tatmadaw went to the edge of the camp for a slash.

Just to make our point, we had a couple of patrols call in mortar fire. Because the patrols were so close to the enemy, they could radio the mortar teams a couple of kilometres away, directing them to lob the shells with pinpoint accuracy. The last patrol directed a shell right onto the roof of the communications hut and the next one onto the armoury, which went up with a huge boom. Knowing it was a mortar attack, the Tatmadaw just huddled in their trenches, giving Wimbo's patrol ample time to sneak out. We heard a week later that the Tatmadaw had abandoned this position. In time the Tatmadaw would be back for sure, but we gave them a real poke in the eye.

The Karen commanders, including General Bo Mya, had let us know how pleased they were with the training. They decided to conduct a grand finale before I left. Fifty kilometres to the west of Manerplaw was a bridge that spanned a ravine on a resupply road used by the Tatmadaw. Dropping the bridge would require good reconnaissance, logistical planning and expert demolitions – all things Baz and I had taught. We couldn't think of a better overall test for our training school.

Baz and I stood at the back of the room, observing as Pacino and Sampson started the planning with a powwow involving all the men. Everyone was briefed on the target and asked to come forward with any suggestions. A couple of blokes spoke up, then another and before long I could see them, as a group, forming a broad plan of how they were going to tackle the mission.

After the plan was sketched out, the officers and NCOs got together with Isaac to thrash out the finer details of logistics and supply. A couple of days later and the entire company was winding its way into the jungle to the west.

Moving more than fifty men through an area crowded with Tatmadaw positions was risky. It took a week to skirt the dozen or so Tatmadaw hilltop forts. Despite all the training it was an exhausting stomp, as on top of our regular kit we were all loaded down with explosives and as much ammo as we could carry.

On the seventh day we came over a ridge and looked down on the bridge for the first time. The Bailey bridge was designed by a British civil servant by the name of (you guessed it) Bailey who worked for the war office during World War Two. The Germans and Italians were blowing up bridges as they retreated and his design meant that the Allied forces could construct temporary bridges quickly and easily. The advantage of a Bailey bridge is that the steel sections are light enough to be transported on individual trucks and put into place on site without the need for heavy machinery. Steel lattice panels bolted to the side make the bridges box-like and strong enough to hold a tank on a single span of up to 65 metres without any supports in the middle. The Tatmadaw had erected a Bailey bridge across a ravine hundreds of metres deep and there was no other way across the river. They were going to miss it.

We scouted around until we secured a LUP, then set up a couple of OPs overlooking the bridge. These were manned round the clock for the next couple of days until we had a good picture of how much traffic was going over the bridge and who was guarding it. Luckily, we were deep enough inside Tatmadaw territory for them to not consider the bridge worth guarding, so it looked like we'd get the job done without any major firefights.

The next step was to measure up the main steel transoms so we could shape the charge that would cut them. The night before the job Wimbo took his team in for a close recon. With a couple of fire-support teams set up to overlook the area and to cover them if there was any trouble, the recon team crept down to the bridge and measured the thickness of the steel. They also checked for landmines on the way in. There was a full moon but visibility was poor due to the jungle canopy; we couldn't keep watch. It was a nervous few hours before an exhausted-looking Wimbo and his team came back in.

The next day was spent preparing. We cut lengths of detonator cord, made up the charges and rigged an electrical-initiator device using an old camera flash. We then ran through a few rehearsals that covered some possible scenarios if things went haywire, such as if the Tatmadaw arrived as the charges were being rigged, if charges failed to go off, or if someone in the blast team got wounded and needed to be rescued. We were relying on plenty of early warning should a truck approach the bridge; we'd need to find cover and lay low as it passed over, then finish the job. If the truck slowed unnecessarily or stopped, we would hit it hard with everything we had, then abort the mission and exfiltrate. Once Baz, the team leaders and I were satisfied that we'd covered every angle, we rested up.

As soon as it was dark, we set up two fire-support teams on ridges high enough that the teams' fields of fire would cover the road on each side of the ravine. Each of these teams had an MG-42, M-79 grenade launcher and a rocket-propelled grenade launcher, with a few spare rockets as well, which would deliver some seriously bad news to any vehicle that looked like it was slowing down more than normal. The teams also had some parachute flares with them in case we needed to light up the area.

There was a possibility that a firefight would break out, in which case we'd have to blow up the bridge earlier than we'd anticipated, perhaps leaving behind men on the wrong side of the ravine. We decided to keep everyone on the eastern bank to avoid the company being split if this eventuated. A couple of men with radios were sent a kilometre up the eastern road to give us early warning should there be any movement in our direction. The demolitions team consisted of six men to set the charges and four more to provide immediate covering fire if their team got bumped on the job. These four also had the crucial job of keeping watch for any approaching trouble from the west. The remainder of the men were split into three ready-reaction teams: one to cover our retreat and two to go either east or west should the lookouts or the demolitions team run into trouble. The lookouts on the eastern road took a while to get into position; the wait was excruciating. We finally got the short message via radio that they were in place. After checking the road for a few minutes, they gave the all-clear and the demolitions crew moved in.

Baz stayed up with the fire-support groups and I accompanied the demolitions team down to the bridge. We lay down flat in a small ditch beside the road just near the bridge as two forward scouts covered the western approaches. They watched the road intently for a few minutes then waved us on. Out from the cover of the jungle the moon seemed unfairly bright and made the bridge shine like silver; the sense of exposure made my scalp tickle. Two days of watching the bridge had revealed that no one was guarding it, but what if the Tatmadaw had a concealed sniper position covering the bridge that we hadn't picked up? Well, I guessed we were about to find out.

The men worked in pairs to place the charges on the transoms under the bridge and then wire them together. The blast team leader was a studious-looking bloke who we had nicknamed Rowdy. Rowdy was the most unflappable, unresponsive person I have ever known. His face never betrayed any emotion apart from serious concentration – well, almost never. When he made something go bang his face would split into a childlike, ear-to-ear grin. Rowdy just loved blowing things up. I found him to be a bit of a soul mate in that respect. Rowdy double-checked his team's work and inspected every charge before giving a 'thumbs-up' signal. We melted back off the bridge, each filing back past Rowdy before entering the bush so he could do a headcount to make sure we had everybody.

The first of the enemy to inspect a damaged bridge will often be the engineers tasked with building the next one. We rigged a few mines on the paths near the road, hoping to put a dent in their number of skilled bridge engineers. After setting the mines, we moved back 100 metres and signalled to everyone else to pull out. The ready-reaction teams scrambled back up to the two fire-support positions, and the lookouts on the east road did the same. As soon as these teams were all together, they started pulling out to the pre-designated rendezvous point a few kilometres away. They would miss the fun of seeing the bridge go down but would be content with hearing it instead.

Squatting in a ditch a safe distance away from the bridge, I did a quick check that we hadn't omitted anything, before allowing myself a moment to savour a job well done. Then I gave Rowdy a light tap on the shoulder and he initiated the blast. There was a blinding flash followed a split-second later by a deafening roar and a mini-earthquake that shook the ground around us. The bridge groaned like it was in pain as the steel buckled and started a slow-motion fall into the ravine. It hit the bottom with a thud that we could feel through the soles of our feet.

I looked across at Rowdy. He was grinning; so was I. We pulled the ends of the blast wires in hand over hand, rolled them up and stashed them in our backpacks before scurrying back up the hill. We caught up to the column an hour later. Everybody was jubilant – the job had gone like clockwork and nobody had been hurt. We were far from safe yet. We marched north to throw the Tatmadaw off our trail; they would have expected us to take the shortest route home and would most likely set up ambushes on the track heading east. After a couple of days heading north, we swung east and made our way towards the river where longboats had been prearranged to pick us up and return the troops to Manerplaw.

We had a passing out parade a few days after we arrived back at the Karen base. I was due back at the Regiment in two weeks and Baz was off back to Queensland to do whatever it was he did there. Most of the men were heading back to their own brigades with plans to set up schools of their own, to teach what they had learned with us. The core of the team, led by Isaac, would stay on to continue the work of our school. Pacino and Sampson planned to join Pepé Le Pew's commando battalion, with hopes to pass on the skills they'd learnt. I thought of the challenge they faced in getting that stubborn Frenchman to change his ways and wished them good luck.

In the parade ground of our little camp we stood at attention as the KNU anthem was played. Isaac gave a moving speech thanking Baz and me for our efforts. We had little cloth badges made up, displaying a symbol of a broken bridge. The men marched up to me one by one and shook my hand as I awarded the badges.

Baz and I had dinner with Isaac and Maggie in Too Wah Loo the night before we left. Isaac didn't once ask me to stay to help the KNU, even though I knew the thought had crossed his mind. We had also dropped in on the General that afternoon and received his warm thanks for our efforts.

The following day after I'd handed in my kit, it was time for Baz and I to be booting off to Australia. It was a sad day. All the blokes from the course who hadn't speared off to the four corners of Kawthoolei came down to the longboat to see us off. Sampson rode with us in the longboat up river to the transit point and into Thailand and then bade us farewell. I felt a bit like a rat leaving a sinking ship. I was heading back to the safety and comfort of my home, leaving my friends to fight it out against the Tatmadaw.

LEAVING THE ARMY

After five months in the southeast Asian jungle, flying back into Perth brought on culture shock all over again. The air was crisp, the terrain flat, brown and featureless. People in the airport were huge, loud and brightly clothed; they barged around clumsily compared to the softer way that Asians move in a crowd. Just retrieving my bag from the carousel felt like I had stuck my head in the back of a rugby scrum. Riding in the taxi back along the causeway, I took in my surroundings: it all seemed impossibly clean and bright – sterile, like a hospital. Apart from the heads I could see in other cars, there were no humans visible; it was like someone had dropped an atom bomb on the place. The newly built white pyramid of the Burswood Casino on the south bank of the Swan River was like a monument to a civilisation already extinct.

I'd just walked in the door and dropped my bag on the ground when the phone rang and one of my mates from Three Squadron invited me to a party at his place that very night. I rocked up with my usual five-dollar cask of wine, bypassed the front door and walked around the back, where a fair bit of noise was coming from. Cold

Chisel's 'Khe San' was playing at full volume; I definitely knew I was back in Australia. I found both the laundry and the bathtub overflowing with ice and beer – exotic beer. I looked down and saw green and blue bottles with funny names like Heineken and Grolsch. I didn't think things could have changed that much in five months, but something must have happened during that time that forced everyone to start drinking yuppie beer.

What happened to good old Emu Export? I thought as I promptly dropped my cheap wine and grabbed a bottle of Heineken and joined the party.

I saw a group from Three Squadron standing around the barbecue and wandered over to join the circle. I didn't say anything – just gave them a big grin and waited for the piss-taking to start. The blokes just ignored me. It wasn't as if I'd expected a tearful reception, but to be blanked by my mates like that was a bit of a shock. I stood there feeling more than a bit awkward while they just kept talking amongst themselves, mostly about what the other squadrons were getting up to on an exercise in New Guinea. I traced back through the weeks before I went away, trying to remember if I'd done anything to piss anyone off. Maybe I'd accidentally shagged someone's girlfriend or something.

I was just about to tell them they could all go and get fucked when Marty, who had been staring at the chest of someone's pretty niece while pretending to have a conversation with her, looked over.

'Dave?' he almost shouted. 'Is that you?'

'Yeah,' I replied. 'Who the bloody else would it be, ya goose?'

He barged through the group, almost broke my hand in a handshake, then pounded me on the back.

'Bloody hell, I didn't recognise you for a moment. Jeez, you're skinny. It's good to see ya, mate. We all thought you'd fallen down the same hole as Donnelly. We thought you were a goner.'

It then dawned on me how different I must have looked. I'd left weighing 83 kilograms and came back weighing 54. I suppose it was a bit dark in the backyard, too. At any rate, the blokes standing around the barbie hadn't recognised me. They'd treated me the same way we treat anyone from outside the Regiment who hasn't got nice tits – with total indifference. It's not that we think we're better than the rest of society; it's just that we haven't got much in common with people who don't know how to shoot or blow up things. It's a peer group thing. That, and the need to stay in the shadows, means we tend to give any outsiders a frosty reception.

All the heads in the group turned as the rest of the blokes slowly worked out who I was. Suddenly, it was a scrum of handshaking and backslapping with Dave the centre of attention. Then the piss-taking started.

'We thought you were fighting up in the jungle, mate. I didn't realise you'd spent five months at Jenny Craig.'

'Got a tape worm, have ya? Jeez, if you were a sheep we'd have to put you down. I thought you went to Burma, not Ethiopia.'

We might be inscrutable to outsiders but within our own ranks we can gossip with the best of them. I spent most of the evening fielding questions like a guest lecturer. It wasn't until later in the night that I got to sit down to have a quiet yarn with Marty. He casually dropped a bombshell.

'Hey, I was talking with one of the blokes who's got a mate in the federal police. He reckons this bloke rang him up asking about you.'

'What do the feds want to know about me for?' I said, mind already racing.

'Dunno, Dave, but the copper wanted to know the phone numbers of all your girlfriends.'

The bloke in question was away in New Guinea with most of the Regiment, so I couldn't speak to him. The next morning I got on the phone and called a few blokes who knew him better than I did. It took most of the day to get the story straight, but I eventually got the message that the feds were interested in talking to me about '*alleged* mercenary activities overseas' and my '*alleged* involvement' in them.

It all stemmed from a bit of a lark. At one point I'd had a photo taken of me posing with an AK-47 in a hut surrounded by crates of ammo, claymore mines, rocket launchers and a host of other weapons. At the time I wasn't even with the Karen; the photo had been taken by one of the Thai officers who Baz and I had been parachuting with in Chiang Mai. I'd mailed the photo to Mal Holloway, a Regiment mate, as a kind of 'look at me being the hard-core mercenary' joke. The letter and photo had been intercepted at the mail exchange and passed onto the feds. How someone at the mail exchange just 'happened' to open this letter, spot the photo and notify the authorities had me stumped. Right from the beginning the whole thing stank of someone within the Regiment notifying the feds, and quite possibly the head shed in Canberra, whenever any of us went travelling on our own. This almost didn't bear thinking about.

I rang the Regiment's Adjutant. He was a little taken aback by the phone call and didn't say much except that 'maybe I should go down to the feds and have a talk to them myself.'

We'd had plenty to do with the feds in the CT team, and I knew their offices were part of the Sheraton Hotel complex in the Perth CBD. I took the train into town and rolled up to their front desk the next morning. Federal police are different from your average copper; they don't have that hard, cold exterior that comes from years of dealing with the nasty side of human nature. The sergeant on duty was quite affable.

'Can I help you, mate?' He even smiled, which is not something I'd seen a copper do to me before – nor have seen since.

I came right out with it.

'Yeah. My name is Everett and I'm from the SAS in Swanbourne. I need to speak to whichever of you blokes has been ringing around asking for my girlfriends' phone numbers.'

He stared at me with his mouth open for a few seconds.

'Just wait here and I'll check for you,' he finally said, then went into their back office. He came out a few minutes later.

'I'm sorry, sir, but no one is aware of any enquiries being made about you or your activities.'

'Bullshit,' I said, keeping my voice even and casual. 'Go back there and ask whoever is *unaware of enquiries being made* if they are also *unaware* of a photograph of me sitting in a hut surrounded by a whole lot of military hardware being intercepted by Australia Post and passed on to them.'

'Wait a minute,' he said. Not so friendly this time as he ducked back out.

I waited another half an hour and was just about to go home when a very worried-looking middle-aged bloke in a suit came out to meet me.

'I'm Federal Agent Longworth,' he said. 'Exactly why are you here?'

'I've come for the interview,' I said. No response from Agent Longworth; I was getting a bit exasperated.

'The interview about my "alleged involvement" in "alleged mercenary activity".'

He jerked his head towards the front door, looking really alarmed now. 'Come for a walk.'

'Listen,' he said as we walked, 'there's been a stuff-up and I'll be in deep shit if this goes up the line to Canberra. Yes, there have been some enquiries about your activities in Burma —'

'Alleged activities,' I interrupted.

'Alleged activities.' He nodded his head in quick agreement. 'But we were supposed to keep the investigation hush-hush and the agent who rang your mate forgot to pass that on. Anyway, the whole thing's gone to shit and we want nothing more to do with it. If it wasn't for that photo, we wouldn't have bothered in the first place.'

'No worries, then,' I said wearily, and left him standing there on the street corner.

I checked in with the Adjutant at Swanbourne later that day. He played dumb and said, 'Well, that's that, then. Better keep your bloody head down for a while, hadn't you?'

With a few days to spare before I was due back at work, I had plenty of time to brood about the Regiment. My squadron was in New Guinea so I was allocated to Base Squadron until they returned. There wasn't much to do besides fitness training, so I got to work in the gym and on the beach, putting back some of that muscle mass I'd left in the jungle.

One week later we were all playing indoor cricket at a local community gym. For us, the game was a combination of cricket, gridiron and full-contact sparring. It was basically shouting, barging mayhem with a cricket bat and ball. I had just got to have a bowl when the Regiment's Intelligence Officer showed up with a couple of suits in tow – they could only have been federal police.

'Go with these blokes, Dave,' said the IO.

'What for?' I asked.

'They are federal police and they want to interview you.'

I knew I was being thrown to the wolves.

There is something distinctive about federal police, ASIO staffers and Canberra people in general. They've all had to survive a culture that, year by year, has less to do with achieving anything useful for the rest of the country and more to do with its own internal bullshit. Standing out in any way probably doesn't help you get by in these places and being honest definitely doesn't, which made Agent Longworth's admission to me a week earlier all the more remarkable. These organisations are made up of bland, grey, slightly podgy characters whose names you can never remember. Maybe it's from the hours spent sitting in meetings, but these people also have this weird way of turning their heads to look at you without the rest of their bodies moving. Their tongues don't flick in and out, but it looks like they should.

The two officers, whose names I cannot remember to this day – I'll call them Lizard One and Lizard Two – drove me back to the Sheraton in total silence. After ushering me into a tiny interrogation room they let fly. Lizard One did the talking while Lizard Two did his best impression of a hard stare.

'You will be charged, Everett,' said Lizard One, 'with carrying out activities that contravene the *Crimes (Foreign Incursion and Recruitment) Act* of 1978. That is, preparing for, and carrying out, hostile activities against a foreign state that is recognised by the Australian government. We know you were involved with Martin Donnelly, we have photographic evidence of your involvement in military activities, and we also have reason to believe that you have perverted the course of justice by trying to influence a federal agent to gain unauthorised information about our investigation.'

This was quite a mouthful, and I was a bit stunned. The *Crimes (Foreign Incursion and Recruitment) Act* was something we had been made aware of very early in the piece with the Regiment. I knew it carried a penalty of fourteen years' imprisonment. Throw in the perverting the course of justice charge and I was looking at a decent stretch.

'Tell us about your relationship with Agent Longworth,' Lizard Two barked. 'How long have you been communicating with him?'

'How long?' I spluttered. 'How bloody long? I only spoke to the bloke a week ago. Before then I didn't know him from Adam!'

'C'mon!' Lizard One laughed. 'We know he's been tipping you off from before you left for Thailand five months ago.'

I didn't know Longworth beyond the five minutes I spent with him, but I knew he was cactus. They really had it in for him and it suddenly occurred to me that they had nothing on me at all – they were fishing for evidence against him. It turned out I was right. After repeating their questions a hundred times in a hundred different ways – standard interrogation technique – they let me go.

Two years later I found out they had charged Longworth. One Saturday afternoon when I was just about to leave home to catch a plane to Thailand, two nervous, beefy-looking bailiffs served me with a subpoena to attend his trial the following Friday. I phoned a lawyer from the airport. We told the feds that I was about to commence a four-month contract in Thailand. Breaking the contract would leave me liable for penalties. These penalties, plus the cost of travelling back to Australia, plus 'think of a number and double it' meant that my lawyer sent them an estimate witness bill of ten thousand dollars. Needless to say, the trial went ahead without me. Longworth was acquitted, as he should have been; he'd done nothing wrong. But I guess the whole drama did help explain the sick look on his face when he first met me: he was anticipating the dive his career would take from that point on.

Once the lizard twins had let me go, I caught a taxi straight back to Swanbourne and stewed about the lack of Regiment support during this whole sorry episode. To my mind, the big question was if this was the way they treated you over a simple matter, then what would happen if an actual government-sanctioned clandestine operation went wrong and you ended up in the shit? It looked like the Regiment would disown you and leave you to the wolves. Not a very comforting thought. I'd also seen the way they had treated guys who had been severely injured during exercises. It was just like selection; it was as if the injured trooper had failed and it would be for the best if they were to disappear as fast as possible, like their presence would stain the Regiment. Let's just say I was getting disillusioned.

Perth is probably one of the worst places in the world to be if you are bored and restless. To live there I recommend you get your adrenal glands surgically removed. With tons of easy money pouring in from the iron-ore deposits in the north, gold in the east and gas offshore, Perth people have turned living comfortably into an art form. Migrants think it's paradise. But after five months of living as a soldier in the jungle, the lack of any meaningful challenge nearly drove me crazy.

I'd drive along the freeway and see sheep crammed into cages on the back of trucks, heading to the port for export to the Middle East, then look at people sitting in buses on their way to work and see the same dead eyes. I kept getting this urge to poke people with a stick to check that they were alive. A six-hour plane flight away was an ancient culture fighting for its very existence against a brutal regime, and all anyone could talk about here was the football and renovating their houses. Even the Regiment made me feel the same way. I was enlisted to play the enemy in one of the patrol courses and being out in the bush with blank ammo and fake bombs seemed unreal. Coming back to Perth and having to take orders from mugs in Base Squadron was the icing on the cake after my brush with the feds.

My heart wasn't in the Regiment or Perth anymore. It probably never had been. My heart was up in the mountains, rivers and jungle with my friends. You couldn't manufacture what we had shared. Being rational, I knew that I couldn't save the Karen from the Tatmadaw single-handedly, but the desire to get back up there and do my bit just took me over.

I was sitting at home one night, so restless that I was flicking the TV channels across every few seconds with the remote control. I settled on the Channel Seven news. Most of the half-hour bulletin was devoted to local issues like the rising burglary rate, how the police were introducing random breath-testing to lower the 'carnage on our roads', and whether some boofhead football star's hamstring was going to be right for the game this week. There was very little on international events and absolutely nothing about the plight of the Karen. Apart from showing how far up its own arse mainstream Aussie culture had its head stuck, it also hit me how I could really help my friends in Kawthoolei. They needed international recognition.

I phoned a few TV producers and news journalists and got a very cold reception. There was nothing I could tell them that they couldn't get off the international wire through an agency like Reuters. Most Aussies couldn't tell the difference between Burma, Cambodia and Vietnam anyway, so the plight of an oppressed minority just blended into the stream of news about overseas troubles and made them even gladder to be living in Australia, where it was 'safe'.

A few more listless nights spent in front of the telly and I had another idea. I can't remember the actual news event – it might have been something to do with the royal family, maybe the beginning of the scandal with Princess Di or perhaps the birth of Prince William – however, the TV station did a live cross to one of their normal newsreaders, who had been flown over to London to report on the event. *What a bloody stupid waste of money*, I thought: flying a highly paid talking head across the world – five star and first class all the way, no doubt – to cover a story that they could have easily paid a local freelance stringer to do. Then the penny dropped. If local people don't have someone who they feel they know (and let's face it, most people think of their favourite newsreader as a member of the family) reporting on an event, then it doesn't seem real to them. To get the media interested in the Karen we would need a local angle – like the story of a young Aussie soldier of fortune helping the Karen people in their fight for liberation.

I called a lawyer to see if there was a way around the *Crimes (Foreign Incursion and Recruitment) Act*. The act was pretty specific as it had been introduced to stop exactly this type of activity. The lawyer's solution was simple: don't take the journalists to Burma; keep them on the Thai side of the border and don't let them work out where they are. They would still be able to collect plenty of footage of displaced refugees to show the Karen's suffering. All I needed to do was to organise some soldiers who'd be willing to appear in footage of me training them and the story could be told – all without setting foot in Burma and contravening the act.

I called the same media types as before with the offer: 'How'd you like to do a story about an Aussie mercenary in Burma?' Lack of media interest was no longer a problem; they almost crawled down the phone line. Nine, the biggest national TV network, signed up their prime-time current affairs show and the *West Australian* newspaper also jumped on board. I had just one more hurdle to cross: the fact that I was still in the army.

My official discharge date was in January the following year, which was still four months off. It may as well have been four years. No way was I waiting that long. I knew I could put in for an early discharge, but I spent a few weeks hesitating. The army had been my life since I was fifteen. As much as I had grown tired of all the bullshit, it was the only security I had known since I'd left home.

I had my mind made up for me in the end. My squadron had just returned from New Guinea and I was about to rejoin them. Who knows? If I'd seen a few familiar faces and got back into the routine of regiment life, the fire to help the Karen may have eventually burned out. I guess our lives can turn on small incidents. I was just getting back from a run when one of base squadron's sergeants called me over.

'Get your hair cut, Everett. That mop is two inches longer than regulation. You're not on holidays any more, son.' The Regiment was usually fairly relaxed about haircuts, especially with the CT team, as a short back and sides could make it harder to blend in with the public. But in the regular roles and tasks squadrons we were expected to look like soldiers.

'Can it wait a week?' I asked. I hadn't hit my first payday since being away and I was down to scratching around underneath my car seat for ten-cent coins and fishing for invites to friends' for dinner every night.

'Get it cut now or you'll be up on a charge,' the sarge said.

'Okay,' I replied. 'Can you lend me seven bucks till payday?'

'Go jump in the lake,' he laughed. 'I'm not lending you any money. Now get your hair cut and report back to me when it's done.'

'If that's your attitude, then I'm quitting. Get me my discharge papers,' I said.

'Yeah, sure.' He thought I was joking. 'Get that haircut or I'll add insubordination to the charge.'

With that, I marched into the orderly room, got the papers, filled them out and handed them in. The whole process took less than twenty minutes, and when I walked out of the orderly room I no longer had any doubts.

The following week the OC of Three Squadron, Major Higgins furious after seeing my application, called me into his office. He thought it was to do with the haircut. The Regiment had lost quite a few good blokes that year – most of them due to disgruntlement with 'management'. They invest more than a million dollars in training each trooper and they weren't happy about blokes not re-signing when their discharge dates came up.

I let the OC know I had reasons for leaving bigger than being unhappy about an order to get my hair cut. But he remained pissed off at me and sent me to do gardening duties for the remainder of my stay. I always seemed to get stuck in the gardens when somebody in the army went sour on me. Not being a slacker, I set to with gusto and proceeded to transform the weed beds into something resembling a decent flower garden. Then I attacked the jungle of weeds and rubbish out the back of the officers' mess and soon it looked like a golfing green. The OC lightened up a bit after that – he must have been getting pats on the back for the improvements to the gardens.

Once I was notified that my discharge had been approved, the ball started rolling with the trip. A journalist from the *West Australian* had already made inroads with a group called Tribal Refugee Welfare (TRW), which helped people who were fleeing Burma to resettle in Australia, as well as helping refugees on the Thai–Burma border.

I had a meeting with the TV station and newspaper journalists in which they agreed to combine resources for the trip. *The West Australian* reporter would accompany the TRW group, while I would go ahead with a photographer/cameraman and reporter from the TV show. I made them all aware of the laws surrounding this type of activity and the fact that the trip was almost certainly going to land me in big trouble, trouble I was glad to wear in order to help the Karen. The trip was booked for October 1986.

The day of my discharge came around, and I was knocking on

the door of the orderly room at Karrakatta Barracks five minutes before they opened for business. I handed in my kit and ticked all of the 'no' boxes on the discharge medical, saying that everything was okay, whether it was or not.

I took my last pay cheque. I was no longer a member of the Australian Defence Forces. But in my mind, I was still a soldier.

THE FISHING EXPEDITION

The two feds who boarded the plane to Bangkok with us stood out straightaway. It was like a casual-dress Friday at the office when those corporate types try to dress down but can't let go completely: you get shirts tucked in that are meant to be left out, long socks with shorts, boat shoes and white hairless legs that have been rubbed smooth by too much trouser wearing. All in all it looks like a bad day at a public golf course. When two late-thirties blokes took the two seats in front of me, looking like a retired gay couple on a cruise, and deliberately avoided eye contact, I knew who they were.

As soon as they buckled in, I leant over and stuck my head in between them.

'Jeez, I thought you feds were too busy to take holidays,' I laughed. One of them was wearing a bright Hawaiian shirt with long cargo shorts and red boat shoes. 'Bugger me, who dresses you, mate? Your missus?'

One of the two reporters I was travelling with also happened to know one of the feds and came up for a chat. The poor fool in the seat in front of me looked decidedly embarrassed about being spotted so quickly, but there was nothing he could do about it now. Losing the feds in Bangkok would be simple, especially if they kept on wearing those bright shirts.

Once we arrived, I booked tickets to Chiang Mai for the two journalists under assumed names. The next day we left for the airport a couple of hours early, via a scenic trip around Bangkok, making a couple of quick tuk-tuk changes. There was no tail and I didn't see anyone watching them take the plane. I took a car up to Mae Sot instead of flying, leaving the two journos to enjoy Chiang Mai for a couple of days while I sorted out the red tape with the Karen military that would allow them safe passage. Once that was done, a quick phone call had them on a plane down to the border town.

About a week later we were given the green light. On the road in we went via the Mae Yuan River instead of the Moei and stopped short of the border at a Karen village in Thailand. I told the crew to sit tight for a few more days while I crossed over and met with Sampson, Isaac and the General. The TV crew only had another week before they had to head home and were getting a little frustrated. I did my best to explain the intricacies of Karen politics and how we'd have to make sure everyone was one hundred per cent happy or else nobody would be filming anything. They didn't seem too convinced.

A couple of days later in Manerplaw, after meeting with the General, I had all the necessary permissions. I also met up with the legendary Captain Hung, a French-Cambodian who was the original commander of the commandos before Pepé Le Pew had weaselled his way in. He was always coming and going and so far we hadn't crossed paths; it was a treat to finally sit down with him for a decent yarn. He was a very well-respected field commander and a humble, generous man. Once I had told him about the film crew, he offered to help in any way he could. The previous year he'd organised a French TV crew to film the plight of the Karen, but they turned out to be from a regional channel and the documentary got no international airplay. Hung could see the benefit in cooperating with a crew from a national broadcaster.

We found a good location to film our 'firefight' inside the Thai border. I never had any intention to take the crew up to the front line and expose them to enemy fire. The Karen were at a constant disadvantage to the superior firepower of the Tatmadaw; speed and concealment were the only things in their favour. Lumbering around with a film crew would just get everybody killed. Ninety per cent of combat footage is staged – anyone who has been there knows that – and that even includes what has been shot by a few 'legendary' combat cameramen.

Hung brought a platoon down to the site of our mock battle, along with them he brought a few thousand rounds of ammo, which he promptly hit up the camera crew to pay for. He's not a man to be refused, so the journos would have had to explain some interesting items on their expense accounts.

We started with a mock demolitions class. Hung's boys were filmed sitting on rows of benches that had been knocked up that morning, listening to my lecture on how to bring down a bridge. Some of the boys even drifted off to sleep during my talk, which added authenticity to proceedings, especially when I booted them awake.

Then we adjourned to a nearby paddock to set off some charges. After that, we had the boys do an assault on some freshly dug trenches while I acted as the enemy and fired tracers over their heads. I rigged a couple of charges to go off some distance back from the trenches as the soldiers advanced, but when filmed through a long lens the short depth of field made it look like the advancing men were right near the explosions, as if they were being attacked by mortar fire. It all looked like the real thing after it had been edited.

In keeping with my idea that a local angle was the only way to give the story the 'legs' it needed back home, the journos focused on those soldiers of fortune, like me, who had thrown their allegiances behind the Karen. I had no intention of disguising my identity, but the news crew decided that my 'fresh-faced boyish' looks didn't enhance the story like a scarred, hard-bitten old soldier's would, so we decided to cover my face with some netting, making me look more like a mercenary. The television footage and newspaper photos that went around the world all show me with this covering, but anyone who knew me could have recognised me straightaway.

Once the interview was in the can, we filmed some of the long-boats on the Mae Yuan River, and then dropped the crew off to be escorted back to Mae Sot. The reporter needed to head back to Australia as soon as possible to file his story using the film already taken, but his cameraman decided to stay with me for another week to get some more footage of the refugee camps.

I told the reporter to fly back under an assumed name and freight his film stock back separately. He ignored my advice and was arrested, with the valuable film in his bag, as soon as he arrived at Don Muang Airport. Hawaii Five-O and his mate – the two feds from our initial Bangkok flight – plus a posse of Thai coppers did the arrest. They told him he'd be charged with aiding and abetting a mercenary, which was just a bullshit charge to try and scare him into giving more information. He was taken to a hotel and placed under 'house arrest', which was more bullshit because he'd broken no Thai laws and they had no authority to hold him. He did the smart thing then and called the Nine Network's Sydney office. They quickly dispatched their local bloke around to his hotel to pick up the film and had their lawyers draft up a strongly worded letter, which was sitting on the feds' fax machine at start of business the next day. They let him go after that.

Once the cameraman had seen the refugee camps and started making his way back to Australia, I had to make my way home as fast as possible. I needed to be there when the story broke so I could answer the charges in person, hopefully getting in the news myself and stretching the story out a bit longer, maximising the exposure for the Karen.

The Nine Network aired the story on its prime-time current affairs show the following Wednesday. The SAS CT team were on an exercise in Nowra, New South Wales, and had crowded into the bar of a local pub when the story came on the TV. Marty saw my head first and shouted out over the noise of the bar, 'Hey, everyone! Dave's on TV!' None of the others knew what I'd been up to since I'd left the Regiment and speculation had been rife. A top PR firm couldn't have stage-managed it better. The story was run in the local newspaper the next morning and nationally the next day.

The Karen suddenly had more media exposure than they'd ever had and the Australian minister for foreign affairs was suddenly facing some very tricky questions about our country's support of the Burmese military junta. A diplomatic row ensued as the Burmese embassy complained strongly about the story. A few people were made to look very bad indeed and nothing strikes fear into the heart of a bureaucrat more. I can only imagine the shit-storm of arse-covering that ensued as all those Canberra pencil necks hunted furiously for someone to blame.

Eventually, of course, this led to a blowtorch being applied to the bum of a few feds, which inevitably would lead them to me. I waited patiently for the door to be kicked in. The offices of the *West Australian* and those of the Nine network in Sydney and Perth were raided. Of course, this bumbling attempt to squash the story just inflamed it further, keeping us all on the front pages well into the next week.

Eventually, the feds found me in a friend's house and accused me of 'hiding out'. I was charged under Section 6.1.A and 6.1.B of the *Crimes (Foreign Incursion and Recruitment) Act* 1978: Section 6.1.A – 'Did enter a foreign country, namely the Union of Burma, with intent to carry out a hostile activity'; and 6.1.B – 'Did enter a foreign country, namely the Union of Burma, and carried out a hostile activity'. I was the first person in Australia ever to have been charged under these particular sections of the Act, which kept me in the news and gave the Karen story the 'legs' we had hoped for.

Bail was set at $40 000 on the condition that I reported to a police station daily. When I returned home it was to three very worried women: my mum, sister and girlfriend. At that point they'd had no idea what I'd been mixed up in and the prospect of a fourteen-year jail term caused them all a lot of heartache.

I'd met Mandy three years before; she was a friend of my sister. Everyone thought she was way too good for me, including me, I suppose. But I took that as a challenge and won her over. We got married in January 1987. It was a fairly subdued celebration as everyone thought I was still going to prison, no matter how hard I tried to convince them otherwise.

We had known that the feds would come after me, but my lawyer and I were both surprised by their first dirty trick. Up until now the only existing evidence against me was a television program and a newspaper article, neither of which was created inside Burmese territory. So the Commonwealth Director of Public Prosecutions (DPP) applied for a special hearing on the charges instead of going straight to trial. The hearing was an attempt to solicit more evidence from the journos by getting them on the stand before a proper trial was held.

On the day of the special hearing, the courtroom was packed with media and there was standing room only for those lucky enough to get in. The right to protect their sources is sacrosanct to all journalists, so the case had generated nationwide interest. So far the government's attempts to squash the story were going really well.

In a nutshell, the Commonwealth DPP could charge me, but the case could not proceed any further without the federal Attorney-General's consent, and this hadn't been given because of the lack of real evidence. Jim Bateman, my lawyer, summed it up perfectly.

'This is a fishing expedition,' he announced to the court.

'Sit down and keep quiet, Mr Bateman, or I'll find you in contempt of court,' was the magistrate Peter Buck's reply.

The hearing nearly didn't even get started. My lawyer and the federal prosecutor engaged in some vicious legal arguments and the magistrate himself had to call a recess six different times to seek judicial advice. Eventually he returned and, looking very uncomfortable, declared that the hearing could go ahead. Again Jim protested and was again told to sit down and shut up.

John Mort, the TV reporter, was called first. He refused to answer any questions. Peter Buck, who was starting to look a little red-faced at this point, threatened him with contempt of court and prison. Jim stood up and protested again and again and each time was told to sit down and shut up. I saw a vein sticking out on Buck's forehead, and I reckoned if we kept protesting he'd explode. I gave Jim a little dig in the ribs next time he sat down, just to egg him on a bit.

The prosecutor resumed his questioning, but Mort still refused to answer. Buck was livid by this stage and gave Mort a verbal spray that would have done a footy coach proud. Magistrates don't take too kindly to someone who challenges them. That vein had a mind of its own, now. Mort stayed cool and simply refused to answer any questions. It was the sacred code of one profession against the sacred code of another and neither would budge. There was a stalemate when Buck asked Mort who his legal representative was.

'I don't have one,' was Mort's reply.

He was excused to seek legal advice. Mark Thornton, the newspaper reporter, was next and he copped the same treatment. Again, Jim stood to protest and a murderous-looking Peter Buck told him to sit down or he would be escorted from the courtroom and taken straight to the East Perth lockup. I was trying not to chuckle at this stage and hoped that Jim would have another go, but he didn't push his luck any further.

Thornton asked for an adjournment to seek further legal advice, to which Buck gladly consented. That afternoon, when we reconvened, there was a repeat of the charade, with Thornton again refusing to answer all but the prosecutor's most basic questions. Just as things were starting to look very grim for Thornton, Buck called another recess and returned to announce a two-week adjournment for Mort and Thornton to get legal advice.

To his credit, Buck said that he was 'uncomfortable with the proceedings' and that he felt the prosecution was 'simply using the court to compel people to give evidence so they could build a case' and this was an 'abuse of process'.

Alan Camp, a fantastic barrister at the Western Australian bar, contacted my lawyer that evening and offered his help, as the proceedings, in his opinion, were a miscarriage of justice. A writ of prohibition was then drafted and filed in to the Supreme Court to stay the proceedings until the Attorney-General gave his consent for the charges to proceed. This was listed for hearing immediately and a stay ordered in the Magistrates Court until the case was heard. The matter was set down for hearing in a month's time.

Come the day of the hearing, the prosecutor tried telling the Supreme Court judge that he didn't have the authority to hear the matter and pass judgement on it; that only a Federal Court could. This really annoyed the judge and he berated the prosecutor for putting forward such a suggestion, as the prosecutor himself wanted the case to be heard in a Magistrates Court rather than the Federal Court. The judge told him he couldn't have his cake and eat it, too. The writ was upheld and a stay put in place until the Attorney-General signed the form.

In May 1987, the Commonwealth DPP dropped the case. The episode was stressful for all involved but my goal was achieved: the Karen cause was getting airplay in Australia and around the globe. The federal government was now investigating what was happening with the equipment it was sending up to Burma for humanitarian projects and keeping closer tabs on its use. A flood of reporters from international media outlets went to Kawthoolei. I can't claim credit for all the exposure the Karen received over the next few years, but I was satisfied that I'd done my bit.

At the time I thought it was fully possible to live two lives. I was planning to continue my involvement with the Karen as well as build a life with Mandy, spending the dry season in Burma and the wet season, when there was no fighting, back in Perth. It's easy to look back and say that I wasn't being realistic, but, as they say, 'It seemed like a good idea at the time.' I spent the next few months driving trucks for a mate before it was time to head back up to Kawthoolei.

THE DAM JOB

Thailand, 1987. A blaring horn snapped me awake, and the front grill of a huge truck filled my vision. I'd nodded off while driving and a collision seemed milliseconds away. I screamed OHBLOODY-SHIT, or something like that, threw the steering wheel hard to the right and braced for a crash.

At speed, what feels like a close shave will often miss by a good metre or more. Riding motocross had taught me that. But when a loose bit of this truck's canvas canopy slapped the side of our car as we flashed past I knew there was just inches in it. I had a brief weird thought that we had somehow driven *through* the truck, but I had no time to dwell on it: we were headed for a deep drain on the other side of the road. Another hard wrench of the wheel and the car was pointing the right way but still sliding at an angle, rally-car style, towards the ditch, as the rear wheels struggled for traction on the wet grass. The rear wheels finally bit into bitumen and we shot straight across the road for a very similar performance on the other side. I edged us back towards the bitumen again, but this time backed off the accelerator to avoid another slingshot across the road into the oncoming traffic. It was all over in a few seconds. I had us back pointing the right way in our own lane again. Before anyone in the car could say anything, I chimed as cheerily as I could, 'Everyone awake?'

I had an American woman, a *New York Times* correspondent, in the back seat and her chaperone, the KNU Foreign Affairs Minister Dr Em Mata, in the passenger seat. The journalist had her face in her hands and kept repeating, 'Oh my God', as Americans do. Dr Mata let fly with a Karen version of ohboodyshit, as well as a few other expletives, the gist of which was, 'Why did we let this Aussie madman drive us down to Bangkok?'

We had been pushing hard, travelling for almost twenty-four hours straight. The journey had started before dawn the day before in Manerplaw with a longboat ride north to Mae Sam Lap, on the Thai bank of the Salween River. From there, we hitched a ride on one of the supply trucks: eight hours of bouncing around on rough, boggy tracks up to Mae Sariang. The truck got bogged every few clicks, so we spent plenty of time knee-deep in mud trying to push it out. After a quick wash and a feed, it was straight back on the road for a drive through the night, going the 700 kilometres down to Bangkok.

We stopped only once for fuel and a couple of times at the Thai police roadblocks, which seemed to operate exclusively at night. I had a well-rehearsed pantomime for these stops. I'd play the dumb tourist and pretend that my passport was in the trunk, under a pile of clothes and other gear, then frantically root around looking for them while a line of cars built up behind us, their drivers honking impatiently. The harried young copper would eventually wave us through without checking anything.

Just after our close shave, the sun rose over the outer suburbs of Bangkok; everyone was wide awake. We dropped off the journalist at the plush Shangri La Hotel before heading back to the outer suburbs to a KNU safe house. There, I fell asleep in my chair with breakfast on my lap.

I'd been back in the country a couple of weeks after a few mind-numbing months of truck driving in Western Australia. On my return to Manerplaw, President Bo Mya congratulated me on my efforts in raising awareness of the Karen people's plight. While he and Dr Mata were pleased, they had no illusions about this little burst of media exposure lasting longer than it took for the international media to latch on to the next big story.

Forget what big Western governments tell you about human rights – if there's nothing in it for them, they won't raise a finger. If oil could be found in the mountains of Kawthoolei, then they'd be all over the Karen cause like a rash. I was amused years later to hear Australian politicians talking with their hands on their hearts about the plight of the poor oppressed peoples of East Timor as justification for helping to kick the Indonesians out – without once mentioning the trillions of dollars' worth of natural gas recently discovered just offshore.

The Thai government would only help up to a point as well. It suited them to have Kawthoolei as a buffer against the Burmese nation on their western border as much as it suited them to have Cambodia, Laos and Vietnam to their east torn with strife. When your neighbours are ripping themselves apart they are much less likely to turn on you. So while the Thais were helping the Karen, they couldn't afford to help them too much.

Apart from giving an update on my media efforts, the other purpose of meeting Bo Mya was to seek his permission to head south to help out the KNLA's 10 Battalion. On my last trip one of the KNLA officers from Manerplaw suggested I go down to the Mergui-Tavoy area of the Tenasserim Division. This is the Burmese side of the mountain spine that runs down the centre of the Malay Peninsula – the thin strip of land separating the Andaman Sea from the Gulf of Thailand. Bo Mya and the KNLA command were concerned about the lack of action down there and were worried that the local commander had grown complacent. Or even worse – that he'd done some sort of 'I'll make you look good to your boss and you make me good to mine' deal with the local Tatmadaw command.

'You are the sort of man who can make a few things happen, Dave,' Isaac had said at dinner one night. There were a few smiles around the table after he said this. I'd already worked out that some of the KNLA colonels thought I was a bit of a loose cannon – someone who might stir things up a bit too much.

Although a couple of the boys from Baz's and my school had returned to the Tenasserim Division, they weren't able to get their own program up and running. One of the boys had quit to become a school teacher, which made me wonder what the kids were being taught in chemistry. The other, Roger, had become a sergeant and was involved in more pressing front-line duties. I figured I could go down to Tenasserim to put in a few months' effort developing the same sort of program that Baz and I had set up in Manerplaw, which was still going strong. The only problem was that Baz was now in Afghanistan, helping the Mujaheddin fight the Russians (this was back in the days when they were on 'our side'), so I'd have to set it up on my own.

General Bo Mya gave the new venture his blessing and sent a message to the commanders of the area to expect my arrival. He also asked me to drive Dr Mata and the *New York Times* correspondent down to Bangkok. He hadn't asked me to scare the shit out of them on the way – that was just a bonus.

I'm not sure how long I slept in the Bangkok safe house, but I was woken by Dr Mata gently shaking my shoulder. Standing with him was a very neat, erect man who was almost comically small. I reckon he would have been four-foot-ten at most. He was Colonel Marvel, the principal governor for the district and my escort to 10 Battalion. With the introductions out of the way, Dr Mata bade me farewell and headed off on another assignment. Colonel Marvel took me out to his luxury air-conditioned Toyota Land Cruiser, complete with Thai driver. I offered to drive but the Colonel laughed and insisted that I sit in the back seat with him. He must have been forewarned by Dr Mata.

We drove to Kanchanaburi, about 100 kilometres west of Bangkok. The Colonel was treating the drive as his chance to interview me. Despite my track record with the Karen, they were still very security conscious and wanted to be sure about me before I was allowed anywhere near the action.

As we drove through the flat sugar-cane country, skirting the top of the river delta, the jungle-covered mountains of the Tenasserim Division loomed in the distance. The car stopped at a small village where the Thai driver jumped out and handed the keys over to a Karen man. We continued on to cross over a Bailey bridge, which had a Thai military checkpoint located at its western end. The area we were about to enter was a military-training zone controlled by the Thai army. Civilian police had no authority here. Our vehicle was waved through and the bitumen soon gave way to gravel as we approached the mountains. There was an abandoned tin mine at the base of the hills and this was where we picked up our armed KNLA escort. The road became a narrow rutted track that wound its way up through the cloud ceiling. We drove past bamboo groves and beneath white limestone peaks with tendrils of clinging vines looming out of the mist.

After a couple of hours of bouncing along, I spied a slash of red and white in the distance. This was the Karen customs checkpoint into Kawthoolei. Colonel Marvel commanded instant respect and he had us through the checkpoint in minutes. Another hour or two and we came to the Karen village of Thee Tha, which was to be my home for the next few months.

After Colonel Marvel sorted me out with a billet, he took me off to Colonel Oliver's barracks for a formal introduction. The local commander was like an Asian Charles Bronson, without a sensitive side. His flat impassive face was pockmarked and he oozed menace. Meeting him was like shaking hands with a tree; he seemed more jungle hardwood than human. He regarded me, unsmilingly, with dark, brooding eyes that had probably seen thousands of deaths and gave the impression that arranging mine would be a very casual matter. Without him saying a word, I knew that in 10 Battalion it wasn't just 'his way or the highway', it was his way or a hole in the ground.

'You've come to teach my men demolitions?' he asked.

'Yes, I hope to —'

'What are your requirements?' he cut in.

I gave him a ten-minute run-down on what I would need to

get a demolitions school started. I could tell by the level of detail in his questions that he was nobody's fool, and that he had seen plenty of fools among the mercenaries who'd made their way to the Karen. I wondered if he'd ever met Pepé Le Pew but didn't think it was the right moment to ask. Once satisfied, he nodded curtly and I was dismissed.

Roger, the battalion's only graduate from the last demolitions course, was taken off active duty and put in charge of the school, with me as head instructor. There was already a barracks and training camp set up at Thee Tha, and the current crop of recruits had one month to go on their basic training before they were to join the fighting. After that, the facilities would be mine, so I used the time to get properly organised. The only thing lacking was a decent running track, so I organised a bulldozer to carve one out of the surrounding jungle.

The barracks were located on the site of an old timber mill at the bottom of a dead-end track. This was ideal for security because there was bound to be the odd BMI spy lurking about. There were also two Thai military intelligence officers permanently based in Thee Tha and it was important to keep them in the dark as much as possible. As far as they were concerned, I was a Baptist missionary by the name of Billy Graham Junior, helping to spread the word of the Lord amongst the spiritually impoverished Karen people – hallelujah!

Before the demolitions school could get started, I needed some explosives, so Colonel Marvel and I took a trip into Bangkok to buy chemicals. Like most Chinatown districts in the world, the one in Bangkok was a teeming maze of gold merchants, food stalls and markets selling anything you could imagine. Anything, it seemed, except the chemicals we needed.

Since I'd last been shopping in 1986, the Thai government had placed most of what we required on the restricted list. The Karen making their own explosives had no doubt cut into the Thai generals' profit margins trading weapons across the border, so none of the normal merchants wanted to deal with us. After a frustrating afternoon tramping around getting one polite rejection after another, we eventually found an old bloke who dealt fertiliser and other farm chemicals out of a surprisingly large warehouse at the back of a restaurant. After walking through the kitchen and out into air thick with that noxious ammonia smell, I made a mental note not to eat at that place when I was next in town.

'You make bombs, yes?' The old bloke knew exactly what the chemicals on our shopping list were for, but something in his toothless smile told us he was open to persuasion. A few US$100 notes later and he was helping us load drums into the back of the van. I made sure we also got a few drums of ammonium nitrate to make some amatol, which would give us more punch per kilo of explosive used. My second demolitions school was open for business.

On the first day a group of fifty young men assembled – some were as young as fourteen and were already experienced fighters. They had been hand-picked by Colonel Oliver and had the stamp of his brand of discipline all over them. It was like having a whole squad of Rowdys. They listened with serious concentration and jumped to perform any instruction I gave at double time. Training these blokes was a breeze.

I'd probably learnt from my past mistakes as well, but for whatever reason progress was rapid. We followed the same basic format as Baz and I had in Manerplaw and within a few weeks I had them patrolling, sniping and laying charges with confidence. The old timber mill was the perfect training venue as it had plenty of steel girders, concrete slabs and timber trusses to blow up.

Early on I had decided to demonstrate the lifting power of a small charge of ammonium nitrate. I got the squad to dig a tunnel under a large boulder that looked as if it weighed more than a few hundred kilograms, maybe even as much as a tonne. A fourteen year old named Po had his whole arm down the hole, scraping out the last of the dirt before we packed in the charge, when he gave a yelp, ripped his hand out and started flapping it wildly. Hanging off his finger was the biggest scorpion I have ever seen, at least the size of my outstretched hand, and Po was madly trying to flick the thing off before it got a chance to sink its stinger in. Scorpion venom attacks the nervous system and, with the slightly malnourished state most of these boys were in, it would probably make him sick for a week or two – as well as hurting like he'd stuck his whole arm into a fire.

The scorpion had done well to attach itself because Po only had a thumb and index finger on his right hand – the other three fingers had been blown off in the Tatmadaw attack on his village that had claimed his whole family. After swinging his arm around in circles like a hammer thrower, he eventually flicked it off, only to see the beast land right in the middle of the squad. It stood there with its claws outstretched and stinger up as if to say, 'C'mon you weak pricks, I'll take you all on.' And so the boys did, launching into it with their rifle butts, smashing the thing into the ground. Maybe the soft earth was cushioning the blows or maybe this Godzilla-scorpion was on steroids, I don't know, but they just couldn't kill it. It scuttled back and forth, trying to get its stinger in somewhere, and rolled with the blows from fifteen rifle butts. Then the group parted as Po came roaring through with a big rock held above his head. He slammed the rock straight down on to the scorpion with a *whump*. He carefully rolled back the rock to reveal the scorpion flattened like a pressed flower.

'Dead now,' he grinned as he looked up at me. His best mate, Kinh, picked the rock up and thumped it down again, just to be sure.

Po and Kinh were the only survivors from a Tatmadaw reprisal attack on their village some years earlier. They'd escaped down to the river when the first shots were fired, but not before a round took half of Po's right hand off. They buried themselves in mud and waited a day after they heard the shooting die down to be sure the soldiers had left. They took one look at the smoking ruins of the village and the remains of their families before walking for three days to Thee Tha. They fronted Colonel Oliver and asked to join up and were adopted by the unit. They were ten years old.

The story of Po and Kinh is not that unusual; thousands of kids had been orphaned by the war and many young boys became soldiers. Po and Kinh were already veterans of several stoushes with the Tatmadaw. These boys had been trained using the standard method: taking the boys in after a Tatmadaw position had been captured and having them shoot bullets into the already-dead enemy soldiers. This reduces their aversion to killing, so they'll do it without hesitation when the time is right.

One day I was trying to teach my group the difference between rigging parallel and serial electrical detonators, and although these boys were fairly smart, they just couldn't get it. Time after time the charges would be set, detonators inserted, and everyone would be standing back a safe distance behind a bunker and click, click – no explosion. We'd then have to wait ten minutes until we could be sure of no delayed detonations, before there'd be the slow, nerve-racking check of all the detonators. Each time I'd find they'd mixed up serial with parallel and failed to complete a circuit. With a parallel set-up, each detonator is in its own circuit. Although this is more complex to rig, it's more likely to be fail-safe as one detonator failing will not affect the rest of the charges. With a serial set-up, all the detonators are connected in the same circuit. This is simpler, but if one fails then the whole lot won't fire. I just couldn't get these boys to appreciate the difference.

As far as one of my tantrums go, on a scale of one to ten I'd give it about a nine. I picked up a shovel and whacked it repeatedly against a steel girder until the head fell off and the handle was just splinters. Then I kicked a box of detonators across the yard, before doubling over and screaming one long garbled swearword at the ground. I looked up for something else to smash and spied Po and Kinh, bent double – mimicking me exactly – silently mouthing my swearwords at each other. Then they fell over laughing. I chased after them but they were too quick for me, and I started laughing after a few yards anyway. The little shits. I ditched the idea of trying to teach parallel circuits after that and stuck to serial.

Po and Kinh did a midday matinee show of my tantrum every day for a week after that. They could mimic the way I walked perfectly and did a fair impression of they way I sounded when I was swearing a blue streak at the squad. If it had been the Aussie army, they would have been put on insubordination charges, and in the Pommie army they probably would have been shot, but I didn't mind because, despite their tendency to turn everything into a joke, they were becoming, very good operators – the best in the squad, in fact.

One night at dinner I got talking with a young captain who turned out to be Colonel Oliver's son-in-law. I didn't get around to asking him what it was like having such a fearsome father-in-law, because he got me interested in an old hydro-electric dam. I had been looking for a target that would serve as the final exam for the demolitions school and this would fit the bill perfectly.

Built in the 1920s by the British, the old dam was just above the plains east of Tavoy, about 80 kilometres from Thee Tha and not far inside Burmese territory. Blowing up a large dam is not as easy as it sounds. The explosives have to be somehow placed deep inside the structure. With solid concrete, you need cratering charges that will blow a hole deep enough so you can set a second round of explosives right inside. It's these ones that will actually do the damage – otherwise you just get an ugly scar on the surface of the structure and not much else. The initial blast would broadcast our presence to anyone within 20 k's of the target and we'd be trying to set the second charge with half the Burmese army shooting at us.

We were lucky enough to have a few blokes in the division who had worked on the dam before crossing over to our side. We quickly found out that it had an internal shaft running down the centre that gave access to a valve system. Blowing up the whole thing in one hit would be a relatively simple matter, if we could get enough explosives down that shaft. After drawing up a rough diagram of the structure and making a few calculations, I reckoned I'd need a thousand kilograms of explosives and the means to carry it more than 80 kilometres through mountainous jungle.

I made sure I had all my facts straight before approaching Colonel Oliver, because I knew he wouldn't need much of an excuse to knock it back. We sat on the verandah of his house and he stared at a copy of my plan for about ten minutes without saying anything. There was a number of things hanging on his decision – my reputation being one of them. If he didn't approve this, then I was pretty sure there wouldn't be much use for me in the 10 Battalion.

He finally spoke.

'You do realise that many people will die as a result of this job.'

'Not necessarily,' I replied. 'They only have a platoon guarding the dam and if we make our way carefully on foot, then split up afterwards —'

'I'm not talking about our casualties,' he interrupted, putting the palm of his hand flat on the table and staring straight at me. 'Many civilians downstream will die and that's before the army's reprisals.'

'I understand that, but I'm more worried about how many people will die if we *don't* take out this dam.' Colonel Oliver raised an eyebrow at this. I couldn't work out whether he was curious about my brilliant idea, or surprised at my lack of respect and wondering who he could get to drive me back to Bangkok, or something worse.

I figured I had nothing to lose and so just ploughed on.

'We know the Tatmadaw are slowly building their numbers and arms and some time in the next few years they will try a major offensive. This will probably happen up north first, not here. But even so, if we don't find a way to damage them economically down here, then we are just making it easier for them to eventually move on Manerplaw. Destroying the dam will take out the tin mine downstream and hurt their ability to irrigate, creating huge headaches for them.'

Oliver was silent for a few more minutes, staring again at my plan. He had the slightest crease of a smile around his eyes when he spoke again.

'So, you need to transport one tonne of explosives, covertly, through 80 kilometres of jungle.' He kept his finger on the part of my plan that mentioned this. 'And you came here seriously expecting me to provide you with the two hundred men it would take to do this, to go on a dangerous mission into enemy territory?'

Hearing him put it that way made me a little embarrassed. The steep terrain and energy-sapping humidity of this country meant that even the fittest soldier couldn't carry more than 20 or 30 kilos. Not to mention the food supplies, weapons and ammunition we'd need. I'd been too conservative in estimating the manpower. We'd need at least two hundred, probably more. Risking a couple of hundred good men on a job like this was too much. *Oh well*, I thought. *Guess I'll head back up north and throw my hat in up there*.

'Have you thought of using elephants?' Oliver asked. 'I'm sure we could pay some of the local *mahouts* (elephant drivers) to carry the explosives most of the way.'

Before I could answer, Oliver told me to get ready for a shopping trip to Bangkok, and to let him know when I was ready to proceed. With a slight nod of his head, he let me know I was dismissed. I couldn't contain my smile as I ran back to the camp with the good news. The next morning Colonel Marvel and I left for Bangkok with enough US dollars to buy everything we needed.

We got into Bangkok too late that afternoon to visit our Chinese fertiliser man, so I decided to check in on the Madrid Bar to see if Jimmy the Belgian had surfaced again. The bar was packed wall to wall with the usual collection of bullshit artists, and I was just about ready to call it a night when I spied two familiar faces. Sitting in the corner, quietly sipping cokes were two blokes who I'd had a bit to do with over the years. I can't reveal where I knew them from, but, like Baz, they were a part of the ex-special forces community.

These fellas came from the same small country town. They weren't twins, but they may as well have been. They talked the same, dressed the same, chased the same women (I'm not sure what went on behind closed doors; it's just not my business) and had managed to score the same postings throughout their military careers. The nicknames 'Bill and Ben' were obvious.

It turned out they had been working in Angola for a couple of years – spreading the good word of the Lord, no doubt, just like I was – and had stopped off in Bangkok for some deep and meaningful relationships with the local ladies before heading home. We had a good catch-up and shared a bit of gossip.

Aside from the occasional R and R in places like Bangkok, Bill and Ben were content in their chosen career and always on the lookout for action. I could tell they didn't have any new jobs lined up and weren't in a hurry to get home. I suggested they come up and help me with the dam job and they agreed instantly. I reckoned a couple of more-experienced hands couldn't hurt, and neither of them had dropped a dam before. I told them to get the bus to Kanchanaburi and meet me there in two days' time.

Colonel Marvel and I did our business with the Chinaman the next morning and sent just over a tonne of ammonium nitrate and other goodies on a truck over the border. I expected the Colonel to be a bit suspicious when I mentioned Bill and Ben, but he said it was no problem and that he'd square things away with Colonel

Oliver by radio. Colonel Oliver would check them out pretty thoroughly when we got back to Thee Tha anyway.

Colonel Marvel dropped me off in Kanchanaburi, and then headed off to Three Pagoda Pass on some private business. When Bill and Ben turned up we jumped on a Bhat bus to the small Thai town on the border of the military-training area. There I hired a four-wheel drive to take us up to the old tin mine; we were waved through at the checkpoint by a Thai officer, as mine was a familiar face by this stage. Colonel Oliver had got word that we were on our way, so by the time we arrived at the Karen checkpoint we had transport waiting for us. As we bumped over the rough track to Thee Tha, I could see Bill and Ben having the same nervous reaction that Baz and I had on our first trip in to Kawthoolei. It was an exhausting enough trip without having to look for ambushes around every corner.

When we got into Thee Tha I formally introduced them to Colonel Oliver, who gave them the same 'my-way-or-a-hole-in-the-ground' stare that I'd received.

'Jeez, he doesn't fuck around,' one of them said as we walked up to the camp.

Even that short walk left Bill and Ben looking knackered. It might have been hot during the day in Angola but it was as dry as a bone; they weren't acclimatised to the humidity at all. It usually takes a month of training before the body will start to store water, increase sweat rates and all the other stuff it does to adapt to humid climates. The boys had two weeks to settle in while I organised the rest of the equipment and had the recruits rehearsing for the job.

The elephants turned up two days before we were due to set off; they lumbered into the clearing nose-to-tail, with the *mahouts* singing and laughing. Then they huddled together as if they were the new kids on the block and were scared of all the bad soldiers with guns. Elephants live about as long as humans, so a *mahout* and his elephant have a lifelong relationship. The level of communication and understanding between the two was amazing to watch. The *mahouts* would take the rope harnesses off the elephants and give them a whack on the bum. The elephants would then trundle off on their own into the jungle, collecting dead wood and ripping out trees until they had a trunk load of firewood. They'd pile this up in the middle of camp before getting fed.

The big top-heavy animals looked ungainly and I wondered how they would handle some of the steep, muddy tracks. I needn't have. They are surprisingly sure-footed for their size, and if the going gets too steep, they use their trunk the same way an off-road vehicle uses a winch – wrapping it around the nearest tree and pulling themselves up. Or else they'd bend down onto their front knees and use their trunk as a third leg to gain more traction in the greasy mud. Men carrying packs would regularly slip backwards, skittling the blokes behind him like tenpins if they didn't step out of the way fast enough. I never saw an elephant do this and I'm glad about that, because there would have been carnage.

The tonne of ammonium nitrate was pre-mixed with diesel to make an ANFO (ammonium nitrate and fuel oil) mix. In this form it was packed into heavy-duty plastic bags, 20 kilograms to a bag. Then half a kilogram of tetrytol was added and a length of detonating cord attached to each bag before they were fully waterproofed. These were then packed into large plastic containers so that they could be easily transported by the elephants without the bags being damaged.

Colonel Oliver supplied us with a platoon of men from his heavy weapons section to provide fire-support if needed. I wanted these boys to be fresh to fight and not knackered from humping their gear, so we loaded that on the elephants as well. This included a couple of homemade 2.75-inch rocket launchers with a dozen phosphorus rockets and a long-range 81-millimetre mortar with fifty rounds. We also took along a couple of extra crates of tetrytol and a few rolls of detonating cord, in case we came across any opportune targets on the way back, and some M-16 'bouncing betty' mines to slow up anyone who might be chasing us.

The *mahouts* were quirky characters to deal with. They were more loyal to their elephants and the centuries-old traditions of their trade than to anyone involved in this fleeting little fifty-year-old war. They had a strange aloofness about them and didn't like being told how to load their elephants. When the interpreter passed on one of my instructions they'd look away and give no indication that they'd understood. It took a lot of work to explain how dangerous their cargo was and how critical it was that they kept the containers sealed from moisture. Eventually I was satisfied, and we headed off across the Tenasserim and up into the mountains.

The dam was 80 kilometres from where we were as the crow flies, but it was easily double that distance when you took into account that we'd be crossing the Bilauktaung mountain range. We'd be marching, sometimes scrambling, up and down some huge hills, and then following intersecting ridge lines. The biggest climb was about 5000 feet, so it wasn't going to be easy. The trip back was going to be a lot quicker. We'd be red-hot after the job and it'd be best to get out as fast as we could, so we'd arranged for a boat pick-up along the Tenasserim on the exfiltration point. There were a few Tatmadaw outposts along the river to be skirted on the way back, but dealing with these would be preferable to a pitched battle with a fighting column.

The head *mahout* reckoned it would take more than a week for the elephants to get over the ranges, so Roger and I decided our boys would head off first. We could get the recon done and be ready to go once the explosives, mortars and extra ammunition arrived. The heavy-weapons boys would stay with the elephant column to provide protection, though it was unlikely that there would be any Tatmadaw units operating this deep inside KNU territory. I still didn't completely trust the *mahouts* to look after the gear and so I was pleased that the heavy-weapons platoon could keep an eye on our stuff. I found out later that the main problem they had was the *mahouts* stealing our rations.

Like most of the rivers in this area, the Tenasserim had carved a steep ravine, so the track up to the first ridge out of the river valley was narrow, muddy and winding; it was so steep in places that we had to either crawl on all fours or grab branches and vines to pull ourselves up. I hung back at the rear of the column with Bill and Ben, and I could tell right from the start that they were struggling physically. But being tired was the least of their worries. They looked up at the loose column of men scrambling up the hill and saw something that looked more like a trekking party than a fighting patrol.

'Jeez, Dave. Where's the security? We'll be chopped up if we're bumped here,' Bill said, with Ben nodding in agreement. 'This looks as bloody dodgy as hell!'

'These tracks are here for a reason, fellas. They're the only way through. If the Tatmadaw have been up here in the last few days we'd know about it.' I tried to be as reassuring as I could; I was pretty keen for them to stick around, as their experience would count for a lot when we did the job.

I scooted off back up the track to catch up to the head of the column. A couple of hours later we were resting at the top of the first mountain, and I started to get a bit worried when Bill and Ben still hadn't shown up half an hour later. I trotted back down the track to see what was up. I found them three-quarters of the way up the hill, parked on their bums and not moving. They were completely stuffed and showing all the signs of heat stress: both had their heads hanging between their knees, with pale, clammy skin, totally soaked with sweat. The huge salt rings around their armpits and crotches were also a giveaway – as you get more acclimatised and 'jungle fit' you lose less salt in your sweat.

'Piss weak, you blokes! Talk about soft as butter. Jeez, if I knew you were this unfit, I'd have left you to your sheilas in Bangkok,' I laughed, trying to make light of the situation as I gave them my spare water and some electrolyte powder satchels.

'Give us a fucken break,' Ben said, somehow raising the energy to be pissed off. 'We haven't been living in the jungle, like a monkey, eating nothing but rice and maggots for the past few years like you have.'

'Ahh, the strong find a way and the weak find excuses,' I said, skipping out of the way as Bill tried to whack me with the butt of his rifle. 'Tell you what, why don't you ladies take your time and I'll leave a couple of my boys with you to hold your hands.' I took off back up the track to find a couple of volunteers before they could reply. We'd gone too far for them to turn back now, and I got the feeling that Bill and Ben wished they were back in Patpong

Road. A couple of boys volunteered to wait and bring them up at their own speed. In the worse case, they could hitch a ride on an elephant. Roger commented that they were suffering from Patpong malaria (too much booze and too many women).

It took four days of hard marching to get where we were going to set up a forward base. The column had stretched out for kilometres, and the boys came in dribs and drabs over the next day. There was a KNLA unit at the camp. Colonel Oliver had advised this unit of our operation and instructed them to help in any way they could. They provided a boat for us to send a recon team to the dam approaches and also came up with a real prize, a Tatmadaw soldier who had switched sides and joined the KNLA the week before. His platoon had just rotated out of guarding the dam site the week before he deserted and, as they say in the movies, he sang like a canary, giving us a wealth of good intelligence on the defences around the dam. We quarantined him after the interview, just in case he was a spy and was tempted to take off to warn his ex-mates.

A recon team that included Po and Kinh set off in the boat. They pulled in a few kilometres downstream and made their way through the bush to a good observation point on a ridge, which overlooked the dam and the Tatmadaw base guarding it. They would spend the next forty-eight hours there, establishing the guards' routine and locating sites for fire-support, plus identifying approach and escape routes.

The rest of the team set about preparing the gear, which was gradually arriving on the backs of the elephants; they'd drop their loads and then turn immediately for home. We also received regular updates from our spy network that the local commander had tracked a Tatmadaw mobile ready-reaction column in the area. The presence of these blokes certainly gave us something to worry about. They were probably the best-trained and most battle-hardened soldiers the enemy had to offer. If they were within a day's march of us, they could certainly spoil our party; we'd have to make sure they were well out of range when the job went down. Once it was over, we'd be travelling light so we figured we could outmarch them.

By the time Po, Kinh and the recon team came in, the rest of the gear had arrived, including two very sick and sorry-looking white fellas who had indeed needed to catch a ride on an elephant. This wasn't the time or place for more piss-taking, so I just made sure they were well rested and fed, ready for the job.

The recon team had done well; they'd supplied detailed maps along with all the other info we needed about the target. But this was an expensive operation by KNLA standards, and my reputation with them was on the line. I needed to confirm everything with my own eyes, especially the escape routes. 'Never walk into something that you don't know how to walk out of' is one of my cardinal rules. Roger and I decided to head out for a look with Bill and Ben.

A few hours later we were hidden in the bush, looking out over the dam. The Tatmadaw encampment was on the eastern side of the dam wall. They had a couple of bunkers overlooking the dam on that side and a bunker on the western bank. We couldn't see any obstacles or the telltale signs of a minefield on the approach to the base of the dam. This was something we'd confirmed with the Tatmadaw deserter – I hoped he was right. The dam wall was a series of raised concrete steps about 1.5 metres high. This was perfect as it would allow us to approach the target from downstream

With my sister Mary, 1964

Storeys Creek, where I was born. Mt Ben Lomond in the background

Me (second from the right) with the Rigby boys, Rossarden, 1966

With David Olsen and Dad, just before the black jay-shooting expedition

Army apprentices school, Balcombe, 1978

With Dad at the march-out parade from Balcombe, 1979

With Dad in Luina on my first leave from the army

On a patrol course, Bindoon, 1983

During the shallow-water dive training in 1984. Posing with an Uzi submachine gun

Freefall-parachuting course in Williamstown. My first sergeant in the Regiment, Maurie Wesson, is second from the left, bottom row; Terry Hewitt sits at far right, bottom row

Receiving my sandy beret from my good mate 'Rock' Roberts

Sniper team, Swanbourne, 1985. Marty McCarthy is at far left, top row; 'Harry' Butler, who disappeared in Queensland in 1990, is second from left, bottom row

Firing the MG-42 captured from the chilli-bomb cave

The first demolitions course with mock-up Bailey bridge in the background

One of the fire-support teams in Mae Tawah

Posing with an 81-mm mortar bomb

Anti-aircraft position at Mae Tawah

Typical jungle-fighting terrain along the Moei River

Karen children at school in Thee Tha

Manerplaw, 1986, at General Bo Mya's headquarters

Test-firing the AK-47

Firing the mortar bomb at Mae Tawah

The 84-mm Charlie Gutsache recoilless rifle

Posing with equipment before the Bailey bridge job

The photo that started all the trouble with the feds

With a 3.5-inch bazooka in Manerplaw

Pacino and Sampson

Buying guns on the Gold Coast

My firstborn, Nicholas, in 1990

In Casuarina Prison's special-handling unit with a couple of mates

Casuarina Prison, 1996

Revisiting Fremantle Prison. This eighteenth-century prison is now a tourist attraction

Sitting on my old bunk inside my original Fremantle prison cell

With close friends (from left) Keith, Debbie, Connie and Shirley Allmark. Connie is the author of *Rebel of Burma*. All are active in helping settle Karen refugees through the organisation Tribal Refugee Welfare

'At home' in the bush on a hunting trip

Siesta time at a bush camp, somewhere east of Kununurra

With Maurie Wesson at the SAS Regiment's fiftieth-anniversary ball, 2007

Catching barra on the Burkley River, in the East Kimberley

and go straight up, rather than moving across the top of the dam, exposing ourselves to machinegun fire from the base.

We watched the target for a day and a half, and in that time, just like during the two days that Po and Kinh's boys had been watching, the Tatmadaw sent out no patrols. The guard changes were supposed to be every two hours, but everyone seemed to knock off about 2000 hours. Some nights there were a couple of checks, which consisted of a stroll along the top of the dam, and on other nights nothing. I made a mental note to organise a couple of hit teams with silenced .22 rifles to guard the eastern and western approaches to the dam wall, in case we caught them on an 'on' night.

The manhole cover on the top of the dam wall, which covered the all-important shaft, wasn't even padlocked shut. There were also a couple of unmanned searchlight towers that didn't look operational. Those would be covered by snipers, and if something were to go wrong, could be knocked out quickly.

We were satisfied with the recon team's work. Their choice of infil and exfil routes, as well as the siting of the fire-support teams, was perfect. The job was set to go down in two days' time, on the blackest night of the month. Roger was placed in overall command of the operation, and a thorough briefing was held with the officers and NCOs before the troops were briefed about their specific jobs.

We were moving into the site with about 140 men in total. The demolitions team had sixty men: fifty for the packhorse work to get the explosives to the top of the dam wall, and eight to provide cover for the two shot-firers who'd initiate the charge once it was in place. After the bags were down the shaft, the remainder of the guys would then form up on the western bank to cover the bunker there, as well as provide close fire-support for the demolitions team.

I got Bill to stay with the fire-support team. I hadn't trained these blokes and so wasn't completely confident of how they'd work under attack. If we were discovered setting the charges, we'd be completely exposed, so I needed someone experienced to direct the mortar fire. Ben was to come in with me so we could cover each other if things got hot.

One of the 2.5-inch phosphorus rockets was rigged up with a charge so it could be fed into the mouth of the bunker on the western bank and cranked off if any trouble came from that direction. Po and Kinh were tasked with leading the team for this job. The remainder of the rockets would be fired into the eastern bank from the fire-support group should a firefight develop. Theoretically that would blanket the defending platoon with smoke and fire, preventing them from getting a bead on any of us on the dam wall. The 81-millimetre would also walk rounds on to the camp to give us time to bail out if needed.

Hand grenades were in short supply, so we pooled all that both units had, and issued one to each of the demolitions team members. If things went wrong during the job, the sacks of explosives could be just dumped down the shaft and a hand grenade thrown down to initiate them. Five seconds is not much time to get off a dam that's about to explode, but you'd be amazed how fast you can sprint with rounds cracking past your head. Also, the dam wall was 40 metres high, and the main force of the blast would be down at the base, giving a few more precious seconds before the top of the wall would start to give way. That was the theory anyway.

You might think we'd be too keyed up before the job to get any proper rest, but a soldier learns to get his head down whenever the opportunity presents – you never know when you will get another chance. The same goes for grabbing a feed. We ate a big lunch of rice and dried meat, with a few other jungle delicacies thrown in, before sleeping for a few hours.

Roger and I roused everybody about 1600 hours, and we used the last of the daylight to recheck our kits. After one last check of all the bags of ANFO to make sure they hadn't been perforated, Roger gave the signal to move out. We were on full patrol discipline now and the training kicked in. The teams had all checked themselves and each other for loose gear that might rattle and anything that might shine. Somewhere behind me in the dark were 140 blokes but I couldn't hear them. This is the most nerve-racking time, being at the head of a group this large, moving on an enemy position, when a single cough, click or any other unnatural sound could mean your death.

We cut straight across and met the river about 1 kilometre below the dam three hours later. As we crept closer along the riverbank and got into position, the roar of the water from the outlet at the bottom of the dam and the mist lifting off the spray made for great cover.

We sent Po and Kinh's team up first. We needed them in position beneath the west bunker before the demolitions team moved into position. They'd be right under the noses of the Tatmadaw troops, so it was too dangerous to communicate by radio. We gave them ample time, thirty minutes, before moving up the wall. We couldn't see them in the mist and the dark, so we had to trust that they'd done just as we'd rehearsed.

Each time I was certain that thirty minutes had passed I'd look down at my watch to see that it'd only been five. I could almost feel the physical pressure of the blokes behind me, leaning forwards like they were straining on a leash, wanting to move or do anything to end the tension of waiting while so exposed. I was just about to lift my arm to signal the demolitions team to move when our careful plan went to shit.

There was a shout, the loud hammering burst from a G3 rifle, and then the solid thump of an explosion from the western bunker. The whole place lit up like a night cricket-match as Po and Kinh's 2.5-inch phosphorus rocket went off. I could see blokes running around, screaming like banshees with blazing clothes and hair, setting fire to the surrounding scrub as they rolled around trying to put themselves out. We couldn't work out what had happened or who was on fire, the Tatmadaw or Po and Kinh.

We had prepared for this eventuality and the demo team leaders snapped into action. Guys started scrambling up the wall. The eastern slope came to life with muzzle flashes and tracer rounds sprayed over our heads. The MG-42 has an almost continuous rate of fire, so it sounds like one long scream rather than the hammering sound you'd normally associate with a machinegun. If they got on target with that, we'd be annihilated. Luckily, they were aiming at the western bunker across the top of the dam. It wasn't looking good for Po and Kinh.

I was about to call on the radio for the fire support when I heard the pop of the 81 going off and the whoosh of the 2.5-inch rocket coming in overhead. The rocket ripped in low, making me duck involuntarily.

Five boys headed to the eastern side of the dam wall to stop any advance on us from that direction. Two others bolted straight up the wall to get in position to open the service shaft's manhole cover. We still hadn't been spotted, and I don't think the Tatmadaw knew what was going on, especially once the mortars and rockets started exploding among them. The firing from the MG had been joined by a dozen or so rifles. It wasn't concentrated on any one spot apart from the western bunker, as the troops couldn't see where they should be firing, and were probably too confused and too busy getting under cover to care. The KNLA often lobbed bombs on to Tatmadaw positions and didn't follow up with attacks; this tactic was mainly to keep them guessing and annoy the hell out of them.

The phosphorus rockets were hitting home and blanketing the eastern bank in smoke and fire, but the mortar rounds were landing too far out. Not being able to lob a few shots to test the range beforehand, we had to estimate and naturally we erred on the side of caution. The last thing we needed was our own bombs landing amongst us while we were carrying a tonne of ANFO. I radioed Bill and requested a range drop to get them closer in, again being cautious, rather than risking a disastrous over-correction – trying to walk the bombs on to the Tatmadaw base. After another few rounds, the bombs were hitting the target, so it was back to the job at hand.

It was my turn to start scaling the dam wall. My heart was hammering so hard that I had the strange thought that it would blow a valve and I'd die right there from a heart attack. I also noticed my rectal muscle squeezing tight. I'm not sure why that happens when we are in danger, but I suppose it's a last-ditch effort to stop the opposite from happening. Normally I'd have found it a bit difficult, having to wriggle over a series of steps almost as tall as I was, while carrying my fighting kit plus my share of the ANFO, but the adrenalin had me climbing like a monkey up a tree.

When I got to the top the lads had the manhole cover open. I leaned in and quickly shone a hooded torch down the shaft, hoping to hell that it couldn't be seen from the other side, especially by the blokes firing the MG.

Something really worked in our favour then; the base of the hole was dry. If it had been wet down there, we would have had to be careful not to rip the bags as we dropped them in. With a dry hole, we could quickly drop them in, not worrying about the occasional bag ripping if it snagged against any machinery on the way down. The charge would definitely be going off. I frantically waved the rest of the boys up the wall.

The demolitions team filed through, threw their bags down the hole, and then scuttled like crabs over to the western bank to take up firing positions. No firing was coming from the area around the burning bunker, but the bushfire was taking hold and it was getting too bright for my liking. We still didn't know what had happened to Po and Kinh.

Only one thing mattered now, and that was to get the ANFO down the shaft as quickly as possible and get the hell out. The fire support team was pumping the mortar rounds and rockets so fast that there was an almost-continuous roar of exploding bombs on the opposite bank and a ripping neon stream of rockets overhead. I figured they were getting as many rounds away as they could so they wouldn't have to carry the bloody things back to base – there'd be no elephants to help on the way home. I was hoping the rounds wouldn't run out before we were clear of the dam wall.

A whooshing roar of flames added to the cacophony coming from the eastern bank. The phosphorus and rocket mortars had set the huts and scrub on fire on that side as well. I could see a couple of wildly thrashing dark spots against the orange flames: some unlucky Tatmadaw soldiers were caught in the open and were burning alive. Their screams sounded more like steam escaping their boiling bodies than anything human.

Those who had made it to the safety of the bunkers over there seemed to be keeping their heads down as their rate of fire decreased. But our fate was still hanging by a thin thread; all it would take was for one of them to get wise and stick their head up and we'd be chopped up by that MG. I was crouched next to the manhole cover; Ben was crouching wild-eyed next to me, as we waved the boys through one by one. I was keeping quiet but shouting with my eyes, if that's possible, for them to get a move on. They really didn't need my encouragement to move fast because we were all feeling like black dots on a white sheet.

We counted the fiftieth guy through and gave him thirty seconds to get clear. Then the blokes in the fire-support team nearest the eastern side of the dam got the message to bug out. They came shooting back past us at a rate of knots, glad to be clear of the exploding ordnance on that bank. There was now over a tonne of explosive down the shaft. If that couldn't blow this old wall down, nothing could.

The Tatmadaw still hadn't cottoned on, and we weren't going to give them a chance to. No time to hang around lighting fuses and lowering initiator charges down the hole now. I set a one-minute fuse on the charge, pulled the twin fuse-igniter pins, made sure it was hissing and threw the lot down the shaft. The detonators were inside a tin can, attached to the detonator cord and padded with foam, so that the thump at the bottom of the drop wouldn't set them off prematurely. Ben and I also pulled the pins on a couple of grenades, threw them down simultaneously and then ran like jack rabbits for the western bank, keeping in what was left of the shadows the whole way.

ANFO has a peculiar way of exploding; unlike the crack of high explosives, it has a lazy blast, especially when it's contained within a confined space. We were just getting to the far bank, and I was mid-stride when the charge went off. The whole dam vibrated, then buckled. A roar that seemed to press directly on my eardrums erupted and knocked both Ben and me off our feet. I bounced straight to my feet again and then scrambled into one of the trenches near the blazing bunker, hugging the dirt at its bottom. Ben crashed in a second later and knocked the wind right out of me.

Giant chunks of concrete rained down everywhere and our trench had no roof, not that a few sticks of bamboo would have stopped much. There was a sustained roar over the crack of exploding mortars and the whoosh of incoming rockets as the dam wall breached and the water burst down the valley. Ben and I were curled up like ring-tailed possums to make smaller targets for any incoming concrete; we were both hoping like hell we wouldn't be squashed flat.

It was a very long minute or two before I uncurled and stuck my head up. A cascade of water was still thundering through a breech in the dam that looked at least 10 metres wide. *Repair that, you bastards*, I thought, indulging in a brief moment of triumph. The rockets had stopped coming in and the mortar was firing at a more conservative rate. It was time to go. Ben and I made our way to the first rendezvous point and did a quick headcount. We were two men short. Po and Kinh hadn't made it to the rendezvous point and they would have by now if they were mobile. We waited another five minutes, by which time our mortar had stopped firing. There wasn't any time to waste looking for them; we had to get moving to make as much distance between us and the dam before daylight.

We made our way up to the fire-support team's position. They had already packed up and were ready to move out. We put in an all-night stomp, almost jogging all the way and only pulling up, just after first light, when we heard aircraft. They were flying a search pattern over the area, but it was a fair way to our north. There was plenty of overhead canopy, but we didn't want to get spotted by accident and have to tangle with that Tatmadaw mobile ready-reaction force. We found good cover and rested up. By the frantic sound of the Tatmadaw radio communications we were listening to, they were pretty annoyed.

I was anxious to find out what had happened to Po and Kinh and assembled the rest of the western-bunker team for a debrief. They told me that Po and Kinh were sliding the rocket into the mouth of the bunker when it must have nudged one of the soldiers inside, waking him up. This led to a tug of war in reverse, as the blokes in the bunker were trying to push the thing out with Po and Kinh trying to push it in. Whether Po and Kinh cranked off the charge in a panic or one of the Tatmadaw trying to fire his G3 out through the same hole set it off, we will never know, but when the rocket went off it took everybody with it.

I felt really sad at losing my little mates, but the other boys were already cracking up as they told the story, especially as they re-enacted the mad panic of the push-of-war. I suppose Po and Kinh would have been honoured that we found some humour in mimicking their last moments. There wouldn't have been much left of Po and Kinh to take home and bury. At least their mothers weren't alive to grieve for them.

Otherwise, we'd got away almost unscathed. A couple from the eastern team had caught some shrapnel during the barrage, and a few from the western-bunker team had burns from being in the vicinity of the rocket, but nothing too debilitating and nothing that would slow anyone down.

We took the long way back to the local company headquarters. The exuberant reception we got on our arrival showed that everyone had already heard what had happened from the radio intercepts of Tatmadaw signals traffic. We had a celebration and a bit of a passing out parade for the boys I'd trained. Most of them were staying on to be dispersed among the various platoons there. A few came back to headquarters with us to attend further duties at the training camp or to be assigned to companies further to the south.

It was much harder to say goodbye to these blokes than the last time I'd done it with the first school I'd run with Baz – maybe because I was more familiar with this war now and knew that most of them would probably be dead or crippled within the next few years. The dam job was also a far more intense operation. I'd had some doubts about the boys' ability to stay cool if things went off-plan, but each one rose to the occasion. They were magnificent. The bond that this sort of experience creates can't be manufactured, and it tore me up inside knowing that it would be the last I would see of most of them. They were in this fight for life, while I was free to come and go as I pleased.

Roger, Bill, Ben and I left the next morning, along with a dozen other blokes, for the trip back to Thee Tha. We were travelling much lighter and the trip back was much faster than the walk in, but it didn't pass without incident. A few months after the dam job a Korean Airlines 747 went down in these parts and hasn't been found to this day, which gives an indication of how rugged the country is. Most of the jungle we passed through hadn't been explored by anyone other than those who had first cut the track along the ridge lines centuries before.

At one point on our trip back I decided to stretch my legs and scoot ahead on my own for a bit. I'd cleared the last ridge of the mountain range, descending the slope that went down to the Great Tenasserim River and our pick-up point. I had switched off a bit and was enjoying the walk – and the fact I was still alive. My mind might have been having a little holiday but my instincts weren't. I suddenly felt a cold shiver through my chest and neck: the classic fight or flight response as the body pumps blood away from the skin and into the working muscles. Then the hairs on the back of my neck stood up all on their own. If it had been an ambush, I would have known about it by now, and I couldn't see any sign of danger. But I couldn't shake the feeling of dread. Something was stalking me.

Then I suddenly remembered having a yarn with a few of the recruits up north about tigers. I had this powerful urge to run headlong down the hill and went a few strides before I realised I'd have no chance. Big cats like their food running and scared. Instead, I slipped the safety catch on my M-16 to full automatic and sprayed a burst of rounds in a 360-degree arc. Then I dropped on a fresh magazine and waited. Something bounded off through the scrub further up the hill. I didn't see what it was, and to this day I don't know if it was a tiger or not. That didn't affect what I did next. I ran. Down the hill as fast as I could, but not quite out of control, head scanning from left to right like it was on a swivel, eyes wide, searching the bush for anything big and furry. After reaching the river, I struck north and eventually came across the track; I perched there to await the arrival of the rest of the blokes, twitching at each jungle noise.

The rest of the guys turned up about two hours later. They were patrolling carefully down the track, weapons at the ready. They'd heard the burst of fire, then nothing, and figured I'd been bumped by the Tatmadaw. It was highly unlikely they'd be patrolling this far inside Karen territory, but the boys weren't taking any chances. When they got close to me, still wanting to keep quiet, they raised their eyebrows as if to say 'what happened?'

'Bloody tiger,' I croaked.

'Bullshit!' they laughed in unison, thinking I was just pulling their legs, trying to wind them up one more time before we got back. But Roger backed me up. Tigers are protected inside the borders of the Karen State and there are plenty about. Bill and Ben were still a bit sceptical, but I didn't need any more convincing. That was the last time I wandered off on my own.

By the time we got back to Thee Tha and sat down with Colonel Oliver, plenty of news had filtered back about the dam job. The Tatmadaw area commander was really pissed off and reprisals against local villagers had been savage. Attacks on Karen positions, including the one we had just left, had also been stepped up. Soldiers had been killed, villages burned, women raped and mutilated as a result of this attack. It was a heavy thing to have on my conscience, but it was Colonel Oliver himself who put it all into perspective. The Tatmadaw had been doing this systematically since 1962 and this just gave them another excuse.

The loss of the dam had put a big dent in the Tatmadaw war-making capacity. Apart from the loss of hydro-electricity, they had lost irrigation water for the rice paddies, which meant they were going to lose a lot of money. Later radio intercepts indicated the Tatmadaw had twenty-three dead and twenty-five wounded as opposed to our two dead. Obviously, the barrage caught a lot of them outdoors. It was a bit sobering to realise what we had stirred up, but overall I was satisfied with the job.

It was just the sort of thing that people like Bill, Ben and I had been trained for, and I figured they'd be keen to do more. After checking first with Roger and Colonel Oliver, I asked the pair if they wanted to stick around and help put through another demolitions school.

'Fuck that,' they said in unison, sounding like they'd expected me to ask and had rehearsed their reply.

'It's too hot,' said Ben.

'The food is shit,' said Bill.

'We can't touch the women,' said Ben.

'And there's no booze,' said Bill.

'We're off back to Patpong Road,' said Ben. 'In forty-eight hours I want to be having a beer, in a bath, with one girl scrubbing my back and another one washing my front.'

They'd obviously thought it through and there was no talking them out of it. I rode back out to Kanchanaburi with them and had a couple of cold beers at the Jolly Frog guesthouse before swapping addresses and parting company. I haven't seen them since, but I did hear a whisper that they ended up in Colombia training drug-cartel blokes in weapons handling. But then again, I heard it in the Madrid Bar, so who knows the truth?

GOLD FOR GUNS

Downtown Pretoria, South Africa, reminds me of those big Australian inland towns: sleepy places that only really wake up on Saturday night. Although it's a city of over three million people, the wide jacaranda-lined streets and solid-stone buildings give it a rural feel. I'd been here for a couple of months, attending meeting after meeting with South African defence force people, some government officials and several arms manufacturers. It was bloody hard being polite all the time so I decided to take a break and see a movie, preferably something loud and featuring a lot of explosions. Walking towards the cinema a few streets away, I got more than I was hoping for.

A sharp cracking sound was followed by a deep boom that I could feel through the soles of my feet. I knew straightaway it was a bomb. The moment of silence afterwards is always a weird contrast. It's as if the world holds its breath before letting loose with a chorus of screaming. Suddenly people were out in the street rushing towards the scene. The IRA or PLO often set off one bomb inside a pub or café to get people running out onto the street. Then a second bomb is detonated, usually in a car, right where everyone is milling about. This was a standard tactic taught in the Libyan terrorist-training camps. Expecting the next detonation any second, I found a little enclave and hung back. Above the screams and sirens I could hear the continuous tinkle of glass as shattered windows in the nearby office buildings slowly cascaded down. People staggered away from the area covered in blood.

I waited until all the emergency vehicles had screamed to a stop and for the parade of bloody people to thin out. There was no second blast. After about half an hour I went closer for a look. Just outside the cinema in the middle of the street was the head of a black man, perfectly unmarked, with eyes open, like it was looking for the rest of his body. His arm was lying on some steps and the rest of him in a charred heap on the footpath; his intestines nearby in a neat steaming pile. There was so much blood and guts it looked like it wouldn't fit if you tried to pack it all back into his body. Obviously the bomber's target was the cinema; luckily the silly bastard set it off before he had gotten there.

The area around the body was taped off and guarded by a huge blond-haired copper in a flack jacket. I caught his eye and walked up to say g'day. He looked down at the mess and shook his head with disgust.

'Bloody ANC get these dumb kaffirs from the hills,' he said. 'They show them how to activate the bomb and tell them they've got a fifteen-minute fuse, when in fact it's an instant trigger. So there's no one left for us to interrogate except this one's head.'

He walked over to the head still lying in the middle of the road and spat. 'Who sent you, you dumb black piece of shit?' Then he booted the head across the road so it skidded into the gutter. I went back to my hotel room and read a book.

Pretoria is the spiritual home of the Afrikaners and site of the biggest South African defence force bases. Afrikaners are South Africans of mostly Dutch and German origin. Fed up with British colonial rule in Cape Town, they set out in the 1830s and '40s on a push north known as the *voortrekk.* Translated literally it means 'pull from the front' – a metaphor of independence. Stand on the top of the huge Voortrekker monument, built entirely by whites from granite quarried in the nearby *koppes*, look down the valley towards the Magaliesberg range, and you can see how the Afrikaners saw themselves as God's chosen people. At the time I was there apartheid was still nearly a decade away from being dismantled and Pretoria was not a good place to be black.

I was in South Africa to do an arms deal for the Karen. The irony of trading with one oppressor while helping fight another hadn't really hit me. I was too young for that sort of introspection.

It was March 1988. I had been involved, on and off, with the Karen for two years. After the dam job, I stayed with Colonel Marvel's battalion and continued my training role. I had escorted a team of journalists deep into southern Burma and helped them find a lost cache of World War Two Japanese weapons and ammunition. One of the journo's stories about 'The Lost Tunnels' made the newspapers back in Australia. After that, I returned to Perth to spend some time with Mandy, who was already tiring of my long absences. Still trying to get some sort of career going that I could juggle with helping the Karen, I decided to be a private eye and got police clearance to act as a licensed enquiry agent.

I had only been home three months and was just beginning to

set up the private-investigation business when I got the call to head back up to Kawthoolie by General Bo Mya himself.

Burma was at boiling point. Civil unrest was erupting right across the country as the economy failed and Ne Win struggled to keep a lid on things. People were beginning to starve.

The time was ripe for the Karen to attack the weakened regime. But if the KNU was going to exploit the opportunity, they'd need to be able to arm a civilian uprising in both the cities and towns. This would take many, many more weapons than the KNU budget could possibly fund.

I'd noticed a few small goldmining operations in my travels around the Karen State. These were mainly alluvial works, kept small and mobile to evade the Tatmadaw and to avoid letting on that the gold was there in the first place. No mineral exploration had ever been undertaken in the areas controlled by the Karen, but with the presence of alluvial gold, you didn't need to be a geologist to guess that there would be plenty underground. The Karen didn't have the sorts of large oil deposits that would bring the Western world running, but if they could tempt someone with the promise of unhindered gold exploration rights in exchange for military aid, then they might stand a chance.

I figured that here would be a good place to start. With heavy gold interests and one of the best-equipped militaries in the world, South Africa, I reckoned, would throw up someone with common interests. I'd initially thought we could bring the arms in by ship through the port at Prachuap Khiri Khan, then truck them the short distance across the border to be carried up into the Karen territories by elephant. But coming through a civilian port in Thailand more than quadrupled the amount of bribes we'd have to pay. We were better off just bribing the Thai military directly.

The area leading into the 10 Battalion's headquarters was under the complete control of the Thai army. Civilian law ceased to apply beyond the military checkpoints. A number of airstrips were located in this area and, with the right contacts, clandestine flights could be made to drop off arms shipments without arousing too much attention. Training exercises created plenty of air traffic and a few more aircraft wouldn't be noticed.

I was appointed a 'Representative Plenipotentiary' for the KNU to the Republic of South Africa for a period of three years. This was my ticket to approach the government in South Africa. Getting their cooperation was a long shot. Despite the fact they were an international pariah and operating under all sorts of trade, arms and sports embargoes, it was very unlikely they would back the Karen rebellion. It probably required too much imagination for a government to be that forward thinking. The next best thing was for me to secure an export licence from them for arms and ammunition, opening the door for a decent supply. Then we wouldn't be so vulnerable to the fluctuating black market controlled by the Thai generals.

Assuming we wouldn't get government backing, I had also arranged to meet with a few large mining companies to see if we could get corporate sponsorship. In effect, I was trying to sell the exploration rights in the future independent Karen State.

I had arrived in South Africa via Zimbabwe. The terminal in Harare was a step back in time – from the eighties to the sixties. It was decrepit and dirty, with surly, slow-moving customs officials whose whole mission in life seemed to be pissing off travellers. I was waiting in line with a bunch of nervous-looking American tourists on their way to the game parks when a squad of soldiers came into the building. The middle-aged Americans shat themselves as these kids came swaggering through with their mirrored sunglasses, tiger-striped camos and belts of ammo wrapped across their chests, Mexican bandit-style. This was precisely the desired effect. No doubt they had grown up on a steady diet of *Rambo* and were doing their best to be menacing. I walked straight up to them and said g'day. The international language of the army prevailed and they all broke into huge grins. They were just kids trying to show off. Pretty harmless, really.

The 100-kilometre road up to Pretoria from Johannesburg had been designed with the idea that, in times of conflict, it could double as a landing strip for fighter jets, so it was as broad and as smooth as a German autobahn. I'd splurged a bit of Karen money on hiring a BMW 515i (to create the right impression when meeting all of these government and corporate types) and sat it on 160 kph the whole way there. I spent the first couple of days in Pretoria at the Four Seasons in the centre of town, but I've never been comfortable in five-star hotels – too sterile – and after living in the bush on and off for the last couple of years, I found all that formality exhausting. As soon as I could, I got a cheap room on the edge of town.

South Africa was in a state of emergency, which had been declared in 1985, and had detained more than 30 000 people without trial, all in an attempt to quell the growing unrest among the black majority. When I rolled up at the Union building for my first meeting with the Far East Office, security was unbelievably tight. The entrance to the building was sandbagged right to the ceiling and there was a bomb squad permanently on duty. They went over the car in impressive detail and over me even more so. The security bloke at the Far East Office was sitting behind bulletproof glass, with a riot shotgun and a bandolier of spare cartridges sitting next to him.

The bloke delegated to meet me was the junior assistant secretary to the assistant minister or some bloody thing. He was thin, nervous and, like all public servants, spent most of the time constructing long sentences about nothing. He was slipperier than a Murray River eel when you tried to get him to make a point. Not that impressed with my proposal, he was more concerned with how another goldfield outside the country would disadvantage the South African economy. They'd rather discourage new gold finds than be a part of them. It was a pretty defensive attitude, but there was not a lot I could do about it.

I wasn't expecting much from the meeting anyway, and if the young public servant had said, 'Why yes, we'd love to finance your revolution on the off-chance that there might be some gold in it for us. How should I make out the cheque?' I'd have probably fallen off the chair. But I guess it paid to go through the right channels. He said that the department would consider the proposal and get back to me. I knew that meant 'no'. On the plus side he was quite happy to give me a letter of introduction to a communications company and one of South Africa's major arms manufacturers. He had these drafted up while I waited.

I pulled up outside the headquarters of the arms manufacturer that afternoon and had to crane my neck to take it all in. The buildings were set amongst lush gardens and, while only ten or so storeys high, they were spread out over several acres. Killing was their business, and apparently business was good. I walked under a tall set of glass windows, through the main foyer and into a circular internal atrium the size of a football field. Military-looking people buzzed around briskly in all directions, looking efficient and professional. They weren't bothered by equal opportunity laws either; every woman who worked there was stunning and blonde.

The sales division chief took me into his office and our bums had barely hit the leather seats before a silver tray of coffee and small cakes was set down in front of us. I asked about the R4 assault rifle. The design of the R4 had been based on the Israeli Galil, which in itself was a copy of the Finnish Rk 62, which had been based on the AK-47, which was, of course, a copy of the German STG-44. The result of this weaponry inbreeding was a very reliable and accurate rifle. In some ways it was the best of both worlds, as we had the option of using either the NATO 5.56 or 7.62 rounds but with the more reliable AK-47 action. Delivery price was US$800; each rifle came with six magazines, a sling and a cleaning kit.

I didn't like their general purpose machineguns (GPMGs), which were MAG 58s. They were too heavy for the Karen troops. They also had .30 calibre Brownings; I wasn't a big fan of either. They finished their firing cycle in the closed breech position, which meant that when they got hot the round would 'cook off'; that is, fire spontaneously because of the heat. The salesman said they had modified these to prevent the problem, but that just added unreliability, I reckoned. I'd have to look elsewhere for GPMGs.

The real bargain there was the cut-price ammunition that had reached the end of its shelf life and was being held in reserve for the South African defence force. This was available at half the cost of brand-new ammo. Even though it was past its expiry date, the ammunition was still in good order. The South Africans weren't shoddy when it came to the manufacture of good-quality munitions; after all, they depended on them for the survival of their state. The sales rep also showed me second-hand arms going for bargain-basement prices, all the merchandise had been captured from the Soviet bloc. You could pick up an AK-47 for as little as US$20, depending on how big a batch you were buying. If I could persuade the right people back in Pretoria, the sale might even be approved by the government.

While we discussed small arms the tone of the meeting had been pretty friendly. But the salesman's whole body language changed when I asked him about rocket artillery. South Africa had just pulled back from invading Angola, so they were touchy about these things. The South Africans had some good systems with ranges of up to 40 kilometres, and these were deadly against infantry and light-armoured vehicles. They could outshoot anything the troops on the other side had, and the South Africans were keen to not let them fall into the wrong hands. The salesman was polite, he was pleasant, but there was absolutely no way we were going to discuss rockets. Pity, they would have been handy against the Tatmadaw.

Just to push my luck I asked about Semtex. There were a number of special projects being planned back in Manerplaw and a hundred or so kilos of the powerful plastic explosive would be perfect for them. At the time this was a restricted item – sniffer dogs couldn't pick up the scent, so you could get it on board aeroplanes and across borders very easily. The South Africans were understandably paranoid about a radical branch of the ANC or one of the small terrorist groups getting hold of it. This was too much for the sales bloke and he abruptly stood up and looked at his watch. I guessed the meeting was over. He escorted me out to my car and just before we shook hands to say goodbye, he took out his pen and wrote a number on a piece of paper. It turned out to be a contact in Singapore who sold Semtex on the black market.

From there, it was off to the communications company. It was a pretty small factory, but they'd developed some exceptional communications gear – miles ahead of anything I'd come across in the Regiment. It was a complete portable one-man communications centre with miniature keypad, printer and frequency-hopping transmitter with data burst capability, and it was all powered by lightweight lithium batteries. A single battery would guarantee seventy-two hours' continuous transmission. This whole set-up weighed less than 5 kilograms, including battery, and measured approximately 30 by 30 centimetres and was 10 centimetres thick. Most people today would laugh at a 5-kilo portable radio, but in the eighties this was amazing technology. It was especially impressive to a bloke like me who had humped the heavy Australian-army F1 HF radio set all over the countryside. The communications company reps were more than helpful and were glad to sell us some units as soon as we came up with the cash. I spent most of my time in South Africa ricocheting from meeting to meeting. When I sought out reps from the big goldmining companies I got the same response as I did from the government. They weren't interested in dealing with the Karen until they had achieved sovereign statehood. Until then, these companies couldn't be seen to be supporting a revolution because it could harm their international interests. Fair enough. Still, zipping around the place in a brand-new BMW wasn't too bad, especially when I found a few excuses to take it on some long runs.

I finally received a summons back to Parliament House in Pretoria, and received a 'thanks but no thanks' letter from the head of the department, which was no surprise. However, I was assured I'd have no problems with government approval for arms exports if I could present an end-user certificate. I had negotiated a possible new source of weapons for the Karen, even if they didn't have the cash to buy them just yet.

That year, 1988, nearly saw the fall of Burma's military government. On 8 August huge pro-democracy rallies were staged. The military murdered over ten thousand civilians by firing into crowds of protesters on the streets of Rangoon, Mandalay and the other big population centres around the country. For the first time this century, Burmese civilians in the cities were receiving a taste of what their military had been doing to the Karen (and a few other minorities) since 1948. Tens of thousands of civilians fled to the sanctuaries of the KNU border areas, prepared to pick up arms and fight the military junta in the wake of the massacres, but the Karen didn't have enough arms, ammunition and food to supply them. If I had somehow managed to make the arms shipments come through, the whole picture today might be different.

THE BATTLE OF MAE TAWAH VALLEY

After three months in South Africa, I'd been looking forward to spending time in Perth with my family. I'd only been home a few days when Rangoon exploded. The brutal military regime looked to be standing right on the edge of a cliff and just needed a little push. I got the call to head back up to Manerplaw and to bring a film crew with me. Derek, a photographer, and his journo mate were free and keen so a few days later we flew to Thailand.

Bangkok was its usual hot, humid, smelly self, but it felt good to be back. We were met by a couple of officials at the airport. They got us through customs, onto a minibus, over the mountains to Mae Sot, then straight down to Manerplaw. Tens of thousands of university students and other civilians from all walks of had begun arriving in Kawthoolei, and we had heard that a similar number had fled to the Kachin and Shan states in the north. We were the first foreign film crew on site in Manerplaw, so there was a scoop in the offing.

After the mad rush to get there, it was frustrating to hit Manerplaw only to be told to sit and wait. Things seem to move at a snail's pace when you really need them to be done fast. I'd volunteered to be the runner back to Bangkok, so the stories, photographs and film stock could be filed as soon as possible, but nothing happened that first week. A lot of Tatmadaw spies had joined the refugees and this created a security nightmare for the Karen. Everyone was being kept well away from headquarters and movement in and out of the front-line areas was restricted.

I spent a day briefing General Bo Mya and a number of his senior diplomatic staff on my trip to South Africa. Obviously they were disappointed about the timing – they could have used a few thousand of those South African R4s right about then. But at least a new supply line of weapons and ammunition was open. I was tasked with making arrangements to establish it further, and they would advise me when they had the funds to make a purchase. The General only wanted to know what was going on once the hardware had actually arrived; the time, date and method of its arrival were up to me. I was keen to get things moving on this project but my first job was to help the film crew get what they came for.

Despite not yet getting close enough to the action to get the world scoop they'd been hoping for, Derek and his mate had managed to collect enough photo and film footage to file a background report. I decided to take what they had down to Bangkok and left strict instructions for them not to move anywhere until my return.

It took me three days to do the round trip, which was pretty quick considering the hassles I faced organising boats, cars and buses. I went via Mae Sot and came back via Mae Sariang to the north to see if I could gather any new information for the media crew. I dashed back up the hill into Manerplaw after almost seventy-two hours without sleep to find that they had shot through. I should have known.

They'd left for Mae Sot to try to interview a student leader of the newly formed All Burma Students Democratic Front (ABSDF). Apparently the student was forming the first armed wing of the ABSDF, and they planned to fight alongside the KLNA and other National Democratic Front (NDF) members, all of whom opposed military rule in Burma. So far no student leaders had been interviewed in the media – this was a hot item.

To cut a long story short, they missed it. You can't go charging around the KNU-controlled territories and expect to be allowed in without a spokesperson or some form of clearance. Because they'd visited once before, they thought they'd have a free ride, not realising how hard I'd worked behind the scenes to gain them access. The whole area was extremely tense; with thousands of strangers blundering about, the Karen were having a difficult time working out friend from foe. As soon as the media crew left our area and tried to enter the next KNLA Brigade's sector, the commander there detained and held them under armed guard. They weren't going anywhere. They dropped my name and the commander sent a runner back to me with a 'please explain'.

It was a major loss of face. Not only had they burnt their bridges with the Karen, they had lost me as their advocate. While I was trying to repair the damage, a French reporter got in and scooped the story. It hit the wires the following day and went all around the world. They knew they'd blown it then. I was pretty pissed off when I finally caught up with them in Mae Sot. I may have been holding a loaded pistol in my lap at the time, I can't quite remember. They were both permanently off my Christmas card list at any rate.

I was more disappointed than angry, I suppose. I would have liked an Australian media crew to break the story rather than some frog reporter. There was no time to dwell on this, however, as the General had decided to strike.

Bo Mya wanted some hydro-electric powerlines to Rangoon cut. The transmission lines ran through areas where the KNU patrolled to the north, and it was decided that turning out the lights on the generals in Rangoon would add to the confusion. Sampson the muscle man, my offsider from the first demolitions school, had just finished a couple of months' training with sixty new recruits. Dropping the powerlines was going to be their final assessment, and I reckon Sampson wanted me to come along to show me how well they had kept the training going.

But all of a sudden I was spoilt for choice. Rowdy, who had also gone through the first demolitions school and helped me drop the Bailey bridge at the end of it, was leading a raid on a place called Mae Tawah, about 40 kilometres south of Manerplaw. He and Tim, a tall, blond ex-New Zealand SAS officer, had planned to bowl over a hilltop position and knock off their ammunition. Tim was one of a few foreigners who had joined the Karen cause in the couple of years since Baz and I had got involved. He'd wandered into Manerplaw not long after we had dropped the Bailey bridge, and I'd bumped into him a few times since. When I first met him he was wearing cheesecloth and beads, having just come from two months in an ashram in Goa. He reckoned he did yoga to pursue enlightenment. I reckoned he did it to score hippie chicks. He was an unlikely soldier anyway, being so softly spoken and gentle. If you got him going, he could talk for hours about the traditions of the ancient Samurai, the poetry writing and flower-arranging they practised in between cutting off peasants' heads – something about balancing the archetypes of warrior and poet. Anyway, he was a good bloke and a very good operator in the bush.

Going with Tim and Rowdy was tempting, but I wouldn't add much to their raid besides being an extra shooter; whereas I was sure my demolitions knowledge would come in handy when dropping the powerlines. I threw my hat in with Sampson's mob. He had a foreigner attached to his unit as well. Stan was a big swarthy Rhodesian who had killed more people than anyone I knew. One of the few paid mercenaries among the rest of us foreigners who were either just there for the fight or caught up in the Karen cause, Stan had a booming voice, which was probably because he was half deaf from firing so many rounds. He carried a MAG 58 over his back on a sling. This was a GPMG normally operated by a two-man crew, but Stan was the strongest bloke I've ever known and he handled it like it was an M-16. He'd picked up where Baz and I had left off – he and Sampson ran an excellent school.

Sampson, Stan and I met with the brigade commander of the sector the powerlines ran through, to get his okay both for the raid and for me to tag along. He said it was fine 'as long as I didn't get shot or blown up' and he made me promise I wouldn't get into any firefights. It always caused lots of unwanted diplomatic hassles in both Thailand and Burma if white blokes got wounded or killed up there. He didn't seem to be too worried about Stan, though.

It took a few days to get organised. The site was near the Karen State, some 80 kilometres up the Salween River to the north, so we had to consider the distance in our calculations of men, explosives, ammo and how to get it all there. We all squashed into a long-tail cattle boat and moved out into the river at first light. It was a good choice of transport as a cattle boat didn't look out of place on a river full of boats smuggling contraband from Thailand into Burma. Tatmadaw spies were everywhere, so we hid under rice sacks as we passed settlements or other river traffic. It was stinking hot as usual, and an awning kept the sun off us.

By late afternoon we had arrived at a small landing on the west bank. It belonged to one of the KNU's goldmining camps and they put us up for the night. The Karen National Defence Organisation (KNDO) militia guarded the camp and restricted all movement in the area to keep word from spreading about the gold they were mining, also creating the perfect cover for us. They kept the gold in an old safe that would have taken any one of the Regiment boys about thirty seconds to crack, and it was guarded by the unlikely sight of two very scrawny-looking German shepherds who looked like they were suffering in the heat.

Heading overland the next morning, we decided to use the network of back tracks to make our way through the hills, rather than the main smuggling route. This added a week to the trip but kept our profile low. It was tough going, especially for this bloke, who had been living off South African hotel food for three months and was finding the change back to bush-tucker a bit rough on the palate. Snake was on the menu, as usual. The big ten-foot-long cobras looked awesome when they reared up and flared their hoods, but a couple of cracks from a bamboo cane took the fight out of them, and then they'd be chucked into the cooking pot.

We normally skirted the hilltops garrisoned by Tatmadaw troops, but this route meant we were much closer to their territory. Around 1500 hours one afternoon Sampson brought the column to a halt on the side of a steep ridge and pointed over towards an enemy position about a kilometre away. He'd been listening to KNLA radio traffic and knew something was up.

'Watch,' he said.

After half an hour, there was a loud thump that frightened a huge flock of birds out of the jungle canopy; this was followed by a column of thick black smoke. A KNLA patrol had rigged a bank of claymore mines and killed an entire Tatmadaw section. They'd been walking down to a stream to replenish water supplies for the position. Now their mates were without water and probably not game to collect any more.

A week of hard slog had us at the area brigade HQ. We still had to keep the operation under wraps, so we set up camp out of sight in the scrub. Sampson and Stan went into the village to make contact and came back the following day with a couple of local guides who knew the area intimately. We sat down and worked out a plan. Tatmadaw troops were stationed at 5-kilometre intervals along the powerlines and they ran periodic patrols along them during the day. The area wasn't mined, which made things easier. We picked two pairs of towers that were on opposite ends of a deep valley, each pair spanning deep ravines, as these lines would be the most difficult to repair. The squad was split into two teams of thirty; Sampson taking one group and Stan leading the other with me. We agreed to hit the towers simultaneously on a zero-hour that was five days away, giving both groups enough time to make the 20-kilometre walk to the targets, and leaving plenty of time to set up OPs and establish the routines of the Tatmadaw patrols.

The walk to the southern end of the valley was heavy going and it took us almost a day and a half to reach a suitable base-camp site. From there we sent five-man teams to set up OPs, watch the lines and log the movements of guard patrols. These teams were rotated every few hours so that everyone got a chance to look over the terrain. Once we had established a safe time to approach, we sent in a team of six to measure the span of one of the towers, as well as the thickness of the steel. We needed to cut the right lengths of detonating cord and get the right-sized blocks of TNT to punch through the steel. One man also had the risky job of climbing up and measuring the height of the live 20 000-volt transmission wires so we would have the right-length cord for the small charges to be pulled onto the lines themselves. The measuring team took less than an hour to complete their tasks and afterwards they swept the dirt around the tower clean of any telltale boot marks. It had only been a couple of years since Baz and I had started the training, but things had come a long way since then. I couldn't help but notice how switched on and professional our troops were.

Once all the details were in, Stan sat down with the NCOs and briefed them on the job. They set about organising the men into demolitions teams and fire-support groups, as well as rigging the charges. We were still forty-eight hours away from zero hour so we had plenty of time for rehearsals. A quick check on the radio with Sampson and we learned that they had almost been bumped by a Tatmadaw patrol after their guide had taken them down the wrong track. After having to go quiet and skirt around the position, they were now three days behind schedule, so we pushed zero hour forward to let them get organised.

We got the message just after sunset on the third night: Sampson was ready to go. By then the plan was well rehearsed. We had decided to rotate the teams through so that everyone had a chance to load up a target. There was a possibility that this could create some confusion in the dark, but it was crucial that the boys had this experience – it could make all the difference down the track.

I moved into position with the southern fire-support team and Stan went with the northern group. We'd only seen one Tatmadaw night patrol from the OPs and they'd been wandering along, talking and using torches, so we weren't expecting any surprises. It was pitch black, so the going was slow, and it took more than two hours before everyone was in place.

We offset 1-pound blocks of TNT on each side of the towers' steel beams to create the cutting charges. These were set both at the base and halfway up the towers in order to wreck as many steel beams as possible. Once these were joined by detonating cord, a couple of the guys used slingshots to shoot steel nuts attached to small pieces of twine over each of the transmission lines. They were careful to only lasso one line at a time to avoid shorting out the wires and creating a shower of sparks that would be seen for miles. Two small blocks of TNT were then hoisted up, positioned so they straddled either side of the transmission line, and then anchored in place by guy ropes. A length of detonating cord ran down from each of these blocks so the simultaneous detonation of both charges would act like a pair of bolt cutters and sever the line. Once both towers were rigged, we ran a trunk-cord between them and joined all the charges. It was now after midnight. We scattered a few mines around the towers in the hope we might disable some of the repair crews, set the initiator on the trunk-cord and waited for word from Sampson.

The code word came over the radios and we gave the youngest bloke in the column the chance to light the fuse – he was fifteen years old. No electric detonators were used on this job, as they could be accidentally fired by the static electricity. The boy lit a cheroot inside one end of a hollow piece of bamboo tubing to shroud its glow. He then slid the fuse into the other end of the tube and sucked for all he was worth to make the cheroot glow red-hot; the lad was desperate to impress and looked worried when nothing happened, but eventually the fuse took with a spluttering hiss.

Waiting for the detonation took forever. Ten minutes came and went and then the nail-biting began. If we'd cocked it up, we'd have to wait at least half an hour before it would be safe to go and check – not something we were too keen on; we wanted to get clear as soon as possible. There was a flash in the sky to the south and then a distant rumble and immediately the humming from the transmission lines ceased. Sampson had beaten us to the punch. I looked over at Stan and rolled my eyes, universal sign language for, 'What the fuck do we do now?'

My answer was a loud crack and thump as our charges went off nearly a minute late; there was the twang of snapping wires, the screech of twisting steel and heavy thuds as the towers hit the ground. The boys started cheering; we had to quickly quieten them down and get them moving. With less than four hours before daylight, we had to be out of the neighbourhood before the aerial search began. You just can't run when it's that dark, and we endured an exhausting few hours trying to move as fast as possible without tripping over, which I seemed to do every few minutes. A badly turned ankle out here would probably be a death sentence.

The dawn light was a relief, even though we knew it would bring the search planes with it. We heard the first engine drone about an hour after sunrise. The jungle provided pretty good protection, and it was a few years before infra-red cameras would be able to peer through the canopy, so we were pretty safe. But by mid-morning the heat had started to rise and some of the boys were really suffering. I was starting to wonder if we'd lose some to heat exhaustion, me included.

At midday Stan got us all together and gave a little pep talk; the topic was what the Tatmadaw would do to us if we got caught. Stan had served with the Selous Scouts, fighting Robert Mugabe's Zimbabwe African National Liberation Army rebels in the old Rhodesia. He'd seen and done all kinds of nasty stuff to captured guerrillas. One trick he told us about was how they'd rig a double bunk and drain the blood from a healthy prisoner on the top bunk into the bloke below; they wanted to keep the latter alive so they could torture him some more. After hearing a few of his stories in graphic detail, the boys found their resolve had hardened and that they were able to keep a good pace the rest of the way. We managed to make the 20 kilometres back to the camp outside the brigade HQ just after sunset without losing anyone. I was more exhausted than I'd ever been, selection included.

Sampson's mob came in during the night and the next morning we all agreed to take a week's rest. Most of the blokes needed to eat and get their strength up or they wouldn't make it back to the Salween. Stan and Sampson went into brigade HQ to pick up any news from the blokes listening to Tatmadaw radio traffic. They heard that the Tatmadaw had eight killed and had fourteen wounded by our land mines, so they must have blundered straight into the area around the downed towers without checking.

Stan and Sampson also brought back news that a big battle was raging around Mae Tawah. Obviously Rowdy and Tim had started a real bunfight. We had orders to return immediately. Our transport would be waiting for us at the village of Sawta in two days' time. That put paid to any plans for recuperation. There was no longer need for concealment, so we just charged down the main trading route. It seemed like a highway compared to the tracks we'd used on the way up. It only took us a day-and-a-half's hard slog to reach the Salween.

The dry season suddenly ended about an hour after we set out. It started raining and didn't stop. The track ran along creek beds in some places and crossed plenty of intersecting gullies. The water in the gullies would build up against the piles of dry-season jungle-floor litter and then these little dams would give way suddenly, creating flash floods. One moment we were sloshing along in ankle-deep water and the next we were swimming as a torrent of brown debris-filled water slammed into the group. We scrambled for the bank and climbed as fast as we could to get above the water. I saw one of the boys cart-wheeling down with the current, but the rest of the squad seemed to have made it up to high ground in time.

We had to perch on the side of the hill for three hours before the creek's flow returned to close to normal. A head count was done, and sure enough there was one missing. As the column moved downstream we found pieces of the missing boy's kit hanging up in branches. His bruised and battered body was eventually discovered wedged in a tree about 3 kilometres downstream. A quick burial service was conducted and the column moved on. We were extremely lucky to only lose the one bloke.

Sawta village was a sprawling, ramshackle trading post perched on the western bank of the Salween River. It abounded with cattle, stockpiles of teak logs, elephants, traders and shops containing all sorts of consumer goods. I'd never seen such a conglomeration of people in the jungle before. It was almost like being in a big city shopping mall, and it was a definite shock to the system after weeks of creeping through the jungle. There were plenty of eyes on us, so I used a bandana to cover my face until I got onto the cattle boat.

Back in Manerplaw we were rushed straight into a briefing from Captain Isaac on the situation at Mae Tawah. Tim and Rowdy's squad had succeeded in capturing the hilltop position, and it had been decided that an all-out effort was going to be made to recapture the entire base, which had fallen to the Tatmadaw in 1984. Sampson and Stan's mobs were to move up and garrison the positions already taken, and so they were to get ready to move out immediately.

Isaac also told us that Tim had been wounded, so after the briefing I headed over to the hospital. I met him halfway there as he was hobbling back along the track to have a yarn with me. His arm was in a sling.

'What happened to you?' I asked.

'Got shot in the hand, didn't I?' he laughed, and gave me the full story.

The position they had captured was on one of the five peaks that surrounded the valley base-camp of Mae Tawah, and was more of a small mountain than a hill. The Tatmadaw post was set on the heights of craggy limestone cliffs that were covered with thick vegetation. The company in position had their wet-season store of ammunition, along with plenty of rations to last them until their next resupply at the start of the dry season. They had an 81-millimetre mortar, as well as a highly prized 84-millimetre Carl Gustav recoilless rifle, although there wasn't much chance of taking possession of this – when facing a large attack the normal Tatmadaw tactic was to spirit the Charlie Gutsache away to stop the KNLA getting their hands on it. But the consolation prize would be the Tatmadaw's crates of ammunition, which wouldn't be able to be carried off in a hurry.

The place was surrounded by the usual three rings of bamboo fencing, and the boys gained entry by blowing up the first fence and crashing through the inner two, which had rotted. Our boys hit fast and hard at 3 a.m. one morning and the Tatmadaw had scampered out in confusion. I think the bloke charged with getting away with the Carl Gustav had a few extra mates on hand to help because practically the whole company took flight, almost without firing a shot. They left the 81-millimetre mortar behind.

Tim said he was amazed by what he found when he inspected the site. The ammunition bunkers were packed to the roof, as were the food stores – there was rice, cans of condensed milk from England and plenty of tinned meat. He was just as stunned by the extensive overlapping defensive trench system; it was straight out of World War One. If the Tatmadaw troops had come out of their bunkers and fought in the trenches, then Tim and Rowdy's mob would have been annihilated. Instead, the few who didn't run stayed put in their bunkers because of the illusion of safety it gave them. However, being a fixed target actually made it easier to put them out of action. Tim and Rowdy had taken a position made up of 120 troops and fixed defences with only fifty men. There's nothing like the element of surprise.

The original plan was to smash, grab and go, but when Tim and Rowdy saw the amount of ammo and supplies, they decided to prop and defend the place, creating extra time for more porters to be organised to carry the loot back to the Karen. They took up defensive positions and held the place for more than a week against several counterattacks.

The Karen boys holding the hill had never seen this much ammunition, let alone been able to shoot with it. They were having a field day, blazing away at anything that moved. Tim and Rowdy had taken a French film crew along, and they were getting what is still regarded as some of the best combat footage ever taken. Firing had died right down and Tim was feeling pretty confident that the enemy had pulled back. Tim had a plan to take the fight to the enemy to prevent them getting too dug in, in which case they'd only become a bigger headache later on. Rowdy didn't agree, and even the French cameraman pleaded with him not to go out, but Tim would not be dissuaded.

Leading the patrol, Tim had only just got beyond the bamboo fence when he walked right into a well-concealed Tatmadaw gun pit. Tim could see right down the barrel of a weapon and thought he was history. His pale skin saved him because the gunner hesitated for just a fraction of a second as he tried to work out what the bloody hell a white fella was doing there. Tim fired and blew the man's head off. The dead man reflexively pulled the trigger and a round went right into the webbing next to Tim's little finger – taking the finger off before travelling up his forearm to exit at the elbow.

Tim then fell down a small slope, another a piece of luck because a split second later the jungle in front of him erupted with enemy gunfire. Most of the rounds went over Tim, but a few clipped the heels of his boots. He was still wearing them when we caught up, and I could see the neat grooves carved by the bullets. A flanking party went out and poured fire onto the Tatmadaw position, forcing the enemy to get their heads down, which gave Tim enough time to crawl to safety.

Luckily, he'd only lost his little finger. A fair chunk of meat was missing from his forearm, but he could still move his remaining four fingers, ruling out nerve damage. It was also fortunate that the Tatmadaw 7.62-millimetre ammunition is substandard. An Australian- or US-made round would have taken his arm off. Tim had a copy of the French film crew's footage, so we went up to General Lah Thoo's house to watch endless re-runs of Tim being knocked on his arse.

The next day Tim and I caught a longboat back up to the action. Hung's commandos, Stan and Rowdy's men – a newly formed company of student soldiers under the banner of the ABSDF – and a heavy-weapons section under the command of a Captain Lowadie had all gathered at the captured base. Lowadie was a twenty-eight-year-old son of the Quarter Master General and had grown up in the hills; he'd never known anything but fighting. The students were a bit of a worry as their training had been rushed through, but they were passionate and committed. I don't mind saying that it takes a certain kind of stupidity to be a good soldier. Thinking too much can get you in trouble when swift action is required. I wasn't sure how these young boffins and their ideology would go in a firefight, but we'd all soon find out.

Tim and I had only just hopped off the boat and started to climb the fire-support hill when we heard the telltale drone of the prop-driven Pilatus Porter PC-7s that the Tatmadaw used as ground-attack aircraft. I dived for cover with everyone else, but every promising log or rock I saw already had a crowd of soldiers and civilian porters competing for every spare inch of protection. I eventually crawled in amongst the roots at the base of a giant teak tree just as the planes started circling overhead. The tree-roots wouldn't protect me from a direct or even a close hit, but at least I would have some barriers against the shrapnel that would spray everywhere as soon as the first bomb hit.

We spent an agonising few minutes trying to find new ways to hug the ground closer as the planes circled, whose pilots were obviously waiting for radio confirmation from their commanders before attacking. The Thai military base just over the border did us a favour by turning on their big transmitters and jamming the frequency. This was to repay a debt from 1984 when, after capturing the Mae Tawah base, the Tatmadaw had crossed over the Thai border and captured the Thai town of Ban Tha Song Yang. It had been the KNLA who had chased the Tatmadaw back across the river. The pilots must have got sick of waiting, though, because they abruptly rolled and dived, the pitch of the propellers changing to a higher whine. The first two planes dropped bombs that fell about 200 metres away. I could feel the thump of their detonation and hear the heavy-rain sound of shrapnel ripping through the foliage, but they were too off-target to cause harm. The next two planes strafed with mini-guns – there was an awesome tearing sound as they sprayed a 50-yard-wide curtain of bullets, most of it absorbed by the foliage. But again, they were wide of our position. It was hard for the pilots to see through the jungle canopy and they must have spotted something shiny and assumed it was our troops. The last two planes peppered both the Thai and Burmese sides of the border with 2.5-inch rockets. They were even further off than the first two, and everyone cheered as the last of the planes flew away.

Tim and I made the climb up to Lowadie's heavy-weapons section. They had their 120-millimetre mortar, a 75-millimetre recoilless and a couple of 81-millimetre tubes set up, and were blasting the enemy hilltop positions and the camp in the valley. The 120-millimetre had been extended to 2.5 metres to increase range and was so heavy that they'd had to weld handles onto the tube so that the fellas could carry it through the scrub. It looked more like a medieval battering ram than a mortar tube. It gave one hell of a thump when it fired and the bombs packed a good wallop at the other end, which more than made up for the discomfort of lugging it around.

Our position was only 500 metres north of Mae Tawah camp, with the Moei River flanking us to the east and the base of a large limestone crag to our immediate west. From the vantage point of the crag we could put the whole northern defences of the Mae Tawah camp out of action, so capturing it was our prime objective. To our south was a smaller defensive position strung with barbed wire and landmines, defended by a single concrete bunker with a commanding field of fire. The Karen had built the bunker when they controlled the base.

Even in a relatively small battle like this there was no point in stretching supply lines too far, so we had to wait for the arrival of food, ammunition and medicine. The boys were cutting bamboo and digging a trench to serve as an aid station for when the fight went full-blown. There were also several two-man recon patrols out sneaking around, trying to get a closer look at the Tatmadaw defences.

Tim was starting to look sick. His weakened state had brought on a bout of malaria. Rowdy came back over from the captured position with Hung for a powwow with Lowadie to plan the assault.

They took one look at Tim and ordered him back to Manerplaw for treatment, which disappointed him as he wanted to be back with his boys. But there was no arguing as everyone knew what a liability he'd become if he really went down.

I left the three commanders to their planning and decided to work my way up to the forward party in front of the bunker position. I'd brought along an old Chinese SKS rifle that I'd fitted with a telescopic sight. I hadn't sighted it in at this stage and the front line was a good place to do this and put the ammo to decent use.

The bunker was located beneath two large teak trees next to the river. Besides the bunker, defences consisted of a couple of coils of barbed wire and probably some scattered mines to the front. There were no trenches that I could see, nor any heads to shoot at. From our position you could look right into the camp itself, as well as towards the Thai town across the river. The place looked deserted, but the Tatmadaw were definitely in the bunker, as evidenced by the occasional shot that would crack over our heads; this was usually followed by a figure scrambling out of the back entrance to lob a 40-millimetre bomb from a grenade launcher in our general direction. The trees absorbed the blast from these.

One particular rocky outcrop provided an excellent firing platform. It was very exposed, but for some reason the Tatmadaw troops couldn't seem to draw a bead on it. I set myself up on the edge of the platform and started putting camouflage cream on my face. This was something the brown-faced Karen boys rarely had to do, so I had to put up with a few taunts of 'green monkey'. The mood amongst the boys was pretty laid-back, which is not unusual for the Karen, but I wasn't taking any chances. In this dark-green environment my white face stood out like a full moon at midnight.

I got into a position, wrapping the rifle's sling around my upper arm to lock it solidly in place as I propped on my elbows; the whole idea being to create a solid platform of rifle to bone to ground. Firing a few test shots into the side of the bunker, I could see the bullets' impact and was able to zero the scope. The bunker had gun slits on each side and I could just see the top left one. I started trying to put rounds into it and after the third shot a ricochet against the back edge pinged inside, which was followed by a brief, loud scream.

The Karen boys cheered and insults flew across the little valley between us and the bunker. Watching me get a result stirred the boys into action and a lieutenant grabbed a 3.5-inch bazooka and decided to have a go. Most of both platoons had gathered around to watch now. The lieutenant's first shot hit one of the trees above the bunker, showering the troops below in wood splinters and leaves, and causing more cheering from our side and a few more insults from theirs. The next round hit the top of the bunker, which shut them up but did little damage. The lieutenant was happy with that and put the bazooka away. Logs soon appeared at the edge of the gun slit I'd been aiming for.

A couple of ABSDF student soldiers came over to our position with a loudhailer and tried to convince the boys in the bunker to give up and join us in overthrowing the generals in Rangoon. All they got for their 'we are brothers-in-arms against a common enemy' speech was another volley of cackling abuse. The students were persistent, though, and kept up their relentless monologue of political propaganda for hours. When one of them got tired he'd hand the loudhailer to another and he'd continue, with us lobbing a few mortar bombs on the bunker in between.

We kept this up for a few days and nights: keeping them awake and on edge, wondering when the attack would come. The shouts coming back from the bunker were getting a little hoarse and manic as their nerves started to go. Occasionally somebody on the mountaintop above us would lean over the edge of the cliffs and send some rounds our way, but nothing hit home. I tried to scope out the culprit but the canopy was too thick to allow a clear view. Apart from these incidents there was no significant action, with the platoon commanders waiting for the go-ahead to storm the bunker as part of a coordinated attack.

Lowadie sent a runner down to fetch me a few days later when they were preparing for the mountaintop assault. The briefings had finished by the time I got there, and the lead elements of the fighting column had already started their ascent. Lowadie said I could tag along, but again told me to stay out of the firefights.

Rowdy was in charge of the operation and was always in the thick of things, directing attacks whenever he went into battle, so sticking near him and taking the occasional pot shot suited me fine. Besides, I didn't want the boys looking out for my safety and disregarding their own in the process.

The mountain was about 350 metres high, and it was a near-vertical climb to reach the top; this was made even more difficult by the tangled undergrowth. The advance party had set off before dawn to clear an approach track. The main body set off at first light, expanding the path as they went. Fixed ropes were put into place so the blokes could get up the steeper sections and over the larger rocky outcrops. The undergrowth started to thin towards the top and so the men fanned out into assault lines.

Like a thunderstorm that's been threatening all day and starts with a few fat drops before the deluge, the battle began with a string of single shots and quickly intensified into a clamour of automatic fire, along with the whoosh-bang of rockets and the thump of grenades. I propped myself behind a rocky outcrop and watched the commotion of running and ducking bodies.

The distinctive paper-ripping scream of the Tatmadaw's MG42s dominated the fusion of sounds. They were the main threat, and knocking them out was the priority. A rocket-propelled grenade took out one of the MG42 crews and the other one got flanked and chopped up by small-arms fire. There were other pockets of resistance, but taking out these two guns gave the blokes the break they needed to push forward.

The Tatmadaw troops started to pull back into their hilltop camp as men ran and crawled from one outcrop to another. Everything was coordinated yet it felt confused; even so, as we pushed forwards, they retreated. I got a couple of shots off but didn't hit anything. Heads were popping up and down all over the place, but nobody was staying up for too long.

Each section commander had been well briefed, so Rowdy didn't have a lot to do except direct reserves into the gaps and keep the fire-support team hosing down the hot spots. It was extremely hard to make out who was who because of the thick foliage, but there was only one objective, and that was to get to the top.

It wasn't long before we were running low on grenades, as they had proved to be the best way of clearing enemy out of the natural bunkers formed by the rocks. Rowdy's 'Plan B' was a typical piece of ingenuity. He had two shotguns and removed the lead from a few dozen cartridges. He then instructed us to make petrol bombs out of old glass bottles with broomsticks attached to their bases; these were then inserted down the shotgun barrels to create homemade grenade launchers. Soap powder had been added to the petrol to turn it into a sticky jelly, just like napalm. It was a surreal sight, watching these singing missiles streaking skyward, like flaming arrows in a Hollywood western. A direct hit would cover the enemy in the flaming sticky gel and, in a screaming fireball, they'd run from their cover before being either cut down or running headlong into a tree with a comical thump. We called it the 'Niki Lauda fire dance', and in the heat of battle we were cackling with laughter. This sounds macabre, but these troops had been chopping our blokes down; we felt nothing for them.

It was getting on towards four in the afternoon and we'd been pushing hard at the Tatmadaw since late morning. They were being driven back and leaving a lot of casualties as they went. The intense fighting came in waves as our boys charged from cover to cover, got their breath back and charged again. Everyone was running low on ammunition and getting dehydrated, so runners carrying sandbags full of loose rounds and jerry cans filled with water were darting around the place. The variety of different weapon calibres made it difficult to accommodate everyone; some just salvaged enemy weapons or took them from KLNA corpses.

The lead sections fought their way to the first knoll of the saddle-shaped mountain top; from where I was, it looked like a massive street brawl: blokes were swinging their rifles like clubs, wrestling hand to hand, and getting the occasional shot off at close quarters. It was desperate and ugly, with blokes doing what they could to kill the enemy. The Tatmadaw retreated onto another knoll less than 100 metres away, hurriedly setting booby-traps as they went. Most of these were easily spotted and defused. Rowdy and I made it to the top of the first knoll.

Each side now occupied an opposite end of the mountaintop, and were separated by a small saddle of land. The fight was still intense and each side had the other pinned; neither had the advantage. Most of the damage to our side was being caused by one particular bloke with an MG42: the MG42's high rate of fire meant that everyone had to keep their heads down while he was firing, and then he'd drop back down again too quick for us to line him up. He was obviously buying time for his mates to get away.

We were out of both the hand grenades and the improvised petrol bombs by now, so when Rowdy crawled over to my position I knew what he was going to ask. I was the only one there with a decent scoped rifle.

'You think you can get him, Dave?'

I took a while to work out where he was firing from, but then I saw him pop up in the crack of a mound of clay that rimmed one of their mortar pits. He was only exposing himself for a few seconds, but once I saw his spot it was a simple matter of putting the crosshairs on the crack and waiting for the first blur of movement before squeezing the trigger. I watched him appear through the scope a few times, and I could tell he had decided to die to save his mates. He was beyond determined and the look in his eyes showed that he knew something that the rest of us will only know when it's our time. My first round caught him in the forehead, the top of his skull flew upwards and he fell back.

With him out of the way, the mountaintop was ours and the boys poured across the open terrain of the saddle to take up defensive positions on the other knoll. From a peak across the valley, I caught a flash out of the corner of my eye and dived, headfirst, into a trench. This was followed by a whoosh and bang as a

Charlie Gutsache 84-millimetre round ploughed into the hilltop and exploded with a deafening hot blast. It caught six of the Karen in the open, sending bits and pieces of them everywhere. Rowdy had landed in the trench behind me and called in fire from Lowadie's heavy-weapons section. Three more shells crashed into our position before we were able to walk the mortar bombs onto their hilltop. When they hit, our bombs turned the Tatmadaw's whole position into a cauldron of fire; I figured we must have hit their ammo dump. The Charlie Gutsache was silenced after that and we didn't lose anyone else.

Rowdy fired out orders and we quickly consolidated our position. We could still see the backs of some of the retreating Tatmadaw as they ran headlong down the hill below us, so some of our boys shot them in the back. Below us we could hear a blazing firefight as my mates from the day before charged the lower bunker. Above the noise I could still hear insults being traded through the loudhailer, but they'd exhausted their vocabularies by now and were down to one-word cracks, like an old married couple.

It was approaching dusk and the blokes were working feverishly to dig in and fortify our position before the lights went out. We needed to be ready for a counterattack or bombardment. Medics handed out heavy-duty green plastic garbage bags and we all helped out collecting the various pieces of the six who had been hit by the Charlie Gutsache. It was a mess. Someone was going to have sort through the limbs and entrails to try to work out 'what belonged to whom' before burial.

There were more than twenty dead Tatmadaw troops. Their uniforms were removed and all their personal effects handed in to the officers before we tossed the bodies over the side of the mountain.

The insects would dispose of them if their mates didn't collect them, and we could do without the sanitary problems they would create. Looking through their belongings, we saw the normal stuff any soldier the world over would carry: pictures of mates during basic training, pictures of family, lockets and wedding rings.

I went through the wallet of the bloke I'd shot; there was a snap of him with his wife and newborn baby. In the second-by-second madness of battle we are all savages, but I felt a stab of regret looking at that picture. It was sad, but still better than the other way around: him standing there getting all sentimental about killing me.

Darkness came with its chorus of insect noises and monkey calls. Rowdy suspended all patrols outside the perimeter, so that anything moving out there was to be considered the enemy. There were too many hiding places in amongst the nearby limestone outcrops to clear them all before nightfall, so we kept a tight defensive position. No fires were lit. Anyone who had food and water left over shared it around. I was completely stuffed. It's one thing to be physically tired, but all that adrenalin pumping through your body over such a long period wears out your nervous system, leaving you bone weary and hellishly thirsty. Apart from the sentries, everyone slept the sleep of the dead until stand-to at first light.

I felt like I'd only just shut my eyes when the sun broke the horizon. Rowdy organised clearing teams to secure the summit and sent an advanced guard down the track to the headquarters in the valley. During the night our boys down the hill had finally taken the bunker. That squad started probing up towards us, with Rowdy's team simultaneously edging down the steep track, while we covered them from above. They found a couple of hastily buried landmines but otherwise it was a clear run to the foot of the hill.

The two teams then joined and began a systematic search of the base camp, which looked completely deserted.

I kept imagining that I could hear the propeller drone of the Pilatus Porter aeroplanes. It was only a matter of time until the Tatmadaw tried an air strike. I got on the radio to Lowadie and suggested they send up a .50 heavy machinegun so we could provide some form of anti-aircraft fire. Half an hour later Tim came strolling up the hill, leading a group of blokes carrying a Chinese 12.7-millimetre heavy machinegun, complete with anti-aircraft sights on it.

'Somebody order an AA gun?' he called out.

It only had a tripod, which wouldn't be stable enough to absorb the recoil, so we set it up on a log and secured it with ropes and big nails. Then we dug a deep trench either side of the log so the gunner could get the right angle to fire at aircraft directly overhead. The AA gun's position was camouflaged, and then the blokes set about reinforcing the roof of each fighting position with anything they could find to improve the overhead protection.

I trekked back up to our summit, which gave a commanding view of the valley and the surrounding hilltop posts. The original hilltop that had been taken by Tim and Rowdy could be seen to the west. South was the opposite mountaintop with the distinctive outline of fortified positions clearly visible. We scanned the bunkers and trenches with our binoculars, and while we couldn't see any movement there, we thought it must have been where the rest of the enemy had retreated to.

Suddenly an intense firefight erupted on the western side of the hill. One of the clearing patrols had come across a cave occupied by a dozen Tatmadaw troops. They had an MG42 and, judging by the almost solid stream of lead exiting the cave, about a year's supply of ammo. They were jabbering away, firing pretty wildly and obviously shitting themselves. Rowdy thought they might be vulnerable to a bit of propaganda, so he got one of the students with his megaphone to see if they could be talked out. Each time he said something they'd let rip with another long burst from the MG. They were not going to surrender; the Tatmadaw commanders must have filled their heads with bedtime stories of Karen soldiers roasting the balls of captives over a fire or something.

We had no bombs of any kind left and were at a loss over what to do next. One of the men suggested gassing them out with a big ball of burning chillies. This probably sounds like a crazy idea – unless you've tried some of the region's chillies. Most of the blokes kept a private stash to liven up the bland bush food; as well as this, the chillies were powerful enough to kill some of the bugs that cause dysentery. A quick whip-round provided a baseball-sized mound of chillies. These were wrapped in a shirt, tied with bamboo strands, and then soaked in a bit of kerosene salvaged from one of the Tatmadaw kitchens.

A two-man team was chosen: one would pitch and one would light the bomb. The bloke whose idea it was in the first place got to be pitcher. He and another bloke carefully crept up to the edge of the cave and the pitcher stood with his arm cocked, ready to throw, while his mate tried to light the bomb. He couldn't get it to ignite and the repeated clicking of the Zippo lighter seemed almost deafening. It was a matter of seconds before the blokes in the cave would work out what the sound was and pop them both with the MG. The tension was agonising.

The ball eventually caught fire, as did the pitcher's shirt sleeve. He hurled the flaming mass into the cave mouth, and then he and his mate danced around in full view in front of the cave, frantically beating at his arm in an attempt to put the flames out. The murderous hammering tear of the MG42 had them both forgetting about the burning arm and diving for cover. They crawled back to safety as rounds chopped through trees. By the time they got back to us they had huge grins on their faces and the rest of us were in hysterics.

Suddenly the MG went quiet. Then, from inside the cave came a long, thin wail, then another, and pretty soon it sounded like someone had woken up a whole room of babies. The Tatmadaw boys came staggering out, screaming at us not to shoot, wiping furiously at their eyes, which probably only made the pain worse. They were completely blinded, walking and tripping over, with their arms stretched out in front. There were six of them and we led them up to the first-aid post where the medics could bandage their eyes. I could see yellowish blisters on their eyeballs, so the pain must have been horrific.

We tried to get into the cave to clear it and salvage the MG42, but we couldn't go near the entrance until the next day. The chilli fumes were the most effective tear gas I'd ever encountered. When we did get inside it was with wet rags over our faces, coughing and sneezing the whole time. It was a mini Aladdin's cave, packed with ammunition and several MG42s, four Heckler & Koch G3s and a couple of G2s. Not a bad haul for the price of a quarter of a kilo of chillies and a dash of kerosene.

That afternoon, down on the valley floor, we could see a lot of movement. As they finished clearing the hills, the Karen boys were congregating at a big teak house on stilts at the centre of the base.

We took our blinded prisoners down, all roped together, stumbling and tripping on the steep descent. The big house must have been the HQ building: inside was a mountain of stores: there were crates of British-made condensed milk, tinned sardines, tinned bully beef and loads of rice sacks. The retreating enemy troops had also left behind a couple of oxen and heaps of chooks. When our boys aren't marching or fighting they are a mobile food-gathering machine and they soon had a few of the chooks in the pot for chicken curry.

I found a wooden crate to dump my webbing on and parked my bum. When I sat down a few of the boys gave me funny looks and muttered to each other. The looks and comments were getting pretty dark, and I was wondering who I had upset when one of the officers came over and told me, very politely, that I was sitting on the coffin containing the remains of the six who'd been chopped up by the Carl Gustav. I hastily vacated the seat and made a few apologies to anyone who'd listen.

The next morning General Bo Mya came up in a longboat to inspect the recaptured base, bringing a hundred reinforcements with him. He stood on the steps of the big house and gave a speech to the boys. I didn't understand much of it but the passion in his voice made the hairs stand-up on my neck; it had been a long time since the Karen had given the Tatmadaw a decent black eye, and recapturing part of their territory was a huge boost for morale.

Just after the General had finished his speech, a Thai boat came across the river, full of journalists and camera crews. I was quickly hidden inside a cupboard under a bench and watched Bo Mya's interview through a crack. The Thais have no love for the Burmese military leaders and when an opportunity to show them in a bad light comes up they take it. The Thai media made sure this defeat was broadcast to the world.

Tim and I spent the next couple of days wandering around the very impressive hilltop fortifications and generally wondering how the hell we'd managed to capture the place. The northern bunker looked solid enough to handle a direct hit from heavy artillery and from just above had a clear view of the positions where our boys and the students with their loudhailer had been hurling insults. The rocky outcrop I'd been taking my pot shots from was also in clear sight. It was a good thing that our boys had done such a good job of keeping the enemy in the bunker, because if they had come out looking for a better firing position, there would have been more casualties, including me.

The set-up was the same down at the southern end of the camp, with a concrete bunker protecting it. The western approaches were an intricate network of trenches and fortified log bunkers, which stretched for about a kilometre, but were completely useless if one didn't have command of the heights above. This was why Tim and Rowdy's effort in taking the first hill gave us such an advantage, and it was the main reason the Tatmadaw commander had cut and run.

Tim and I were strolling back down to the big house when a bloke popped up out of nowhere wearing a red bandanna, pointed a camera at us and started snapping pictures. Tim and I reacted instinctively, snapping our rifles into the firing position. Tim growled.

'You press that shutter again and I squeeze this trigger.'

Mr Bandana was obviously playing the big-time war correspondent, with cameras slung over his shoulder and a vest full of film. It must have been his first time in a war zone – an experienced photographer would never take a picture without asking permission first. The sight of two angry blokes leaning into rifles aimed straight at him turned him white and he dropped the camera like it was suddenly red-hot. I walked over, picked up the camera, gave it a bit of a wipe and popped the back to remove the film before returning it to him.

We'd given him a serious fright and he couldn't say much, so we had a quick word to his Karen guide, who was acutely embarrassed, and told him to escort our mate back over the river and to never let him set foot here again.

'Why didn't you box his ears?' Tim asked as we continued down the hill.

'Because he'll still file a story,' I said. 'I don't want any bad press for the Karen if I can avoid it. Besides, we should have been more switched on.'

Despite the celebrations and the visit from Bo Mya, there was still work to do. The southern mountaintop was still occupied and the Tatmadaw could call down air strikes on us at any time. Rowdy put together a fighting column and we headed out in the evening to get into position for an approach the following morning. I teamed up with a section that was commanded by Wimbo, the student from the first demolitions course who had suffered through most of it with tuberculosis. The approach here was much more difficult than the one to the northern hill, with more vertical cliff faces. We moved slowly, each section leap-frogging the one in front so constant fire support could be called on if somebody made enemy contact.

We came across wild banana trees with the trunks stripped down to their edible core; a good indication that the Tatmadaw were running low on food. Rowdy figured they must be struggling by now and decided to leave a gate open for them. While our group was probing from the south, another probed from the north. With the Karen-occupied camp to the east we hoped they would run through an open route to the west rather than stand and fight to the last man. This suited everyone as we were more interested in their ammo and supplies than dead bodies.

Approaching on multiple fronts is always risky because of cross-fire. This was less concerning here because we'd be firing uphill and most ricochets would fly off into the heavens. The plan was to stay in close radio contact and once a group had made contact the rest would stay in place and do their best to provide fire support.

We spent an hour or two moving about two-thirds of the way up the hill and then waited for Lowadie's heavy-weapons boys to start shelling the hill before moving further. Under the earth-shaking boom of the 120-millimetre mortars we moved closer to the top, everyone tense about the first contact. Along with the thump of the big bombs I heard a few smaller pops that soon blew into a mad rattle as our group's lead patrol made first contact. The shelling was stopped immediately and the eastern and northern groups poured fire into the hilltop so they wouldn't know what direction the drive was coming from.

I saw one bloke in our section fire an RPG7 rocket at a bunker. As the rocket ignited, the venturi, located halfway along the launch tube, exploded and tore half of his face off and he fell back screaming. The metal must have fatigued over the years and finally decided to let go. One of the medics quickly gave him a shot of morphine to quieten him and stuck a field dressing on what was left of his face.

Our attack was ferocious and numbers were in our favour. Soon the return fire from Tatmadaw dwindled and we continued to push forward. A message from Rowdy came over the radio relaying an intercept they had picked up from the enemy commander, ordering his men to pull back. We slowed the advance to give them a chance to run without any heroes putting up last-ditch attempts to buy their mates time. I saw glimpses of olive-green bodies scrambling out of bunkers and into the bush and sent a few parting shots their way just to hurry them up.

After half an hour it was decided we should start moving in again. It's always an unnerving experience moving into a recently deserted enemy position. You walk on eggshells, every sense turned up high looking for a barrel, booby trap or some sign of movement. The boys called out gently in Burmese 'Anyone home?', and a couple of replies came back from badly wounded soldiers who'd been left behind. Otherwise, the place was deserted. A couple of booby traps had been laid and an ammunition bunker had been rigged to explode, but they'd been in too much of a hurry to light the fuses before they ran.

The whole of the Mae Tawah valley was now in KNLA hands, but to the west there was still intense fighting. The remnants of the Tatmadaw battalion had regrouped in an attempt to retake Tim and Rowdy's mountain. Its strategic height was obviously the key to holding the whole valley. I took some binoculars to a perch on the northern mountaintop and watched the firefight from there, though there wasn't a lot to see except for the occasional shell burst or flash from small-arms fire; the boys seemed to be holding fast.

About midday I heard the dreaded drone of the Pilatus Porter PC-7s. Six of them had returned to attack the western hilltop. Everyone dived for cover and word of their arrival was flashed around the radio net. I heard a thick Kiwi accent shout 'Dave, get your arse over here' as Tim threw the camouflage off the Chinese

12.7-millimetre heavy machinegun. His hand was still too sore to fire the gun and he needed me to shoot while he directed fire. I jumped in behind the gun, which had a wooden stock and a pistol grip, and let fly at the circling aircraft. This must have come as a bit of a shock to the pilots as the tracer began arcing towards them, because it sent them scattering in all directions. The big gun had a vicious kick and the tripod came loose. A couple of the boys jumped to hold it in place, which restricted my field of fire, as they had to try to move with me as I swung it around. The muzzle blast was fierce, as were the hot cases ejecting onto their bare backs, but they didn't complain and held onto the bucking gun grimly.

Soon everyone was caught up in the excitement and started blazing away, sending criss-crosses of red and green tracer floating into the air. Someone let go with an RPG7 round and that exploded some 400 metres up in the air, leaving a large black cloud. I don't know whether that or the tracer flying among them did the trick but the aircraft headed off into the west, still carrying their payload under their wings. A Tatmadaw commander was shouting at them over the radio to come back and do their job, but with no result, and the planes disappeared to a huge cheer from everyone at the base. Having so few planes and a lack of spare parts, the Tatmadaw flyboys are very reluctant to expose the aircraft to heavy ground fire. After much backslapping and laughter, we arranged for thicker ropes and big steel spikes so that the 12.7-millimetre could be securely strapped in place. I wish some of those journalists had stuck around, because they would have scored great action footage with the blokes dodging about trying to hold the gun in position.

The Tatmadaw attack on the west mountain faded and everyone went to work setting up defences for the whole valley. We could be sure the Tatmadaw would try to take it back at some point. I wasn't needed in the valley anymore so I took the boat back down to Manerplaw. If I had known it was the last time I would see Rowdy, Wimbo, Tim and a host of my other Karen brothers, I might have said a longer goodbye. They are all dead now.

I decided I'd better head back home to see how the family was getting along and to find out if I was still married. Forty-eight hours later I was on a Qantas flight back to Perth. I wanted to get a few things sorted back home before I started rolling out my plan for the next five years.

In the ensuing months the military regime in Burma wasn't toppled, despite the widely held protests across the country during the democracy uprising. In 1989 the collapse of the Communist Party of Burma, one of the largest and best-equipped insurgent groups in the country, saw a major shift in the military junta's strategic situation. The communists had not only tied up several divisions of Tatmadaw troops, they'd also been receiving military aid from China. The military leaders rebranded themselves as the State Law and Order Restoration Council and struck a billion-dollar arms deal with China. They now had the manpower and military muscle to attack the Karen in an all-out conventional war.

Mae Tawah was recaptured a year later after a two-month siege, which saw the biggest-ever bombardment of any one position by Burmese artillery in the history of the entire conflict. In less than one hour they poured more than three thousand shells into the hilltop position that Tim and Rowdy had captured. The KNLA troops had to pull out before they were annihilated. Once this strategic height was taken, the rest of the mountaintop positions fell, along with the valley base.

PART III

Crossing the Line

THE CINEMA JOB

Returning to Perth, I walked into an ambush as good as anything I'd seen in the jungle. Mandy, my wife, told me she no longer wanted to be married to a soldier. It was an ultimatum: either I established a civilian life or she'd walk. I bought a truck and started carting cars all over the state as a subcontractor for TNT. It was pretty much a seven-days-a-week job and my longest run was over 4000 kilometres one way. If I got a Sunday off, it was spent servicing the truck and welding up the decking on the semitrailer. I started off with a clapped-out ten-year-old Isuzu prime-mover and a semitrailer that was just about falling apart. I nursed both through the next three months and managed to earn enough to keep the debtors at bay and purchase a new Mitsubishi prime mover and replace the running gear on the trailer. The new truck had air-conditioning, which felt like heaven as I was driving in 40-degree Celsius temperatures.

During this time we had our first son. We named him after one of my Karen lieutenants and sent lots of pictures of him to my mates up in Kawthoolei. It didn't seem that long before he was twelve months old and we had another baby on the way. The sheer joy of having kids caught me by surprise and my biggest regret is not playing a bigger part in their lives while they grew up.

That same year my dad passed away after a long battle with supra-bulbar palsy, which has similar effects to Parkinson's disease. Mum had nursed him at home for the last four years. She, and a few of the people closest to me, say that I went a bit wild after his death. I don't completely agree, but I suppose my dad was the one person I never wanted to disappoint. Having him gone might have influenced a few of my choices. He was cremated at Karrakatta cemetery and that day I had the sense I'd lost some grounding. There was no one to ask for guidance any more – life was up to me.

Despite the demands of the trucking business, I'd stayed involved with the Karen cause, chiefly through my good friends Connie and Keith Almark and the Tribal Refugee Welfare in Southeast Asia committee. This committee raised funds for the Karen refugees in Thailand and helped sponsor refugees from war-torn Burma to come out to Australia. Connie and Keith had left Burma soon after Ne Win came to power in 1962. They had devoted their lives to the Karen cause.

Over this time I'd also done a couple of short trips up to Thailand. The first was to track down a bloke who'd run off with over 30 million Thai baht of the Karen's money. This bloke was an American I had crossed paths with a few times. He was ex-US Special Forces from the Vietnam era and had proved himself trustworthy to me. When he approached the Karen with a proposal to ship surplus arms from Cambodia they jumped at the chance. They still had a sizeable number of students to equip with weapons. Having been ripped off in the past, they sought a few assurances about this bloke, one of which was given by me. When he disappeared with their money it was a major loss of face for me, and I jumped on the first plane up there to help track him down.

I used a few of my Thai military intelligence contacts and we found him holed up in a hotel in Bangkok. He had to do some pretty fast talking to stay alive and his story was that the Thai military had confiscated the ten truckloads of gear as it crossed the military zone adjacent to Colonel Oliver's 10 Battalion sector. A Thai general had told him to piss off, so he did and was hiding in fear of his life – with good cause. I left a couple of blokes minding him and went out to Kanchanaburi to check out his story. It turned out to be true. The local Thai general was making money on the side by shipping arms to the Tamil Tigers in Sri Lanka. He was going through, of all places, the tourist resort of Phuket. After snooping around Phuket for a few days, I located a suspect warehouse and did a night-time recce of the place. It was stacked up to the roof with crates of weapons, much more than the ten truckloads' worth that the Karen was missing. Not wanting to get my hands dirty in Thailand, I left the recovery job to a team organised by Isaac and led by Stan.

A week later Stan and his team, wearing Thai police uniforms, raided the place and took seventeen ten-tonne trucks' worth of gear. They were back over the border before the Thais could even raise the alarm. They headed up through Mawdaung, and then transported the gear up the peninsula on elephants. I heard that the Thai general was more than a little pissed off, but the Karen had solved their arms supply problem in the short term.

The fact that it didn't solve the problem in the long term led me to get involved again in 1990. Stan had contacted me to see about starting a regular munitions supply run for the KNU. Setting anything up had to be done face to face as telephones couldn't be trusted at either end. To bypass any legal hassles caused by my supplying arms to a non-recognised government we had a front company set up in Thailand and generated an end-user certificate. This was at huge cost but was still cheaper than dealing through the Thai military. I went to Colonel Oliver and revisited the idea of using the small Thai airstrips near his sector. The fearsome old man was surprisingly keen. The strip he had in mind was very remote, so we could bypass the greedy Thai generals by putting some money in the right pockets.

Singapore had the closest reliable airport, so we sketched out a plan where a plane from Singapore would be met in midair with another plane coming from Chiang Mai. The planes would switch transponder frequencies at precisely the right time so that our flight would appear to be continuing to Chiang Mai while we dropped off the radar screens and landed at our strip in the mountains. A quick touchdown and unload and we could catch up with the Chiang Mai-bound plane, switch transponder codes back and continue on to Chiang Mai to pick up a load for Singapore, thus establishing a regular cargo run in the minds of the air-traffic controllers. Drug smugglers do this all the time so we were hardly reinventing the wheel.

The supply side was simple. Singapore has arms manufacturers as well. I went knocking on a few doors. After a couple of long lunches that turned into dinners, and then into huge hangovers the next morning, a contact agreed to sell me military ordnance as long as my end-user certificate was legitimate and met with government approval. He didn't think the Singapore government would stand in the way since we were talking about million-dollar sales each month. This manufacturer was also supplying the Tatmadaw with ammunition, so it was in their best economic interests to supply both sides of the fence, stopping it from becoming a one-sided contest, so they could continue to enjoy huge demand.

Towards the tail end of one long dinner, I mentioned to my salesman about my South African contacts and my plans just to use Singapore as a transhipment base if I couldn't work out a suitable deal with them. He offered me a US$10 000 retainer on the spot, just to keep my business from going elsewhere. The ten grand was a nice kick-start, but it didn't go far. There was warehousing, bond stores, office space, tarmac space and a host of other requirements to set up a business in Singapore. I was going to need more cash.

Loose lips would sink this enterprise faster than they would any ship. Not just the Singaporean authorities but the Thais, too, had to be kept in the dark or the whole thing would be shut down fast. It made sense that I would fly the weapons in from Singapore, rather than risk adding a commercial pilot to the small list of people in the know. I decided to get my commercial pilot's licence when I got back home and do the job myself.

Back in Perth I spoke with my wife about moving to Singapore and setting up an air-charter business. As usual, I wasn't telling her the whole truth, something we'd both become used to. It seemed like a good way forward for the family as the seven-days-a-week truck driving wasn't allowing me to be a much better father than when I was a soldier. I sold the trucking business in December, enrolled in flight school and hit the books. It was hard work getting back into studying again, but I was determined to get my jet endorsement, my air transport pilot's licence and my commercial pilot's licence, all inside six months.

The cost of commercial pilot training was at least A$40 000 at the time. Selling the trucking business for a small profit, plus the ten-grand retainer from Singapore would get me started, but I'd need a lot more to get everything set up. I could have asked the KNU for the money and they may well have given it. But something made me reluctant to do this – probably pride after nearly losing them that 30 million Baht with my last recommendation, not to mention the costs I had run up with my fruitless South African trip. I decided to raise the cash the quickest way possible – by stealing it.

Some people still ask me about crossing the line, as if I had made some momentous moral decision to become an outlaw. I didn't. Governments, international boundaries and laws didn't mean that much to me back then. I was a soldier on a mission and my mission was to help the Karen.

I took my time picking a target for the robbery. I needed the best combination of high cash turnover and ease of penetration. The penny dropped when the wife and I were at the new Hoyts Cinema Complex that had opened near the Carousel Shopping Mall in the Perth suburb of Bentley. Big shopping malls and multiplexes are commonplace today, but this was the first one in the state to appear. The place was crowded with thousands of punters, all paying cash. It was still an undeveloped suburb, surrounded by plenty of vacant land, full of good staging points, OPs and escape routes.

It took me a couple of days and a few trips to the movies to pinpoint the location of the safe. The cluster of security company stickers on one of the office windows eventually gave it away. It was an above-ground 'two-key' safe. Management can open the main door of the safe, but there is a smaller inner-door that can only be opened with two keys; one is held by the armoured car company and the other by a staff member. There is a one-way slot in the inside of the safe where money envelopes can be slipped in. Defeating the locks on both doors wasn't beyond me, but it would take hours. The whole scenario would become simpler if I could get the key to the outer door.

Once I decided on taking the manager at home, I knew it would be a two-man job. I hadn't heard from Baz for a couple of years, but used the grapevine to track him down. He was in Townsville. He'd given up soldiering and was trying to make a go of a fish-and-chip shop – badly, by the sound of it. I gave him the run-down on the job and he said, '. . . 'ken oath I'm in', almost before I'd even finished speaking. I sent him the plane fare and he flew in a few days later. Waiting in the arrivals lounge at Perth airport, I didn't see him get off the plane and was thinking that he must have missed the flight when this huge, fat, red-headed bloke walked up to me.

'G'day, Dave,' he smiled. He'd been running a fish-and-chip shop all right, and eating his own produce every night by the look of him. He looked like a carrot-topped Michelin man with freckles.

'Jeez, have you been stung by something?' I blurted.

'Fuck off. You're not so slim yourself.'

He had a point; trucking had put a few kilos of flab around my middle. 'Looks like we both could do with the fish-paste-and-rice diet again,' I said.

'Fuck that, I can still move okay. I've just got a verandah over the tool shed, that's all.'

I put Baz up in a motel room and after a few days of careful planning, we were ready.

It had been easy to find the manager's house. I rang the cinema a couple of times, pretending to be a university student doing a PhD on consumer recreational behaviour. I asked a few questions about the difference in the number of people using cinemas during the week as compared to weekends. Included in this survey were the times that the heaviest number of users passed through the doors. I asked to speak to the manager and soon had his name. I rang back during the week and asked for the assistant manager, saying I needed some follow up information for my survey. Then I used the phone book to match name and initial. Neither of them had a silent number. I'd seen the car that each was driving, so it had been easy to check out the addresses and match them to the cars in the driveways, getting a quick visual of their faces to confirm. A couple of nights watching the manager's house and I was able to confirm that there were no kids.

If we'd known the woman was pregnant, we would never have started the job. In all the scenarios we rehearsed – scoping out the backyard, neutralising the pet, gaining access to the house, subduing the manager – we hadn't prepared 'actions-on' for 'She's bloody pregnant!' It took us a few seconds to react. Eventually I jumped up and stood away, but kept my hand across her mouth. I suppose it was a gesture that suggested we were civilised enough to go easy on a pregnant woman, because it settled hubby down, which, in turn, calmed her down. Baz got off the hubby and told him to calm his wife. I turned the light off to make it a bit more comfortable for them. We reassured them that they wouldn't be harmed in any way as long as they followed instructions. After taking the phone out of the wall, we let them comfort each other and get themselves together, while we sat in the corner and got our shit together.

'Fuck this, let's can it,' whispered Baz. 'No way am I being responsible for the loss of a baby.'

I spoke to the manager.

'Hey, how many weeks pregnant is she, mate?'

'Six weeks.'

No wonder we couldn't tell, she'd hadn't started to show.

'Listen,' I said to Baz under my breath. 'You look after her, make her as comfortable as you can, be nice and turn on the old Baz charm. She's not going to be any more scared than she was five minutes ago. I reckon we press on.'

He nodded and we decided to keep going. Baz moved out to check the street. I looked over at the neighbour's house to make sure no lights had come on. Baz came in to say all was clear out the front. We'd wired up Baz's earpiece to a radio scanner as well. Part of the planning had been to punch in and verify the radio frequencies of all police and security companies in the area. All frequencies were quiet, apart from the normal procedural chatter, but we waited thirty minutes to be sure.

The shell-shocked young couple had experienced enough surprises for one night, so we deliberately ran through the rest of the job with them, making it clear what we needed them to do and repeating that they wouldn't be hurt. Once people have been frightened, they have this strong desire to please; it's part of the survival mechanism, so if you give them little jobs they tend to be very cooperative.

Time was ticking away, so things had to start moving along. The manager got dressed in a suit, all tidied up like he was off to work. We then told his wife to get dressed in warm, dark clothes. Once they were ready, we had them sit on the lounge while I got ready.

I'd noticed in my reconnaissance that the manager was roughly my size, and that he wore a few different suits to work, which solved the problem of me having to bring one to wear. I took one of his suits from his wardrobe and moved to the bathroom to begin my transformation. I sprayed my eyebrows and hair black with a wash-off hair dye, then put on my black wig and stuck on a big, bushy black moustache. I popped on a pair of clear spectacles to further break up the outline of my face, and then donned the suit. It was a little baggy around the middle, but looked acceptable at a glance. The disguise needed only to get me past a cursory look from a patrolling police or security car. Even a quick chat with them wouldn't present a problem. A briefcase topped off the disguise of an overworked manager pulling a late one.

We found some insect repellent, blankets and pillows for the wife, and then moved them both out to the car. Hubby kindly showed me how to unlock the car without setting off the alarm and we got them organised in the back seat, with her lying down, head in his lap. Baz flicked the child-proof locks to prevent the doors being opened from the inside. We had covered the scenario of his car being low on fuel by stashing a jerry can of our own in the backyard. I checked and he had a full tank, so we left the jerry can where it was.

I drove steadily, taking the almost-deserted main roads and staying on the speed limit all the way over to Cannington. I'd timed the route a few times in the past week, so we'd have an accurate ETA. Part of the pre-job planning was to set up a staging area, near enough to the job for Baz and I to stay in radio communication and where we could hold the hostages without drawing any attention our way. I found the perfect spot for this in a derelict house that was near the cinema complex. It was on the edge of a park with lots of bush around to provide a screen and offer numerous escape routes that we could take on foot. It looked like it had been used by squatters at one time, but even squatters have standards and the place was so busted up and shat in that it had been deserted. I'd stashed my safe-cracking kit there the day before, buried in the backyard.

We pulled in behind the house and killed the car's lights but kept the engine running. Baz guarded our new friends as I retrieved my job bag and found a dry, comfortable place for the missus under a tree. I left her with Baz and jumped in the car, but she started crying and making too much noise, distressed at her husband leaving. I kicked myself because we'd done something unpredictable and broken our little contract of trust with them. I hadn't mentioned that we'd be splitting them up.

I pulled the hubby out of the car and we all sat down under the tree and had a powwow. We assured the manager's wife that everything would be okay and this was the safest way to do the job. I told her we wouldn't be very long and to just sit tight until we got back. She calmed down again and the manager and I set off. Baz's job was now to keep her safe and quiet, but, more importantly, to stay in radio contact with me over anything he heard on the scanner.

On the three-minute drive to the cinema I again briefed the manager so the job ahead would be clear in his mind. This included our cover story. He only had to verify what I was saying if we were stopped and questioned; otherwise, I'd be doing all the talking.

I drove straight into the car park, pulled up and let the manager out. I took my balaclava off. I was pleased to see that the manager averted his eyes from my face without me having to tell him, which showed that the manager was switched on and cooperating. He went towards the office first, carrying my bag and the keys, while I followed with the briefcase. Once he opened the main doors, he went straight to the alarm keypad, punching in the deactivation code.

'Stand by,' I said to Baz on the radio. Warning him to watch the scanner if he wasn't already.

If the silent alarm was going to be tripped, either by the manager inputting a special code or maybe even walking on certain pressure-sensitive pads, it was now. He didn't look like he was playing hopscotch, or looking for a certain place to tread, so if he was going to pull a fast one, it'd be by entering the wrong code. If the alarm had gone out, we'd know soon enough and I reckoned I'd still have time to get away.

There were numerous fire-escapes all over the building and the only trap was the safe-room, where there were only two ways in and out. The office windows also gave me a good view of anyone rolling up at the front of the building to spoil the party. In that case the furthest I'd have to run before getting into the scrub was about 100 metres; in there I was sure I could lose whoever was chasing me. I'd also scoped out a large underground storm-water drain that I could get to from several different directions. Once in there, I could go for kilometres undetected and pop out of any number of different drain openings. It was the ideal way to avoid helicopters, infra-red detection equipment and tracker dogs, as well as foot and vehicle pursuit.

So far so good. We locked the main door and made our way into the safe-room, me still walking directly behind the manager so he couldn't get a good look at me. There were two safes and probably a few thousand dollars' worth of coins lying around in bags; these were of no interest because of their weight. The manager had the main safe open in less than a minute. He was really playing his part well. He only had the keys to the outer door, and I had to blow the inner one. I made him lie on the floor just outside the safe-room, with his legs in the doorway touching my feet, so I'd know where he was at all times. I quickly made sure there were no telephones within his reach. I took out the only loaded weapon we used on the job – a cut-down .303 rifle – then put on a set of safety goggles and some earmuffs to muffle the deafening blast that the .303 was going to make in the tiny room.

A quick look out the window to make sure no cars were cruising past and a single word to Baz on the radio, and I was ready. I told the manager to jam his fingers hard into his ears, then I worked the bolt to chamber a round in the .303 and placed the barrel squarely against the keyhole of the inner safe door. The alignment was crucial; the opening of the keyhole and the inside opening of the barrel had to match up exactly, as I didn't want the round to ricochet outwards from the hardened casing of the inner door. This also ensured that the full force of the projectile and muzzle blast were concentrated on the small keyhole.

Even though I'd braced for it as best I could, the .303 jerked back savagely in my hands as the blast recoiled off the lock with a thunderous roar. I shook my head to clear the ringing sound, chambered another round and blasted the lower lock. I checked the handle and it was still locked solid. Bugger. I gave each keyhole another blast, before giving the handle another good yank. This time it swung open and I was looking at a great stack of envelopes stuffed full of money shrouded in cordite smoke and confetti. A couple of the envelopes had been shredded, but there was more cash in there than I had anticipated, much more.

A large plastic bag held most of the envelopes, but after it was full I had to stuff more into my suit pockets. I crammed the bulging plastic bag into my bag, along with the shell cases and mangled projectiles. With the rifle, safety glasses and earmuffs, it was a tight fit and I had to battle to do up the zip.

Time to move. A quick glance out the window showed that the coast was still clear. I got the manager to stand up, and I marched him out, standing close behind him. We reset the alarm on the way out and locked the front door. I got him into the back of the car again, this time lying on the floor, then got behind the wheel and drove off. It had been less than four minutes from the time we entered the building. I radioed the code word to Baz and he fired back, 'Jeez, that was quick.'

A few minutes later we were back in the driveway of the derelict house. The manager and his wife were pretty pleased to see each other, and when we told them that it was all over they collapsed together and sobbed with relief. Baz and I were both combat veterans rather than hardened crims, and the guilt started to hit about how much distress we'd caused these folks. We made a few bumbling attempts at making them feel better, telling them there was nothing personal in our choice of the cinema as a target.

'Mate, I know you're going to get down on yourself,' Baz said to the manager. 'About how well you can protect your wife and kid. But there's nothing you could have done.' Very sensitive on the part of the big Queenslander, I thought.

We used flex-cuffs, which are really just the oversized plastic zip-ties that electricians use, to loosely restrain them both. Later, both the media and police made a big deal about this, saying that using plastic ties was unique to the SAS, choosing to ignore the fact that police, paramilitary forces and prison departments all over the world use plastic ties to secure people.

We asked the couple to give us a couple of minutes to get out of the area before raising the alarm, knowing full well that they would be free in no time because of the loose cuffs. It would take them a few minutes to untangle themselves and that was all we needed.

We drove south for a couple of kilometres and as soon as we were out of visual and aural range, turned and headed north. We'd picked a block of flats just up the road from the target's house as a place to leave our car, as the high frequency of comings and goings would make our movements less likely to be noticed. I dropped Baz a few blocks away and waited for him to signal on the radio that he was free and clear in our vehicle before heading over to the domestic airport to dump the manager's car.

I'd also scouted out this location prior to the job. It was a back street not far from a pedestrian bridge over the highway. I hoped that the car's proximity to the airport would throw the police off the scent, and create just a bit more confusion to clog up the investigation. Also, by using the pedestrian bridge to cross the major highway, Baz could pick me up in an entirely different district to the one the car was left in. This, I hoped, would all make it harder for an investigator to 'connect the dots'.

Just after I pulled up near the airport, I got the call from Baz that the police were on their way to the cinema and had broadcast the plates of the manager's car. I had to move fast. I got all of my gear out of the car and, at the last minute, I took off the manager's suit and left it in the car for him to get later. I figured the poor bugger had been through enough, and I didn't want to steal his personal property. It was a stupid mistake. The police forensic team had a field day with it.

After one last check for anything left behind in the car, I made my way toward the footbridge. I waited until there were no oncoming headlights in either direction on the highway, then scooted across. We'd chosen the pick-up point carefully as well – a small park with plenty of bush and a roundabout at one end. The roundabout was perfect as it was something that would naturally slow a car. Baz could drop his speed, I could dive in and close the door a few blocks down the road. It was a pick-up that wouldn't sound like a pick-up, just in case the coppers went door knocking in the area later on.

I sat down amongst the trees and absorbed the sights and sounds of the neighbourhood, making sure that nothing was likely to trip us up. It was quiet, with no lights on in any houses. Baz was in a holding pattern a few blocks away; I called him in for the pick-up. As soon as I eyeballed the car, I talked him in so we could time it perfectly. As the car drew level, I opened the rear door, climbed in and quickly lay on the floor, still holding the door handle. A couple of blocks away I pulled the door fully shut and covered myself with a blanket.

We went straight to our cache spot and got down to the business of cleaning and stashing. Everything was counted off into garbage bags: gloves, balaclavas, clothing, makeup, moustache, glasses, earmuffs, shoes, job bag, handcuff keys, weapons, scanners and radios. We had a wash and got dressed in our normal clothing, leaving our gloves on the whole time. We then set about counting up all the loot. The empty money envelopes, cheques and any paraphernalia from the safe went into the garbage bag as well. There was enough money to cover costs, pay Baz and set my Singapore project in motion.

We took the garbage bags containing all the material and took a drive off into the bush to another quiet location. Once we were there, we dug a hole, doused the bags in fuel and burnt everything, making sure it was all reduced to ash. Then we filled in the hole and camouflaged it. If by some fluke it was ever dug up, it would be a one-in-a-billion chance that it could be linked to the crime, and by that time any evidence, such as tyre tracks linking the remains to us, would have long vanished. Then, we drove for another hour or so to another site where we had stashed a set of oxyacetylene bottles and some cutting equipment. We cut up the weapons into small, unrecognisable pieces. These were then taken to a couple of different locations and buried in scattered holes. Everything to do with the crime was now disposed of, except for the gloves, which were the very last thing we burnt.

We were both knackered. It had been a big night's work and the sun was just rising over the Darling Scarp as we parted company. Baz was planning to hang around in Perth to let things cool down for a few weeks before flying home. It was the last time I saw him. When I tried to track him down in Queensland a couple of years later he'd disappeared and left absolutely no trail.

I hid my share of the money and slid back into bed with my wife not long after sunrise. She'd barely noticed I'd been gone, and was used to not asking questions about anything I did in the wee small hours. I had told her I was working security at the fireworks display that night in any case.

I hadn't even heard of PTSD (post-traumatic stress disorder) at that time, and I've only come to understand it after hearing about it while I was in prison. But that night I did have the sense that the manager and his wife's lives would never be the same again.

THE FIRST TASTE OF PRISON

Fremantle prison was built in the 1850s out of huge limestone blocks quarried on site. In those days they built prisons to punish, not to rehabilitate, and this place was pretty punishing. Oppressively hot in summer, it had once reached 52 degrees Celsius inside; the inmates rioted and nearly burned the place down. I wasn't there in the middle of winter, but they reckon the cold wind of Fremantle harbour blew right through the place.

I was in solitary confinement, which was a 2 by 3-metre cell with a dirty foam mattress on the floor and a bucket to shit in. Incredibly, the smell of the recently deposited turd in my bucket was being overpowered by the body odour of the 500 other men nearby, who only got to shower once every three days. Prison is the noisiest place I have ever been. It groans, screams and clanks like a big wounded metal monster twenty-four hours a day. There is no predictable rhythm to the sound; you never adjust and never get a decent night's sleep.

It was quite the predicament, but I was still in pretty high spirits. It was just another adventure and, one way or another, I didn't reckon I'd be in there very long. I was being held in solitary while the prison authorities worked out where to put me and Jim. We had been transferred here from the East Perth lockup after thirty-six hours of interrogation, a few punches to the face and a brief court hearing.

So I leave the family, go off to join the army, cross the continent to join the Regiment, spend a few years in southeast Asia, get mixed up in some trouble, walk into a 150-year-old prison and who should I meet? My bloody older sister, Mary, on her first few months in the job as a prison warden, that's who.

'You're in the shit this time, little brother,' she smirked as I walked past.

'Where's an air rifle when you need one?' I shot back. They transferred her after that. Seeing her standing there in the line of screws, watching us walk to the Initial Orientation Unit (IOU), just added to the surreal feel of the whole day. Looking back, I suppose the 'not-quite-real feeling' was partly responsible for the high spirits. I was left scratching my head about the whole deal.

There is no doubt that a few of us who had left the Regiment around the same time had got mixed up in trouble. Much of that has since been put down to us leaving the CT team all charged up with no place to go. I spoke to a psychologist many years later who said that people like us, those who existed in a high state of readiness for months on end, actually had part of our brains grow larger; there was a physical change to cope with the adrenalin, dopamine, cortisol and the rest of the cocktail of chemicals that keeps you switched on in times of danger. Take an operator out of that environment after he's become conditioned to it and he'll exist, day to day, in a profound state of restlessness. There is a compulsive need to get close to the edge and take risks. None of us could really settle down. Being colleagues and mates we caught up regularly, and I'm sure a few of the blokes did the occasional 'job' together, much like Baz and myself. Some creative copper must have connected the dots and floated the theory that we were an organised ex-military crime gang, which had led to our arrests on the Albany highway a few nights earlier.

My mate Jim, an ex-Regiment man, didn't have a B-class licence, so he had asked me to drive a water truck for him. I owed him a few favours; he'd always helped with fixing my busted-up old semi-trailer, which needed work almost once every couple of weeks. We were returning from dumping a load of water in a dam on a property owned by one of his mates; water-carting was a common practice towards the end of a long, hot WA summer.

We'd just come down Armadale hill, part of the scarp that rings the flat coastal plains of Perth, when a battered, resprayed old Ford transit van pulled alongside of us and began nudging us to within inches of our bull bar.

'Shit,' I said. 'Someone's had a few too many drinks.' And I steered us into the gutter.

'Dave! Watch out! Power pole!' Jim shouted. I steered us back onto the road and smacked the van out of the way like a ping-pong ball, at the same time leaning out the window, shaking my fist and hurling abuse. He came back for another go, and, again, was sent bouncing back onto the other side of the road – talk about road rage. Just then, a Holden commodore shot out around our duelling vehicles, mounted the grass verge of the median strip and threw a blue light on its roof. It was probably the one time in my life I was glad to see a copper.

'Now this dickhead will get sorted out,' I said.

'Let's make a run for it, Dave,' Jim said quickly. 'Plant it and let's get the fuck out of here, we can get to some bush and lose them on foot.'

'We haven't done anything wrong,' I said. 'Relax, mate, and let's see that dickhead in the van try and talk his way out of it.'

I looked via my side mirror at the van and saw that it wasn't one staggering drunk coming out of it but about a dozen big blokes in black combat gear carrying 12-gauge shotguns. That's when I realised that they were the TRG (police tactical response group), that their van was in fact an armoured van, and that we were getting rolled. Seconds later we were staring down the gaping barrels of five or six shotguns and being told to get down out of the truck slowly.

'I haven't been drinking officers. I'm as sober as a judge,' I said.

There was stunned silence for a moment and then they dragged me down, threw me on the ground, cuffed me and frisked me before one of them stood on my legs. Obviously none of them had a sense of humour.

The next thirty-six hours were a blur. Arresting Jim and I had been part of a larger operation that caught a host of other blokes and involved three different branches of law enforcement. First the CIB took me home, woke up the wife and kids and made me watch while they tore the house apart. They got excited when they found $12 000 in a floor safe; that was money I was holding to buy some radio equipment for the Karen.

From there, it was back to the East Perth lockup where I was formally charged with conspiracy to cultivate marijuana. With my hands cuffed tightly behind my back, I was left in the interrogation room for the rest of the night. I just curled up under the table and went to sleep. The next morning one of the young coppers unlocked the interrogation room door and couldn't see me; his voice cracked like he was going through puberty as he nervously called out, 'You there, Everett?' He probably thought I'd used my phantom SAS skills to escape. He seemed pretty relieved when I sat back up in my seat and said, 'Morning' as cheerily as I could.

Then I was driven out to a look at a marijuana crop, which I had never seen before and which I had supposedly taken part in cultivating. The water we'd carted the day before may well have been used to irrigate it, but this was the first I knew of it. Brod, another ex-Regiment bloke, was already there, accompanied by several coppers, so it looked like he was in the shit, too.

Then it was back to East Perth for another snooze. My tightly bound hands didn't hurt any more because they'd gone numb. A few hours later a couple of lizard men, who could only have been federal coppers, came in brandishing two steel cylinders that they said I had made. They claimed that these had been used in an attempt to import 3 kilograms of heroin into the country. They said that someone had dobbed me in. This was getting out of hand, but I knew it was bullshit and figured all I needed to do was wait for the truth to come out. I'd had enough of talking and just slipped into a trance – something that the Karen boys had taught me – and blocked them out of my mind.

After another few hours, I was taken down to the armed robbery squad for questioning over what seemed like every unsolved armed robbery that had taken place in Perth in the last two years. They didn't mention the cinema job specifically, but I guessed they had me lined up for that as well. They got boring after a while, asking the same questions over and over again, so I went back to my trance. I snapped back out of this when one of the coppers punched me hard in the face and then whacked me in the guts; I was pretty good at zoning out, but not that good. Overall I'd say their interrogation techniques were fair to medium; I noted the direct approach, the incentive approach, fear up, fear down, ego down, futility technique and a nice variation on the 'Mutt and Jeff' approach, otherwise known as good cop–bad cop, where one of the coppers is as nice as pie and the other just wants to bash you.

Despite what the coppers will tell you, they regularly bashed people during interrogation back then. They did it because: one, their profession is known to attract playground bullies; and two, it makes the person being interrogated feel hopeless and very alone, as if the law and order system has failed him and there is no way out. The problem for them was that they couldn't beat us too badly or the press would be wondering about all the bruises and such. So they were still constrained by some rules, whereas in the interrogation training we did in the Regiment it was 'no holds barred' and much, much worse than anything the boys in blue could dish out.

When they put me back in the lockup I made a formal complaint about my treatment. I still remember the names of the coppers who belted me when my hands were tied behind my back. I wrote them all down on a piece of paper when I was on the run. When this list was found they called it my 'hit list' and made a big noise about how I was planning to seek revenge on each one of them. I wasn't, but the fact that they spent two years shitting themselves while I was at large was revenge enough.

The next day it was into court to hear the charges; bail was refused. After the hearing, they took me back in and tried questioning me again, but I just went into my trance and blocked it all out. From there, it was down to the Fremantle Prison to be deloused, scrubbed up and issued with prison garb.

They kept us in the 'boneyard' for the first day. All new blokes were kept here until they were processed into the mainstream population. It was also where they kept the child molesters and informants, known as rock spiders and dogs, and anyone else who'd be attacked if they were in the main population.

Jim and I were then moved into a double cell in the main division. I still wasn't too worried at this stage and was expecting to be released fairly soon. Jim, on the other hand, was pretty sick with worry; he reckoned that our names had been given to the cops to protect a few people high up in a drug distribution chain. Jim was worried they'd pay someone inside the prison to knock us off. It all sounded a bit fanciful to me, and at the time I reckoned Jim was just having a paranoid reaction to being locked up.

Jim also reckoned the coppers themselves were in on it, which I also doubted. Suggesting that they were involved in drug running was drawing a long bow, I thought. Although, years later, quite a few members of the CIB and armed-robbery squad, including the two blokes who initially arrested us, left the police service in disgrace.

We soon slipped into the prison routine. Most of the day was spent in the yard, which was the size of a couple of tennis courts and was crammed with more than a hundred blokes. An open-sided shed in the middle provided relief from the sun and rain, and the three toilets located at the end wall were alternatives to the cell bucket. You could only use the toilets on the left and right sides as all the junkies used the middle toilet as their 'office'. There were clothing issues once a day. When they brought the bins around containing fresh clothes, jocks and socks, there was a wild free-for-all down to the steel grill to grab something.

Another rush of bodies occurred when medication parade was called. They handed out liquid Valium and Largactil to anyone who asked and most blokes were addicted. Within ten minutes they were all zombies, walking into walls and each other. One day I was returning to the division just prior to medication and walked past the medic who had a table full of white plastic cups next to a 10-litre jug of liquid Valium. I could only shake my head.

There wasn't much in the way of exercise gear in the yard. Some 20-litre detergent containers had been converted into improvised weights: they were filled with water and either a towel or a broken broom handle was used as means to lift them. There were a few heave beams around, as well as some sit-up benches. I still had that bit of weight around the belly from truck driving, so decided to get into a regular exercise routine to try and lose it. I got stuck into sit-ups, heaves, push-ups and pumping the water bottles when I could get a hold of them. I managed to get a bit of a suntan, too.

Lockup was at 4 p.m. and you got your meal as you went up to your cell. The food was fresh and not too bad all told, and you were even given half a loaf of freshly baked bread to go with it. Once in the cell, you had a choice of having your light on or off all night; there were no switches inside. There was a great view of Fremantle Harbour from our slot windows.

For fun, I'd blind the screws in the gun towers with my mirror by directing the setting sun's reflection into their faces, then I'd duck down quickly so they couldn't work out which cell it was coming from. But, otherwise, Jim and I didn't get into any strife. We were used to playing the grey man and blending in. I wasn't sure whether our SAS reputation would count for or against us, with blokes feeling like they should bash us to show who ran the place, or being scared of the super-secret Ninja skills we were supposed to have. We didn't really find out either way – most blokes just left us alone.

Despite the overcrowding and archaic conditions, it was a fairly relaxed joint. Many of the blokes had been there for more than ten years and had learned to exist in a kind of robotic daze with the lights on but nobody really home. Also, the place was so confined that a riot there would have had devastating consequences, so most blokes had a sense of not wanting to push the boundaries. If you count boarding school and the army, I'd been in one sort of institution or another on and off since I was twelve, so it wasn't a huge adjustment for me. But Jim got more miserable as time went on, really missing his missus and newborn kid.

I'd told my wife plenty of times that if I got in the shit for anything, she should divorce me as fast as she could, organise a lawyer and bring me the papers so I could sign everything over to her. That way, if she and I still had a relationship, we could sort it out down the track, but in the meantime she and the kids would still have a roof over their heads – one that the police couldn't touch. She brought the papers in a week after I ended up in jail and that was that. For her, it was the last straw, and we never reunited. I wasn't that upset about it because I knew it would be the best thing for the kids. I told Jim to do the same thing, but he was advised against it because it would look like an admission of guilt and strengthen the case for the prosecution. It was bad advice because the coppers used it to bring huge pressure to bear on him later on.

I put in for a transfer to the O'Connor Remand Centre at the Canning Vale Prison; I wanted to get a chance to walk on grass again and go running. One day Jim and I were at work in the shoe shop when a screw came up out of the blue and told me to pack my kit. It was like stepping out of the Stone Age and into modern times. There, I had my own cell and even a flushing toilet and a sink with running water. And grass! To be able to lie on the grass and go for a run felt amazing.

Strangely, despite the much better conditions, Canning Vale had the opposite atmosphere to Fremantle. Being a remand centre, it had people coming and going all the time. Nobody could settle into a routine and there were always fights to establish the pecking order each time fresh heads came in. A few of us from Fremantle went up at the same time, and they put us all in A-wing in Unit One, nicknamed 'The Bronx'.

Putting a bloke 'on the dog' was to let on that he was some sort of informant who had given his mates up. There is nothing in the criminal world lower than a dog, besides a rock spider. One idiot in A-wing had styled himself as a bit of a gang leader and hard man. He'd told everyone he'd done armed robberies and had shot a copper. He'd pick blokes, almost at random, and put them on the dog as an excuse for his little tribe to give them a savage bashing. I could tell he was a weak prick but didn't bother with him, just stayed out of the way and did my grey man thing. Three weeks later the so-called cop-killer went to court and the next day the papers reported what he had *actually* been charged with. It turned out he'd enticed a thirteen-year-old boy out of a Jesus People shelter with the promise of a few drinks and a good feed, got him drunk, bashed him and then raped him. So he wasn't a pistol-packing hero at all, just a scungy rock spider.

The atmosphere in the yard the day after the trial was so tense it was palpable. The balance of power had been wrecked as this bloke's former gang had lost their leader. One by one they were picked off and had the shit kicked out of them. When the leader came back he spent all day in front of the screw's box. Eventually, someone got him in a quiet spot alone and half an hour later he was stretchered out, covered in blood, never to be seen again.

I was looking forward to Jim being transferred up as well. But when he did things changed for the worse overnight. Someone had decided to put some pressure on us and this changed our privileges drastically. We got banned from running on the oval and were moved from outside-facing cells into one that faced an inner courtyard; we were surrounded by concrete again after a brief taste of greenery. They also moved us into a different cell every second day.

One morning I had a crack at one of the guards about this, 'C'mon mate, how am I going to get a tunnel started if you keep moving me around?' but he didn't think it was funny. No sense of humour at all, those blokes.

I wasn't planning anything drastic, but I couldn't say the same for Jim; his morale was getting lower by the day. I wondered if he'd made some plans to escape that had been leaked to the cops, but he insisted he hadn't. It got tougher for Jim after the screws started strip-searching our families every time they came to visit, children included. Having his newborn baby stripped naked by a screw before each visit really got to him. Mary had told my family to expect such treatment, so they weren't too fazed when it happened. It is humiliating to have to strip naked in front of a bunch of total strangers, and it just degrades your loved ones until they feel like criminals as well.

Most blokes didn't take the option of going to court every eight days on the remand cycle because being trucked into the city and spending the whole day in the cramped lockup there was a hassle. But I made a point of going. I wasn't going to take these charges lying down. The young cops at the Central Law Courts had got to know my face by now. They were taken aback when I rocked up in chains with my little squad of shotgun-toting escorts.

'Shit, Dave, what did you do wrong?' one of the young ones asked.

'Don't go telling anyone,' I said. 'But I sneaked into the superintendent's office and pinched his milk.'

No sooner had I been delivered back to the prison than the superintendent came storming up and told me off for telling lies to the coppers at the courts about pinching his milk. Obviously somebody had made enquiries and he lost some face amongst his cronies. It was my first taste of how rumours can fly around in a paranoia-fuelled prison. It wasn't a bad first effort and in later years I learnt to conduct the grapevine like an orchestra. It was Dave's ministry of propaganda, all right.

The night before we were due to go to court for an election date, Jim had a visit that changed everything. His lawyer, Max Crispe, told him that the crown were going to ask for thirty-five years for him if he didn't roll over and give them some people higher up the food chain. He'd also lose his house, yacht and all his assets, which the coppers had frozen. His wife would be charged as an accessory and his baby would be made a ward of the state.

'I'm fucked either way, Dave,' he said with his head in his hands. I don't reckon he'd eaten in days and he looked pale and sick.

I had a go at cheering him up.

'It's bullshit, mate. They are trying to scare you into making a confession. They've put a lot of time and money into this; the whole thing's in the newspapers and they are going to look stupid if we walk. I reckon they're getting desperate, mate. Stay strong and it'll blow over.' We had a game of table-tennis to get his mind off it. He seemed pretty relaxed and cheery when we parted ways at lockup.

Next morning I was called into a meeting with the senior officer from our block and the assistant superintendent. They were pretty polite – even offered me a seat, which was unusual. Then they dropped the bombshell.

'Your mate is dead.'

'Who?'

'Jim.'

'How?'

'Suicide. He suffocated himself with a plastic bag. We found him in his cell this morning.'

I don't remember much of the next few minutes; it was a huge shock. I felt terrible for his family. It wasn't a game any more. Something was definitely not right. In my mind there was just no way Jim would top himself. I reckoned he'd been killed, and if someone had gotten to Jim, they could just as easily get to me.

No one would show me the suicide note either. I tried to figure out what had gone wrong, but the harder I tried the less information I was told. I knew the cops had been leaning on Jim for more information and that he wouldn't help out. There were a few people, cops included, who were better off with Jim dead. I didn't sleep much after that realisation and spent every night in my cell waiting for someone to try something on with me. I isolated myself and watched my back at all times. It was a long time before I slept well.

I wasn't allowed to attend Jim's funeral because I wasn't family, and it was a year or two before I got to say goodbye to my mate. They eventually granted me bail because they were worried about my going down the same path as Jim. I might have been better off staying locked up. The bail conditions were the strictest ever imposed on anyone in Australia: $200 000 bail and another $200 000 surety. My mum put up her house and Mary put up hers, which was originally my grandmother's. Home detention was imposed, which meant an electronic bracelet was fitted to my wrist, and every time the security company rang I had to insert into a special machine that verified my presence. Sixteen random calls were made over each twenty-four hour period, and they also made a twice-nightly face-to-face security check.

I stayed with my sister but I couldn't settle. Strange noises kept setting the dogs off at all hours and this, combined with the intermittent phone calls, none of which I was allowed to miss or it would be straight back to prison, started to do my head in. Jim had mentioned a couple of names to me. These were the people he was keeping from the coppers. I'd never had anything to do with these blokes, but I wondered if they felt it necessary to shut me up as well. No way was I going to be a sitting duck in home detention, waiting for them to bump me. There was only one way to sort this out. I needed to get free and go after them.

HOME INVASION

Sleep deprivation is one of the best methods of breaking someone down mentally. Go for a week without the normal five to eight hours of restful sleep a night and your brain stops learning, you have worse coordination than when you are drunk, and you don't process blood sugar as well and so begin showing the symptoms of diabetes. You also feel anxious and depressed, take more risks and show less caution. In interrogations sleep deprivation will break down someone's resistance and they'll stop withholding information. I knew most of this first-hand because it was one of the things we had trained for, but after a few weeks of home detention I was going into uncharted territory.

Sometimes I'd get four calls in a row at two-thirty in the morning, then again at five, then at six. I'd just get to sleep again when the phone would ring. I only had to miss one of those calls to violate my bail conditions, so I was like a hair trigger waiting for the sound of the phone. Then there were the two random physical security checks at night, which meant having to answer a knock at the front door, be identified and have my electronic bracelet checked.

Added to this was my siege mentality – thinking that someone could try to bump me at any time. I needed to sort this shit out, and there was no way I could do that from there. Of course, I could have just run, but that would have meant my mum and sister losing their homes, and I couldn't have lived with that. I'd made it clear to anyone who would listen that I thought I was next on someone's list, so I figured the best solution would be to fake it – make it look like someone had smashed into the house and shot me, and disposed of the body elsewhere. It didn't need to be perfect, as I was sure the first thing the coppers would assume was that I'd done a runner. I just had to put enough doubt in their minds and not give them any evidence to prove that I had faked it. I tried to view it from an investigator's angle.

I considered how cruel this would be to my mum and to Mary – letting them think I was dead – but there was no way I could let them in on it. An experienced copper would pick that they were lying straightaway. Better they thought me dead for a while than actually having me dead, and I was sure I'd be able to pass on a message once I was free. Best of all, they wouldn't have to forfeit the 200 grand if it couldn't be proved that I'd absconded.

Finding access to a weapon was easy. I had stayed in this house for a while after my grandmother had died in 1983 and I'd buried a gun at the bottom of a 30-metre deep bore in the backyard. It was a Stirling semi-automatic.22 that I'd shortened back to pistol length and replaced the butt and stock with forward and rear pistol grips. With a twenty-round magazine and silencer, it was a very handy piece of kit. It was good for pinging the rogue cats that were killing the birds in our backyard without arousing the neighbour's suspicions. I'd greased and packed it pretty well, so when I pulled it up and checked it over it was in good order. I'd stored the rounds in a small glass jar and the original packaging was gone, but I was pretty sure they were low-velocity rounds. Fire high-velocity rounds out of a suppressed weapon and they'll still make quite a racket. I test-fired it into a block of wood from 6 inches away and it made a nice muffled *ker-thunk* sound, so I figured they were low velocity.

After a bit of scouting around, I spied an old pair of size twelve work boots in the next door neighbour's rubbish bin. I found a smaller pair in our back shed. I also found an old pair of overalls and some flip-flops that would not be missed by anyone. I'd have to stomp about 35 kilometres on the night I disappeared, so I collected a 2-litre plastic soft drink bottle for water and a bag of sweets and nuts.

I couldn't choose the timing as I would have to wait until I was sure nobody would be home for a few hours, but it had to be at night. My sister's social life provided an opportunity one Friday night when she came home from work at about 6 p.m. and announced she was heading out to dinner with her boyfriend. Not long after she was gone, one of the security guards came around and did one of his nightly inspections of my electronic bracelet. He left at about seven-thirty and I flew into action.

First I retrieved the cat gun from the bore, being careful not to leave any footprints in the sand that I'd just spread over the back lawn. Then I put on the old overalls and the size-twelve boots and grabbed our wheelie bin from the frontyard. It was half full with rubbish; I tipped that onto the front lawn and scattered it around a bit. Then I ran the bin over the lawn, through the gate and over the sand on the verge, making sure I put as much body weight on it as I could so its tracks would give the impression it was carrying something heavy, like my dead or unconscious self. Once I'd run the tracks to the concrete pathway outside, I hoisted the bin onto my shoulders and carried it back into the yard. I then climbed onto the side fence and traversed it, keeping the bin off the ground, ensuring that I didn't leave any scrape marks or signs of my movement. Once I reached the rear fence, I climbed over and went along the neighbour's back fence to a car park next to a doctor's clinic. I laid the bin on its side in the far corner of the park, hopefully giving the impression that my abductors had parked there and wheeled my body around before loading it into their car.

After carefully traversing the fences back to our place, I put the smaller shoes on and walked around the frontyard and into the house, leaving footprints everywhere. I made plenty of scuffmarks in the hallway and lounge room to make it look like a struggle had taken place. I'd been eating my dinner in front of the TV when the security guard had visited so I sat down to finish eating and contemplate what my reaction would be if an intruder crashed through the front door.

A bit of method acting was required, so I jumped up, knocking the table over and sending the food all over the floor. I then stepped backwards through it, grabbed the curtains off the window and pulled them from their track. Next I stepped towards the lounge-room door. It was here that I figured I'd be shot, so I fell to the floor and nicked a vein in my arm, letting the blood drip on the floor, then flailing my arm around a bit to create some blood spray. Once a small puddle and plenty of splatter marks of blood were on the floor, I quickly taped the vein shut and stood up, careful not to step in my blood-splattered Jackson Pollock-style artwork.

Then I went back outside and turned the mains power off.

I wrenched the lounge-room window open and climbed inside, leaving a few scrape marks. Any assaulter worth a damn would make sure to conduct a simultaneous double entry to maximise surprise and close off escape routes. I jumped onto the large lounge chair that sat beneath the window and dislodged some cushions onto the floor, then walked around in the room, stepping in the blood and leaving a faint footprint from the sole of the smaller shoes on the floor.

I then switched back to the size-twelve boots, putting the smaller shoes into a plastic bag, and climbed back out of the window with the cat gun. I needed to make some noise now, so I did a chin-up on the brick wall in the frontyard to check the street for activity. A party was going on across the street, but nobody was walking down the footpath on our side. I stomped back in, hoping the deeper footprints would indicate a heavier man. I gave the front door an almighty kick, smashing the lock out and sending the door flying open; I then rushed into the lounge room and fired a round into the back wall. Instead of the muffled *ker-thunk*, there was a loud crack, which echoed right up the street.

Shit! It wasn't subsonic ammo after all. In the test shots I'd fired the cat gun too close to the block of wood and hadn't given enough distance for the round to create its mini-sonic boom. All hell broke loose as every dog in the neighbourhood started up, including my sister's alsatian and doberman that I'd managed to keep quiet up until then by locking them in the backyard. I panicked for a second before realising what was done was done and that the extra noise might count in my favour – if I worked fast.

Now for the two shots that were supposed to hit me. I stepped further into the room and fired a round into the wood, the shell casing flying over onto the lounge chair. Then I went over to where my body would have fallen onto the floor, angled the barrel down and fired another round into the wooden block. This time the spent cartridge pinged over in the far back corner of the room. So now the position of the spent casings and the powder traces from the muzzle blast would indicate firing from three different spots and on the move, instead of one position.

I then walked through the blood drips with the size-twelve boots on and scuffed about as though I was stuffing a body into a bag. My glasses had come off when I did my falling-to-the-floor-after-being-shot routine, so I trod on them for added effect. Into the plastic bag containing the smaller boots, I put my water, food and a spare pair of thongs. I also chucked in one of the thongs I'd been wearing and left the other one amid the mess on the floor. Then I ripped the phone out of the wall and walked backwards out of the house, like I was carrying the body out to the wheelie bin.

So, the scene was set: bullet holes, empty shell cases, smashed-in doors and windows, upturned furniture, bloodstains, crushed spectacles, a half-eaten meal, one shoe missing, the other left at the scene, no clothes or personal effects taken, money left lying around, phone ripped out of the wall, wheelie bin missing, large and small footprints that didn't match my foot size or those of any visitors to the house. All the ingredients for a dastardly deed committed against my good self.

I had to move fast now. Even if no one had reported the shots, I could expect a security call any minute. I jumped from the verandah onto the side fence and travelled along it to the back fence. I gave the dogs a pat on the way to say goodbye.

We were only a few blocks from the main north–south railway

line and this was a perfect way to traverse the city unseen. When I heard the first train coming I cut the electronic bracelet from my wrist and laid it on the track. After the train rolled over it, I buried the mangled remains in a muddy puddle. I hadn't been in the open for more than six months and it felt strange to see that velvety-black sky overhead and have all this space around me. There was no time to be sentimental, however, as I had a long hard walk to get to my gear cache before sunrise.

The back-up cache was something I'd set up when planning the cinema job with Baz and its location will surprise some people. It was in an expanse of low, scrubby dunes behind the rifle range at the SAS barracks in Swanbourne. Apart from being right under everyone's nose and the last place anyone would look, it was an almost-perfect LUP. It was restricted territory and off limits to the general public, bordered by the ocean, the barracks and a busy road with a golf course on the other side. It wasn't the sort of place kids would come exploring and, besides that, the rifle range was in almost constant use and most people were well aware of the danger. We did occasionally run through the area when I was in the Regiment, but we stuck to the tracks because the scrub was too thick and covered a lot of old World War Two barbed wire in the area, making it hard to spot.

Most often, going bush is the worse thing an escapee can do. In an unpopulated area the movement of strangers is usually tracked by the grapevine and locals who know the place can spot something unusual pretty fast. Crowds of people are the best camouflage and this spot was close to both the city and major transit points. There were multiple escape routes if I needed them and there was abundant fresh water and bush tucker; not only that, but there was plenty of tucker to be scavenged out of the rubbish bins from nearby fast-food places as well as the Swanbourne barracks' messes. There was no way I'd starve out there.

An added bonus was that I could have a shower and wash my clothes at the rifle range showers. There were several of these as each rifle club had their own facilities and none of them were kept locked up. There was no roving security around these premises back then, so if I used them at night, there wasn't a problem. Keeping clean wasn't a luxury; I'd be moving amongst the public and a dirty, bedraggled bushman would stand out, especially in the wealthy western suburbs of Perth.

I walked across the city without major incident. Following the railway bridge over the busy Great Eastern Highway allowed me to stay unseen. Once I hit the Swan River, I found a long thin piece of cane and tied a coke tin to the thick end of it with a reed. With that and my plastic bag over my shoulder, I would pass for just another late-evening fisherman on his way to a favourite spot. I wasn't stopping or talking to anyone, so nobody could really have got a close enough look at my fishing tackle to realise it was fake. I walked past fewer than a dozen people the whole way and apart from saying a casual 'evening' to the odd person, I drifted on through, blending into my surroundings.

The main north–south freeway crosses the Swan River via the Narrows bridge. It was humming with traffic as city workers headed home after Friday-night drinks and others came in for a night out. I tried to stay casual and unhurried as I walked across, but I felt hugely exposed; it seemed like every head in every car was turning to look at me. I suppose it was a natural thing for them to do, but it didn't help my paranoia. I knew the alarm must have been raised by now and that every copper in the city would be on the look out for me, but I was comforted by the thought that I was well out of the range of any grid search they'd be looking in and their resources were already stretched pretty tight on Friday nights.

Once across the bridge, I climbed the steep sides of Mount Eliza into Kings Park. One thousand acres of natural bushland right on the edge of the city centre: great for recreation, great for tourists and great cover for recently escaped prisoners on the run. Once in the cover of the bush at the top of the hill, I discarded my fake fishing rod, had a drink of water and feed of nuts and gazed out over the lights of the city. My legs and the soles of my feet were aching badly from the unfamiliar exercise, so I did a few stretches to freshen the muscles, and then kept moving. Once I crossed the park, I used the leafy back streets of the western suburbs to make my way to Swanbourne.

It was a huge relief to climb the fence into the rifle range complex. I was careful to fold the wire, bent by my climb over the fence, back into place and cover any of my tracks in the sand around the fence and on the perimeter road. It took a bit of looking around in the dark to find my reference point, a distinctive Y-shaped bush that led to the cache site. After digging down a few feet, I found the container. I pulled out a sleeping bag, ground sheet, camouflaged shelter, small radio, pocket television, steel mug, spoon, pocket knife, a couple of packets of dehydrated food, water bottles, a set of camouflaged clothing, military boots and a small gas stove. I then covered up and recamouflaged the cache and all signs of the tracks leading to it. I only had a couple of hours of darkness up my sleeve and had to move quickly – I still needed to pick a spot for my LUP. This needed to be a considerable distance away from my main cache in case I got sprung and had to run.

I found a nice dense thicket and crawled inside. My familiarity with this place meant I could trust it, and I wasn't expecting any surprise visitors. A wave of weariness swept over me, both from the longest walk I'd done in a couple of years of sitting on my arse in trucks and prison, and from the fact I hadn't slept well in half a year. I slept the rest of that night and most of the next day.

The following evening I flicked on the radio to listen to the news and found myself to be the lead item.

'Police are investigating the violent abduction of a prisoner on home detention in Victoria Park last night. David Francis Everett, an ex-SAS soldier who was to stand trial on a number charges, including armed robbery and drug smuggling and cultivation, was found missing during a routine check by police. Mr Everett —'

I flicked it off after that. It was being investigated as an abduction and that was all that mattered. I didn't reckon I was so clever that I'd fool everyone but that didn't matter. Until they could prove otherwise, my mum and Mary's homes were safe. I didn't want to dwell on the drama I'd created either: what was done was done, and I needed to stay switched on.

I got dressed in my camouflage gear, including a hat and a face veil. If someone did spot me, they would more than likely think it was another SAS trooper going about his business. Scouting round for a more suitable LUP than the last night's thicket, I soon found a good position on the side of a low hill. It was covered by very thick scrub and I could see plenty of barbed wire and other nasty obstacles surrounding it: these would make any bushwalker take a detour around.

I dug a little ledge into the side of the hill so I would have a sleeping pad and somewhere to store my gear. Then I strung up the camouflaged shelter over it and covered it with natural vegetation, leaving about 6 inches between the ground and the shelter for vision and air circulation. Next, I dug a small latrine pit and constructed a camouflaged lid.

Once satisfied with the LUP, I worked out what supplies I'd need from the cache to get through the next couple of weeks. I wanted to make the fewest trips back to it as possible so the vegetation wouldn't get trampled down around the hide. Keeping strict track discipline also meant taking alternative routes in and out all the time so no paths led to the area. I did this by crawling about 50 metres through the low-hanging scrub before standing up and walking. The thick scrub really was a great security blanket; nobody would be able to come through it fast without making enough noise to warn me.

I raided my cache again, then explored the area for something that would serve as a water container; I needed something larger than the soft-drink bottle. I found an old plastic fire extinguisher lying amongst a pile of rubbish at the back of the firing butts. It held about 25 litres, which would last a couple of weeks at a pinch, and it would save me going out each night in search of water. On the walk back to my LUP that night I disturbed a couple of rabbits, and one got itself snagged in the chain-link fence. I took it back to the hide with me, where I tethered it for a couple of days before knocking it on the head and cooking it up.

Now that everything was set up, it was just a matter of sitting and waiting. I checked the news on the radio daily, and I was off the main bulletin within a matter of days, and I was sure it wouldn't be long before the public would forget about me and start worrying about their footy teams again. I still needed to give it a few weeks before I moved, until the police search died down, so it was just a matter of sitting, waiting and playing a game of patience. I did a lot of isometric exercises during the day and went for long walks along the beach late in the night when nobody was around. I even had a few swims but the water was pretty cold that time of year. It was a mundane time but the sleep, exercise and solitude did me good. I could feel my brain clearing after the battery-hen existence of detention.

The rifle range was running hot for the first fortnight; I suppose only a soldier would find that a comforting sound. The annual Queens Cup rifle competition was on and the extra firing added to the secure feeling as it made my LUP more of a no-go zone. There was the chance that I'd catch a stray round, I suppose, but I couldn't get all worked up over a one-in-a-million chance like that. I guess it would have been pretty ironic to have been hit and to have died out there, probably never to be discovered, although if my body was found with a bullet in it, it may even have been evidence of my abduction.

After a few weeks, I was getting confident about moving around undetected and started doing a few daytime excursions. I could hear thumping explosions and the rapid popping of small arms coming from the old CT kill house. I figured they must be either training for something big or having a VIP visit. I knew that a new multi-million dollar training facility had been built for the Counter Terrorism role, which was being expanded every year. I'd also heard that Prime Minister Bob Hawke was in Perth and put two and two together, figuring that he must be the guest of honour to open the new facility.

We often gave demonstrations to visiting VIPs when I was in

the CT team, especially to politicians, and we did our best to scare the pants off them with lots of loud explosions and fast, deadly-seeming action, just so they knew their tax dollars were being well spent. We made a little platform for them to stand on during the demonstrations and would often rig a small charge under it, timed to go off when we entered the kill house. This wasn't enough to harm anyone, but it'd make them jump a few feet in the air each and every time.

I crept up to a good vantage point on one of the scrub-covered dunes near the training complex, keeping myself well hidden. Using the detached telescopic sight from the cat gun as a viewing glass, I watched for most of the afternoon as the boys stormed the various mock-up buildings in the complex, all with live ammo and plenty of big bangs. Sure enough, after a few hours, I saw a convoy of long black cars enter the complex and the little grey-haired silver bodgie himself, our prime minister, step out of his limo. I'm sure he enjoyed the demonstration over the next hour as the boys did their best to impress him and his little entourage, but I wonder if he felt the hairs prickling on the back of his neck. The whole time he was in the crosshairs of Australia's most dangerous fugitive. Lucky for him I vote Labor.

The prime minister's visit was the highlight of my stay, but I curtailed my daytime excursions after that, except for one last visit to the nudist beach to remind myself that breasts did, in fact, still exist. I let five weeks elapse before I figured it was safe to move again. The plan was to get to Adelaide first and use that as a base to make some enquiries about the blokes Jim was involved with, then move on to Sydney and organise a new ID, before making a move out of the country. A few weeks' clear thinking in the sea air made me realise there was no going back and that there was nothing I could do to clear my name. The best thing for me and my family was if I got out of the country and started a new life. But before I did that, I had to find out if I was on anyone's hit list; in which case whoever it was would be on mine. They say the best form of defence is attack.

I had a decent backpack stored in the cache, as well as enough dehydrated food and vitamin tablets for at least three months, good civilian clothes, hair dye, footwear and a daypack. There were also maps of all the states in Australia and air, bus, ship and train timetables for most states in the country. I wouldn't be imposing myself on any of my truckie mates. I was sure the coppers would have even the most remote acquaintances of mine under some sort of observation, and even good blokes can't help themselves in blabbering eventually. I had to stay officially dead for the time being.

I stowed what was needed into my backpack and closed the cache for what would hopefully be the last time. I left the cat gun stowed there, packing a 9-millimetre SIG Sauer pistol with a couple of boxes of rounds into my daypack instead. I would have preferred to travel without the pistol, but I still wasn't sure who was gunning for me and I figured a bit of last-ditch protection wouldn't go astray until I'd sorted everything out.

The night before leaving I went for a final clean-up and to dye my eyebrows and hair black. I'd done this up in Thailand while travelling and it made me look completely different; nobody would recognise me at a glance. The next day I returned the hide to its natural state – virtually undetectable. As night fell I gathered my kit and headed off across town.

My plan was to hop on an interstate freight train from the Forrestfield marshalling yards. I'd delivered and received freight from there when I was trucking, so I knew the layout of the place and had a rough idea of the security set-up. On Mondays and Tuesdays the yards were busy unloading freight and from Wednesday onwards they were loading east-bound wagons. I set out Saturday night so I had a couple of days up my sleeve to check the place out in more detail. Perth airport was right next door to the marshalling yards, so my plan was to play the penniless English backpacker waiting for his flight home and sleeping rough in the meantime. If anyone asked any questions, my Pommie accent would pass casual inspection. There is also a lot of swamp around the airport that is off limits to the general public and would make for a perfect LUP for a few days.

Despite the training I'd been doing in Swanbourne, I still found the 40-kilometre cross-town stomp with my fully loaded pack murder on the legs. Scouting around the bush near the airport, I found a small island in the middle of a swamp that was surrounded by paperbark trees where I could set up my LUP. I was a bit worried that, being a Sunday, kids might come and play on the island, but I had it to myself all day.

On Monday night I went over to the marshalling yard to scout around and was pretty discouraged. They must have caught a lot of stowaways boarding freight cars in this area, or else thieves stealing things, because the area was lit up like the fourth of July – too hot for me. I headed down to the unloading yard where it was much quieter. I noticed the security guard doing his rounds here at about the same time on successive nights and it wasn't as brightly floodlit as the marshalling yard, so there were plenty of places to hide. I decided to board a car here before it went to the marshalling yard and conceal myself well while it was being loaded. I'd also noticed that the workers in the main marshalling yard had been checking the inside of the open freight wagons, so I figured I had to somehow deposit myself amongst the freight to be safely concealed.

I spied some circus rides that were going back east on flat-bed rail wagons after being in Perth for the Royal Agricultural Show. The octopus ride had plenty of hidey holes and I checked its dispatch card to verify it was going to Adelaide. The only problem with my hide was its open top exposed me to overhead inspection. I found some scrap tarpaulin that, at a glance, would just look like an equipment cover. I figured I'd only have to pass a cursory look as most people are that busy they don't have the time to look under every piece of canvas lashed to freight.

I had no idea how long I'd be stuck in the wagon in the marshalling yards, so I needed plenty of water and something to shit in without the stink attracting too much attention. On the way back to my hide I managed to find myself a plastic 20-litre water drum and an old metal bucket that would make do for a toilet. The place was a scavenger's paradise: I also found a stack of magazines to while away the hours and an old shovel I could use to bury some of my gear. I had to move quickly to get stowed on board, though, as there weren't any departure times on the freight labels.

The following evening I started moving my gear down to the freight terminal in stages since there was too much to carry all at once. I'd just dumped the water container, bucket and shovel and was jogging back for my backpack when I saw a line of torches moving along the fence. I stood in cover and watched them move inevitably closer to my gear; they were obviously following my tracks, which were pretty clear in the sand. I had to think fast and I realised that the fact they were yet to discover the backpack still gave me a slim hope of talking my way out of being a stowaway. Just as the two blokes at the end of the line stumbled across the bucket, water container and shovel I stepped up to them out of the dark and said, 'G'day. You blokes looking for me?'

'Hey! Over here!' one of them shouted to the rest before giving me the obligatory bright light in the eyes. Pretty soon there was a crowd of them all doing the same thing with their torches. Obviously, they were on the lookout for a potential stowaway or thief.

'What are you hanging around here for, mate?' one of them asked, pointing to the bucket and shovel. 'And what's the gear for?'

'Ah, well, I've got nowhere to stay so I'm living in the swamp over there . . . and the farmer down the road . . . whose place I normally get my water from . . . well, his dog bit me you see . . . so I'm looking for a tap over here somewhere.'

'So why'd you leave the bucket and shovel there?'

'Well, there's this potato patch over the road that I wanted to raid and I was looking for a hole in the fence to get over to it.' I was adlibbing furiously and hoping they wouldn't ask any more questions.

'Okay, mate, if we catch you trespassing again, we'll call the cops. Follow us down to this gate and you can walk down the road.'

I was amazed that they believed my story but I guess the bucket and shovel must have thrown them slightly. If they'd seen the backpack, I'm sure they would have called the cops. I hung off in the shadows for a while and watched the posse depart. After a few hours, I climbed back over the fence and made my way to my ride. After walking back to collect the water container, bucket and shovel and then the pack, I'd covered more than 15 kilometres. Before I could settle into my hide, I had to check for surveillance. The bonus of faking my abduction was that I wasn't the subject of a major nationwide manhunt, so my only real concern was the regular security patrol and he came in a car that I could see from miles away. The coast was clear for me to get on board.

The sun was just rising, so after viewing my little hide on one of the octopus arms from a few different angles to make sure it was concealed, I crawled in and waited. For the next ten hours I sat there as people walked and drove past within metres of me. At around four in the afternoon, a big bang and a tremor ran through the wagon as the shunting locomotive was hitched up. Then we started to roll.

I had a tiny peephole to look through at the outside world and as the train rolled past TNT's car carrying depot, I saw Frank and Mick, two of my trucking mates, standing next to their rigs, shooting the breeze. I would have waved and said g'day but I was supposed to be dead.

The train got stuck in the marshalling yards for another few hours while blokes walked the length of the train ticking items off the manifest and checking the couplings. Finally, at about 8:30 p.m., another locomotive was hooked up and we clanked out of the yards, slowly building up speed as we hit the open track. I was finally on my way. As the train picked up speed, the wind started buffeting the canvas shelter and the volume of the noise steadily increased. I could see us climb the Darling Scarp out of the city and begin the steady climb up the Avon Valley. I was positioned roughly in the centre of the train, so I allowed myself a brief respite from my hide and stood on the tray, letting the wind buffet me. I think they call it train surfing. As every kilometre put Perth further behind me, I could feel a growing excitement about being free.

The trip across took a couple of days. It was uncomfortable rocking back and forth in the heat and dust in my octopus arm, but I only ventured out at night to empty the bucket. I made sure to empty this between the cars so that there would be no telltale brown stain down the side of the car. Even though I was nearly half a kilometre back from the locomotive, if I stuck my head out at the wrong time I would have been seen; this was the longest stretch of straight railway in the world. The flat, arid Nullabor plain was the last place I wanted to try to run and hide in if I were spotted.

The train entered the main marshalling yard in Adelaide at about four in the afternoon. Sure enough, we passed under an overhead container lifter and there was a guy in there staring right at my canvas, so my knowledge of rail freight saved me there. There was no panic, though, as he didn't give it more than a bored passing glance. There was no waiting around at this end of the line and within about ten minutes they were unchaining the semitrailer from the flat bed. Next thing, the truck started and we went bumping off the wagon and parked in a holding yard. With luck, the owners would be there so that they'd drive the truck out of the yard and I could debus at a truck stop. But the truck didn't move off. I was parked in the middle of a huge marshalling yard that was dispatching trains to Alice Springs, Perth, Melbourne, Sydney and Brisbane. There was a tremendous amount of activity going on and I felt very conspicuous and vulnerable; all I could do was to pray for night to fall quickly.

The security at Adelaide was much more professional than Perth and they didn't stick to a set pattern of patrolling. To make things worse the truck was parked next to the administration offices and workers' canteen. To add to the challenge, I could see that I would have to cross a number of railway lines and another good 100 metres to the fence over open flat ground. I wouldn't be moving too fast with my 50-kilogram backpack, so I was going to have to choose the moment carefully. All my essential items were in the small daypack and nothing in the big pack could be traced back to WA, so in the event of being spotted I could just dump the big load and run. None of the staff here looked less than six-months pregnant, blokes included, so I fancied myself in a footrace.

It was like waiting for a break in the traffic that never comes. I stayed on edge for hours but no time window of more than a minute or two came. People were coming and going from the canteen constantly and that bloody efficient security guard was giving me the shits with his zipping all over the place. Where's a fat and lazy security guard when you need one? It was getting on to midnight when I decided to risk a dash anyway. My nervous stomach required me to use the bucket one more time, so I felt sorry for the poor roadie who had to unpack 'The Octopus' in Adelaide.

I dropped my pack under the semi and followed it down, then crawled up onto the axles until I was ready, just in case someone took a look under the trailer. It wasn't long before I heard the shunting locos pulling up near the crib rooms and saw the drivers head in for a feed. I gave them about fifteen minutes to get settled in, then started to make my move.

I'd just shouldered my pack when the bloody security guard's car came past again. He drove around at such high speed that every time he came my way I thought he was on to me. I bailed straight back under the trailer, my heart tripping at a million miles an hour. Just as he approached the truck, he threw a U-turn and charged off into the night in the opposite direction. I wasn't waiting this time; I crawled out from under the trailer and hobbled off as quickly as my little legs could carry me.

Although the shunting locomotives were parked, their huge diesel engines were left running, so I didn't need to worry about making a noise. I had to crawl and then push the pack under a row of wagons. I prayed that the loco didn't kick into gear and cut me in half. I had just heaved myself through the last one and shouldered the pack when I saw the security car doing another Starsky and Hutch dash towards the crib hut again. I just put my head down and shuffled as fast as I could with my load. It was like that dream where you run as fast as you can but can't seem to move, and I was expecting a shout of 'STOP!' or to hear the security car accelerating towards me.

I made it to the fence without being seen and found a shadowy section to lie down in, snuggling in at the fence's base. I used the pliers from my survival pack to cut a small slit along the bottom of the wire and wriggled through. Once on the other side, I covered the slit with grass and twigs, and then made for a highway overpass that was a few hundred metres away. This little assault course scramble had been going for a while now and my lungs and legs were burning from the effort. The overpass had an alcove underneath and I scrambled up into the darkness a relieved man.

LIFE'S TOUGH ON THE RUN

The girl was obviously terrified as she stood with her toes on the edge of the vertical cliff face.

'No, no. I can't do it,' she said in an appealing Liverpudlian accent as her friends egged her on. They were a hard-partying little squad of English backpackers, all aged twenty-two or younger.

'Go on, Georgie, yer pillock. Yer big strong man there'll help.'

I knelt down next to her and put my hand on the small of her back. She had on tight denim shorts and a little singlet that exposed her midriff so I got a bit distracted for a second. That's got to be one of my favourite parts of a woman's body, the way the two buttocks curve like a delicate sine wave into the small of the back. I rubbed my hand up and down there reassuringly and spoke as soothingly as I could.

'Now, Georgina, I want you to look at me.'

She turned and looked at me with these huge, trusting blue eyes. She had a little overbite and slightly bucked teeth but was as cute as they come.

'You're at the most difficult bit right now. Every step you take from here will make it easier. Just let out a little bit of rope and lean out over the edge.'

Lean out over the edge of a cliff and your body will instinctively want to do the only sane thing – lean back. One of the hardest things to teach people in abseiling is to keep leaning out as it's the weight of their body pushing into the cliff face that makes their feet stick to the edge. Lean back at the wrong moment and the feet slip, leaving a very terrified client pinned upside-down at the top of the cliff face and the rest of the paying customers afraid to take their turn. The trick is baby steps: a little bit of rope, a little step and they are on their way.

Women are much more fun to teach because they aren't as reluctant to say they're scared; whereas men often will just freeze up as they try to fight the fear. The cute little Pommie backpacker was a case in point; she took hold of herself mentally and her features became set with determination. She let out some rope and started leaning forward, breathing hard to stay in control of the trembling in her arms and legs. Soon she was leaning out at just over 45 degrees with her pert little boobs almost falling out of her singlet. There is enormous pressure coming through the harness at this point and it's very hard to take a step.

'That's good, Georgie. Good girl. Now rock to the side slightly and put a bit more weight on your right foot. Okay, now take a small step with your left. Good, now rock your weight onto the left and take a small step with the right. Excellent. Okay, a bit more rope. Good, feeling more comfortable now?'

'Yes,' she peeped.

Once they are over the edge they start to hang in the harness and feel a little more secure. Despite the fact they are staring face down at a 40-metre drop, they start to enjoy it. From there it is just a matter of playing the rope through the friction device and walking down. I could hear her giving little squeals of delight all the way to the bottom.

Once on the ground, she staggered around, experiencing that almost-orgasmic rush of adrenalin that seems to clean every negative sensation right out of your body. She gazed back up the cliff face at me with a look that said she held me personally responsible and, if I were to give her the opportunity, she would like to repay me later on that night. I smiled back; something told me they were not the last delighted little squeals I'd be hearing from her.

Jeez, life on the run is tough, I thought to myself.

How I'd ended up as a rap-jumping instructor in tropical north Queensland while on the run was one of those little twists of fate that my life seems to turn on. I'd been in Adelaide for a few days after hopping the train across the Nullabor, blending in with the crowd as just another slightly shabby backpacker. I'd got my eyebrows and hair professionally dyed brown and ordered brown contact lenses to match. This, coupled with my long hair, made me almost unrecognisable as I'd always been a blue-eyed blond. I paid my yearly subscription to the nearest Youth Hostels of Australia office and had a photo ID made up as Chris Roberts – my old friend the Regiment CO's name. I figured I'd tell everyone my nickname was 'Rock' just for a laugh. The ID was my ticket to cheap accommodation around the country and would also pass any cursory checks by the law.

My second night in Adelaide and I was having a counter meal at a pub while watching the TV news when a familiar face filled the screen with his boof-head. It was Macka, one of my mates from the Regiment. He'd set up the rap-jumping business after he left and it had been going gangbusters. He was in Adelaide giving demonstrations as part of a state-wide tourist promotion. As it was the perfect novelty item to show at the end of a news bulletin, the promotion took care of itself.

I recognised the logo of the hotel chain they were demonstrating from and had a strong impulse to go and catch up with him. He's a top bloke, and I was interested to see how he was making a go of the business. It was a bit of a deviation from my plan to stay out of contact, but I was encouraged by the absolute lack of any news reporting on my story over this way. SAS blokes are used to working on a 'need to know' basis anyway and I knew Macka wouldn't ask any questions, so I wouldn't be exposing him to any charges of aiding and abetting a fugitive. Bugger it, I thought. I'll go and say g'day.

I grabbed the daypack from my hostel room and headed down to the hotel in Glenelg. I phoned his room from the lobby; he answered in his usual gruff manner.

'Macka here.'

'G'day, Macka. It's Dave.'

He knew who it was straightaway. We hadn't seen each other for a few years, but Macka wasn't big on sentiment.

'Yeah, mate. What can I do you for?'

'Listen, can you meet me out the front at the end of the pier in about five minutes. I don't want to talk on the phone.'

'Will do.' And he hung up.

I watched him walk to the end of the pier and look around. He knew I'd be watching him for a couple of minutes so he wasn't fazed when I wasn't there. He didn't recognise me when I walked up to him, which showed how dependent most people's memories were on me being blond and blue eyed. I told him I was on the run from a messy divorce and needed to lay low for a while, and he immediately offered me a job and somewhere to stay. He didn't bat an eye when I asked him to call me Chris Roberts; he didn't even ask why. This might seem strange to most people but in the Regiment this 'what you don't know can't be used against you' mindset is standard. He was unaware of my recent troubles anyway as he'd cut most of his ties with the Regiment in order to make a fresh start in Queensland.

When he took me back up to his hotel room to introduce me to the rest of the team my eyes nearly fell out of my head: here were more gorgeous half-dressed women than I'd ever seen in one place, and they outnumbered the blokes by at least two to one.

'Someone call for reinforcements?'

The blokes on his rap-jumping team were all fit, tanned and dressed in uniform – company T-shirt with cargo pants. Having been on TV the night before, they'd attracted a few groupies and I reckoned Macka didn't need to pay these blokes because the look on their faces told me they'd have done it for free.

Macka had taken something simple and made it fun. Abseiling and rappelling are just sliding down ropes. The rope travels through a friction device like a figure eight. The pressure on the friction device controls the speed of your descent. We sometimes did forward rappelling in the Regiment, with the figure eight at the back of the harness, so we could face down towards the target as we descended. Rap-jumping was forward rappelling with a couple of metres of slack in the rope at the top. You'd leap face-first into space, free fall for a metre or ten and then brake the fall by putting pressure on the rope. As with all rappelling, the backup system is someone on the ground who can pull as hard on the rope as you can, so they can brake the descent if you forget or faint or whatever. It looks totally out of control, but it's pretty safe.

Macka was one of the first entrepreneurs to recognise the potential of the backpacker market. The tourism industry in the eighties dismissed them as skinflints, but people like Macka saw that they had money to spend; they just wanted to spend it on having fun instead of stuffy, overpriced hotel rooms. The team all had black shirts with 'RAP JUMPING' in white letters across the front and back with the company's motif. The T-shirt was a badge of courage and not only did Macka make a killing by selling them, but he also got his business promoted everywhere the T-shirts went.

I was introduced as one of Macka's old crew, so the next day I had to perform. I hadn't rappelled for years but it would be a major loss of face if I stuffed up. There is a bit of a sensitive touch required once you are free falling because if you apply the brake too hard, the sudden stop will cause you to smack into the wall like a pendulum. I figured the best way around this was to not apply my brake at all and just leave it up to the bloke on the ground, since he'd be pulling the rope away from the wall. On my first jump I left about ten metres of rope as slack, and I can still see my brake man's eyes – as wide as dinner plates – as I hurtled towards him before he pulled down hard on the rope, stopping me well above the ground. They probably all thought I was crazy at first, but I was soon one of the boys.

The rap-jumping team packed up and headed for Queensland the next day and I arranged to meet up with Macka in Magnetic Island in a few weeks. His plan was to put me in charge of his operation there. I organised a discount bus trip to Sydney with my YHA card and felt quite comfortable travelling openly as a young backpacker. I didn't need to isolate myself and the more I conversed with other travellers, the more detail I was able to add to my backup story. Although I was in my late twenties, I looked a fair bit younger so I blended in easily. It would have hardly mattered if I hadn't anyway, as young people travelling independently tend to prize individuality, and a few eccentricities aren't noticed. It was quite a relaxing trip.

I checked into the main youth hostel in Glebe after arriving in Sydney. Sharing a dorm room with eight other guys made me a bit nervous about my gear, so I kept my run cash and ID in a money belt that went everywhere with me, including the shower. My daypack had the pistol (which had been disassembled and stored in a tin box in case anyone glanced inside the pack), camouflage paint, a change of clothes and a couple of days' worth of dried food in case I needed to do a runner. I never left the daypack unguarded but figured that anyone who wanted to steal out of the large pack could help themselves. Youth hostels were pretty honest places in those days anyway, and I didn't lose anything.

While I was in Sydney, I made contact with a couple of people. I had to be extremely careful as the wrong word in the wrong ear would alert the cops that I was still around, which would mean the loss of Mum's and Mary's houses and would probably trigger a nationwide manhunt. Eventually, I got the story about how I ended up in the shit, and it was as I suspected. A couple of blokes who barely knew me had dropped my name to the police to throw off attention from themselves. When they found out I was ex-Regiment they shat themselves and had been slinking around, wondering if

I was coming for them; while at the same time I was trying to find out if they were coming for me. As what was done was done, there was no value in getting revenge so I passed on the word that all was square. I got on the plane for Queensland.

I hadn't stepped off a plane into a blast of tropical heat for a while, so arriving in Townsville a few days later was a nice reminder of my other travels. The place looked as barren as it had six years ago when I was there as a soldier. After catching a bus into town, it was a quick trip across Cleveland Bay to Magnetic Island on a sleek catamaran ferry.

The rap-jumping base was set up in a house in Arcadia, one of the small seaside villages on the island. Given that my last experience in management was with a company of Karen soldiers, I think it's fair to say the motley collection of European travellers who Macka had trained as instructors got a bit of a shock when I arrived. They were living on takeaway food, so the first changes were to organise a cooking roster and to purchase a large wok and gas burner. We planted a vegetable garden and I organised regular diving and bush-foraging expeditions to supplement our diet with fresh meat. Physical-training sessions were run every weekday morning, and the team was up at the crack of dawn, the coolest time in the tropics, for an hour of running or swimming.

The team vehicles used a lot of fuel, and I began ordering it from the mainland in 200-litre drums, which cut the fuel bill by a third. I cut the plugs off the air-conditioning units to lower the power bills and got into the habit of unplugging the telephone whenever I left and taking it with me so the team couldn't run up big phone bills calling home. I knew it wasn't going to make me too popular, but I wasn't there to make friends. Instead of slacking off between rap-jumping trips, we visited as many hostels as would allow us to hold demonstrations. The extra marketing effort soon had us booked solid and we were turning away customers. With the extra business and lower costs, profits soon soared and Macka was very pleased.

The team enjoyed our forays into the bush to collect food and I imparted a few survival skills while we were out there. The trips also came in handy for me as I was able to set up a couple of survival caches and plan a few escape routes in case things went to mud again. I noticed that some of the team like to smoke marijuana from time to time and I soon put a stop to that as well. Of course, I didn't want any excuse for the law to pay us a visit, but putting paid to the pot wasn't just for selfish reasons: our safety standards had to be above reproach. Stoned instructors were dangerous, which was unsafe for customers, bad for our reputation and consequently bad for business.

We were open for business seven days a week and it was a pretty punishing routine. After an hour of PT, followed by breakfast, we would run through a thorough safety check on all of the equipment. Then we'd load up the vehicles with the gear and drive to all the backpacker hostels to pick up our customers for the day, before holding a briefing for the whole group at the last pick-up point.

The cliffs we used were a 1-kilometre climb through the scrub and it took about half an hour before we would have the whole group in place ready to start the morning's fun. We'd start with the small cliffs and progress to the large overhangs. By the time we dropped the last tired but happy punter back at their accommodation it would be time for lunch and a long siesta. In the late afternoon we'd go diving, fishing or foraging in the bush before cooking dinner. After dinner, it was back out to the hostels for promotional activities and to party with the people we'd been with that day. Generally we'd hit the sack about midnight, sometimes alone, sometimes not. We rotated the one much-needed day off per week between us.

After a couple of months, Macka asked me to join him up in Cairns. The jump site there was the magnificent Barron Gorge, which was featured in the film *Sniper*. While I was there we took a couple of *Sports Illustrated* journalists through the ropes so they would give us a plug in their magazine. I managed to fade into the background whenever photos were taken, just in case.

Macka showed me a great time over the next few weeks; we did a tour of the Great Barrier Reef and a few scuba-diving trips. I could have lost myself in this sort of thing for a few years, but I reckoned I'd get found out eventually. I decided to head down to Sydney to organise a better ID and start thinking about getting out of the country. Macka and I travelled down together as he had a plan to expand into the massive Sydney backpacker market and needed to scout a few locations on Sydney Harbour and in the Blue Mountains.

My contacts in Sydney were able to arrange a completely clean false passport that would stand up to all the normal customs and immigration scrutiny. It took quite a bit of running around, including a trip to Canberra, to set up. Once this had been established, I needed to wait at least three weeks for it to be cross-checked by an independent source to make absolutely sure it would pass as legitimate.

So, with a few weeks up my sleeve before I'd be disappearing completely, I decided to head back up to Queensland with Macka.

In Townsville I had the choice of heading up to the main base in Cairns or back across to Magnetic Island. I opted for Maggie Island because it was closer and I figured I'd be the most use to Macka over there. It was a simple choice that would make a massive difference to the rest of my life.

I was keen to see if the Maggie Island crew had held up their standards or slackened off. One of the boys, Cain, picked me up at the ferry and told me about a new crew member, Melissa, who they had hired while I was gone.

'She'll be good for the team, I reckon,' said Cain. 'She's enthusiastic and a really hard worker.'

Yeah, right. When I met Melissa I took one look at her and knew she hadn't been hired for her ability or experience. She was gorgeous and had spectacular tits. Cain had fallen head over heels in lust. Still, she seemed like a nice kid and I didn't mind having a bit of extra eye-candy around the place for a few weeks. I was well out of party mode myself and had begun to mentally switch on for my overseas travel, but I couldn't begrudge the boys a bit of fun.

Unfortunately, no one had thought to advise Melissa of our strict no-drugs policy and that morning she had bought a small bag of dope from an undercover copper. The local drug squad had been working the island in the lead-up to Christmas, hoping to stem the flow of party drugs that seemed to follow the tide of backpackers onto the island at that time of year.

My normal practice following a trip away was to take the Sig Sauer 9-millimetre out of my daypack and stash it in my survival cache up in the hills. But I was tired from the trip and watching Melissa leaning over the wok in a bikini top, cooking our evening meal, seemed to hypnotise me slightly; the steam from the wok had created a lustrous sheen on her cleavage. I decided to head up into the bush after dinner. I'd just finished my shower, eaten Melissa's delicious stir-fry and flopped on the lounge in a sarong when I heard crunching gravel on the driveway. I looked out the door and saw shadows hurrying down the driveway.

Shit, I thought. *It's the cops. How the hell did they find me here?*

I made a half-lunge for the front door but had no time as three coppers burst in. At the same time others came in the back way. My mind raced over the last few weeks, trying to find where I had slipped up. After a couple of seconds of panic, I settled down. These blokes had hardly kicked the door down and their guns weren't drawn; it slowly dawned on me that they were here for someone else.

'Where's Melissa?' one of the coppers asked.

They had a search warrant for drugs, which one of them gave to me, but I refused to take it from him saying that I didn't own the house. He then tried giving it to Cain, who said the same thing, so the copper just threw it on the floor. They asked Melissa to show them her room and she led them out the back to the shed she was staying in. Six of the coppers followed her out so they either thought she was a dangerous criminal who might need restraining or they were just as hypnotised as the rest of us by the sight of those boobs straining that little bikini top. It was a good distraction and it tipped the odds in my favour.

Two other coppers took one of the other young blokes, Jamie, into his room for a search, which left the guy who had tried to serve the warrant with Cain and I in the lounge. Talking to the copper gave me the excuse to stand up and put myself in a better position to make a hasty exit. My daypack was sitting on a chair in the middle of the room. It may as well have had a 'please search me first' sign written on it, and I knew I'd be stuffed the moment they found the pistol. I contemplated making a grab for the pack before I ran; it would have been a smart move if I'd been able to pull it off. The coppers would have assumed I'd done a runner with a bag full of drugs, which would have been preferable to them finding the Sig Sauer.

The cop made my decision for me as he made a beeline for the daypack. I made a couple of slow, casual moves towards the door. He was a friendly bloke and had probably heard about our operation being fairly clean so he didn't have the beady-eyed glare of someone expecting to find criminal activity. But his eyes bulged when he looked inside the pack and fished out the pistol.

'Who the bloody hell owns this?' he almost shouted at us both.

'Dunno,' we both said in unison.

He gave us his best hard stare, then looked back in the pack. That was it, I was gone like the wind. Out the front door, over the side fence and up into the jungle. I ran like a maniac, knees and arms pumping high like those blokes on *Chariots of Fire*, only I was wearing a sarong.

No bullets cracked past me, no sound of drumming feet, no shouting voices, all of which usually accompanies a posse chasing you. Soon I was at the base of the hills and deep into the dark jungle where no one could follow me.

I heard later that the cop wasn't too worried about me taking off. A concealed pistol in a bag was hardly big news in redneck Queensland, after all. He simply asked Cain where I'd gone and continued the search. But I knew it would only be a matter of time before they would trace the pistol by its serial number back to WA. Then they'd fax a copy of my YHA card to the WA police and someone would be able to identify me. I was really on the run now. There'd be a nationwide manhunt and heaps of media attention, and I could forget skipping the country for the time being. Plus, my mum and sister would lose their houses. My world had turned to shit in a matter of seconds, all because I was too lazy to stash my pistol before relaxing.

There was no time to dwell on that just yet. My immediate concern was to secure water for the rest of the night and to find somewhere to lay-up. In the yard of an old house on the edge of the bushland I found some empty 2-litre plastic soft-drink bottles. I filled these up with water and trotted back into the bush. Cold was not a problem, but I was being eaten alive by mosquitoes. Mangrove swamps were nearby, so I covered myself in foul-smelling mud, which kept the bugs away. I found myself a shelter in amongst some big boulders up in the hills, built a bit of a nest to lie down on, curled up and went to sleep.

The next day was stinking hot and I was glad I'd sourced the water. It was the start of the march-fly season and they were swarming all around me. These bastards are as big as blowflies and try to drill you with a proboscis that feels as thick as a safety pin – they give the worst bite I've had from any insect. I spent the day killing them by the hundreds, while watching the back of the house. There were no cops around and my backpack had been put out on the back verandah.

Towards dusk I set out to find my cache and it took a while. It was steep terrain strewn with large boulders and densely covered with vegetation. It was good country to go to ground in and I reckon

I could have hidden out there for years. I found my buried shovel first, then went and uncovered the cache. I had camouflaged clothing, boots, binoculars, dehydrated tucker, hammock, water purifiers, water bottles, vitamin tablets and enough equipment to keep me going for a few months. It was good to get some clothes back over my insect-ravaged skin.

After concealing the cache, I moved back over to my spot overlooking the house and lined up a good approach route while I waited for the sun to set. There were still no cops about and everyone else seemed to be out, probably doing that night's promotional visits. It took about an hour to stalk up to the house, watch it for a while, and then do a complete circuit of it before I crawled up and retrieved the pack from the verandah. I took a 10-kilogram dumbbell as well. My plan wasn't to run just yet, since I was sure the coppers would be watching every highway, ferry terminal and airport for me. The best thing was to lie low for a while before moving, just as I had in Perth. The dumbbell was to help me keep fit while I waited.

The next day I looked for a good LUP. Magnetic is an old volcano so there are plenty of caves, but I avoided them because they only had one entry. I found a large overhang under a massive shelf of steep rock. A small 10-metre-high rock face had to be climbed to reach the opening, so there was no chance of someone stumbling onto it or being able to sneak up without me hearing them first. A number of large vertical fissures at the rear of the overhang gave me different escape route options and there was enough room to stand, do my exercises and lay out my kit comfortably.

Nobody came into the bush much on the island anyway. The tourists were barely fit enough to stagger from the beach to their bungalows in the heat and the locals didn't give a stuff about the bush. Even so, I was careful not to leave any signs of my presence on the rock and kept good track discipline around the base of the little cliff. The overhang gave me sweeping views of Arcadia and the shipping channel over to Cape Cleveland. It was spectacular scenery with plenty of passing boats to keep me entertained.

I estimated it would take the wheels of justice two days to spit out my identity and I was spot on. On Wednesday, after the team had headed off to work, a bunch of unmarked police cars pulled up to the backyard. The plain-clothed cops broke into the house and set to work – searching and dusting for fingerprints. I recognised one of the cops from Perth. He was probably thanking me for scoring him the free trip to Queensland to the envy of all his Perth mates. I wondered how he'd feel when he found his name on the list in my bag.

Within the next twenty-four hours, news of my appearance must have hit the airwaves, as suddenly there was a swarm of TV helicopters circling the island, and film crews with their presenters doing stand-ups in front of the house. At one stage the cameras were pointed straight at me as they did a pan of the surrounding hills. The news on the radio that night confirmed that I had been 'working in the business of an SAS colleague' while on the run. So, there was no doubt that I'd landed Macka in the shit and he would have some explaining to do. He wasn't charged with anything in the end, which was a relief to me.

I spent a couple of weeks on my little ledge, waiting for the media and police circus to move on, before planning my next move. Swimming to the mainland wasn't a great idea. It was across a 10-kilometre channel filled with all sorts of unfriendly marine life, like bull sharks, crocodiles and deadly box jellyfish. Besides that,

I reasoned that the coppers would be expecting me to run to the mainland, and they'd be watching every road, rail and air option for a while.

A few weeks back I'd been about to catch the ferry from the mainland when an old hippie offered to sell me his boat for twenty bucks. It was a little flat-bottomed dinghy that wasn't much use for anything besides cruising up tidal creeks, but I figured at the time that it would make a good diving platform for catching dinner. It was a bit underpriced – I reckoned the old fella's head was still back in 1970 – and I planned to sell it on to a backpacker for a hundred or so whenever I booted off. I had left it on the mainland for a few days before motoring it over to the island one clear day. I had it stashed on the beach about a kilometre away from the backpackers. Now it would be my means of escape.

I planned to motor a long way south, in the shelter of the Great Barrier Reef, before moving overland again. Gladstone was the farthest town south I could get to before I'd be exposed to the full swells of the Pacific and smashed to pieces in my small boat. That was more than 1000 kilometres away and would put me well outside the police's search radius.

It took another week to collect the fuel I needed by siphoning off small amounts from different vehicles, so as not to arouse any suspicion amongst the locals. Mixing this with engine oil, I soon had 100 litres of two-stroke that I could store in 20-litre drums that I'd scavenged from the local rubbish dump. I'd also found an old set of oars there. I used an old wheelbarrow to transport these, along with all the other gear I'd need for a trip, down to a cache that I'd set up in the bush near a local backpackers. I took the wheelbarrow with me on the trip, as it would be a good way to quickly get my gear off the beach, up into the bush and out of sight when I laid-up each day.

My gear also included a stinger suit – a one-piece Lycra wetsuit that I could use for diving and swimming amongst the deadly box jellyfish. It also provided good all-over sun protection. I had a mask, snorkel, swim fins, a hand spear and some fishing line so I could supplement my diet with fish. I took a 40-litre drum of water, as well as a tarp that could be rigged to catch water when it rained. I already had cooking gear and a decent supply of dried food from my existing cache, and had added to this by snaring a few rock wallabies and drying their meat in strips, as well as collecting a good pile of new-season mangoes. I was ready to go.

I didn't take the big items like the tarp and oars until the night of departure for obvious reasons. That night I had to put in a big effort, collecting them in the wheelbarrow and taking them down to the backpackers cache, before running over to collect the dinghy. I rowed it out through the surf before trying to start the outboard. After a bit of anxiety on my part, it kicked on the third pull and I was away.

I noticed that the dinghy didn't have a bung for its drainage hole at the stern, so I carved a piece of soft wood to fit. Once parked in front of my cache, I had to race the tide to load the gear. Each time I came back out with an armful, I had to push the boat further out to avoid being stranded. By the time I'd grunted and puffed everything on board, the little dinghy was almost pushed down to the gunwales with 200 kilos' worth of gear. I lashed the wheelbarrow to the bow upside-down to serve as a wave deflector. It looked strange but it did the trick.

I strapped a watertight barrel, loaded with food, water and

a few other essentials, to my waist in case I was knocked overboard. I also wore the mask, wetsuit and swim fins while I was motoring at night for the same reason. It was 2 a.m. by the time I motored out into Cleveland Bay, using the faint shape of a mountain on the mainland as my navigation point.

The little flat-bottomed dinghy turned out to be a poor choice of craft. Water splashed over the sides at an alarming volume and bailing furiously with my small plastic bucket couldn't keep the water from gradually filling the boat. Normally this would be the time to remove the bung from the stern and let the speed of the boat naturally drain the water out, but the little outboard couldn't propel us fast enough. I was fighting a losing battle. Then the motor died and I was left wallowing in the swells, trying to figure out what was wrong with the motor. I soon found that it was just that the fuel line had come loose, which was easily fixed. As I got closer to the coast, the swells died down and I was able to keep the dinghy afloat by bailing continuously.

The horizon was just starting to colour as I got within clear view of the coast. By some fluke of navigation, I could see that the boat was aimed straight at a tiny beach no more than 15 metres in width. A couple of hundred metres either side of the beach was rock. There was a very narrow scrub-covered gully running back into the hills, which was perfect for my purposes. As soon as I skidded up the sand bank, I leapt out of the boat and started running gear up into the gully, flinging it into the bush to be sorted later. I had to get off this beach and leave no sign that I'd been on it before it got too light. Even though I was stuffed from being on the go all night, I had no time to rest. I was glad of the dumbbell training I'd been doing on my rock ledge, as it took a huge amount of strength to muscle the dinghy up on to the sand, pushing it end over end, before tipping it on its side and spearing it into the bush. Then, I grabbed a branch and swept the sand clean of any disturbance, walking backwards into my hide as I went. From there, I climbed halfway up the hill and found a spot to watch the beach; I took a moment to feel relieved that I was finally off the island. I slung my hammock and in it I had one of the deepest sleeps that I can ever remember.

I decided to stay put for a couple of days to rest up, plan the remainder of the trip and fill up on protein – fresh fish and mud-crabs were everywhere. I hiked up to the top of the hill one morning and could see Cape Bowling Green 50 k's to the south, which was my next navigation point. I'd found an old BP road map, which, while showing the shape of the coast, was hardly a navigation chart. I'd have to be on constant lookout for submerged reefs.

Just after sunset on the third day, I set out for what was to become an epic ten-day journey. Not being a seaman, I tended to hug the coastline, which was fine in the bays but got me in trouble as I rounded the headlands and nearly ran aground on reefs a couple of times. Each time I had to point the little dinghy out to sea and head out across swells that were often over 2 metres high, causing the hull to groan and creak as it twisted under the load. Having to motor away from the reefs also used extra fuel and, as I only had a couple of 20-litre tanks, I was forced to refuel from the drums while at sea, being careful not to get any seawater in the fuel. The little outboard also nearly seized a couple of times and I realised that I hadn't put enough oil in the fuel mix. Again, this was a scary experience: bobbing around in the middle of the ocean in the dark, trying to oil the cylinders to get the motor going again.

Once I was more than 100 kilometres south of Magnetic Island, I wasn't so worried about being seen in public. During my rest-ups, I'd tie the dinghy to a tree on the high-tide line and rig the canvas as a sun shade, while I fished and snoozed the day away; I'd even light a small camp fire. Zinc cream all over my face was good camouflage, along with a baseball cap and sunglasses. A few boats cruised past and waved, and I'd give them a lazy one-hander in return – just another Queenslander out enjoying all this perfection.

In the early part of the trip I saw some huge sharks. One hammerhead in particular was as long as the boat and cruised behind me for a few minutes. Even when I was furthest out to sea in the middle of the bays, I was less than 30 kilometres from shore. I knew that with the stinger suit, mask and fins I was within swimming range should the boat break down, but it would be a nervous half a day in the water with those big bastards around.

On the fourth day the onshore wind picked up and started whipping white-capped waves over the side of the boat. The hull started to fill up fast and there was no way I could keep up by bailing. I had no option but to head to shore, well short of where I had planned to stop, and hope to find a decent lay-up spot. It doesn't matter about the size of the boat – from a surf ski or sea kayak to an ocean liner – the difference between a river boat and an ocean-going vessel is the curved bottom of the hull, known as the dead rise. In flat water a dead rise just creates unnecessary drag, but on the ocean it allows the boat to ride over the waves while holding a straight track. Trying to pilot a flat-bottomed boat with a following sea is like pushing one of those demented shopping trolleys that won't go straight. I was madly screwing left and right while water washed over the stern.

After half an hour of this exhausting battle, I could see the white strip of sand looming. The waves were over head height, so just before I hit sand I swung the bow around to face out from the beach and into the waves. I'd just lifted the motor and was preparing to jump ashore when a wave caught the bow and swung the boat broadside to the waves. It was only the sheer weight of all my gear that kept it from flipping. Instead, the waves just washed over the side and sank the boat a few feet. Luckily the tide was on its way out so the boat didn't sink any deeper; with a rising tide I would have lost everything. I frantically pitched my survival barrel up the beach followed by the rest of the gear. By the time I was battling to unhook the motor, it looked like a shipwreck. Once again, I had to shuttle-run everything up into the scrub and out of sight in case some hero saw me and thought I needed rescuing.

By this time, the tide had receded and left the dinghy half full of sand. After half an hour of digging, I was able to tip it on its side. I then saw the explanation for the sudden, rapid water intake. There was a metre-long split in the hull. It was another miraculous escape in a week of miraculous escapes; the dinghy surely couldn't have sailed more than another few yards like that. There wasn't time to dwell on this, however, as I had to twist and drag the boat through the sand above the high-tide line again; I was actually getting stronger from this daily exercise and didn't find it too hard this time.

That night I was lucky enough to catch a young kangaroo by setting a wire snare in one of the holes they used to get under a farmer's fence. I threw it on the fire to cook in its own juices and had a delicious feed a few hours later. I took a long walk up the beach just after sunset and found a string of old foam fishing-net floats. I cut and shaped these so they could be jammed into the split in the hull, hopefully caulking it so I could travel a bit further south – at least far enough to find another boat.

The repair job held up well over the next couple of days as I motored over smooth, flat seas. Water did seep in through the crack, but I was able to maintain enough speed for the drainage system to work and, besides, using my plastic bucket to bail one-handed had become as second nature to me as swatting flies. I passed under the huge Abbot Point jetty and past the Port of Bowen. Ahead was Gloucester Island, another huge undersea mountain whose peak jutted out of the sea like a monstrous shark fin. On its west side I found another crystal-clear bay with a tiny white uninhabited beach. I stayed there for a few days, enjoying the fishing and diving in between recaulking the split in the hull.

I noticed the wind picking up after a couple of days and the radio forecast warned of 2-metre-plus swells, so I decided to make a 65-kilometre night run across open water to the Whitsunday passage, which is probably the most sheltered water inside the Great Barrier Reef. One hour into the trip, I was motoring along comfortably between Gloucester Island and the towering cliffs of George Point when the boat was suddenly picked up and smashed back down onto the water. I was flung off my little bench seat and nearly thrown overboard. For a few crazy minutes I had my back on the gunwale, one leg in the water and the other desperately feeling around, trying to find something to hook on to so I could tip myself back into the boat. All the while I was clinging to the rudder and trying to steer the boat away from the cliffs.

After what seemed like ages, I was clear of the boiling water and absolutely clueless as to what had happened. The dinghy was almost half full of water and the gunwales were only inches above the water line. Finally back in the boat, I bailed like a madman and twisted the throttle to maximum revs, hoping to get enough speed up to drain some water out of the bunghole. The way the water was pouring in made it obvious the caulking must have broken loose from the impact. The fuel tanks were floating about next to my legs, but at least their vent-holes were above water.

After twenty minutes, the water level dropped a few inches and for the first time I thought that I might be able to make it out of there with all my gear, instead of having to swim to shore. I was totally reliant on the engine. If it stopped, I would be swimming. I spied the lighthouse on George Point and knew it wouldn't be long before I entered the protection of the Whitsunday Passage.

I realised later that I'd run into a tidal surge between the two bays; billions of litres of water simultaneously converging from two different directions causing a maelstrom of white water. I decided to stay the hell away from any headlands in future. No more moving at night either.

Once I reached the calmer waters of the passage, I pulled ashore a couple of kilometres up the beach from a small holiday spot called Earlando, which housed quite a large caravan park. I found a small inlet surrounded by scrub which was an ideal lying-up place. As I slowed in preparation for beaching, the little dinghy sank in half a metre of water. It met its end gallantly. I quickly unloaded all the gear, set up camp and left the hull where it was. There would be plenty of time to pull it ashore once the tide had gone out. A quick scout around showed that all was clear. I wrapped myself in the canvas sheet and sank into what might as well have been a coma.

A few hours later I was woken by a deep, pulsating throb.

I scrambled to the mouth of the inlet just in time to see a massive pleasure boat that looked like a mini-Titanic. It was easily an 80-footer and probably burned a thousand bucks' worth of fuel per hour. It had teak decks, a tall superstructure and all kinds of radio antennae and satellite dishes. There were people relaxing on the back deck and sunbathing on the bow, and by the look of the number of fake boobs on display, the ratio of men to women on board was about seven to one. Just as it went past the inlet mouth, I heard the big engines throttle down and a crew member dressed all in white came out and lowered an anchor.

The aluminium-hulled tender trailing behind the cruiser would be my next boat. It was about 18 feet long and looked to be very sturdy. The only drawback was the huge effort it would take to roll it up a beach to hide, but the further south I moved the less critical that would become.

Just after midnight that night I crawled out to the inlet and waited for the partying on the boat to die down. By about 3 a.m. the music had gone quiet and they had stopped shouting, laughing and chasing each other around the deck. In my stinger suit, with mask and fins donned and a diver's knife strapped to my calf, I swam out under the cover of a convenient shower of rain. I cut the mooring line off the 18-footer just below the water line, then frayed it to look like it had come loose on its own. I let the tide help me swim the big tinny away from its mothership, before slipping aboard and rowing, as quietly as I could, back to the mouth of the inlet.

Moving my gear into the new boat was like stepping out of a Mini Minor and into a transit van. I was able to stack everything in and have it only flush with the gunwales. Even with the wheelbarrow lashed aboard I had room to move my feet around and sprawl out a bit. Once everything was stowed, I emptied the water out of the old dinghy and towed it out into the main channel. Once in deep water, I pulled the balsa-wood plug out of the bunghole in the stern. A bit of rocking from side to side and it sank suddenly, with a relieved plop.

Whether I had fooled the 18-footer's owners about it being stolen or not, the boat was going to be missed, and searched for, the next morning. I had to put as much distance between me and the settlement as possible. I took off into the seaward side of the grassy island and was soon smashing into huge swells, the land disappearing each time I went into the troughs. After an hour of punching into the waves, the outboard quit. I could hear the deep bass boom of the waves hitting the cliffs as I was being blown towards them. The small auxiliary motor on the boat barely made a difference, so I unshipped the oars and rowed as hard as I could, just holding my own against the swell. I didn't have the time to inspect the motor properly, but I could see that the fuel lines were okay. I assumed I had overheated it, just like in the other boat, and sure enough, when I tried it again half an hour later it roared to life.

An hour after that I was back on the lee side of the islands and belting along in almost dead-flat conditions. The famous tourist spots like Hayman Island, Daydream Island, Long Island and Shute Harbour all shot past in the dark. Then it was past the bottom end of Long Island and back into the open sea and big swells again. My new vessel handled the big seas remarkably well, and I realised that even without the tear in the hull my old little punt would have been sunk by now.

Late that afternoon, after a few hours' lay-up on a tidal flat just past Cape Conway, I cooked the motor yet again. I didn't rush this time and decided to give it a while to cool and take the opportunity to refuel the tank. A tiny swell rocked the boat just as I was tipping in the fuel and some of it splashed on my crotch. I barely gave it a second thought and just rinsed it off with some seawater. The motor fired again once it had cooled off and ten minutes later I was motoring along happily when my privates started burning as if they'd been rubbed with chilli powder. Talk about great balls of fire – within a few minutes I was in agony. I forgot about trying to make Port Mackay and desperately searched the coast for a place to land. I didn't dare look, but it felt like my balls were covered in hot blisters.

I spotted a bay with a small island at one end of it and headed for that. The coast looked deserted, although the line of palm trees looked suspiciously uniform. No chance for a closer look; I was almost blind with agony. There was a small beach about 30 metres long on the island. I ran the boat onto the beach, leapt out, stripped off the stinger suit and streaked naked into the water.

I was expecting instant relief but it took another ten minutes or so for the stinging to stop. I took a hesitant look down at my privates, fully expecting to be hideously scarred for life, only to find a slight redness in the skin. The pain was way out of proportion to the injury and it was a relief to be unharmed. I waded back to the boat and decided to have a brew. As the billy was boiling, I looked up to see a young family walking up the beach, with Mum covering her two daughters' faces with her hat. I wondered why she'd do that before I realised I was still naked, with my red balls swinging in the wind like a baboon's. I grabbed the stinger suit and wrapped it around me, apologising as they walked past, noses in the air. Once they were facing the other way, I dug into one of the barrels for some shorts, all the time wondering where the fuck the family had come from.

I had a closer look at the row of palm trees through my binoculars and, sure enough, I could see buildings and caravans. I hadn't planned to go public again on the trip, but I figured I was far enough from the scene of the most recent crime. That evening I went to the general store at the park and bought myself a paintbrush and a small tin of black paint, went back to camp and proceeded to alter the registration number on the boat, just in case someone did a registration check. I felt a bit more comfortable after that.

I stayed the night, and the next day did another 100 kilometres to Hay Point, an ore-loading facility. Just down from the loading facility in the shelter of its long jetty, there was a caravan park and pub right on the beach. I was halfway to Gladstone now, and the next 550 k's would be mostly uninhabited coastline, so I needed to stock up on fuel, water and food, and consult a few maps. I took most of the afternoon to ferry my supplies from the general store down to the boat.

I was under way well before sun-up, and once I was well out to sea, I ditched the faithful wheelbarrow. I wouldn't need to take on any more supplies and there was no longer any point in hiding in the bush. From here on, I wanted to travel as light as possible to conserve fuel. I pointed the nose towards Cape Palmerston, 30-odd kilometres away, and opened the throttle wide. The sea was oily smooth, but I could feel the humidity rising and see dark thunderclouds on the horizon, all classic signs of a big storm, maybe even a cyclone.

I was almost flying across the surface of the water and Cape

Palmerston soon went past. I then entered the Northumberland Island chain, which is a sparsely scattered set of islands that stretches for a 100 kilometres to the next big landfall of Long Island. This point was at the northern extremity of the Shoalwater Bay military training area, a huge expanse of territory that was out of bounds to the civilian population in Australia. I'd trained here more than a few times with the Regiment and the coastline started to look familiar in places.

I seemed to be going faster all the time as the boat shed the extra fuel weight, and it was a good feeling to be covering so much territory so quickly. I was soon passing Wild Duck Island, rounding Long Island and making for Cape Townsend. The glassy water allowed me to motor right up to Pine Tree Point, a long finger of land jutting out into the sea, about 40 k's down from Cape Townsend. Around the back of the point was a long, narrow estuary that went inland for kilometres. I figured that here I could make a good sheltered camp if there was a storm.

As I rounded the point, another boat came out of nowhere and sat right on my tail. It was a 20-footer with a big canopy and there were a bunch of blokes with straggly beards and unhappy faces on it, giving me hard stares. I peeled off to let them pass, gave them a goofy expression and a wave but got nothing in return.I figured they probably had a big dope crop growing nearby, and weren't keen on having strangers around. They had some serious horsepower because once they passed me the boat almost stood on its tail before it roared away out of sight.

I doubled back to find a camping spot and made a mental note to keep an eye out for them. Many an unsuspecting traveller has gone missing after stumbling across someone's illegal dope crop in Queensland. That night I secured the boat by burying some driftwood in the sand and tying it off to the bow and stern. It was secure, but I could make a quick getaway if needed. Then I camped a way back in the bush after burying the supplies.

I spent another two days there, snorkelling in the clear water and pigging out on fresh seafood. I came across half a dozen sea turtles one morning. They were suspended underwater and I thought at first they were dead, but when I grabbed one its eyes snapped open and it towed me along with amazing power for such short, stubby flippers. I was just as surprised as the turtle and let go. I played around with them for a while but didn't have the heart to knock one off and eat it. It was the same with some big bug-eyed gropers that swam up and nudged me with a solemn curiously, like puppies. Just when I thought I'd be opening a can for dinner, a sleek, aggressive Spanish mackerel charged at me, scaring the life out of me because I thought it was a shark. The next time it came around it copped a spear in the head for its trouble. I baked it under coals wrapped in wild banana leaves for three hours and it took me two sittings to eat it all.

As I sat around my little campfire under a shining tropical moon, listening to the heavy sigh of the water on the white sand, I thought that there would be worse places to be on the run. With the good boat and first-hand knowledge of secluded spots, I started to think I could live this idyllic existence for a while. I had enough cash to keep me in basic foodstuffs and fuel for years and the ocean would provide everything else I needed. After a year or two of this, I could drift back to WA as an almost-forgotten man and sort a few things out before heading overseas.

But like on all holidays, reality bites in the end. I couldn't have known that my story had gained some legs and that the tabloid TV shows and newspapers were having a field day, trying to out-do each other with sensationalist pieces about the psycho-robot-commando-killer on the run. I'd been avoiding most news bulletins up until then, because I needed to be without the distractions and had only been listening in on weather reports. This day I listened to the full bulletin. I was surprised that I was still one of the top items. Somebody had spotted me at a national park near Cairns and police were swooping on the area. I was supposedly travelling in a white panel van with the word 'chubbo' tattooed on my hand. I smiled at that, knowing the coppers were concentrating their efforts more than 2000 k's away. Then, I heard Mary's voice come through the speaker. That made me sit up.

'Come in, Dave. Give yourself up. Mum and I are going to lose our houses.' She sounded really upset. Apparently, most TV and radio stations had been broadcasting her plea almost daily since I'd been discovered.

I went from being pretty content to feeling like shit in about two seconds. The challenges of being on the run had allowed me to forget about the havoc I had brought into my family's lives. Not that turning myself in would make much difference; they'd forfeit the $200 000 anyway.

The news snapped me out of my little tropical daydream. I had to take action to see if I could get enough money to pay them back. Looking back, this was probably the first sign that I was getting a touch irrational. It was the classic gamblers' mistake of trying to play themselves out of trouble, or throwing good money after bad. I decided to do a couple more jobs before I left the country.

I broke camp in the early hours of the morning and headed off on the outgoing tide. It was another magnificent day and I had a dream run on flat, still water. The boat just ate up the last 250 k's. I passed Great Keppel Island, then Curtis Island, before spying the town of Gladstone on the shore. Past the town was the entrance to the Boyne River, which cut inland to the Bruce Highway and the main north–south railway line. After cruising 25 kilometres upstream, I spotted the first railway bridge, which meant the highway was nearby as well. I nosed the boat up a small tributary and prepared to go overland again.

The place was barren except for the scrub along the creek line, but I decided to have a little wander up the creek each way to check for habitation. There wasn't a soul within sight or earshot, so it was safe to destroy the boat and most of my gear. I removed my personal kit and changed into some camos before piling everything else into the middle of the boat. I smashed the engine number off the motor and the maker's badges off the hull before emptying a petrol drum over the lot. The blaze was fierce enough to melt the aluminium hull down to the water line, all but dissolving the motor, as well as vaporising the rest of the gear. While I waited a couple of hours for it to cool, I dug a big hole, then threw the charred remains of everything in it, before chopping up the molten skeleton of the hull and burying that as well. After the hole was camouflaged, you'd have never have known the boat even existed.

I'd kept a 20-litre water container as the creek was pretty muddy and I was covered in soot. I had a good scrub and changed into a clean set of jeans and a T-shirt, ready to rejoin society. My time in the tropics was over.

FUNDRAISING

With a couple of stops on the way, I eventually hitched down to Brisbane and sorted out a new ID at a youth hostel. I used the new card as an opportunity to go on a bit of a spending spree. Using the local *Trading Post*, I acquired a semi-automatic .22, a pump-action riot shotgun with pistol grip, a Swedish .223 assault rifle, a double-barrelled shotgun, a .303/25 rifle, a brand-new Aussie SLR, which was the derivative of the Belgian 7.62-millimetre Fabrique National FAL, with telescopic sight and extra 30-round magazines, a ballistics vest, a silencer for the .22, and an American Kevlar battle helmet. Everything was purchased legitimately with my fake ID and the whole lot set me back about $5000. The SLR alone was $3000 but it was worth the money. These rifles are rare in civi street and still rated highly by infantrymen the world over. I've heard that some operators in Baghdad are still using them to this day in preference to more modern assault rifles. I had no plans for the SLR in Australia, but figured it would become my personal weapon if I ever made it back to Burma.

I tooled up for one simple reason. All the sensationalist media coverage, particularly some of the tabloid newspapers I'd had a chance to scan since coming ashore, had built me up as a dangerous Rambo-type who would kill on sight. If I were a tactical response group copper with a wife and kids who was heading to arrest someone with my kind of reputation, I reckoned I'd shoot first and ask questions later. I just wanted to secure the two-hundred grand for Mum and Mary, stay alive and get overseas. If the coppers were going to play, I was going to have to play, too. Besides, a couple of the jobs I had in mind would take a bit more firepower than I'd needed previously.

From Brisbane, I took the train down to Sydney and rented a one-room apartment for a month. There, I bought all the necessary dried food and other kit I'd need to live in isolation for three months. I was planning to use my old camp in the scrub in Swanbourne again, and this time I was determined to make no contact with anyone who knew me. I'd need to be completely self-sufficient. I also took some time out in the Snowy Mountains, hiking up to an isolated spot and spending a few days getting the weapons zeroed in, particularly the laser site on the .22, which I'd shortened and modified into an updated version of my old cat gun. I had a great few days in an old hut, pinging away to my heart's content, with nobody around and the snow muffling the reports.

Once I was back in Sydney, I packed up everything except a few travelling essentials and the new cat gun. The gear was sent to Perth with a freight-forwarding company, timed to arrive in a few weeks, allowing me enough time to get across the country.

Hitchhiking had been fairly uneventful until I reached just outside Gundagai. I was travelling with a cook from Melbourne when a traffic copper coming the other way flicked on his lights and siren.

'Shit,' the bloke said. 'He's seen my radar detector.'

These are illegal in New South Wales, so he unclipped it from its mount and threw it across the seat to me.

'Hide it somewhere!'

I had no choice but to stuff it in my jacket as we pulled over and the copper strode up to the car. The only problem was that he'd seen the bloke pass something over to me. He walked around to my side and held out his hand.

'Hand it over,' he said wearily. 'C'mon, mate. I saw him hand you something, now let's have it or I'll do you for hindering a police officer.'

You could do me for a lot more than that, I thought as I gave him my best sheepish look and handed him the detector. The copper proceeded to give the driver a long lecture about being a smart arse, while I just sat there and stared straight ahead. After we got the ticket and were allowed to drive on, the cook wouldn't talk to me. He let me off at the next town. I guess he didn't like me after that.

After a few short rides, I got lucky in Port Augusta and scored a ride all the way across to Kalgoorlie. The bloke was in his seventies and was heading across from Melbourne to visit relatives in Perth and all the way up in Kununnura. Luckily, he stopped to stay the night in motels at both Ceduna and Norseman, where the main east–west checkpoints and quarantine stations are. I was able to box around each checkpoint in the dark and spend the night in the bush. I'd walk down the highway with my thumb out early the next morning ready for when he came past. He probably thought it was coincidence, picking me up each day like that. I enjoyed his company all the way across the Nullabor. There are not many genial, humble old Aussie characters left like him nowadays.

It was a bit of a risk taking the bus from Kalgoorlie to Perth, but I did the sums and figured it would mean less exposure. Western Australia has such a small population that you can bump into someone you know almost anywhere, so I thought I'd just take one risk, rather than a new one each time I was picked up. I got friendly with a young German bloke in the youth hostel that night. He was going the same way, so to other the passengers on the bus it looked like we were travelling together.

Debussing in Perth was another risk, as the station was right in the city centre. I made sure I was almost the last person off the bus and walked straight across the street to jump in a taxi. I let the taxi driver speak first to make sure he wasn't Irish before bunging on my best brogue and asking him to take me to the Floreat Hotel, where I was to meet a mate from old County Kilkenny.

'Ah, the old country,' I said, 'it makes you want to get drunk and sing songs, to be sure.' He gave me a funny look after that one, so I shut up and let him give me a running commentary on the sights of Perth all the way to the Floreat. A couple of hours later I was back in my hide in Swanbourne, ready to start some fundraising.

Society is full of weird paradoxes and they don't come much weirder than the prison system. As a way of punishing people, it's at best limited because there are plenty of worse places to be than prison. But as a way of preventing crime they are downright absurd. What is the logic in taking a criminal and locking him in a compound full of other criminals and expecting him to mend his ways? What do you reckon the main topic of conversation is in prison, day after day, night after night? The perfect crime, of course. I had only been in remand for a couple of months when some blokes I'd met inside had given me the ideas for both jobs I intended to take on next. I'd been to Crime University.

Two blokes in particular were full of useful information. Desmond Reynolds, an ex-British paratrooper who'd been jailed for stealing gold from the Youanmi goldmine, and Mike, a manager from the Farmer Jack's supermarket chain who'd let an amphetamine habit get the better of him, emptied the safe out after work one night and tried to do a runner across the country, only to get pulled over for speeding near Eucla, with the cash from the job still on the back seat of his car.

Mike reckoned that a typical Farmer Jack's supermarket had at least a quarter of a million dollars in the safe on a Saturday night. He'd been manager at two different stores, one in Armadale on the southern fringe of the urban sprawl and the other in Dianella, which was on the northern edge of the inner city. He told me the routines of the managers, locations of the safes, types of alarms used, locations of the keypads and which alarms were on the safe itself.

Des had worked as a process operator in the gold room at the mine, so he knew how to go about breaking in there, as well as the day the gold shipment regularly departed and the routines of the security guards. I decided to leave the gold job till last, because it would take a bit more time and effort than knocking over the supermarkets. And I would have to get my hands on some explosives.

Step one was to organise some transport, scope out unoccupied houses, and pick up my kit from the freight company. I bought a good-quality mountain bike in town to solve my transport problem; I fitted it with panniers and racks. A law had just been passed in WA making bicycle helmets mandatory and this worked in my favour, as a helmet and sunglasses make anyone unrecognisable. Perth has an excellent network of cycle paths that allows you to move from suburb to suburb independently of the main roads, making for an inconspicuous way to get around. The bike also allowed me to scout around for a vacant house without looking too suspicious – I was just another fitness freak out doing his thing.

I found the perfect vacant house in Swanbourne, just a few blocks from camp. It was set back from the road and obscured by shrubs and a high hedge. I contacted the freight depot at Kewdale and asked them to drop the gear off at the house after 5 p.m. That way the driver would probably be in a hurry to get home. I made sure I was there well before five and watched the house and road for any sign of police activity before he turned up, then jumped on the bike and pedalled up the street just as he was arriving, to create the impression that I was just getting home from work. I left the bike helmet and glasses on and he didn't bother to check my signature too closely.

I stashed the gear under the house, and it took a few trips to carry it all back to the camp on the bike. To help store the gear I pinched a wheelie bin and dug it into the side of a small hill a few hundred yards from my lying-up place at the camp. I found another good spot to hide the bike and masked it with camouflage netting. Once I'd covered my tracks, paying particular attention to the telltale wheel ruts, it was time for phase two.

My plan was to knock over both supermarkets on the same night. That was the only way to get them both, because they'd surely tighten security at all their stores after one had been done. It was a bit of a stretch to do both jobs on the one night without backup, but I needed a lot of cash and once these jobs were done, it wouldn't take the cops long to work out who was back in town. I'd need to hit hard and then clear out fast. I spent a couple of weeks shopping at both stores, taking my time to confirm Mike's information and identify the back and side entrances, alarm isolation pad and alarm sensors, as well as escape routes around both suburbs. Once I'd see the layout of both places, I started to formulate a plan.

On the night of the job I'd take the manager of the Armadale store as he was locking up for the night. With a partner on the job, I would have had a few more options. We could have taken him in his car, as he was leaving work, or at home. But going solo restricted my choices to hiding amongst a stack of milk crates near the back door and surprising him just as he came out. I briefly considered hiding in one of the storerooms, but that would leave me way too exposed and cut down my escape options at critical moments. Once I'd blown the Armadale safe, I'd make my way up to Dianella and take the second manager in his home, just as Baz and I had done in the cinema job.

I made a few bogus phone calls and obtained names and addresses of managers and assistant managers for both places. Just to complicate matters, the Dianella manager lived across the river in the southern suburbs and the Armadale manager lived up north. But I figured this might work in my favour and add to the police's confusion on the night. I chose the Dianella manager for the home invasion because he looked like a single bloke and didn't appear to have a dog or anyone else at home, so I concentrated most of my surveillance on his place. I did have a brief look at the Armadale manager's house but didn't spend too much time because I didn't plan to take him there.

Spring was getting close and the days were getting longer.

I needed to act soon or there would be too much evening light, meaning more exposure.

I sorted my gear for the job. As I'd be loitering around the car park at the Armadale store for at least a few minutes, a balaclava was out of the question, so I bought a fairly realistic-looking human-face mask from a novelty shop. This would pass a glance at a distance, especially if I were covered in dust and plaster, looking just like a builder on his way home after work. I also had a workman's blue hairnet, overalls, work gloves and a balaclava as backup. From my arms cache I took a Colt M-16 carbine, with a collapsible butt, homemade perforated steel stock, and a severely shortened barrel-less than was 30 centimetres long. It's an awesome weapon at close quarters, and it looked the part. Added to this was a Sig Sauer .45 auto pistol and a Gerber fighting knife. All these weapons were easily concealable and looked fearsome enough to command respect. For the safes, I took a cut-down .303 to blast the lock and a jimmy bar. I bought some large plastic cable-ties to secure people and added my police scanner with earpiece. The gear was sterilised, packed into the job bag and sealed up.

I'd spied another unoccupied house in Armadale that was half gutted – a renovation in progress. On the night before the job I took a couple of hours to pedal the 50 clicks over there, then stashed the bike in bushland over the road and hid in the roof space. If I got discovered during the day, I could easily enough pass myself off as a vagrant needing a place to sleep. An icy southerly wind blew up during the night and the planks I was lying on weren't too comfortable. I didn't get much sleep. The renovation crew started work at 7 a.m. the next day and worked right up until mid-afternoon. I hadn't planned on them working late, and if they'd still been there when it was time for the job, I'd have aborted. I didn't move while they were working for fear that the slightest creak would give my position away, so I was as stiff as a board when I finally got out of the roof.

I waited until 5:45 p.m., when it was dark, before moving down to my hiding place amongst the milk crates near the back door of the shopping complex. There was a single car parked at the rear, but I didn't recognise it as the manager's. I was waiting there with my pistol out, trying to remember the make of the manager's girlfriend's car, when a carload of plain-clothed police detectives rolled into the car park. I straightaway tensed up and got ready to run – mind racing back over the last couple of days, trying to pinpoint where they had picked up my trail. But they swung past my hiding spot without even glancing my way and pulled around to the front of the shopping complex, no doubt indulging that other great passion all coppers have apart from chasing crooks – fast food. I checked the scanner and there was no traffic that sounded as if it would warrant a carload of detectives attending a crime scene. I let out a long, quiet sigh of relief and focused back on the rear door.

When I looked back after those few crucial seconds a bloke was already at the lone car, unlocking it and getting in. I couldn't see if he was the manager or not, and had to decide in a split second whether to nab him or let him go. He had an armful of papers and a big bundle of keys, so it was a fair guess he was my man. But if it wasn't the manager, then I'd be stuffed because he wouldn't have the right keys for the safe. If he was the manager, then I was missing my chance, because the assistant would be rostered on the next week. He must have come out the front door, or had locked up prior to my arrival and been getting a burger himself. In the end it was the freaky surprise of seeing that carload of coppers that swayed my decision. I let him drive away. I walked back to the bush, retrieved my bike and rode back to Swanbourne, irritated but already planning take-two in a couple of weeks.

Have you ever seen one of those idiotic bike tourists out in the desert? Trying to find themselves as they pedal through extreme heat on a fat-tyred bike, loaded up with an impossible amount of gear. Well, two days after the botched supermarket job that was me. I had a fortnight to wait for both managers to be rostered on weekends again, so I decided to use the time to scope out the gold job. After packing the bike with two weeks' worth of food, camouflage gear, sleeping bag and the new cat gun, I pedalled over to Midland and took a bus out to the fringe of the wheatbelt, to a small town called Wubin. After a four-hour bus ride, I unpacked the bike at sunset and set out for Paynes Find and Youanmi Downs, the location of the goldmine.

I rode through the night to Paynes Find, reaching the tiny town just as the sun was rising. It was a bit of a stretch to call it a town, actually, as it consisted of a cluster of mostly uninhabited tin-and-asbestos shacks and a single general store that sold everything from petrol to beer. I was right out on the edge of the Western Desert and the terrain was covered with small hills and head-high mulga scrub. I filled up on water and left the main road, taking a dusty, rutted track east towards the mine. The going was much harder now, with long stretches of soft sand that couldn't be ridden through, so I spent most of the first four hours just pushing the bike. The daytime temperatures were getting up to 38 degrees Celsius this time of the year, so it made sense to limit travelling in the middle of the day. I also didn't want to be seen by too many locals – have the bush telegraph talking about a 'mad cyclist' on the Youanmi track and before you'd know it, I'd be getting rescued.

I made camp in a clump of scrub and slept through the heat of the day. The next night I covered 70 kilometres, filling up on water at one of the station windmills at Red Bluff. There where plenty of windmills along the track; the water tasted rusty and muddy, but it was wet and that was the main thing. There wasn't much traffic along the track, and I could hear vehicles coming well before they got close enough to spot me, leaving me plenty of time to spear off the track and hide. As it was, I only saw one Toyota Land Cruiser all day.

There had been some decent winter rains and the wildflowers were in full bloom. In places the desert was covered with a purple, red and green carpet. Without the competition from city lights and smog, the stars were so bright that they provided enough light for me to follow the road easily. Although it was hard work, pedalling and pushing the bike through the soft sand, I somehow felt at peace out there alone.

After another day of hiding from the heat and fitful dozing, I was in range of the mine. I pushed hard on the third night to cover the last 80 k's and pretty soon I could see a glow on the horizon and hear the telltale *beep beep* of trucks reversing. It was 2 a.m. by the time I got close enough to hide the bike and do my recon on foot. It was a typical goldmine setup, with a crusher, mill, processing lab, huge mixing tank, tailings dam and gold room. The big open pit next to the plant wasn't in operation, so I assumed they'd be trucking the ore in from elsewhere. I also saw a diamond drill rig operating; it was lit up like a Christmas tree, so I gave it a wide berth. I noticed all the vehicles were left unlocked and parked facing out, as per standard safety requirements in case of an evacuation. This would work in my favour in case I, too, needed to evacuate in a hurry.

I set up my camp halfway between the mine and accommodation camp, just off the access road that ran between the two. The trees were pretty sparse in that area but there was a knee-high carpet of wildflowers, which was a huge bonus. Lie down amongst them and nobody would see you unless they tripped over you. I found a small clump of scrub to serve as a hide and did a bit of landscaping to make it less conspicuous. I also checked the sight lines from my spot to the camp, mine and closest bit of road, and I moved some dead trees to block the lines of sight. It's a big mistake to cover one spot completely, because the density will stand out against the rest of the vegetation. Carefully positioning branches and sticks further out from a hide is far more effective. Just before I settled in for a sleep, I heard a couple of light vehicles coming up the access road. A minibus and Toyota four-wheel drive, carrying ten people went past. The vehicles passed back the other way about ten minutes later, carrying four people. It was 6 p.m., time for shift change, and it looked like night shift was only a skeleton crew.

A small mob of emus woke me the next afternoon as they wandered right on top of my camp. On another day I would have knocked one on the head and cooked him up, but I had plenty of food so I just shooed them away with a couple of well-aimed rocks. After a brew and a feed, I waited for the sun to set and right on 6 p.m. I saw the minibus and Toyota pass with the four night-shift staff, and return ten minutes later with the day-shift-workers who had knocked off.

It took seven-and-a-half hours to do a 360-degree recon of the site. I spotted an unused helmet and pair of underground miner's gumboots as I first approached, so I put these on. The boots would ensure I didn't leave any unfamiliar footprints in the dust and the helmet might come in handy later if I were challenged and had to try to bluff my way out. Climbing the huge waste dumps was treacherous; rain had carved deep crevices in the sides and the proximity of the floodlights covering the plant ruined my night vision. If I were impatient, I'd surely break a leg so I went carefully. I was looking for the perfect OP that could be used to safely view the whole site during the day, but couldn't find one. I had to settle for a spot halfway up one of the waste dumps, which gave me a clear view of the airstrip but only a partial view of the mine.

It was Wednesday and normal roster change for most mine sites happens on Tuesdays and Thursdays, so I guessed a plane was due the next morning. Most mines collect all the gold particles that have been mined, melt them down in a furnace and pour them into moulds to make gold bars at least once a week. The information Des had given me also indicated that a gold pour would have been done that night and the fresh bars would also be catching the same flight down as the outgoing workers.

I finished my tour of the mine at about 2 a.m. and immediately organised my kit for a move to the OP. I slipped into my camos, took some water, food, binoculars and camouflage cream and made my way up to the spot. It took about an hour to get organised since I had to ensure I had good overhead cover in case someone on the inbound plane looked directly at my spot at the wrong moment.

Most mining companies make the gold room as inconspicuous as they can for obvious reasons. But close inspection soon revealed a heavily built box-like structure with a visible burglar alarm. It was exactly where Des said it would be. At about 6 a.m. a vehicle came onto the mine-site from the camp, pulled up at the gold room and backed inside. Half an hour later a plane flew right over my OP, before swinging around to land on the strip. At the same moment the vehicle pulled out of the gold room and drove over to the landing strip, parking at one end. As the plane was touching down, a bus appeared from around the corner and headed to the strip, but it parked some distance away from the vehicle with the bullion on board.

The plane taxied over to where the outgoing crew were lined up, holding their luggage. It took about ten minutes for the incoming crew to leave and the outgoing crew to board the plane. As soon as the last bloke was on board, the gold truck roared up to the plane from where it had been waiting, and three blokes jumped out to load a number of heavy boxes into the plane's hold. The total elapsed time from the plane touching down to lifting off again, loaded with passengers and gold, was less than twenty minutes.

I stayed in my OP amongst the wildflowers for the rest of the day and well into the night. I noticed that ore was being hauled to the mill in triple-roadtrain loads, with a regular turnaround of about ninety minutes. A few quick sums in my head and I worked out that this meant the pit they were digging in was roughly 40 k's away. This was another advantage to the job, as the bulk of the workforce – those drilling, blasting, digging and loading the ore – wasn't where I was moving around. The trucks dumped the ore at the head of the crusher, and a bloke operating a Caterpillar 988 front-end loader would tip the ore into a huge hopper that fed the crusher. In between trucks he'd also use the loader to keep the ramp and pad smooth for the trucks. Some people like to watch a nice sunset, but for me the sight of a huge, smoking machine roaring and clanking about was pretty relaxing; I guess it reminded me of Macka's bulldozer back in Tassie. I waited for the night shift to come on and for the cleaner to knock off at 10 p.m. before heading back to my camp.

The rest of the week was spent moving in and around the site in the dark, getting familiar with the routine of the place and endlessly rehearsing the different scenarios that might occur during the job. It became obvious that this was a two-man job. I needed to neutralise the operator of the big Cat 988 at the crusher first, probably by tying him up, putting him in the bucket of the dozer and driving him back down to the plant. Then the two mill operators would have to be bailed up and restrained. The mill operators stayed mobile throughout the night, checking machinery, cleaning up ore spills and doing small repairs, so their movements were hard to predict. Once they were detained, I would then have to move on the bloke who spent most of the night sitting on his arse in the control room. If I had a partner manning an OP overlooking the site, he could keep me updated by radio on the movements of the two mill operators, allowing me to bail them up one at a time, without having one of them run to raise the alarm.

Prior to the assault, I'd have to isolate the entire mine site from the outside world, giving us enough time to get to Great Northern Highway before the alarm was raised. Once there, we could disappear in any number of directions without being caught. The mines' main communications were through a microwave link, with a tower on site, and a link to another tower 15 kilometres away. A small charge placed here with a timing device would sever the cable between the dish and the transmission unit just as we were going in. They had high-frequency radios on all vehicles, but I only needed to worry abut the ones at the mine-site, and I could disable the antennas on these easily enough. The base HF antenna at the camp could also be disabled with a pair of pliers. The telephone lines between the mine and the camp would also have to be cut. On one of my patrols I cut these lines and left them severed for half an hour as a test. If any security people came up to the mine in a hurry, then I'd know they had an alarm linked to the site. They didn't, so I knew that the alarm on the gold room was a visual alarm for the people on site only. I rejoined the lines and sealed them back into their pipe.

To cut off road access, I needed to make up a few dozen star spikes by cutting short lengths of the 5-millimetre-thick steel bar used to reinforce concrete; these could be welded into an X-shape with the ends sharpened, so no matter which way they landed on the road there would always be a pointed end to stick up into a tyre. Scattering these over all the access road would prevent anyone from getting away to raise the alarm and would also stop the triple-roadtrains from entering the site while the job was on. On the way out we'd also spike the road to Paynes Find. A smaller track that headed north to the town of Sandstone would also have to be spiked, just to add confusion about our escape route.

The night before the arrival of the gold plane was the obvious time to do the job. Not only would we get the bars that had already been smelted, but there would be some gold in the collection tanks, still impregnated in steel wool, ready to be melted down. This was the gold that Des had been caught pilfering.

Once we secured the four staff, it would be a matter of cutting through the side of the gold room with an oxy-acetylene torch, after I'd smashed the alarm unit off the side of the building with a sledgehammer. The walls of the gold room were corrugated iron with arc mesh on the inside, which I figured would take less than ten minutes to get through with the oxyacetylene. If we cut into the wall behind the safe, we could then drag the safe out with a chain attached to the front-end loader and lift it into our vehicle. I figured we'd use a Ford V8 F350 four-wheel drive for the job. It would have enough power to handle the weight of the gold and could do 160 k's per hour on the gravel road back to Paynes Find. Then we would race up and grab the racks of gold-impregnated steel wool from the acid tanks and throw them in the car as well. I'd then get my partner to follow me in one of the company's Toyotas for a few kilometres, before he'd dump it somewhere it wouldn't be found straightaway. The tyre tracks would have everyone searching for a Toyota instead of a Ford, which would buy us more precious time.

Plan B, if we didn't manage to secure all four staff, was to smash into the gold room with the front-end loader and scoop up the safe in the bucket, then load it into the F350. This way we'd be halfway down the Paynes Find track before the alarm could be raised. While one of us drove down the track, the other would fit a shaped charge to the safe door. Once we were far enough away, we'd fit a blast shield over the rear window of the Ford, blow open the safe, load the gold bars and then dump the safe in the scrub.

I reckoned we could get to Paynes Find in less than ninety minutes. Travelling fast with the headlights off in that open country would give us plenty of time to pull off into the bush if we saw headlights coming the other way, especially if we saw the flashing candy lights of the Dalwallinu police heading north towards the mine. First light should see us on the outskirts of Perth, where we could find some bush cover to stop off in to wash all the telltale red dust off the Ford. After that, we could cruise into the suburbs looking like any other tradesmen starting their day.

It was a simple plan, really. With the right backup, I reckoned it would work a treat. After five days of sneaking around the mine site, it was time to head home again. I decided to give the bus a miss this time and ride all the way back. Riding through the night on the track to Paynes Find took me two days. I then switched to 'idiot long-distance bike-tourer' mode, and riding during the day along the highway had me back in Perth the following Thursday, leaving a couple of days up my sleeve before I was set to try the supermarket jobs again.

After a good night's sleep at the Swanbourne camp, I grabbed the supermarket job bag, which hadn't been opened and so didn't need to be sterilised a second time, and pedalled out to Armadale. The only change to my gear was the addition of a space blanket to avoid another freezing night's sleep in the roof of the Armadale house. A quick check showed that the renovations were still in progress, so gaining access to the roof on the Friday night was easy. The builders didn't turn up to work on the Saturday, so I was able to move around a bit while I waited out the day, which made it much more comfortable.

At five-thirty I made my way down from the roof and across the car park to my hiding place amongst the milk crates at the back of the store. The car park was mostly deserted and the manager's parking spot was conspicuously empty. I waited a few minutes but there was no action at the back door. I had a sinking feeling that

I was late again. By half-past six it was obvious he'd gone. I'd stuffed up again. I wondered whether I should just bin the job altogether and just do the gold mine. If I didn't do the supermarkets tonight, it was going to be too light in the evenings to risk a confrontation in the car park. I sat staring at the milk crates for a few minutes, mulling over my options. I'd just go for it. I hadn't rehearsed taking the Armadale manager at his house too carefully, but I knew where he lived and had checked out the house from the outside.

I retrieved my bike from its hiding spot in the bush and rode to the nearest train station. Perth metropolitan railways will allow you to take your bike on the train if it's not peak hour, so I was able to wheel it straight on. I got off in the city and pumped hard up through the northern suburbs to the manager's house. I did a couple of rides past to check if he was home. I could see a couple of lights on and his car was in the driveway. Down the end of his street was an industrial site that had emptied out for the night, so I stashed the bike in some bushes there.

The manager's neighbour on the right side was a slack gardener, so there was plenty of cover in his yard. I moved down the side of the house, grateful for the cold night; they had their windows and doors closed tight. Rain had been forecast, but it was one of those crisp, dead-still late winter nights in Perth, when sound travels easily, so I moved extra slowly to the backyard and found a place to set up near the manager's back fence. I sat for a while and listened to the police scanner in case someone had reported me as a prowler.

My previous recon had shown no signs of a dog at either manager's place, but a lot can change in two weeks so I spent a few minutes staring over the fence. Once satisfied, I slid over and crawled up to the house. I went slowly from window to window, trying to see inside to get numbers and locations of people, but every curtain was pulled shut, and, apart from the sound of the TV, I couldn't hear any other voices. I knew I should be spending more time establishing what was going on in the house. This was really flying by the seat of my pants, but I was committed now and there was no backing out.

The back door was closed and also had a heavy security screen on the outside. The security screen would be easy enough to pick, but I would undoubtedly make a bit of noise picking the inner door. Luckily, they had only locked the screen door and the inner door was unlocked. I retrieved my job bag from where I had stashed it on the way in and got the balaclava, face mask and M-16 ready. I slowly opened the screen door, keeping pressure on the hinges to avoid them squeaking. I carefully closed both doors behind me to avoid any telltale cold drafts and moved into the small laundry. The laundry opened into a passageway, which appeared to have the lounge room and its blaring TV at one end and a cluster of bedrooms at the other. I decided to check the bedrooms first. They were all empty, but worryingly, there were fluffy toys on the beds.

I crept slowly up the hallway and pressed my ear to the other door. The sound of the TV was muffled, so I figured it was one more room away. The bloke definitely oiled his hinges because this door opened quietly as well. I was now in a kitchen, and on one side was an open archway that surely led to the lounge room. There was no point sneaking a peek first as I'd probably be seen. For maximum shock value I just stepped straight into the room, gun at the ready, right into my worst nightmare.

So much for my pre-job recon: the manager had a small family.

The wife was lying asleep on the couch with a six-month-old baby in her arms and he was sitting on the floor, leaning on the couch, with an eighteen-month-old girl asleep on his lap. For a second I wavered, trying to decide whether just to run out the front door. This would be messy and stressful for all involved, but I decided to plough on. I'd need to secure them to get away cleanly and that was no better than going through with the whole job. Once you've been tied up and had a gun pointed at your face, the rest is just details.

The manager sitting on the floor looked at me dumfounded; I guess he was trying to fit the vision of a heavily armed, black-clad, masked man appearing in his lounge room in with his existing idea of suburban life. It didn't mesh, and he cracked up laughing, thinking it was one of his mates playing a prank. One rack of the slide on the M-16 – that 'lock-and-load' sound made so popular in the movies – and he was convinced the gun was real. He went so pale he was green. I thought he was going to pass out. I kept the M-16 aimed at him with the right hand, and used the left to make a palm down motion, and then said the two most useless words in the English language.

'Calm down.'

I'd entered his domain with a dangerous weapon and was threatening his family – this cuts right against the instincts of most blokes to be a protector. The look he gave me was a tortured combination of fear and anger; I was sure he would have liked the gun to be in his hands. There was a paralysed moment where we both wondered what to do next before his wife woke up. There was a sharp intake of breath that I don't reckon she let out again properly for the next four hours. The thin, breathless voice came from high in her chest.

'What? Who are you? Oh, my baby. Please don't hurt my baby.' She curled up around the baby on the couch. Then the eighteen month old woke up, and straightaway picking up on Mum and Dad's fear, took one look at me and started howling. I've held my nerve under incoming fire, been bombed and strafed by aircraft, but nothing tests the nerves in a tense situation like a screeching kid. She had an impressive set of lungs and was going at it like a chainsaw, so I looked straight at the dad and spoke to him through the din.

'Look, mate. I'm not going to hurt anyone. I just want the money from the safe at work. I'm just going to step back into the kitchen so I don't frighten the kids and you settle them down. Then we're going to drive out to Armadale.'

He nodded his head. I waited in the kitchen for a few moments as Mum and Dad soothed their little girl. They both showed great courage, keeping the fear out of their voices and pretty soon the little girl was making curious noises about the man in the other room.

I can look back on this now and see it from their perspective. A bloke enters your lounge room with a fearsome-looking gun and says, 'It's okay. I'm not here to hurt you'. I guess it's pretty hard to take his word for it and some deep, instinctive part of your mind must be wondering if you are going to die tonight. I've still got a lot of respect for the way they handled it.

Waiting in the kitchen, I had a decision to make. Do I tie up Mum and the kids and drive back to Armadale with Dad? Or take them all with me? It was pretty obvious we all had to go. I'd need to restrain Mum pretty strongly to stop her raising the alarm while we were opening the safe. This would make her unable to attend to the kids, who I'd probably need to restrain as well. On the other hand, controlling two adults and two small children while I blew the safe would be difficult. I chose the lesser of two nightmares. The crying had stopped so I moved back into the lounge room. I spoke as slowly and patiently as I could.

'Okay, now, I'm only after the company's money, not your money. I don't want to hurt anyone. We are all going to get in your car and drive out to the supermarket and open the safe. Get the kids organised, make sure you've got plenty of blankets and pillows because you'll be spending the night there. Let's go.'

'But I haven't got the keys and I don't know the alarm codes. I'm not rostered on tonight,' said Dad.

Okay, so he'd handled it well up till then, but that was a stupid move. Why risk your life in an armed robbery when it's not your money? Why risk your life even if it *is* your money?

'Don't be fucking stupid: I just saw you leave work and followed you here. I know the safe is in the back corner of your office. I know the alarm keypads are just inside the door on the right-hand side, and I know you've got about a quarter of a mil in the safe. If you're going to risk the life of you and your family, then do it for something that matters, you fucking idiot.'

He toed the line after that. The other bluff I had was the earpiece of the police scanner. I paused a couple of times to listen in on this and adjusted the squelch knob up and down to give the impression that I was receiving transmissions on a two-way radio and had one or more partners on the job.

After food and blankets for the kids had been organised, we moved out to the car. My plan was to sit in the back with the two kids, while Mum and Dad sat in the front. I'd be less visible that way. Even without the balaclava, which would have been a dead giveaway, the rubber face mask only worked at a distance and someone peering closely into the car would have probably thought something was amiss; pity it wasn't Halloween.

'She'll cry if she can't sit with me,' Mum said, pointing to the eighteen-month-old.

'It's not a bloody negotiation,' I said. 'Now get in the front and let's go.'

I should have listened to her; we were only one block away from home and the kid was crying at full volume again. I tried to talk to the little kid and handed her a couple of stuffed toys, but surprisingly the masked bandit was no substitute for Mum. After ten minutes, the crying had put everyone on edge. The baby started up, then Mum started sobbing, and then Dad joined in. If it went on much longer, I reckoned I'd be bloody crying, too.

'Okay, find somewhere to pull in and let's swap over.'

We pulled in to a factory driveway and quickly swapped seats. That solved the minor crisis and the kid was quite happy after that. Dad had a bit of a lead foot and I had to tell him to slow down a couple of times, but otherwise the trip out to Armadale went smoothly. After everyone had stopped bawling, there was a long silence, which was broken by Dad asking a question.

'So, how did you get in the house?'

Fair question, I thought. So I spent the rest of the journey giving them a long lecture on how to improve home security. A bit of a hard way to learn a lesson, I suppose, but I reckon every home they lived in after that was like Fort Knox.

When we arrived I got Dad to pull in close to the back door. He and I went in the back way and disabled the alarm at the keypad.

Then we got Mum and the kids out of the car, raided the confectionery aisle for the eighteen-month-old and moved everyone into the office. The floor safe was cleared easily enough, but that was small takings compared to the main tank. I knew the manager wouldn't have both keys to this and I could see he was bracing for another confrontation. He was relieved when I took his word for it.

After trying to force the safe's inner door open with the jimmy bar a few times, I realised I'd have to blow the lock out with the .303. I moved the family into the toilet block at the back of the supermarket and warned them that a loud bang was coming. A child's hearing is very sensitive and there was no way they could stay in the office as the .303 went off. I also told them to wait until 10 p.m. before raising the alarm, which would be well past the time I finished the Dianella job – hopefully.

I locked the door to the toilet block and started moving back towards the office. On a whim I decided to check the back windows. It was lucky I did: there was another car in the car park. Two security guards had parked right next to our car. We'd left the car unlocked and the padlock on the supermarket's rear door hanging loose to create the impression that someone authorised had popped back in to the supermarket after hours. If the security guards did their jobs, they would stick their heads in the door and verify this anyway, so I quickly moved to the back door and got ready to bail them both up, hurriedly running through a couple of possible scenarios in my mind. I was going to have to get both of them inside somehow. Maybe by bailing the first one up and keeping him quiet until the second one came looking. I found a spot between produce aisles that had a good view of the back door and waited for it to open. The next sound I heard was a couple of car doors slamming and a car driving off. I waited for a few more minutes before taking another peek out of the window. The security guards had driven off without checking inside the supermarket. Good old private security guards, eh? Lazy one day and useless the next.

But I couldn't just assume they had gone. They might have been cunning instead of stupid and pulled back to contact the police once they saw something was awry. I carefully opened a side door to see if they were hiding further up the street and jumped in fright when a clanging alarm went off right next to my ear. *Shit!* I closed the door fast and ran back to the ablution block where the manager and his wife were sitting down, looking a bit wide eyed. As soon as I motioned to the manager, he knew what I wanted and scurried over to the nearest keypad to shut down the alarm without me even having to ask.

'It's okay,' he said. 'That's just for stopping shoplifters sneaking out of the side exit. The alarm's not monitored.'

I wasn't so sure, but I didn't have time to grill him any further. I locked him back in with his family and got to work. I blasted the locks six more times with the .303; the cordite smoke was filling the office. Still no luck; the locks on the safe wouldn't budge. I had to save a few rounds for the next job and so decided on the more laborious process of wedging it open one millimetre at a time. Five minutes later the phone on the office desk rang. The side door might have been monitored or the security guards might have followed up. Either way it was now too hot. I threw everything into the job bag, moved quietly back to the ablution block and carefully unlocked the door so the family wouldn't be locked in there all night if I was wrong about the phone call, and then slipped out of the back entrance. I needed some time-delay before the manager realised I was gone, so I slipped the car into neutral and rolled out of the car park before I started it up and drove away.

In the half hour it took to get over to the Dianella manager's place there was no mention of Armadale on the police scanner. There were plenty of apartment complexes near the house, so it was easy to find somewhere to dump the car where it wouldn't be noticed for a while. The weather turned and heavy rain started falling as I walked away from the car. Bad weather is always a bonus because it dampens noise and keeps people inside. I found some thick hedges opposite the house and sat for a while to observe the street and clear my head from thinking about what a fuck-up this night had been so far.

The carport was open at the side of the house, so I took a casual stroll up the street and ducked in there after checking there was nobody else on the footpath. I left the job bag in the carport, took the M-16 and the jimmy bar and hopped a low steel-railed fence into the backyard. My feet had barely hit the dirt when I heard a deep-throated growl. I swung around and saw a huge black shape streaking towards me like a freight train and a set of white teeth bared and coming straight at my throat. I had time to make one movement, and that was to bring the jimmy bar down in a hard overhand swing. It cracked the dog right on the top of the skull and it sank to its knees in front of me. I cracked it hard another three or four times before I could see that it was well and truly dead. It was a doberman. The shock of it nearly ripping out my throat had given me huge strength and I'd made a mess of its skull.

I hadn't seen feeding bowls or any other signs of a dog on my initial recon, so this was a surprise to say the least. Surely the householders must have heard the dog growl; I heaved its carcass over the fence into the carport and waited for the back door to open, ready to barge in and bail them up as soon as someone came to investigate. I waited for ten minutes, but no sound came from inside the house.

That was no guarantee they hadn't heard me. They might have just been smart. I once read a story about a martial arts champion who'd charged out of the house when he heard someone breaking into his car. As soon as he opened the back door, he walked straight into the business end of a swinging star picket and is now a vegetable, fed by a drip in hospital. Smart people don't barge out of the back door when they hear a noise; they sneak a peek through a window and call the police.

In my highly aware state even the slightest noise sounded like a bomb going off. But no curtains twitched and the police scanner stayed quiet, so the drumming of the rain on the tin roof must have worked in my favour.

I was just getting ready to make my entry into the house when it occurred to me that we'd be exiting via the sidedoor into the carport. The last thing my hostages would want to see was their beloved pet with its skull smashed in. I jumped back over the side fence and lifted the big doberman into the backyard. Without the benefit of adrenalin, he was bloody heavy and I had to use a fireman's lift to get him over the fence. Then the big fella had his revenge. Just as I was about to drop him over the fence, his bowels evacuated all over my neck and shoulders. Covered in foul-smelling shit, I finished the job of dragging him under a bush and out of sight before going back across the street to my hiding place and using the rain and a few leaves to clean some of the shit off me.

After the clean-up, I went back to the house and slowly crept from window to window, checking the interior layout. The lights were all off and it seemed everyone was in bed. I found an unlocked window in one of the front rooms and slipped inside, after I'd checked for both alarm sensors and obstacles that I might knock over as I entered. Coming in from the hammering rain outside meant that it took a few minutes for my senses to adjust to the silence of a household after bedtime. Once comfortable, I unlocked the front and back doors in case I needed a hasty exit, then I slowly worked my way from room to room.

Through the door of the first room I could see the telltale signs of a kid, probably a boy, if the racing-car posters and dinosaur toys were anything to go by. Sure enough, looking past the doorway, I could see a tousled blond head moving softly under a thick doona. This night was just going from bad to worse. I really started to doubt myself here. My recon of this place had me convinced there were no kids or dogs, and I was wrong on both counts. I checked the next room and saw another little blonde head, this time a girl. I stood in the hallway for a second and considered walking away. But since there were no babies involved, I figured I could get Mum and Dad away without waking the kids and have them back before morning.

In the third and last bedroom were the manager and his wife, sound asleep. It was pitch-black inside the room, aside from the red digits of a digital alarm clock. I had a small flashlight that I'd used my tape and pinprick trick on, which gave me a tiny needle of light. I didn't want a repeat of the cinema job, so I decided to wake the manager up slowly and let him wake his wife up. I pulled the covers off his feet while shining the light in one of his eyes, then gave his toe a little tweak.

He slowly woke, probably thinking it was one of his kids needing a glass of water. I decided to keep the mood as calm as possible and spoke very quietly.

'G'day, mate. I need you to stay really calm and wake up your wife.' I shone the light onto the M-16 as I said this so he'd know the score. He looked at me for a moment with his mouth open, trying to compute the situation, then nodded slowly and turned to shake his wife's shoulder. The first thing he said to her when she woke up was 'Stay quiet, honey. Don't wake the kids', which impressed me. When I had their attention I told them how it was going to play out, keeping my voice calm but firm.

'We're going to get dressed and drive over to the supermarket in Dianella and you are going to help me get to the safe. I know you can't unlock the safe but you can disable the alarm keypads and get me into your office. Don't play any silly games 'cos I'm not here to hurt you or your family. I just want the company's money, not yours.'

'I've just gone on annual leave,' the manager said. 'I don't have the keys or the codes.'

I'd already practised my 'don't be a fucking idiot; why risk your life when it's not your money' speech once that night, so I reckon this time I was even more menacing. But he didn't fold.

'Seriously, mate. I can't help you; I've just gone on holidays. The keys would be hanging on the hook in the kitchen if they were here.' He pointed down the hall.

Sure enough, there was a hook in the kitchen that said 'keys', which was conspicuously empty. I checked every drawer and cupboard in the kitchen, then the bedroom, but couldn't find any keys. I loosely restrained the couple in their bed while I took the car keys out to the carport and searched their vehicle from back to front. Still no keys. I went back to the bedroom for one last try. The couple were remarkably calm and assured me again that I was out of luck. That was the last straw. For a second I considered taking the manager out of his bed and forcing him over to the acting manager's place at gunpoint, but that would mean another family – and, knowing my luck, another set of kids and probably another bloody dog – it would have just spun out of control. I tied them both up a bit more securely, told them not to raise the alarm for at least half an hour and took their car.

Just after I crossed the river on the freeway heading towards the northern suburbs, the scanner came alive with talk of the Armadale job. Five minutes later the whistle went up about the South Perth house I'd just left. They hadn't broadcast the make and model of the car yet so time was still on my side. I picked up my bike from where I'd left it earlier in the night, put it in the car and then doubled back towards Herdsman Lake, where I knew there were a few high-rise apartment blocks. I was just skirting the lake on Herdsman Parade when they gave the details of the car over the scanner. I pulled into the first large car park I saw, locked the car and took off on the bike towards the Swanbourne camp.

It was still hammering with cold wet rain so I had a miserable ride back. I'd probably alerted the coppers that I was back in town, wasted a bunch of ammo, and traumatised a couple of families and kids – all for the petty cash from the Armadale supermarket. I should have quit right then and left town. But in my mind I still needed to raise that money to pay back Mum and Mary. I had no choice but to press on with plans for the gold job.

GOING DOWN

After a restless sleep in the damp Swanbourne scrub, I woke to hear my Mum crying on the radio. I had switched it on to check for news and found out I *was* the news. The cops had, as predicted, taken about five minutes to make me their prime suspect in both jobs and were warning the innocent citizens of Perth about the dangerous, heavily armed psychopath in their midst. Mum was on Howard Sattler's (WA's local shock jock) daytime talkback show begging me to give myself up, in between saying that the bloke who took those families hostage 'couldn't have possibly been my son'. It was still raining heavily and the weather matched my mood. I sat in the bush with my head in my hands, pondering how the night before had become one giant shit-fight from start to finish. I've never allowed myself to dwell on the downside of any situation; I don't see the point. Being morose never got me anywhere. Pretty soon my mind turned to the gold job.

Success in the gold job required two things that I didn't have: shaped charges and an experienced partner. My recon of the mine had already shown that I needed a partner, but the previous night's debacle confirmed it. Doing a big job without help was difficult, especially when it came down to crowd control. Once I secured the explosives, I'd contact Des, who'd tipped me off about the gold in the first place. This was breaking another rule but I figured it could have been worse. Besides, an ex-military bloke would be a pro at handling both weapons and people, and having been through the police wringer already, the cops would have trouble putting pressure on him in an interrogation – or so I reasoned.

The best place to steal explosives from was pretty obvious. The State Explosives Reserve in Baldivis held everything I needed in one convenient location. It was set up by the government in 1984 as a place to stockpile and control the distribution of explosives – so they didn't fall into the hands of ratbags like me, I suppose. I wasn't sure how secure the place was, but there was only one way to find out.

I'd need some linear-shaped charges similar to the type we used to blow holes in walls when entering buildings in the Regiment. Failing that, I'd need some plastic explosives to make my own. Civilians use shaped charges to fracture boulders and seismic charges for oil exploration. They also use a sheet explosive called metabel or datasheet; this plastic explosive is used to case-harden the rock-crusher jaws on mining or quarry sites, and its velocity of detonation is almost the same as military-grade plastic explosives, so it would be perfect for my needs. The only real difference between civilian and military explosives is quantity. In civilian applications they tend to go for precision for safety's sake and to keep costs down. In the military we went for overkill and maximum damage.

The reserve is a series of storage bunkers, set in the middle of a large pine plantation a safe distance from any private residences.

I'd never been near the place, so I planned on spending a few days on site doing a detailed recon. My recon had been a bit slack with the supermarkets, so I was determined to cover every contingency this time. With rations packed, as well as some camouflaged bush gear and the pair of gumboots from the mine site, the next night I rode the 60 clicks through the rain to get to Baldivis. Finding a lying-up place in the pine forest was easy enough. I chose a spot that was in a small depression amidst a thick stand of trees. After camouflaging the lines of sight and trading my wet running shoes for gumboots and dry socks, I set out on foot to do the recon.

I couldn't believe this place didn't have a permanent guard on site. There was enough blasting capacity here to level Perth's central business district, and it was all stored out in the middle of nowhere with nobody looking after it. I checked the empty guardhouse and could see the alarm panel through the window. It showed sixty lights, meaning there were sixty bunkers on site, and I had to check them all to find what I needed. It looked like it was going to be a long night. I expected there would be motion sensors in each bunker and reed switches that would signal any door being opened, so I'd need to be careful.

I did a quick tour of the grounds and quickly realised I'd need more than a week to cut my way in, negotiate the alarms, check each bunker and then conceal my entry point. I also had to somehow get my hands on an inventory. The guardhouse was rigged with its own alarm so looking in there was out of the question. The two companies that used the site for storing their explosives both had offices in little transportable cabins, or 'dongers' as they are called in the mining game, on site.

The first donger had one of its sliding windows open a crack, so I was able to get in there without leaving a sign. It was just a bare desk and a single filing cabinet with company receipts stored alphabetically. It took less than ten minutes to search through everything – no itemised list or inventory there. The second donger had its sliding windows locked with lengths of dowelling laid in the tracks to stop anyone just popping the lock with a hard slap on the window. The door locks were not the type that were easily tackled with a basic lock-picking kit either, so I decided to smash the window and climb in. I opened the door from the inside and then broke off a low-hanging branch from the closest pine tree and stuck it through the broken glass. There was a fair bit of wind accompanying the sheets of rain, so I figured it might look like the window died of natural causes.

The second office looked less temporary than the first. There were a few more filing cabinets and a computer was sitting on the desk. I hit the power switch on the computer and it only booted up part of the way before asking me for a password. It was an IMB machine and looked to be either a 286 or 386 generation with a password program in the BIOS, which are the tiny set of instructions kept by a little battery when it's turned off. The password box was eight characters, so I tried a few obvious ones like: 00000000, EXPLOSIV, EXPLODE1 and each time got the message PASSWORD IS INVALID. PLEASE TRY AGAIN. Then I flicked through the top drawer of the filing cabinet and sure enough, under 'P' was a sheet of paper with the password written on it. It was the company name. I probably should have guessed that one.

I typed in the password and the machine finished booting up. This was in the days before Windows, and I didn't know much about computers apart from a few basic instructions. At the C:\

prompt I typed DIR and a list of directories immediately scrolled down the screen. One of these was INVENTRY, so I typed DIR INVENTRY and in that directory was a spreadsheet file with a list of different types of detonators and explosives, each assigned a bunker number. A quick scan through and it was obvious that bunker numbers three and five were the ones with the detonators and plastic explosives that I needed.

I cleaned my bootprints from the floor and locked the front door before doing a quick recon of the bunkers. Both were above-ground sheds with audible alarms and blue lights on them. I figured there would be trembler switches on the doors and motion sensors inside the buildings, so I'd have to move fairly fast once they had been breached. Although the distance of the site from the city and the series of gates that an investigating security guard would need to unlock before reaching the site would give me enough time to gather what I needed and get away. The horizon was starting to colour by this time; it was time to get back to the lying-up place and have a snooze.

A couple of hours later the sound of chainsaws and heavy machinery woke me. I cammed-up and stalked over in the direction of the noise. There were a crew of blokes felling some of the pine trees more than a kilometre away; it was unlikely they'd stumble across my camp.

Three days on site gave me plenty of time to observe the security patrols and have a more detailed look at the bunkers. There was only one patrol each night and they came at exactly the same time, so I reckoned I'd have about three hours to set up and do the job. The roof looked like the easiest place to make entry into the bunkers. Tin snips would cut a hole in the corrugated-iron roof and if there was arc mesh reinforcing the inside, I could cut through that with bolt cutters. I had spied an aluminium ladder in an unlocked gardener's shed on my recon and that would get me up on the roof. I decided to make the entry right on the stroke of midnight in the hope that the security company would be distracted by their shift change at that time.

Midnight on night three and it was pouring with rain, the burglar's friend. After retrieving the ladder, I moved over to bunker three, which held the detonators, being careful to stick to the gravel path and avoid leaving footprints in the sand. Once on the roof, I made a V-shaped cut in the tin and peeled back the flap for a look. The shed had a high roof and the needle of light from my taped-up penlight wasn't strong enough to make out any detail near the floor. Then I remembered a light switch on the outside of the building, so I dropped down and turned the lights on. The bunkers didn't have any windows, but shafts of light were visible through the front door. This caught me for a second, but the security guard would have to be passing close by to see the light. Back on the roof, I now had a clear view inside the shed. Unbelievably there weren't any motion detectors. I could see the reed switches on the doors and a smoke detector, but none of the little infra-red sensors high in the corners where they should have been. The job had suddenly gotten a lot easier.

I did the same with bunker five and saw that it was packed almost to the roof with different types of explosives. There was anzomex, AN60, powergel, det-cord, tetratayl-seismic shaped charges and plenty of detasheet; even a couple of tonnes of ball powder on a pallet; this was for police use so they could reload their pistol ammumition. It was a treasure chest of nearly anything that went bang, and no motion detectors here either.

Once I'd checked out what I needed, I made a bigger hole in the tin and used the bolt cutters to make an entry hole in the arc mesh. Then I returned to bunker three and did the same. I wrapped the blue lights and audible alarms in hessian bags that I'd also salvaged from the gardener's shed. In the instance that I did set off the alarms, this should dampen the sound enough to not alert any one nearby. Covering the lights also meant that the guard was less likely to rush straight to the bunker; he'd have to check the alarm panel in the guardhouse first, buying me some more precious time.

Now for a test run. Just because I hadn't seen any motion sensors didn't mean they weren't there. I climbed down into bunker three, walked across the floor, then climbed back out, down the ladder and ran over to the guardhouse to check the alarm panel. No lights came on, so it looked like I had plenty of time to go shopping, as long as I didn't hit one of the reed switches on the doors.

From bunker three I selected a couple of hundred safety-fuse detonators and a similar amount of electrically initiated ones. I climbed down from bunker three's roof, switched off the lights and was just making my way over to bunker five when I heard the front gate rattle. Through the rain I hadn't even heard the security guard's car come up the track. He wasn't on schedule, which made me think straightaway about having triggered a silent alarm. I quickly climbed onto the roof and pulled the ladder up behind me, lying prone but keeping watch on him. He seemed pretty relaxed so maybe he wasn't responding to anything, I hoped. Lucky I wasn't inside one of the sheds with the light on when he turned up. As I lay watching him, I could hear a rhythmic *tic tic tic* sound. It was coming from close by, so I looked inside the bag for whatever was making the noise. Then I realised that the hammering of my heart was so strong that with my mouth open it was making a ticking noise in my throat: not good for my blood pressure, this criminal business.

The guard's car pulled into the reserve and he started a slow drive around, shining a spotlight on each and every building as he went. It took him about half an hour to get around the whole complex, before pulling out and locking the front gate behind me. Luckily, he hadn't noticed the hessian bags wrapped around the alarm lights and boxes on two of the bunkers. I gave it ten minutes and then set to work again.

It didn't take me long to find the detasheet, seismic charges and high-velocity detonating cord that I needed. Then I made another one of those rash decisions that I had started to favour so much. In hindsight the smartest thing I could have done was to disguise my point of entry on each bunker. With their occasional use, it might have been days, or even weeks, before someone bothered to look close enough to spot the holes I'd made. Then they'd have to do a stocktake to work out what was missing. It would only be then they'd realise that the thief was experienced in demolitions, which would have inevitably pointed the finger at me. By which time I'd have already done the gold job. But no, instead of thinking it through logically I decided just to blow the whole place up.

There were about 55 tonnes of explosive in the shed. If it were the movies, I would have lit a long fuse on a single stick of dynamite and run like hell before watching it go up in a mushroom cloud. But different explosives have different methods of ignition and the result of only setting off one lot would have been lots of dangerous munitions scattered far and wide, possibly onto private properties, making the clean up a nightmare.

I was careful to link up the various stacks of explosives with detonating cord, so they'd all ignite simultaneously. I placed a couple of crates of gelignite on the police academy's ball powder to make sure it went as well. The seismic charges were a bit tricky as there were thousands of these small separated charges. I doubted they'd go off without being initiated separately, which would have taken longer than the rest of the night to rig. After a bit of mucking around, I decided to place a couple of detasheets right on top of them so that the majority would ignite instantaneously, and hopefully the heat would set the rest off before they could be scattered too far. Where possible I arranged the blasts to travel down and in, rather than outwards, to prevent the charges being scattered before they could ignite. But with such a range of detonating velocities it wouldn't be perfect. It took a good hour to set up and there was a spiderweb of det-cord running all over the shed when I'd finished.

Lighting the fuse inside the building would set off the smoke alarm, so once I'd joined everything together I ran a length of det-cord under the front door and connected it to a fuse outside. I lit a small length of fuse and timed its burn rate so I could calculate how much to use. In the Regiment we took pride in being able to set a fuse that would ignite a charge at the exact moment required: not one second before or after. Most fuses burn at about one centimetre per second but it pays to test it as there is always slight variation. Once the burning fuse hit the primary detonator, an ignition blast would travel into the shed at eight kilometres a second, hopefully hitting each stack almost simultaneously.

I figured a five-minute fuse would allow me time to get to the boom gate at the front of the compound. I'd need to be there in case another unannounced security guard turned up while the fuse was burning. I'd have to bail up and restrain him rather than risk having his death on my hands. Sometimes a fuse can double up on itself and the flame can take a short cut leading to an unexpected detonation before you've had time to get away, so I strung it along the external support girders on the side of the shed.

Everything was set now. I had a quick look around to check the place was still deserted, then tossed the ladder up on to the roof of the bunker and lit the fuse. The boom gate was just a kilometre away so a quick run had me up there with plenty of time to go. I ducked into the scrub next to the boom gate and checked my watch; thirty seconds to go.

It was coming up to 4 a.m. and I could see that the houses and small farmsteads down the road were still dark and quiet. It was the darkest hour, just before dawn, and there was a constant drizzle of rain and a mist in the upper branches of the pine forest. The only other sound was the frogs in the nearby swamp.

Ten seconds to go. I looked over towards the reserve and counted down the seconds under my breath. *Zero*, no bang. Doubt crept in. Maybe the safety fuse had got wet? Maybe I'd stepped on it in the dark? Every blaster's nightmare: thinking about having to walk back up to a hot site, not sure if the thing will go up.

Suddenly there was a flash so bright everything looked X-rayed. Then two painfully loud sounds: a sharp crack, then a thunderous boom. A searing wave of hot air blew over, knocking me down. It was an intense experience. I had a few seconds with my face in the dirt, wondering first if I was still alive, then waiting for the pain to really start because I assumed I'd burnt all of my skin off.

They reckon the bang could be heard up to 40 kilometres away. It still holds the record for the largest 'criminal-initiated explosion' in Australia, which is nothing to be proud of, I suppose. There was a dead silence for what seemed like ages, and I was convinced I'd blown my eardrums. Then a dog barked; horses whinnied in panic and kicked the sides of their stalls. Time for me to get moving. I was still pissed off it had blown four seconds late.

I crawled across the road and under a fence. I saw a small hill with a thin stand of trees a few hundred yards away and so crept up there to get a better view. The site was glowing and there was the occasional muffled explosion – either from the tins of ball powder or seismic charges that hadn't ignited in the initial blast and were now being set off by the heat. I prayed some security guard didn't roar up to the site and play hero. They all needed to wait for a demolitions expert to arrive.

Fifteen minutes later I heard the distant wail of a police siren and once on site, they immediately blocked the gate – much to my relief as there were still regular explosions going off. I could see that bunker five had been obliterated except for a very buckled and dented concrete floor. The pine trees had done their job well and had insulated the impact to the surrounding area. Satisfied that nobody was hurt, I boxed around to where my bike was stashed and rode over to my new LUP.

As usual, I didn't try to leave the area immediately but waited out the initial shit-storm for a couple of days. I'd camouflaged a good spot in thick scrub that had no tracks through it. I didn't see a soul for the whole time I was there. This 'stay in the area and stay low' policy has always worked for me. I heard the police helicopter flying over the area a few times but otherwise it was quiet. The radio news bulletins were full of stories about the blast, along with plenty of speculation that somebody had triggered it to hide a theft, along with plenty of speculation that somebody was me. It wasn't long before the coppers were saying that I'd taken the explosives to conduct a one-man war against the Western Australian authorities. Not even nearly true, but it made good headlines.

Less than a week later I was shuffling along the bike path near Canning Bridge, which crosses the Swan River just near the Raffles Hotel, one of Perth's art deco landmarks. Hunched over in a black duffel coat and beanie, wearing my trusty mining gumboots and carrying fishing gear, I looked like any of the hundreds of blokes you see fishing for bream and mullet around the riverbanks. I was four hours early for my meeting with Des, which gave me plenty of time to check for any coppers who might be setting up surveillance.

It hadn't taken me long to track Des down. I knew he'd still be on parole so a couple of bogus calls to the Department of Justice and I had his phone number and home address. In prison we'd agreed to use 'Pegasus', a significant name to a couple of former paratroopers, if we ever needed to make contact. When I called him and said it was 'John Pegasus' needing a quote on some bricklaying he was a little bit stunned.

'Is that who I think it is?'

'Sure is, bloke. Meet me on the Canning Bridge near the Raffles at 9:30 p.m. Bye.'

The police were, of course, looking under every rock in WA trying to find me and had been grilling anyone who might have had anything to do with me over the past few years. Even 'mates of mates' were being questioned; for example, Raj, a mate of Marty's whom I'd only met once, had the coppers knocking on his parents' door at 2 a.m. and sitting on his bed for four hours, asking where I was. They had Des down as a known associate of mine and my bogus enquiries through the Department of Justice had raised a red flag. They had phone-tapped our first conversation and my 'go straight to jail, do not pass go' card had been turned up without my knowing it.

Des was in his early forties; he had a short and solid build and receding dark-brown hair. He had that squat waddle that comes from miles of stomping with heavy loads. He was right on time and I picked him walking up to the bridge straightaway. I walked towards him and we crossed paths without him recognising me. I had a straggly beard, my hair was long and I looked like an old hippy in my fishing get-up. I spun around and then walked up behind to give his elbow a tug.

'Keep walking, mate. Don't look back,' I muttered and let a ten metre gap open up between us before calling out a couple more instructions. 'Get back in your car. Drive to the South Perth Yacht Club. Wait for me there.'

The yacht club was about ten minutes' walk away and Des's car was the only one in the car park when I got there. I waited in the bushes on the verge for another ten minutes to check for suspicious activity before quickly walking over and getting in the passenger's side.

After going solo for so long, it was bloody good to catch up with someone familiar. We shared a crushing handshake and had a good long yarn about old times. Des had been doing well on the outside, picking up plenty of casual bricklaying work and keeping himself out of trouble. I almost couldn't stop myself from babbling – it was that good to talk. I can still remember how happy I felt at the time, which goes to show that as much as we'd like to think we can go without human contact, we can't. Eventually, we got down to business.

'Mate, I'm going to do over the mine,' I said. 'I'll give you a brick of gold for your info, or you can come in with me on the job and I'll go ya halves.'

He probably knew I was going to ask and so didn't look too surprised. But I could understand when he hesitated for a while. It's not as if he were desperate or struggling for money. But I knew he hadn't been the only bloke pilfering gold from Youanmi and that a couple of other blokes had dobbed him in to save their own skins. Those same blokes had threatened to bash his family while he was inside if he ratted them out.

'Fuck 'em,' he said after a while. 'I'd love to do those fuckers over. Besides, I'll be fucked if I'm laying bricks for the rest of my life.'

'Well, mate. Have a think about it. It's a big thing to step over the line again and you'll have to sort out a rock-solid alibi for a few days. Meet me in Kings Park on Sunday and if you're still keen, we'll go from there.'

'No, fuck that. I'm keen. Let's go now.'

'No, mate. Don't make a rash decision. Think it over and I'll see you in a couple of days.'

I got him to hold his hand over the interior light while I slipped back out into the night.

Back in Swanbourne there was plenty of work to do. I had to turn the detasheet into some linear-shaped charges that would cleanly cut a hole in the back of the gold safe. Scrounging around the back of the rifle range, I found some aluminium Coke cans and an old manhole cover made of 5-centimetre-thick steel. The steel was bound to be thicker than the safe, so if my shaped charges cut through it, then I'd know they'd work on the night.

Beneath the rifle range was a network of storm-water drainage tunnels that were 30 metres deep in places. The entrance to the system was a shaft with a heavy concrete lid that was hidden amongst a thick crop of bushes. I'd often used the system to get in and out of the rifle range. I figured this would be a good place to test fire the charges after I made them up. A shaped charge is a V-shaped or conical wedge with explosives packed around it. When ignited, the explosives push in to the space and create a 'jet' of plasma travelling at supersonic speed. It will bore through anything, even concrete or armoured steel.

Making a linear-shaped charge to cut a hole in a steel plate is simpler than making the conical shape needed to bore into concrete. The jet of plasma doesn't have to cut very far so a triangular void made by strips of detasheet set at right angles is sufficient. I made the V-shaped channels using aluminium from the Coke cans. The cans were cut into 2-centimetre-wide strips, which were joined together, then bent at a 90-degree angle. The detasheet was then cut into 2.3-centimetre-wide strips and glued along the length of the aluminium strips, with ports in the end for the detonators to fit into. The lengths were then strengthened by binding them up with gaffer tape so they wouldn't bend out of shape.

After carrying my handiwork down into the tunnels, I set a shaped charge on the steel manhole cover, connected an electrical initiator and ran a wire back out to the hidden entrance amongst the trees. After sliding the heavy concrete cover back in place, I took a seat and waited for activity at the range to pick up. With the amount of rifle fire at the range and the occasional explosion echoing over from the CT training at the barracks, I figured the muffled thump of my charge going off 30 metres below ground wouldn't seem too out of place.

Firing at a range occurs in carefully controlled time brackets, then halted while the targets are checked, so the noise comes in intermittent loud volleys. As the next volley sounded I cranked the charge off. As far as 'muffled thumps' go this one wasn't very muffled. A deep rumble shook the earth. This was followed by a queer sensation in my stomach, similar to taking a fast elevator, as the tunnel lid was lifted and thrown about 10 metres clear, with me still sitting on it. It was the second time in a week that I'd underestimated the strength of a charge and had nearly blown myself up. The pressure of the blast coming out of the tunnel mouth was enough to lift me and the 100-kilo concrete lid and blow us away like dry leaves.

That's surprising, I thought as I lay on my back spitting out sand and looking up at a mini-mushroom cloud billowing out of the tunnel. *I must see if I can go a day without blowing myself up sometime soon.*

I'd figured that since the tunnels were big enough to walk through without crouching, and extended for hundreds of yards in each direction that the blast would have plenty of room to disperse horizontally. I scratched my chin for a second and then thought, *Shit! The smoke!* and ran around madly through the scrub, flapping my shirt to disperse the smoke that was like a neon sign saying 'Dave Everett – hiding here'. Soon after this, another volley rang out from the firing range. It was a relief to hear it was business as usual up there. Then a deep boom sounded from the CT training area and it seemed my little test had gone unnoticed.

After the smoke had cleared, I scrambled back down the shaft to check my work. The steel manhole cover had a 60-centimetre-square hole in it. The charge had gone through it like it was soft cheese. There was no need for a second test, although I made a mental note to stand well back when we blew the safe. I man-handled the scorched-looking concrete lid back into place, then camouflaged the site and worked my way back to camp.

The rest of the day was spent making up the charges for the safe and getting all the kit together for the job. I still had some armour-piercing rounds for the SLR I'd bought on the Gold Coast. I'd issue this to Des so he'd have enough firepower to knock out the engine block of any vehicle trying to escape the mine site, while I'd use the modified M-16 for intimidation value.

By mid-afternoon I had the job bag prepared and sterilised. That night I rode back up to the War Memorial in Kings Park, meeting up with Des only a few hundred metres from the spot where I'd first laid-up after faking my abduction nearly a year before. We stuck the bike in the boot of Des's car and drove over the other side of the river to South Perth. The public toilets near the river just off Berwick Street are a common meeting place for gay men, so a couple of blokes sitting in a car didn't look too out of place, although any bloke who knocked on our windows looking for love would have been in for a rude shock.

I wasn't expecting Des to back out, but I gave him one last chance.

'So, what's it to be, mate? Are you keen or what? Last chance to say no.'

'When do we kick off, mate?' He smiled and with that we started going through the job in detail. Des had already come up with a good alibi; he would start a bricklaying job in the southern suburb of Gosnells early on the morning following the job. This was near the spot we'd picked to melt down the gold, so I'd be able to drop him off and get busy while he would spend the day at work. He'd probably look knackered, but otherwise it would be bloody hard for the coppers to link him to an armed robbery the night before nearly a thousand kilometres away.

The first of many signs I missed was that Des seemed to react a bit nervously every time a different car pulled into the car park, and he nearly froze when a police car roared past us up the highway with its sirens blaring. The next was when I gave him the money to go shopping. He was to buy the timing devices we needed to drop the communications towers, a good secondhand F350, fuel, power jacks, spare tyres and food for the trip.

'Now, the radios,' he said. 'Have you got 'em?'

'Yep, radios are sorted.'

'Now, listen. Instead of you fucking about breaking into things, let me buy them legally.'

This came out of left field and surprised me a bit. 'You'll buy them? No —'

Des cut me off.

'No, don't worry about it. I'll get them; I need them for my job.'

'I don't need to break in anywhere, Des; I need the radios for another job.'

'I'll buy 'em for ya, mate; let me buy 'em for ya. Just give me the model number and I'll get 'em.'

We went on like this for another ten minutes before I managed to convince Des to forget the radios. It turned out he was trying to get me to use a set that were supplied by the police. This way they'd be able to monitor our coms and increase their chances of taking me in without it turning into a shooting match. The police had actually kicked Des's door in about two hours after he had met me near the Raffles on Canning Bridge. I was wrong to think that they wouldn't have been able to put the frighteners on him, because they made him an offer he couldn't refuse. They fitted a listening device to his car and almost everything that had been said between us was recorded from that point on. My gabbing about the two botched supermarket jobs and the Baldivis job gave them plenty of juicy evidence for later on. It would have also given one copper some sleepless nights. In a roundabout way Des asked me about the list they'd found in the bag on Magnetic Island.

'You planning to do a few people?'

'I beg your pardon?' I said

'You know, coppers. You're not planning to do them before the job, are you?'

'No, fuck that. If I started killing people around here, it'd bring too much shit down on my family. Shame, I wouldn't mind paying that Solomon a visit.'

'Who?'

'Frank *bloody* Solomon. The one who set me up: 20 Candle Way, Willeton, drives a Commodore, has a double garage, comes home about seven most nights.'

'Oh, that Solomon,' Des laughed.

I got to listen to the surveillance tapes a few months later in court. My lawyer made them play the tape to the jury because on the strength of the transcript alone it sounded like I was plotting to overthrow the government, but not before my murderous rampage.

But Des and I were just bullshitting like a couple of blokes will do when they get revved up and start raving. No different than the story that the bloke at the pub tells about his grand final-winning goal that gets kicked from ten yards further out each year. We were talking about bombing police headquarters as a diversion and robbing the Reserve Bank of Australia with a team of mercenaries I'd bring in by boat from Burma – killing anyone who got in our way. It was pure fantasy and when the court heard the tape they could hear us laughing at ourselves as we were crapping on. But I suppose to a bunch of coppers who still didn't know how much explosive I had stolen from Baldivis, listening in would have been worrying to say the least.

But all the court drama was a fair way off. Des and I set a date to meet the Wednesday after we had the radio conversation. Des would hand over the timing device and give me an update on the purchase of all the other gear, including the car, then we'd meet again to drive up and do the job the Tuesday after that. He dropped me off at the back of Kings Park and I rode back to Swanbourne. The next few days I spent rechecking the gear, packing up my hide for the last time and removing any trace of my presence from the area.

Wednesday came around pretty fast and I rode back up to Kings Park, stashed the bike in the bush and walked up to where Des's car was parked. Des is normally a funny bloke and can get a laugh out of almost anything. Despite the serious nature of what we were about to do, we'd had fun talking through the planning. I should have picked that something was wrong when he seemed strained and awkward. He had only driven a short distance when he said he needed to pull over to take a leak. When he got back into the car I quizzed him.

'You okay, mate? You seem a bit jumpy. You sure you want to go through with this?'

'No, I'm okay. I was just busting for a leak waiting for you to turn up.'

I told him to drive over to Nedlands and park near the outdoor cinema at the University of Western Australia. Movies were showing that night so the car park would have plenty of people coming and going, allowing us to blend in. Des was still as stiff as a board and not saying much; his driving was jerky as well. I looked in the mirror and saw a police patrol car following right behind us. There was a car park entry about 30 metres in front of us and I made a quick decision.

'Pull in here. Pull in here now,' I almost shouted, not giving him any warning.

The police car put on its flashing indicators to follow us in, then it stopped flashing suddenly and the coppers roared away: clue number five that something was up. The coppers must have been just about to pull us over for a traffic infringement but been warned off by the tactical response group, who I assume had been following us from a long way back. I had missed that as well. I suppose it was a bit like being at the pub and meeting some sheila who is really average. You've got your beer goggles on and it's been a while since you've had a shag, so you choose to ignore the bumpy nose, bucked teeth and screeching voice. I was so keen to get this job done that I was overlooking every warning sign, and because Des was the first bloke I'd shared any action with in the past year, he was my best mate in the whole world who couldn't possibly do the wrong thing by me.

We sat in the car park for a few minutes after the patrol car had disappeared and went over the plan again. It was like trying to teach a kid with ADHD; Des was so jumpy it was hard to get him to concentrate, but eventually we nailed all the details down. I'd planned for us to meet up the following night in some bushland near Gosnells. I was going to spend the next day carting all of the gear over there from Swanbourne, and then I'd be ready to go. Loading the car with the explosives and guns was one of the highest risk points in the operation, as anyone who saw us could note a few different details that would come in handy in the police's enquiries.

'I'd prefer we met up in daylight,' said Des.

'Fuck off, Des, that's a stupid idea. C'mon, mate! Get your thinking cap on for fuck's sake.'

'No, I'd prefer we did it in daylight, Dave. That way we'll be able to see anyone coming.'

I almost couldn't believe I was hearing this.

'See anyone coming? I'm more worried about anyone bloody seeing us going. How do you reckon we can spear off if we are compromised in broad daylight?'

'No, Dave. I just think it would better all round if we did the meet in daylight.'

I ran out of patience after that. Des had got so fixated on a daylight meet it was ridiculous. Again, my 'good mate Des' goggles had blinded me to the fact that he was operating under police instructions. They were as nervous as hell about taking me down and wanted to tip the odds in their favour. Even though they now had plenty of evidence, they wanted to take me as late in the game as possible. Operating on the theory I had a few other accomplices, they figured that taking us at the final meeting might reveal someone else. Of course, they didn't consider that if I'd had other people in my team, I'd never have contacted a virtual stranger like Des in the first place. But they had to take us before we got on the road up to Youanmi, when we'd be armed to the teeth with a whole desert to hide in.

'Des, read my fucking lips: we are not going to meet up in broad fucking daylight. You'll meet me at 7 p.m. and that's the end of it.'

The words were barely out of my mouth when I heard an engine roar. I turned to see a white van mount the kerb behind and accelerate towards us. It smashed into the back of Des's car with a *boom* that threw us a few yards forward, smacking my forehead hard into the dash. Black-suited coppers carrying pump-action shotguns swarmed out of the back of the van towards us.

I looked across at Des and he said, 'Oh, what's this?'

I knew at that moment he'd ratted me out.

I thought about reaching for the .45 in my daypack on the back seat. I knew I was going to be executed; no way were the coppers taking me alive. They'd declared war on me a year ago and would have made a pact to knock me for sure. *May as well go down shooting*, I thought. Then things slowed right down. Those seconds lasted about five minutes each. I reached back for the gun as I saw the tactical response coppers barrelling towards the car in the left-hand mirror.

Just then, my gaze wandered up along the bank of the Swan River. I saw a young couple walking towards the cinema. Too far away too hear or see what was happening, they were getting on with their picture-perfect lives and enjoying a warm night at the movies. The woman carried a young girl who looked about eight months old – the same age as my daughter – and she was looking over her mum's shoulder straight at me. She had big blue eyes. The fight just drained out of me. I decided to spend my last free moments looking at something beautiful instead of doing something ugly.

It was a good op, the takeout. There was no shooting. Just me getting ripped out of the car, knocked around a bit, stripped, cuffed and thrown in the back of the van with a bag over my head. The coppers spent eight hours in a marathon tag-team interrogation session, but I just went into a trance for most of it – blurring my vision and tuning out their voices. I just let my mind wander over all the times and places I'd felt truly free in the past few years, while they were still fresh in my memory.

The main emotion I felt, knowing I was in custody again, was relief. Life on the run had been starting to do me in. All the plotting, planning and constant second-guessing myself could stop. I knew from here on in at least I'd sleep on clean sheets and get a regular feed. I'd also get to see my kids from time to time. That was all that mattered for now.

THE MONASTERY

Prison? Prison was boring. Apart from a few highlights, it was the same day four thousand times over. I was a criminal; there is no escaping that fact. But unlike most blokes doing long sentences, I've got mostly non-criminal friends. Nowadays these people shake their heads when they try to comprehend what being locked up for over a decade is like. For me it wasn't that out of the ordinary; it was just like boarding school or the army: you get up when it's time to get up, clean your room, work when it's time to work, eat when it's time to eat, sleep when it's time to sleep and try not to piss anybody off.

I was put into the special-handling unit (SHU) at Casuarina Prison and it was the last time I saw grass or sky for nearly three years. The SHU, or shu-box as we called it, was created to house the worst of the worst and so far has been escape proof. The complex cost more than $12 million to build and more than $100 000 a year to house each inmate; it has a ratio of three screws to each prisoner. It comprises two square blocks of eight heavily fortified cells, accessible only through several steel doors and an airlock.

There were closed-circuit cameras everywhere I looked and every door was remote operated from a security post manned twenty-four hours a day. The shu-box had only been built the year before I moved in, so I was the first occupant of my cell. It was sparkling clean with fresh sheets and a pillow on the bunk, a new stainless-steel washbasin and even my own shower. After living like an animal in the bush, it felt like a luxury hotel room.

My arrival in the prison created a stir amongst all the screws. When I was being processed a small crowd of them gathered to check out the newest celebrity. The guard who was entering my details asked for any aliases I had used, so I gave them a few: Chris Roberts, Fred Smith, Bill Benson (after Bill and Ben), Pepé Le Pew and a few others that I can't remember now. Put that in your computer and smoke it, I thought.

Almost as soon as I arrived, rumours started circulating about how a gang of ex-SAS cronies and mercenaries from Burma were going to attack the prison and bust me out. The screws in the shu-box were even given extra self-defence training in case I tried to kill them with my little finger or some other Ninja trick we were supposed to have learnt in the Regiment. This was a never-ending source of fun for me, and I would occasionally drop the odd hint just to fire up their paranoia and stave off boredom.

Every time I was transported to court it cost the government more than $160 000. A small convoy of armoured cars, along with several other escort vehicles, would all barrel down the freeway with lights and sirens blaring. Helicopters with snipers circled overhead and as well as the MSU (Metropolitan Security Unit – the prison system's special armed squad), the police TRG and a whole SAS team were deployed each time I was on the road. I heard later that the Regiment boys brought a M-60 machine-gun, M-79 grenade launchers and 66-millimetre anti-tank rockets with them for the job; someone had definitely convinced them to expect trouble. It might have been something to do with the first time I rode in with the MSU boys and saw they were carrying 12-gauge shotguns and .38 revolvers. 'How do you expect to stop an armoured personnel carrier with those pop guns?' was all I asked; but they must have taken me seriously.

It took almost a year to clear my court cases. Both the State and Commonwealth DPPs spent hundreds of thousands of dollars prosecuting me. After an eight-day trial, I was found innocent of the marijuana charge. The Commonwealth flew over their top prosecutor, Brian Martin QC, from South Australia for the heroin case. Eight days later I was found innocent again. Eight must have been my lucky number. My solicitor, Richard Bayly, from Bayly and O'Brien, acted for me. Paul O'Brien and Richard are the best criminal lawyers in Western Australia.

Richard had spoken with the DPP prior to the heroin trial and they had agreed to drop four of the original armed robbery charges as long as I pleaded guilty to the cinema job, the supermarket jobs and the Baldivis blast, and to planning the goldmine job (incitement to commit armed robbery). They had no evidence on a number of other armed robberies I'd been charged with in an attempt to tie me in with their 'ex-military gang' theory.

There were a string of associated charges dealing with each robbery, such as breaking and entering premises, unlawful use of motor vehicles, kidnapping, etcetera. The police were also keen to charge me with incitement to murder based on the things Des and I had talked about in the car when they were recording us. But as soon as the tapes were played in court, it was obvious we were just a couple of blokes having fun bullshitting each other. Even so, I had to fight the charge hard and it wasn't until the end of 1993 that it was dropped.

Justice Wallwork, who had presided over the heroin trial, was the sentencing judge. The initial sentence was eighteen years, which was then reduced to fifteen years after considering the time already spent in custody, my guilty plea and the lack of a prior criminal record. The DPP appealed the sentence immediately; the media had built me into a monster and the relatively 'light' sentence made them look stupid. They wanted at least thirty-five years based on my supposed danger to society. A different set of judges heard the appeal and handed down a twenty-year sentence, with a two-year discount for time already served and no consideration for the lack of a prior criminal record, public service or guilty plea.

Out of that eighteen-year sentence, I would have to do a minimum of ten and a half years on the bottom (jail slang for time actually spent behind bars). Dealing with the thousands of details relating to the trial had taken most of my attention in that first year; once it was all over, I decided to do something I'd never have had the time to do on the outside. I set my sights on getting a Bachelor of Arts degree, majoring in journalism, international relations and strategic studies; my goal was to get a PhD in Asian Studies.

Life in the shu-box wasn't easy. Their main tactic to keep everybody docile was sleep deprivation. Every two hours during the night they'd come in, banging and clanging their way through the airlocks, switching on the lights and kicking our cell doors. When I finally joined the rest of the prison population the one thing I looked forward to was a decent night's sleep.

Sixteen dangerous prisoners and dozens of screws all existing in a tiny concrete box sounds like a recipe for chaos, but it seemed that this had the opposite effect in the shu-box, and most of the time it was deathly quiet. An American bloke in the cell next door said it was like a monastery and that became how I decided to treat it. I disciplined myself to exercise every morning and study hard during the day. I didn't bother with a television or any other contact with the outside world for nearly a year and a half, before my studies required me to become better acquainted with current affairs.

It took less than a day in prison and a few exchanges with my fellow inmates to realise that long-term incarceration will drive you mad. Forget rehabilitation, that's just token bullshit to keep the politicians happy. The purpose of prison is to strip you of your will by taking away all your choices, so you end up defeated and docile. In that isolated environment you lose your reference points in the world; if you take your cue from what's going on around you, all sorts of weirdness can result. Small things, like having the type of bread you eat changed or being unlocked ten minutes late, can consume some blokes until it's all they can think and talk about. I made a conscious decision to not get dragged down by things like this, and to avoid negative talk at all costs, so I wouldn't become bitter and twisted. At one point the coordinator of the shu-box pulled me up for smiling too much; he reckoned I was freaking out the guards and other inmates, and giving the impression that I was hiding something. I guess it's possible to be too positive.

It's probably hard for people on the outside to believe, but the freedom from making any real decisions from day to day can make for a cosy little zone. The thought of having to decide what to do with your day, what to wear, what to eat and the million other choices free people take for granted can become overwhelming. Even the difference between the shu-box and the rest of the prison was marked.

One bloke, who we called Maggot, after spending a couple of years in the shu-box, found the general prison environment so stressful that he climbed onto the roof of the complex and tried to break back in. The roof of the central atrium had tubular steel bars that were injected with bright red dye, sealed and pressurised, so that anyone who tried sawing through them would end up literally red faced. Maggot managed to break off one of the bars and was covered in red dye; he jumped up and down like an orangutan, screaming at the guards to let him back in. Eventually, they called in the MSU, who lost patience with his shouted insults, climbed up onto the roof, dragged him into the unit and beat him senseless with their truncheons and boots, with the seven shu-box inmates as witnesses.

We all wrote letters to the Ombudsman, protesting about this and, while nothing happened at the time, a couple of years later – after a few more complaints of brutality – the MSU was disbanded. I was bashed myself a few months later and spent a couple of months in hospital recovering from skull fractures. One bloke who shouldn't have been in my area was let in and I was king-hit from behind while in the shower and given a good kicking while I was on the ground. I have my suspicions about who let him in and that it might have had something to do with the complaints I had made about the bashing of Maggot. The bloke who did it is still in prison and will be there for a few more years yet.

I broke the stretch up into attainable goals. First was my security review in October 1997, in which I could be dropped down to medium security if I had been behaving myself. The next review was four years after that, and there I would have a chance to go to a minimum-security prison farm. Once I passed the entrance exam at Deakin University, I was able to break the time up into mini six-month sentences, corresponding with each semester. My majors were an easy choice, as the courses gave me a chance to explore the historical background to something I was naturally interested in – the use of military force by governments to oppress minorities; I'd had some first-hand experience, after all.

Things between the shu-box inmates were so harmonious that the authorities became suspicious at one point. One of my fellow inmates was an old Italian bloke, Bruno 'The Fox' Romeo, with strong family connections. Someone had started a rumour that a few shu-box screws had been given Mercedes Benz cars by him. The truth was that the old bloke was wheelchair bound and everyone, inmates included, tended to chip in to help him get around. What started as a joke about him being a 'mafia don' who would reward everyone for their help was taken seriously somewhere along the line – a full internal investigation resulted. Never let the truth get in the way of a good rumour.

The prison management began rotating guards in and out of the place more frequently to avoid any chance of Stockholm syndrome, where the good guys start developing empathy for the bad guys. They began monitoring calls from the unit and even sprang the occasional random strip-search on the guards on their way out. This stuff was all just bullshit dreamed up by someone trying to make a name for themselves within the Ministry of Justice.

In March 1995 someone turned off my 'danger' light and I was released back into the general prison community. That same afternoon I lay on the incredibly sweet-smelling grass and just stared at the sky for hours, giving myself severe sunburn in the process. Walking to the dining hall that night, I felt my chest tighten and had trouble breathing. It took me a while to realise I was having a panic attack. There were sixty blokes in there and the noise they made was deafening. I was a bit of a curiosity for a while – I was very thin, my skin was yellow-grey from lack of sun exposure, and I shuffled along, stooped over like an old man. One bloke reckoned I looked like Papillon. It took a few weeks to adjust to the noise and human contact, and it was a month or two before I could walk across the open courtyard without having a panic attack. I reckon if I didn't have a few bigger-picture goals, like finishing my studies, I might have tried to break back into the shu-box myself.

Once the panic subsided, I couldn't get enough of being outside. I paced the expansive lawns at every opportunity. After a while, a couple of screws came and talked to me, asking how long and wide I reckoned the grassed area was. After the third time they asked this, I worked out they were fishing for info on whether I was measuring it out to see if a plane or helicopter could land there. Their fantasy escape scenarios for me knew no bounds. Still, I suppose it gave them something to talk about.

In 1997 my review for medium security came up and I elected to go down to Albany Regional Prison, which is in the south-west corner of Western Australia and about 400 kilometres from Perth. I especially wanted to go down there so I'd be able to start my resocialisation before hitting a minimum-security prison farm. Albany had a reputation for treating prisoners like humans rather than like numbers, and that was the sort of place I wanted to be. It's the best-kept secret in the whole of WA's prison system. I remember when I first got off the escort vehicle at Albany one of the screws called me by my first name, which made me suspicious until I realised that was how they treated everyone.

I finished my BA in 1998, then enrolled for my Honours and did that over a two-year period, along with some basic computer courses and a Teaching English as a Second or Foreign Language certificate. I applied to do a PhD after that, but couldn't get past the requirement to be on campus for at least three months of the year. I decided instead to do a Masters and then transfer over to a doctorate after my release. My thesis for this project was the history and tactics of the Karen National Liberation Army.

Transferring to Albany turned out to be a good choice. The guards were fair and decent in their treatment of the prisoners; even the visitors I had down there commented on how polite the prison staff were, particularly as compared with the screws in Casuarina. The odd bloke did incur their wrath, but you would have to be a complete dickhead to get on their bad sides, as they gave plenty of gentle warnings to 'pull your head in' before they got tough.

I was walking back from the volleyball court with one of the screws one day when he said, 'Where's your other head, Dave?'

'What d'ya mean?'

'Oh, we were told before you came down to be bloody careful 'cos you were a two-headed monster who could flip out without any warning.'

'You shouldn't believe every rumour you hear,' was all I could think to say.

The Ministry of Justice had, at this time, been trialling a behavioural psychology-based violent offenders treatment program (VOTP). The basic theory behind it was that men like me, who chose violent means to reach our goals in life, did so because we lacked other skills to get what we wanted. All we needed was some training in 'pro-social behaviour' and help with our communication skills and we could go on to become valued members of society. I thought it was a load of bullshit and refused to go, saying that it would interfere with my studies, which were giving me a far more important skill set than how to turn the other cheek when some dickhead is giving you the shits. Besides, I wasn't forced into violent behaviour because I lacked any other skills; I chose it as a career because I liked shooting and blowing things up.

But I was only delaying the inevitable; I knew I'd need a good performance on the VOTP to make my parole date. The problem was that when I did apply I was assessed as unsuitable. They had a 'violence scale' of zero to thirty, with thirty being the most extreme, and you had to be at least a fifteen to get in. I was assessed by a clinical psychologist on two different occasions as a three; I made sure I had that in writing. Then the head of the VOTP received a complaint that I didn't have to do the program, probably from someone high up in the department. The decision to exempt me was overruled and I was ordered to pack my bags for a six-month stay in the city. I wasn't too happy about it at the time; it interrupted my studies and it meant moving back to a larger prison and encountering more wankers on a daily basis.

The remand centre that Jim and I had originally been moved to from Fremantle – the place where he had ended his life – had been redeveloped and was now called Hakea Prison. I moved up there in February 2001; I even got my old cell back. A Wing, Unit One. It was like stepping back into the dark ages. The place was filthy and most of the screws were the same constipated shitheads they were a decade ago. Luckily, I was only there for two days before they speared me up to Unit Nine, a newly built block. The atmosphere there was much better: the place was only a year old, there was hot running water and a remote-controlled colour TV, and the screws were a bit more 'user friendly'.

I was wrong about the VOTP; surprisingly, I found it valuable. The people running the program were genuinely committed and hardworking, and they stood out like beacons amid the cynical, defeated prison staff. Much of what we learnt was not new to me, but it was good to work through this stuff with other blokes on the program; it was the first real camaraderie I'd felt since my time with the Karen. I can see the sense in the idea now – that plenty of criminals box themselves in with bad choices because they haven't mastered a few skills that the rest of the population take for granted: like asking for help, basic negotiation skills, and the like.

The facilitators reckoned I was an anomaly. None of the psych tests showed any classically criminal-thinking patterns or abnormal brain functions and my family background had been basically normal. One facilitator, Cherie, recognised my symptoms of post-traumatic stress disorder, as her brother was a Vietnam-war veteran. She said to find help once I'd gotten out; they couldn't help me in prison.

There was a graduation ceremony at the end of the program, attended by all of the Ministry of Justice bigwigs. My mum was allowed to attend and I directed part of my speech to her. It went a bit like this.

My crimes were only a small part of my life, just a kink in the line, or an aberration, as somebody put it once. But it was enough to cause a huge derailment that sent my little trolley bouncing off the track and spiralling into a black hole. I was in big strife.

Unfortunately, at the time, sticking a gun in somebody's face and telling them what to do was second nature to me. People were just objects. I'd had it done to me and did the same to hundreds of people over my years in the military. The intensive training over those years tends to wire you up to that pattern of thinking.

So what, I thought. It's no big deal.

I couldn't understand what all of the fuss was about; I wasn't going to shoot anybody and nobody was getting hurt. Without realising it, I had already fallen into the trap of justifying my criminal actions.

Of course, the victims of my crimes didn't know they weren't going to be shot or hurt, and the consequences of those actions to their psychological wellbeing was pretty devastating, as it was for my family when I was arrested and sent to prison. I had absolutely no idea at the time what long-term impact my actions would have on others. What I thought was EDM (effective decision making) was actually DDM (defective or dumb decision making), which I seemed to excel at.

This dysfunctional and distorted thinking brought me unstuck really badly and I hit the floor with a mighty thump. I've been trying to pick myself up ever since.

Mum knew I'd changed after I'd been in the Regiment; I didn't think I had and wouldn't accept it. I guess I just didn't want to hear it and filtered it out. I kept thinking it was Mum who had changed – not me. I'd simply convinced myself that

I didn't have a problem; but that was the problem in itself. I didn't fully realise this until I did the VOTP, which brought reality home.

It's hard for me to admit it, Mum, especially in front of all these people, but you were right all along; the Regiment did change me and it has taken a hell of a lot of time to finally admit it. I guess it was a case of having too much pride and blaming bad luck on everything.

Anyway, it was a pretty deep hole I'd fallen into and it has taken a lot of effort to crawl back out. How did I do it? Firstly, with the help, support and faith of my mum.

I'm finally admitting that I had a problem. This is the final leg up out of the hole, and it has allowed me to slam the lid shut so that I won't fall back in.

I'm not a soldier any more. I'm a husband, a father, brother and a son.

A few months later I was transferred to a minimum-security prison farm. As soon as the prison truck pulled up, a brightly coloured parrot flew down and eyeballed me from a few metres away; it was a good omen. That night I asked one of the blokes what time lock-up was. He laughed. I had twelve months to serve but I knew then I was on my way home.

EPILOGUE

By Kingsley Flett

It's a practical boat, an aluminium-hulled 20-footer, small enough to manoeuvre the tidal creeks yet big enough for the long fast runs across the Cambridge Gulf. The deep hull can handle the standing waves created by the king tides and its high sides keep the crocodiles out. We chug up the centre of a tributary feeding one of the five rivers that drain into the gulf; its flow volume on a par with the Nile delta and the Amazon. Dirty green mangroves crowd in on each side and a pale-blue sky presses the humid air down.

Dave sits at the helm, one arm draped casually on the throttle and finger on the bottom of the wheel. He's wearing a battered felt hat, an Akubra, which is standard head-wear in the Kimberley; an old paint-spattered olive-green army shirt, board shorts and rubber flip-flops. His face is weathered and shows a few lines, but remains surprisingly youthful for someone in his mid-forties. If the photographs of Dave from his days in the Regiment make him look like a sixteen-year-old boy among men; then now he looks barely thirty.

It's not surprising to have found Dave here in one of the last truly wild places on earth. If you can think of the opposite of a prison cell, then this would be it. To the Aboriginal people the land is their story, and in Western Australia's Kimberley the eye travels from horizon to horizon and never fails to reveal an epic: fierce heat, heavy thunderstorms, blood-red mountain ranges, hundred-mile wide bushfires and big rivers with massive crocodiles lurking in the waterholes. Only the most accomplished and determined manage to carve a life up here. As Dave says, 'There's lots of elbow room.'

'Okay', he says quietly. 'Let's pull 'er up here.' He throttles down and swings us in a smooth arc towards the bank. The rest of us, Dave's wife Donna, her two teenage sons and I, get ropes ready to tie us off.

Dave is pure military: in that world one person barks the orders and everyone else scrambles to comply. I've got no problem with this. Even my most easygoing mates become grumpy bastards when they get in charge of a boat and Dave is no different. Donna has a problem though. She's a local, one of the Miriwoong Gajerrong language group and her great-grandfather is a Gajerrong man from the Northern Territory. Her people have been on this land for thousands of years and are surely one of the most communal societies on the planet; she's used to debating every small decision at length.

'Don't tie us up that way,' she says. 'Just hook up on those branches. That'll do.'

'Donna,' says Dave, his voice going thick and hard, like he's on the verge of a tantrum, which he is. 'If you tie up like that, the boat will get caught in the current and spin us around.'

'Nah, well, it doesn't bloody matter, does it?' she says back casually, giving me a wink and a smile.

The debate rolls back and forth like this for at least half an hour; it's more a clash of cultures than one of personalities. The boys are too smart to get involved. They exchange a knowing look and find somewhere to lie down for the duration.

Eventually, we tie off and settle in for an afternoon's fishing. Donna and the boys sit like stones, lines in the water. The only sounds are the occasional buzz of a fly and the plops of fish breaking the surface. We can't see any crocs but their telltale tracks are in the mud on the bank. They'd have slipped into the water as soon as they heard us coming and were now most probably sitting on the bottom of the river, their hundred-million-year-old metabolisms ticking over at a couple of calories per minute, waiting for us to make the first move. No one is going for a swim.

It's just a fishing trip to Dave and me, but to Donna and the boys it's a way to connect with the land. I remember Donna saying once, 'If I don't go out bush every few weeks, it feels like I start to fade away. Getting out here fills me up and makes me feel good.'

Donna hooks up first – a nice fat salmon. Not the barramundi we are here for but good eating anyway. Not much else breaks the silence and the patient meditation of waiting for a bite.

'This place is shit,' says Dave suddenly; the stillness is too much for him. 'Let's get 'er untied and go up that other creek.' He starts to move.

'David,' says Donna in that perfectly firm, stern tone that only mothers can produce. 'We'll just stay here and relax.'

That's the final word on the matter. Dave stomps up to the bow, leans against the windscreen, pulls his hat over his eyes and goes to sleep. There is part of Dave that's still eight years old, and like most little boys he has two speeds: flat-out and sleeping. Typical of all soldiers, he can also fall asleep anywhere. He looks at peace.

There was no glorious Hollywood moment where Dave one day walked into the sunlight and freedom. From the low-security prison farm he began a gradual reintegration back into society. First with day visits, then overnight stays, eventually leading to his final release. He and Donna had met in prison while she was teaching English to some of the inmates. He moved in with her after he got out and they moved north a year later.

People's reactions to Dave and his story are rarely moderate. They either see him as a hero or a villain. The truth is he's both. Australians have a history of romanticising outlaws, and then there are the war-junkies and chair-borne commandos who like to live vicariously through the combat experiences of soldiers. Those people should see the full picture: Dave shuffling the hallways at three in the morning, unable to sleep after another nightmare where he's been visited by one of the men he's killed in combat. Donna says that sharing the bed with him during one of these nightmares is a contact sport.

They should see him freaking out when plans are changed at the last minute. After more than ten years in prison, he is so conditioned to predictability that to be late, or not keep an appointment with him, causes physical distress.

They also need to see him in his reflective moments. There is a reason that criminals are flippant about their crimes and give the impression they lack remorse; it's too painful to think about it all the time. Dave's been trained to compartmentalise his feelings, putting away what is unnecessary and irrelevant. But when the memories of those deeds rear their heads, he can look haggard and old. He has to carry that guilt for the rest of his life.

It's been called Erichsen's disease, soldier's heart, shell shock, combat fatigue, war neurosis and operational exhaustion. Now known as post traumatic stress disorder, PTSD has been accepted worldwide as a valid psychiatric condition. The constant over-stimulation of the adrenal glands and the amygdale area of the brain permanently change the way emotions are processed. Sufferers of PTSD are alternately hyperactive and depressed; they block out their own emotions and those of people around them; they can also be extremely jumpy and react violently to sudden noises. For Dave it's 'all of the above'. It was his mum and one of his old SAS mates, Fess Parker, who pushed him to see a psychiatrist. He checks himself into the 'funny farm' regularly now to keep his medication in balance and to make sure he's travelling steadily.

His mother noticed a change in his personality as early on as his first year in the Regiment. Dave admits now that if he had listened to his mum and sought help, then the third part of his story would never have happened.

'But I was a young bloke then,' he says. 'What young bloke has ever listened to anyone?'

On a balmy late summer's evening, at an impeccably restored old beachside house in Perth, I went with Dave to a gathering of 'the old and bold', the Australian SAS Association. From Vietnam-era vets right through to those currently serving in Iraq and Afghanistan, they all get together from time to time at 'the house'. The most remarkable thing about them is how unremarkable they are. It could be a gathering of a local footy team, with the ruddy-faced old veterans talking about the glory days and the lean, super-fit, young brigade humouring them, laughing at their stories. The difference is the photos on the walls: portraits and group shots of young men in dirty fatigues and camo paint, holding rifles, with jungles, mountains and deserts as the backdrop; it's definitely not a footy club.

There is a reserved welcome for outsiders. They're not openly aloof, but not fully relaxed either – polite but distant. Dave had been back to the house a few times now. He wasn't too popular in the Campbell Barracks at the height of his notoriety because of the bad press he was bringing to the Regiment. But there is no sign of that now as his old mates from Three Squadron and the CT team come up and say g'day, stir him up about how young he's still looking and ask him what he's up to. I get the sense that no one here has passed judgment. There is a lot of compassion for the different paths blokes have trodden after the Regiment, and this sits alongside the knowledge that it hasn't been easy for many.

Being welcomed back was a big step for Dave. He now keeps in regular contact with his closest mates, like Marty, and his first troop sergeant in the Regiment, Maurie Wesson. He's also part of a network of ex-SAS soldiers that helps each other through hard times. There have been a few who've committed suicide and a host of others who fight the same psychological demons as Dave.

Dave's life is good now and in many ways he's blessed. He spends most of his time in the bush, where he is happiest. He has an extended family and, unlike most ex-criminals, his best friends are 'straight', leading lawful and successful lives. There isn't that peer-group pull to return to a life of crime. He has a close relationship with his two children from his first marriage and it's a credit to his first wife that she allowed him to stay in touch with them while he was in prison and to re-establish contact when he came out. They are both fine kids on the verge of adulthood.

People often ask me what kind of man Dave is. It's a question I can't answer definitively. Those who read this book will have to make up their own minds. Everyone has their own experience of Dave, and those who love him will think differently to those who have looked at him down a gun barrel.

The *excitable boy*, as Dave was nicknamed in the Regiment days, still shines through though – he's very mischievous. During the 2007 Australian federal election, both Prime Minister John Howard and soon-to-be-elected Kevin Rudd visit Campbell Barracks for an official function. Dave walks straight up to Kevin Rudd and says, 'G'day'. Standing a few metres away at the top of a flight of stairs is John Howard. Dave leans in close to Mr Rudd, points over to where Mr Howard is standing, and says quietly, 'You want me to push him down those stairs?'

Rudd licks his lips and with a nervous laugh says, 'Oh no, there's no need for violence, ha ha.'

'Joke, Joyce,' says Dave as he walks away from a puzzled-looking future prime minister.

Dave then walks over to talk to a mate who is standing with the Regiment's commanding officer. The CO cringes visibly when the penny drops and he realises who Dave is. Everyone looks even more worried when Dave walks up to John Howard and introduces himself; there are more than a few interested heads turned towards the group now. Mr Howard introduces Dave to his wife, Jeanette, and they have a polite chat about pensions before Dave wanders off – to everyone's relief. Three out of four prime ministers of the last twenty years have had a close brush with Dave, one way or another.

Postscript 2008

In the space of twelve months Dave lost his younger sister, Kate, and then Donna lost her eldest son, Adam, in a car accident. Their relationship didn't survive the grieving. Like all break-ups, it was difficult and painful for them both.

Late one night during one of our marathon chats, Dave revealed that he's started to feel the tremors, the early signs of the neurological disease that claimed his dad at a young age.

'It's in the mail, mate.'

So the bloke who nobody could ever picture as an old man probably won't get to be one. He doesn't see this as tragic. For someone who fully expected to die as a soldier every day is a bonus.

Regardless of what the future holds, I'll have one lasting memory of Dave. It's from when I was first getting to know him and we were on a hunting trip in a remote part of the Kimberley. Dave's walking ahead with a 7.62-millimetre rifle held at the ready position (SAS troopers never sling their rifles). A dirty orange sunset is painting the horizon. The pandanas grass seems to collect the last of the fading light and takes on a surreal yellow glow as we stalk through, looking for scrub bulls. Dave, who I'd never usually describe as having a cat-like grace, is moving with a perfect economy and balance. Me? I'm stumbling along, stubbing my toes, tripping and panting just to keep up. For his apparent lack of effort, he moves incredibly fast through the bush. In this most primal of worlds he's confident and capable.

He's never impatient with my slow pace. From time to time he just stops and waits, like a statue, for me to catch up. I'll always have that image of him silhouetted against the sunset, with his bush hat and a rifle, perfectly at home.

ACKNOWLEDGEMENTS

This book was written for my dad, Snowy Everett, my sister, Kate, young Adam, and the Karen people of Burma, past and present.

I express my sincere thanks to the following people: Marty McCarthy, for being a great mate and loyal friend; Fess and Moya Parker, for all their help and great advice (including boxing my ears when I needed it); my former troop Sergeant, Maurie Wesson, and Squadron Sergeant Major Ian Rasmussen, for their friendship and rock-solid support; Oleh Kay, for helping to squash my brain back into place; Keith, Connie, Shirley and Debbie Almark, my second family and dearest friends; Mum, for her patience, faith and unwavering love for me; and John, for keeping the home fires burning when I couldn't. Nic and Jess: this is how it really happened. Thank you for being great kids and a constant source of pride and joy to me.

Kingsley and I gratefully acknowledge Tara Wynne at Curtis Brown and Sarah Walsh for their support and valuable advice; both Tara and Sarah are bonza sheilas, even if they are Poms. Thanks also to Bob Sessions from Penguin for seeing the potential of the story, and for his fantastic choice of editor, Bridget Maidment, the velvet sledgehammer.

Kingsley would like to thank a number of his friends who read early versions of the manuscript and offered constructive advice: Cameron Hay, Mick and Tracey Fyfe, Alf Kandiah, Bree Van de Zuidwind, Wendy Schultze, Jinny Sharp, Simon Longworth, Bradley Flett and Jeremy England. Kingsley also thanks his parents, Gloria and Malcolm Flett, for their support.

ALSO FROM PENGUIN

Big Shots

Adam Shand

'This is the biggest happening in the underworld since Jackie Twist got the Frog back in '58. This is going to unleash merry hell, son...'

In 2003 Adam Shand, until then a finance journalist, naively set out to unravel Melbourne's bloody gangland wars. A few months' research, a guaranteed cover story. But his foray into the underworld took him deeper than that. He became embroiled in a complex world where feuds raged between rival families, and where a new generation was clashing with the criminal Establishment. Before long, he found himself counted as a friend by those who sometimes ended friendships with a hail of bullets.

Big Shots takes the reader into the heart of the city's multi-billion dollar 'disorganised crime' scene, as Shand meets the key figures and suspects, including Carl and Roberta Williams, Mick Gatto, and many others. He discovers the human drama behind the brutal slayings that were splashed across the front pages, and in the process comes to question his objectivity. And even whether he is being used to further the players' murderous ends.

'If you only read one book about this subject, make it this one'
– *Sun Herald*

The Mascot

Mark Kurzem

'I want to know who I am. I want to know who my people are before I die . . . I want to place a flower on my mother's grave. Wherever that may be.' Alex Kurzem

One summer's day in 1997, Mark Kurzem returned home to find his father on his doorstep. Alex Kurzem had travelled halfway round the world to reveal a long-kept secret, and now wanted his son's help to piece together his past and his identity.

As a five-year-old during the Second World War, Alex Kurzem had watched from a tree as his entire village, including his family, were murdered by a German-led execution squad. He scavenged in the forests of Russia for several months before falling into the hands of a Latvian SS company. After one soldier discovered this young boy was actually Jewish, Alex was made to promise never to reveal his true identity – to forget his old life, his family, and even his name. The young boy became the company's mascot and part of the Nazi propaganda machine responsible for killing his own people.

After the war Alex was adopted and his new family made a home in Australia, far from the sites of wartime atrocities. But after fifty years of holding onto this childhood secret, Alex needed to discover and share the astonishing truth about his past.

read more

my penguin e-newsletter

Subscribe to receive *read more*, your monthly e-newsletter from Penguin Australia. As a *read more* subscriber you'll receive sneak peeks of new books, be kept up to date with what's hot, have the opportunity to meet your favourite authors, download reading guides for your book club, receive special offers, be in the running to win exclusive subscriber-only prizes, plus much more.

Visit penguin.com.au/readmore to subscribe